# ALPHABETICAL INDEX.

NOTICE. — The blank leaves between each department are intended for additional receipts, which may be either written or pasted.

## A

| | PAGE. | | PAGE. |
|---|---|---|---|
| Abgenehrter Gugel- | | Apple Dumplings, | 187 |
| hopf, | 325 | Jelly, | 411 |
| Almond hills, | 486 | Jelly cake, | 295 |
| Cake, | 295, 307 | Meringue, | 205 |
| Candy, | 392 | Pie, | 200 |
| Icing, | 339 | Pudding, 218,219,220,478 | |
| Macaroons. | 353, 854 | Sauce, | 266 |
| Almonds, burnt, | 384 | Slump, | 217 |
| Cream, | 385 | Souffles, | 264 |
| For confectionery, | 495 | Strudel, | 248, 249 |
| Salted, | 889 | Toddy, | 471 |
| Ambrosia, | 422 | Torte, | 204 |
| Angel food bread, | 166 | Apples, baked, | 265 |
| Food cake, | 279 | Jellied, | 266, 269 |
| Aniseed cakes, | 858 | Spiced, | 458 |
| Apfel charlotte, | 479 | With rice, | 194 |
| Appetite silds, | 154 | Apricot ice, | 898 |
| Apple butter, | 405 | Ice-cream, | 852 |
| Cake, | 328 | Asparagus salad, | 137 |
| Charlotte, | 217 | Canned, | 125 |
| Compote. | 264 | Aspic, | 104 |
| Custard, | 210 | | |

# B

| | PAGE. |
|---|---|
| Baba la Parisienne, | 320 |
| Bairische Dampf- | |
| nudeln, | 188, 189 |
| Baked apples, | 265 |
| Beans, | 105 |
| Eggs, | 110 |
| Omelet, | 108 |
| Potatoes, | 114, 116 |
| Shad, | 39 |
| Tomatoes, | 129 |
| Banana ice cream, | 372 |
| Bananas, how to serve, | 423 |
| Barbecued rabbit, | 88 |
| Barley, egg, | 111 |
| Soup, | 18, 19 |
| Water, | 472 |
| Bass, sea, | 40 |
| Batter, chocolate, | 253 |
| Sponge, | 253 |
| With prunes, | 253 |
| Bean Soup, | 24 |
| Beans, baked, | 105 |
| Dried, | 131 |
| Lima, | 129 |
| Pickled, | 44 |
| Snap, | 127, 128 |
| Sour, | 131 |
| String, pickled, | 444, 445 |
| To keep fresh, | 444 |
| Beef a la Julienne | |
| Soup, | 19 |
| Brisket, | 58, 59 |
| Roast, | 60 |
| Soup, | 13 |
| Beefsteak, broiled, | 55 |
| Fried, | 56 |
| Beer, hot, | 470 |
| Soup, | 27 |

| | PAGE. |
|---|---|
| Beets, how to cook, | 127 |
| Bergamot ice cream, | 378 |
| Berliner Pfankuchen, | 323 |
| Beverages, | 462 |
| Bills of fare, | 491, 497 |
| Birds, reed, | 82 |
| Bisque pineapple, | 377 |
| Cake, marbled, | 311 |
| Biscuit tart cake, | 309 |
| Biscuits, Graham, | 169 |
| White, | 168, 169 |
| Black bass, boiled, | 42 |
| Blackberry brandy, | 462 |
| Cordial, | 473 |
| Jam, | 402 |
| Preserves, | 403 |
| Syrup, | 403 |
| Blackberries, canning. | 431 |
| Black cake, | 284 |
| Blanc mange, | 256 |
| Blanc mange, cherry, | 256 |
| Blueberries, canning, | |
| | 430, 431 |
| How to serve, | 423 |
| Bohemian potato puffs, | 120 |
| Boiled black bass, | 42 |
| Eggs, | 107 |
| Fritters, | 175 |
| Hominy. | 184 |
| Pickled beans, | 444 |
| Potatoes, | 114, 115 |
| Sweet potatoes, | 119 |
| Tongue, | 100 |
| Bordelaise sauce, | 50 |
| Boston baked beans, | 105 |
| Brown bread, | 166 |
| Fry. | 44 |
| Bouillon soup, | 21 |

PAGE.

Brandied cherries, 418
Brandied French
  prunes, 419
Fruits, 416
Melange, 416
Peaches, 417
Pears, 417
Quinces, 418
Brains, calf, 68 94
Bread, angel food, 166
  Boston brown, 166
  Buns, 171
  Butterbarches, 162
  Chicago brown, 171, 172
  Corn Muffins, 170
  Family white, 160
  Family Graham, 165
  French rolls, 167, 169
  Graham biscuits, 169
  Graham gems, 169
  Graham muffins, 170
  Hints on making. 159
  Individual loaves, 162
  Kinsley's muffins, 171

PAGE.

Bread, Plain rolls, 167
  Rye, 164
  Twisted, 163
  White biscuits, 168, 169
Bread, wheat muffins, 170
  Yeast, 160
  Zwiebel, Platz, 165
Brod Torte, 307, 309
Broiled beefsteak, 55
  Squabs, 70
Brown bread, Boston, 166
Brandy, blackberry, 462
  Cherry, 471
  Huckleberry, 462
Broth, mutton, 25
  Rice, 28
Buns, 171
Burnt almond cake, 295
Burnt almonds. 384
Butter Barches, 169
Butter taffy, 387
Butternut candy, 392
Butterscotch, 386

## C

PAGE.

Cabbage, pickled, 453
  Red, 126
  Salad, 142
Cake, Abgeruehrter
  Gugelhopf, 325
  Almond cake, 307, 295
  Almond macaroons, 353, 354
  Angel food, 279
  Aniseseed, 341
  Appel, 328

PAGE.

Cake, Apple jelly 303
  Baba la Parisienne, 320
  Berliner Pfankuchen, 328
  Biscuit tart. 309
  Brod Torte 307, 308, 309
  Burnt almond, 295
  Caramel, 303. 304
  Caraway seed cookies347
  Cardamom cookies, 349, 350
  Cheap black, 284

PAGE.

Cake, Cherry,                330
     Cheese,                 327
     Citron,                 348
     Chocolate eclaires,     357
     Chocolate,              280
     Chocolate cream,        305
     Chocolate coffee,       336
     Chocolate tart,         309
     Chocolate wafers,       351
     Chocolate puffs,        355
     Cocoanut,        286, 287
     Coffee fruit,           269
     Cottage cheese,         333
     Cream,           301, 303
     Cup                     288
     Cup cookies,            347
     Currant gems            338
     Date,                   282
     Date tarts,             312
     Dominoes,               338
     Filbert tart,           310
     Filled tart,            310
     French coffee,          320
     French puffs,           322
     Fruit            288, 289
     Garfield,               281
     German fruit,           336
     Gingerbread,            291
     Ginger cookies.         347
     Ginger wafers,          356
     Gold,                   283
     Hickory nut,            286
     Hickory nut maca-
        roons,        355, 362
     Hints on making.
               316, 317, 318
     Honey,                  333
     Huckleberry kuchen,
                     330, 335
     Huckleberry,            285
     Ice Cream,              300

PAGE.

Cake, Jelly roll,            295
     Kaffee kuchen,          329
     Kisses or Meringues,    341
     Kreugel,                332
     Lady,                   287
     Loaf cocoanut,          286
     Layer pound,            297
     Love,                   298
     Marble,                 287
     Marbled biscuit,        311
     Mohn kuchen,            328
     Mohn tarts,             330
     Mohn wachteln,          334
     Mohn maultaschen,       352
     Molasses cookies,       358
     Mother's   delicious
        cookies,             345
     Napfkuchen,             328
     Nutmeg,                 359
     One egg,                284
     Orange,                 299
     Peach shortcake,        305
     Peach Kuchen,           333
     Pink cream,             294
     Plain bunt.             326
     Poppy seed cookies,     353
     Pound plum,             284
     Pound,                  285
     Prune,                  327
     Quickly-made sponge     281
     Railroad                299
     Roley poley,            331
     Russian punch tart,     306
     Seed,                   285
     Shavings,               351
     Silver,                 283
     Simple.                 299
     Sour milk cookies,      348
     Spice,                  287
     Spice roll,             331
     Spice wafers,           350

PAGE.

Cake Sponge, 282
Stollen, 332
Strawberry, 306
Sunshine, 278
Tutti frutti, 302
Va illa cookies, 358
Walnut, 297, 298
White cream, 294
White mountain, 296
Weiner Kipfel, 321
Weiner Studenten,
  Kipfel, 322
Windbeutel, 322
Yum Yums, 348
Calf's brains, 94
Lung and heart, 66
Liver and onions, 63 64 65
Candies, (see confectionery)
Canning, 426
Blackberries, 431
Blueberries, 430, 431
Cherries, 428
Currants, 430
Damsons, 432
French plums, 433
German plums, 433
Green corn, 434
Peaches, 422, 433
Pears, 435
Peas, 435
Pine Apples, 436, 437, 438
Quinces, 429
Rhubarb, 428
Strawberries, 427
Tomatoes, 434
Cantaloupe, pickled, 432
Canvas back duck, 82
Caramel ice-cream, 328
Cardamom cookies, 349, 350
Carrots, 128

PAGE.

Carroway sauce, 50
Carroway seed cookies, 347
Catsup. tomato, 451, 452
Cauliflower 454
Pickled, 454
Salad, 146, 147
Champagne ice, 375
Chand'eau sauce, 241
Charlotte, apple, 217
Cheese cake, 327
Cottage, 333
Quince, 405
With noodles, 181
Cherry blanc mange, 256
Brandy, 471
Cake, 330
Ice, 371
Pie, 204
Pudding. 226
Roley poley, 331
Soup, 26
Strudel, 249, 250
Syrup, 471
Cherries brandied, 418
Candied. 389
How to can, 428
Marmalade, 400
Pickled, 458
Preserved. 400
Chicken croquettes, 79
Fricassee, 99
Prairie, 90
Pressed, 99
Salad, 141
Sandwich, 153
Soup, 14
Steamed, 78
With rice. 72
Chocolate, 368
Batter, 253

| | PAGE. | | PAGE |
|---|---|---|---|
| Chocol'te cake, 280,302,336 | | Confectionery, | 382 |
| Cream cake, | 300 | Almond candy, | 392 |
| Cream candy, | 384 | Burnt almonds, | 384 |
| Coffee cake, | 336 | Butternut candy, | 392 |
| Eclaires, | 357 | Butterscotch, | 386 |
| Ice-cream, | 368 | Butter taffy, | 387 |
| Icing, 340, 341, 342 | | Candied prunes, | 391 |
| Macaroons, | 484 | Candied dates, | 391 |
| Pudding, 232, 283 | | Candied figs, | 391 |
| Puffs, | 388 | Candied cherries, | 389 |
| Tart, | 309 | Chocolate creams, | 385 |
| Wafers, | 361 | Cocoanut caramels, | 388 |
| Chow chow, | 449 | Cocoanut cones, | 386 |
| Chrimsel, | 479 | Cocoanut drops, | 388 |
| Cider, to keep sweet, | 518 | Cocoanut creams, | 392 |
| Cinnamon sticks, | 487 | Cream almonds, | 385 |
| Citron cookies, | 348 | Cream candy, | 384 |
| Preserves, | 401 | Cream caramels, | 391 |
| Clove cookies, | 347 | French creams, | 390 |
| Clover leaf macaroons, | 487 | Filbert creams, | 291 |
| Cockroaches, to exterm- | | Hoarhound candy, | 389 |
| inate, | 519 | Ice cream candy, | 387 |
| Cocoa, | 463 | Maple creams, | 387 |
| Shells, | 468 | Maple nut candy, | 388 |
| Cocoanut cake, 301, 302 | | Marshmallows, | 390 |
| Caramels, | 383 | Molasses candy, | 390 |
| Creams, | 392 | Nougat, | 392 |
| Cones, | 386 | Nut candy, | 388 |
| Drops, | 388 | Peanut candy, | 391 |
| Loaf cake, | 298 | Salted almonds, | 389 |
| Pie, | 200 | Tutti frutti candy, | 392 |
| Codfish balls, | 95 | Walnut chocolate | |
| Coffee cake (see cakes) | | drops, | 385 |
| Cold slaw, | 451 | Wax paper for, | 387 |
| Compote, apple. | 264 | Cookies, caraway seed, | 347 |
| Huckleberry, | 257 | Cardamom, 349, 350 | |
| Peach, | 262 | Citron, | 348 |
| Pears, | 262 | Clove, | 347 |
| Raspberry, | 267 | Cup, | 347 |
| Cones, cocoanut, | 386 | Ginger, | 347 |

PAGE.
Cookies, Macaroon, 353, 354
Molasses, 355
Mother's delicious, 345
Poppy seed, 353
Sour milk, 248
Vanilla, 353
Colds, 510
Cordial, blackberry, 473
Corn, canned, 473
Muffins, 170, 171
Corn, pickled, 446
Cottage cheese cake, 338
Crab apple jelly, 184
Crab apple preserves, 396
Crabs, soft shell, 46
Cranberry sauce, 52, 245
Pudding, 232
Cream almonds, 385
Cake, white, 294
Candy, 284
Caramels, 391
Gooseberry, 270
Pineapple, 269
Pistachio, 263
Raspberry, 261
Soup, 27
Strawberry, 259
Tapioca, 257

PAGE.
Cream, Whipped, 258
Creams, cocoanut, 392
Filbert, 291
Maple, 387
Croquettes, 89
Of calf's brains, 68
Of chicken, 79
Of potato, 125
Croutons, 24
Croup, 508
Crullers, 178
Cucumber, salad, 143
Cup cookies, 347
Currant float, 267
Gems, 355
Ice, 871
Jelly, 408
Preserves, 394
Wine, 414
Currants, frosted, 424
How to can, 430
How to serve, 423
Custard, orange, 258
Peach, 266
Pie, 210
Pudding, 215
Rice, 263
Cutlets, veal, 64

# D

PAGE.
Damsons, to can, 432
Danish grits, 262
Date tart cake, 312
Tarts, 309
Dates, candied, 391
Delicious fritters, 175

PAGE.
Dill pickles, 440, 441
Dish washing, 9
Dominoes, 356
Doughnuts, 177
Dressing for salads, 148
Dried beans, 131

PAGE.

Drop dumplings, 17
Drops, cocoanut, 366
Duck, 82
  Canvas back, 82
  Roast, 84
  Wild, 84
Dumplings, apple 194
Bairische Dampfnu-
  deln, 188, 189
  Calf's liver, 193
  Drop, 17

PAGE

Dumplings, Kartoffel-
  kloesse, 191
  Leberknaedel, 193
  Peach, 189
  Potato, 190
  Rice, 191
  Schwaemchen, 192
  Snowballs, 187
  Wiener Kartoffel
    Kloesse, 193
Dutch cheese, 252
  Sauce, 50

# E

PAGE

Easter Dishes, 475
  Almond hills, 486
  Apple charlotte, 479
  Apple pudding, 478
  Brod torte, 486
  Chaud'eau sauce, 477
  Chocolate cake, 485, 486
  Chocolate macaroons 484
  Chrimsel, 479
  Cinnamon sticks, 487
  Clover leaf maca-
    roons, 487
  Filled chrimsel, 480
  Grated apple pud-
    ding, 479
  Hasty pudding, 488
  Macaroons, 487
  Macaroon cookies, 484
  Mandeltorte, 486
  Matzo Kloesse, 482, 483
  Matzo pudding, 476
  Matzo Kugel 476
  Pies, 481

PAGE.

Easter Dishes, Potato
  Flour pudding, 478
  Potato pudding, 477
  Prunes, 480
  Raisin wine, 481, 482
  Sponge cake, 484
  Strawberry short-
    cake, 483
  Strawberry dessert, 480
  Table for 475
  Tart cake, 485
  Ueberschlagen Mat-
    zes, 481
  Wine sauce, 442
Eclaires, chocolate, 357
Egg lemonade, 402
Egg nogg, 409
Egg plant, 132
  Sandwich, 154
  Wine, 482
Eggs, baked, 110
  Baked omelet, 109
  Barley, 111
  Boiled, 107

| | PAGE | | PAGE |
|---|---|---|---|
| Eggs, Herb omelet, | 109 | Entrees, Gefillte Milz, | 101 |
| Omelet plain, 107, | 108 | Goose liver, | 96, 97 |
| Piquant, | 110 | Paprica, | 100 |
| Poached, | 111 | Pressed chicken, | 99 |
| Sweet omelet. | 109 | Smoked tongue, | 100 |
| Eierbier, | 470 | Sulze von Kalbsfues- | |
| Entrees. | | sen, | 97 |
| Aspic, | 104 | Sweetbread glace, | 98 |
| Boiled tongue, | 103 | Sweetbreads, | 94 |
| Boston baked beans, | 105 | Stewed milt, | 102 |
| Calf brains, | 94 | Tripe, | 104 |
| Chicken fricassee, | 99 | Erbsen Lievansen, | 170 |
| Codfish balls, | 95 | Escaloped oysters, | 43 |
| Gansleber in Sulz, | 105 | Peaches, | 269 |
| Gansleber Puree in | | Tomatoes, | 129 |
| Sulz, | 105 | Extract, punch, | 470 |

# F

| | PAGE. | | PAGE. |
|---|---|---|---|
| Family bread, | 160 | Fish, Boneless filled, | 82 |
| Graham bread, | 165 | Crabs, | 46 |
| Farina mush, | 184 | Croquettes, | 89 |
| Pudding, | 227 | Flounders, | 41 |
| Soup, | 22 | Hecht, | 87 |
| Fig Pudding, | 216 | Herring, | 41 |
| Preserves, | 399 | Perch. | 84 |
| Sauce, | 220 | Pickerel, | 87 |
| Figs, candied. | 391 | Pike. | 86 |
| Filet de boeuf and | | Redsnapper, | 40 |
| champignons. | 54 | Sauces, | 48, 52 |
| Filbert creams, | 391 | Shad, | 39 |
| Tart cakes, | 310 | Smelt, | 42 |
| Filled fish, | 32, 39 | Sunfish, | 40 |
| Matzo Kloesse, | 482 | Trout. | 33, 35, 38 |
| Filbert cake, | 310 | White. | 35. 39 |
| Fish. a la Brunswick, | 38 | Flaxseed lemonade, | 471 |
| Bass, | 34, 40, 42 | Fleisch Kugel, | 58 |
| | | Float, currant, | 267 |

| | PAGE. | | PAGE. |
|---|---|---|---|
| Float, Raspberry, | 267 | Fried, potatoes, | 117 |
| Floating island, | 268 | Smelts, | 42 |
| Flour and milk soup, | 27 | Sweet potatoes, | 119 |
| Frapees fruit, | 378 | Spring chicken, | 77 |
| French coffee cake, | 320 | Tomatoes, | 130 |
| Creams, uncooked, | 390 | Fritters, boiled, | 175 |
| Plums, how to can, | 433 | Delicious, | 175 |
| Prunes, brandied, | 419 | Lemon, | 176 |
| Puff paste, | 199 | Orange, | 176 |
| Puffs, | 322 | Peach, | 185 |
| Rolls, | 167, 169 | Pineapple, | 185 |
| Toast, | 174 | Frosted currants, | 424 |
| Waffles, | 179 | Frosting, boiled, | 339 |
| Fricasseed chicken, | 77, 99 | Frozen fruits, | 371 |
| Veal, | 65 | Fruit cake, | 288, 289 |
| Fried beefsteak, | 56 | Cake, German, | 335, 336 |
| Oysters, | 43 | Fruit sauce, | 244, 245 |
| Perch, | 34 | | |

# G

| | PAGE. | | PAGE. |
|---|---|---|---|
| Gänseklein, | 74 | Game, Rabbit, with caper sauce, | 85 |
| Game, | 80 | Rabbit ragout, sweet and sour, | 88 |
| Barbecued rabbit, | 80 | Reed birds, | 82 |
| Broiled squirrels, | 88 | Ragout of rabbit | 86 |
| Canvas-back duck roasted, | 82 | Spiced rabbit (Hasenpfeffer), | 85 |
| Fricasseed rabbit, | 87 | To keep game fresh, | 92 |
| Fried rabbit, | 88 | Venison roast, | 88 |
| Pigeon pie, | 90 | Venison steak, | 89 |
| Prairie chicken, | 90 | Venison and rabbit pie, | 89 |
| Quail roasted, | 83 | Wild pigeons, | 83 |
| Quail on toast, | 91 | Wild turkey, | 83 |
| Quail pie, | 91 | Wild goose, | 84 |
| Rabbit, | 83 | | |
| Rabbit, roasted | 85 | | |

| | PAGE. |
|---|---|
| Game, wild duck. | 84 |
| Gansleber in Sulz, | 105 |
| Puree in Sulz, | 105 |
| Garfield cake, | 281 |
| Gargle for sore throat, | |
| | 508, 511 |
| Garlic sauce, | 50 |
| Gefillte Milz, | 101 |
| Gems, currant, | 335 |
| Gems, Graham, | 169 |
| Geraucherte Gansbrust | 77 |
| German fruit cake, | 335 |
| Waffles, | 179,180 |
| Geschundene Gans, | 75 |
| Gherkins, pickled, | 449 |
| Ginger cookies, | 347 |
| Wafers, | 356 |
| Gold cake, | 283 |
| Goose liver, | 96, 97 |
| Minced, | 76 |
| Roast, | 78 |
| Stewed, | 77 |
| Wild, | 84 |
| Gooseberry cream, | 270 |

| | PAGE. |
|---|---|
| Gooseberry, Fool, | 257 |
| Jam, | 404 |
| Graham biscuits, | 169 |
| Bread, | 165 |
| Gems, | 169 |
| Muffins, | 170 |
| Pudding, | 217 |
| Grape jelly, | 410 |
| Pie, | 210 |
| Preserves, | 406 |
| Grated apple pie. | 205 |
| Greengages, preserved | 395 |
| Green corn, | 120 |
| Green corn, pickled, | 446 |
| Green corn, to can, | 434 |
| Green kern soup, | 20 |
| Green pea soup, | 17 |
| Grieben, | 75 |
| Grimslich, | 221 |
| Grits, Danish, | 262 |
| Groceries, how to store | 10 |
| Grog, | 470 |
| Gruel, oatmeal, | 184 |
| Gumbo soup, | 18 |

# H

| | PAGE |
|---|---|
| Haringsalat, | 145 |
| Hamburger steak | 56 |
| Ham sandwiches, | 153 |
| Toast, | 155 |
| Hard sauce, | 243 |
| Hasenpfeffer, | 85 |
| Hashed calf's lung and | |
| heart, | 66 |
| Hasty pudding, | 488 |
| Hazelnut ice, | 374 |

| | PAGE. |
|---|---|
| Herb omelet, | 109 |
| Hecht, | 87 |
| Herring, Marinirter, | 41 |
| Sauce, | 50 |
| Hickory-nut cake, | 286 |
| Macaroons. | 355,362 |
| Hills, almond, | 486 |
| Hoarhound candy, | 389 |
| Hollandaise sauce. | 51 |
| Hominy, boiled, | 184 |

| | PAGE. | | PAGE. |
|---|---|---|---|
| Honey cakes, | 351 | Huckleberry brandy, | 462 |
| Horseradish, | 127 | Cake, | 285 |
| Sauce, | 50 | Compote, | 257 |
| Hot beer, | 470 | Kuchen, | 330,335 |
| Hot pickles, | 450 | Husk tomatoes, pickled | 459 |

# I

| | PAGE. | | PAGE. |
|---|---|---|---|
| Ice-cream candy, | 387 | Ices, Currant, | 371 |
| Cake, | 300 | Currant raspberry, | 372 |
| Ice-creams, | 365 | Lemon, | 372 |
| Apricot, | 373 | Orange, | 371 |
| Banana, | 372 | Peach, | 373 |
| Bergamot, | 878 | Pineapple, | 369 |
| Caramel, | 328 | Raspberry, | 373 |
| Chocolate, | 368 | Strawberry, | 369 |
| Coffee, | 370 | Iced tea, | 465 |
| Hazelnut, | 374 | Icing for cakes, | 339 |
| Lemon, | 370 | Almond, | 339 |
| Nesselrode, | 326 | Boiled frosting, | 339 |
| New York, | 367 | Caramel, | 343 |
| Orange, | 372 | Chocolate, | 340,341,342 |
| Peach, | 369 | Cocoanut, | 343 |
| Pineapple, | 369 | Lemon extract, | 341 |
| Pistache, | 374 | Lemon peel, | 342 |
| Raspberry, | 375 | Pink, | 340 |
| Strawberry, | 377 | Unboiled, | 342 |
| Tea, | 370 | Vanilla, | 341 |
| Tutti frutti, | 374 | Yellow, | 340 |
| Vanilla, | 375 | Yellow or golden, | 342 |
| Ices, | 369 | Imitation cauliflower, | 122 |
| A la tutti-frutti, | 373 | New potatoes, | 118 |
| Apricot, | 373 | Pate de foi gra, | 155 |
| Champagne, | 375 | Italian salad, | 188 |
| Cherry, | 371 | | |

# J

| | PAGE. | | PAGE. |
|---|---|---|---|
| Jam, blackberry, | 402 | Jelly, Fruit, | 413 |
| Gooseberry, | 404 | Grape. | 410 |
| Raspberry, | 404 | Neapolitan, | 412 |
| Strawberry, | 399 | Peach, | 409 |
| Jellied apples, | 266,269 | Raspberry, | 411 |
| Jelly, | 408 | Raspberry-curran', | 410 |
| Apple, | 411 | Roll, | 295 |
| Cake, | 295 | Sauce. | 242 |
| Crab-apple, | 134 | Strawberry, | 408 |
| Currant, | 410 | Raspberry syrup, | 412 |
| | | Wine, | 411 |

# K

| | PAGE | | PAGE. |
|---|---|---|---|
| Kaese Kraepfil, | 182 | Kitchen utensils, | 10 |
| Kaffee Kuchen, | 329 | Knoblauch Sauce, | 50 |
| Kalbslunge Strudel, | 252 | Kohlraben, | 121 |
| Kartoffel Kloesse. | 191,193 | Kraut Kugel, | 231 |
| Kern, green, soup, | 20 | Strudel, | 254 |
| Kimmel Sauce, | 50 | Kreugel, | 832 |
| Kinsley's muffins, | 171 | Kugel, Matzo, | 476 |
| Kloesse, matzo, | 482 | | |

# L

| | PAGE. | | PAGE. |
|---|---|---|---|
| Lady cake, | 287 | Lemonade. Flaxseed, | 471 |
| Lamb chops, | 59 | For invalids, | 466 |
| Roast, | 61 | Milk, | 468 |
| Layer cake, | 293 | Lemon cake, | 287 |
| Pound cake: | 297 | Fritters, | 176 |
| Leberknaedel, | 193 | Ice. | 372 |
| Lemonade, | 465 | Ice-cream, | 370 |
| Egg, | 462 | Icing, | 872 |

PAGE.

| | PAGE. | | PAGE. |
|---|---|---|---|
| Lemon Jelly, | 303 | Liver, Goose, | 96, 97 |
| Pie, | 206 | Loaf cake, 'cocoanut, | 286 |
| Sauce, | 242, 243 | Lobster salad, | 137 |
| Lettuce salad, | 143, 144 | Love cake, | 298 |
| Lintel Soup, | 25 | Lunches, how to pre- | |
| Linsen Soup, | 25 | pare, | 10, 496 |
| Liver, calf's, | 63 | | |
| Dumplings, | 193 | | |

# M

PAGE.

| | PAGE. | | PAGE. |
|---|---|---|---|
| Macaroon cookies, | 484 | Meats, Broiled beefsteak, | 55 |
| | | Brisket of beef, | 58, 59 |
| Macaroons, | 487 | Calf's liver, | 63, 65 |
| Almond, | 353,354 | Croquettes of calf's | |
| Clover leaf, | 487 | brains, | 68 |
| Hickory-nut, | 355, 362 | Filet de boeuf au | |
| Maitre d'hotel sauce, | 48 | champignons, | 54 |
| Mandeltorte, | 486 | Fried beefsteak, | 56 |
| Mandel Strudel, | 254 | Fleisch Kugel, | 58 |
| Mangoes, pickled, | 454 | Fricasseed veal, | 65 |
| Maple Cream, | 387 | Hamburger Steak | 56 |
| Nut candy, | 388 | Hashed calf's lung | |
| Marble cake, | 287 | and heart | 66 |
| Marbled biscuit cake, | 311 | Lamb chops, | 59 |
| Marinirter Herring, | 41 | Mutton chops, | 59 |
| Marketing, hints on, | 9 | Roast beef, | 60 |
| Marmalade,Strawberry | 400 | Round beefsteak, | 56 |
| Marshmallows, | 390 | Roast mutton, | 62 |
| Mashed potatoes, | 115 | Roast lamb, | 61 |
| Matzo Kloesse, | 482 | Roast veal, | 63, 64 |
| Kugel, | 476 | Sauerbraten, | 62 |
| Schalet, | 476 | Soup meat, | 57 |
| Pudding, | 476 | Spiced veal loaf | 66 |
| Mayonnaise salad, | 142 | Stewed veal, | 67 |
| Measures and weights | 520 | Time-table for roasts, | 54 |
| Meat ball, | 58 | Veal cutlets, | 64 |
| Meat Sauces, | 48, 52 | Veal sweetbreads, | 67 |
| Meats, breast of mut- | | Wiener Braten | 57 |
| ton, | 59 | Medical case, family, | 507 |

| | PAGE. | | PAGE. |
|---|---|---|---|
| Mehlsuppen, | 28 | Molasses candy, | 390 |
| Melange, brandied, | 416 | Cookies, | 345 |
| Menu, wedding, | 501,505 | Mothers's delicious | |
| Meringue, apple, | 205 | cookies, | 345 |
| Milk lemonade, | 468 | Dill pickles, | 441 |
| Punch, | 468 | Muffins, corn, | 170 |
| Soup, | 27 | Graham, | 170 |
| Toast, | 175 | Kinsley's, | 171 |
| Milk and flour soup, | 27 | Wheat, | 170 |
| Milt, stewed, | 102 | Mush, farina, | 184 |
| Mince pie. | 201,202 | Oatmeal, | 184 |
| Minced goose, | 76 | Mush and milk, | 188 |
| Tongue, | 153 | Mushroom Sauce, | 48 |
| Mint sauce, | 52 | Mustard pickles, 447, 448 | |
| Mock turtle soup, | 14 | Prepared. | 445 |
| Mohntorte, | 299 | Mutton breast, stewed, | 59 |
| Mohntorts, | 330 | Broth, | 25 |
| Mohn, Kuchen, | 328 | Chops, | 59 |
| Maultaschen, | 352 | Roast, | 62 |
| Wachteln, | 884 | | |

# N

| | PAGE. | | PAGE. |
|---|---|---|---|
| Napfkuchen, | 826 | Noodles with cheese. | 181 |
| Neapolitan blanc | | Nose bleeding, how to | |
| mange, | 259, 260, 261 | stop, | 512 |
| Neapolitan Jelly. | 412 | Nougat, | 392 |
| Salad, | 140 | Nut Candy. | 388 |
| Nervousness, remedy | | Candy, maple, | 388 |
| for. | 511 | Nutmeg cakes, | 359 |
| New potatoes, imita- | | Nutmegs, pickled, | 456 |
| tion of, | 118 | | |
| Noodle pudding, | 224 | | |
| Soup, | 16 | | |

# O

| | PAGE. | | PAGE. |
|---|---|---|---|
| Oatmeal gruel, | 184 | Ox-tail soup, | 15 |
| Mush, | 184 | Oyster dressing, | 79 |
| Okra gumbo soup, | 18 | Plant, | 182 |
| Omelet, egg, | 108, 109 | Patties, | 45 |
| One egg cake, | 284 | Salad, | 137 |
| Onion sauce, | 48 | Soup, | 22 |
| Onions, pickled, | 453 | Oysters, Boston fry, | 44 |
| Spanish, | 131 | Cream stew, | 44 |
| Orangeade, | 469 | Cream on shell, | 45 |
| Orange cake, | 299 | Dry stew, | 44 |
| Custard, | 258 | Escaloped, | 43 |
| Fritters, | 176 | Fried, | 43 |
| Ice, | 371 | How to serve, | 42 |
| Ice cream, | 372 | Stewed, | 42 |
| Pudding, | 233 | With noodles, | 180 |

# P

| | PAGE. | | PAGE. |
|---|---|---|---|
| Pancakes, potato, | 178 | Peach, Short cake, | 305 |
| Bread, | 179 | Syrup, | 248 |
| Paprica, | 100 | Peaches, brandied, | 417 |
| Patties, oyster, | 45 | Escaloped, | 269 |
| Pea soup, | 17, 19 | How to can, | 432, 433 |
| Peach butter, | 404 | How to serve, | 423 |
| Compote, | 268 | Pickled, | 457 |
| Cream pie, | 209 | Peanut candy, | 391 |
| Custard, | 256 | Pear compote, | 262 |
| Dumplings, | 189 | Preserves, | 395, 403 |
| Ice, | 373 | Pears, brandied, | 417 |
| Ice cream, | 369 | How to can, | 435 |
| Jelly, | 409 | Pickled | 456 |
| Kuchen, | 333 | Peas, how to can | 435 |
| Pie, | 203, 204 212 | Pepper mangoes, | 454 |
| Preserves, | 394 | Perch, fried, | 34 |
| Pudding, | 315, 216 | Piccalilli, | 450 |

|  | PAGE. |  | PAGE. |
|---|---|---|---|
| Pickerel, | 87 | Pie, Cream, | 209 |
| Pickles, relishes, etc., | 440 | Custard, | 210 |
| Boiled beans, | 444 | Easter, | 458 |
| Cabbage, | 453 | French puff paste, | 199 |
| Cantaloupe, | 432 | Grape, | 210 |
| Cauliflower, | 454 | Grated apple, | 205 |
| Cherries, | 458 | Lemon, | 206 |
| Chow chow, | 449 | Mince, | 201, 202 |
| Cold slaw, | 451 | Peach, 203, 204, 212 | |
| Dill pickles, | 441 | Pigeon, | 91 |
| Early fall vegetables, | 443 | Plum, | 200 |
| Gherkins, | 426 | Pumpkin, | 206 |
| Green corn, | 446 | Quail, | 91 |
| Hot Pickles, | 427 | Raspberry cream, | 201 |
| Husk tomatoes, | 459 | Rhubarb, | 207 |
| Mustard pickles, | 447, 448 | Rhubarb custard, | 208 |
| Nutmegs, | 456 | Veal and rabbit, | 88 |
| Onions, | 453 | Vinegar, | 209 |
| Peaches, | 457 | Whipped cream, | 209 |
| Pears, | 456 | Wine, or Mirror, | 213 |
| Pepper mangoes, | 454 | Pigeon soup, | 22 |
| Piccalilli, | 450 | Pigeons, | 83 |
| Plums, | 455 | Wild, | 83 |
| Prepared mustard, | 455 | Pike, with egg sauce, | 36 |
| Salt pickles, | 419 | Pineapple bisque, | 377 |
| Salzgurken, | 442 | Cream, | 269 |
| Sauerkraut, | 444, 445 | How to serve, | 422 |
| Spiced apples, | 458 | Ice, | 369 |
| String beans, | 443 | Ice cream, | 369 |
| Teufelsgurken, | 450 | Pink icing, | 340 |
| Tomato catsup, | 451, 452 | Piquant eggs, | 110 |
| Picnic lunches, | 10 | Pistache ice cream, | 374 |
| Pie, | 198 | Pistachio cream, | 263 |
| Apple, | 200 | Plain bunt, | 326 |
| Apple tort, | 204 | Rolls, | 167 |
| Apple meringue, | 205 | Plum pie, | 200 |
| Apple custard, | 210 | Preserves, | 395 |
| Cherry, | 204 | Pudding, 221, 222, 223 | |
| Cheese, | 208 | Pudding sauce, | 244 |
| Cheese straws, | 209 | Plums, how to can, | 488 |
| Cocoanut, | 200 | | |

| | PAGE. | | PAGE. |
|---|---|---|---|
| Plums, Pickled, · | 455 | Pound cake, | 285 |
| Poached eggs, | 111 | Pound cake, plum, | 284 |
| Polish salad. | 147 | Prairie chicken, | 90 |
| Poppy seed cookies, | 353 | Prepared mustard, | 455 |
| Potatoes dumplings, | 190 | Preserves, | 394 |
| Flour pudding, | 478 | Apple butter, | 405 |
| New, imitation of, | 118 | Blackberry jam, | 402 |
| Pancakes, | 178 | Blackberry syrup, | 403 |
| Pudding, | 223, 477 | Cherry, | 400 |
| Salad, | 145 | Cherry marmalade, | 400 |
| Soup, | 25 | Citron, | 401 |
| Baked, | 114, 116 | Crab apple. | 396 |
| Fried, | 117 | Currant-raspberry | 397 |
| How to prepare, | 113 | Fig, | 399 |
| Mashed, | 115 | Gooseberry jam, | 404 |
| Puff, Bohemian, | 120 | Grape, | 406 |
| Ribbon, | 118 | Greengages, | 395 |
| Stewed, | 115, 116 | Peach butter, | 404 |
| Sweet, fried, | 119 | Peach, | 394 |
| Sweet, boiled, | 119 | Pear, | 395, 403 |
| Sweet, roasted, | 119, 126 | Plum, | 374 |
| Poultry, boiled squabs, | 70 | Quince cheese, | 405 |
| Chicken fricassee, | 78 | Quince, | 396 |
| Chicken croquette, | 79 | Raspberry, | 404 |
| Chicken with rice, | 72 | Raspberry jam, | 404 |
| Dressing for, | 79 | Strawberry, | 398 |
| Duck, | 72 | Strawberry jam, | 399 |
| Gaenseklein, | 74 | Strawberry marma- | |
| Geschundene Gans, | 75 | lade, | 400 |
| Grieben, . | 75 | Tomato, green, | 401 |
| Geraeucherte Gans- | | Tomato, ripe, | 402 |
| brust, | 77 | Watermelon rind, | 401 |
| Minced Goose, | 76 | Pressed chicken, | 99 |
| Oyster dressing for, | 79 | Prince Albert Pudding, | 230 |
| Roast turkey, | 71 | Prune Cake, | 327 |
| Roast goose, | 73 | Sauce, | 246 |
| Squabs, | 70 | Prunes, | 269 |
| Spring chicken, | 77 | Candied, | 391 |
| Steamed chicken, | 78 | French brandied. | 419 |
| Stewed Goose, | 77 | | |

| | PAGE. | | PAGE. |
|---|---|---|---|
| Prunes, stewed, | 480 | Pudding, Plum,221, 222, 223 | |
| With batter | 253 | Potato, | 223 |
| Pudding, Apfel Char- | | Prince Albert, | 230 |
| lotte, | 217 | Queen of Plum Pud- | |
| Apple Slump, | 217 | dings, | 238 |
| Apple, 218, 219, 220 | | Rhubarb, | 230 |
| Almond Roley Poley.237 | | Rice, | 228 |
| Bread, | 225 | Sponge, | 223 |
| Cherry, | 226 | Suet, 220, 221 | |
| Children's favorite, | 227 | Sweet potato, | 231 |
| Chocolate, 232, 233 | | Tipsey, | 229 |
| Cranberry, | 232 | Yorkshire, | 60 |
| Custard, | 231 | Yum Yum. | 234 |
| Farina, | 227 | Pudding Sauces, | 241 |
| Fig, | 216 | Puff Paste, French, | 199 |
| Graham, | 217 | Puffs, chocolate, | 355 |
| Grimselich, | 221 | French, | 222 |
| Hasty. | 488 | Spanish. | 176 |
| Kraut Kugel, | 231 | Pumpkin pie, | 206 |
| Metropolitan Apple, | 235 | Punch extract, | 470 |
| Matzo, | 476 | Milk, | 472 |
| Nesselrode, | 376 | Roman. | 371 |
| Noodle, | 224 | Tart, Russian. | 306 |
| Peach, 215, 216, | | Puree of Tomato, | 46 |
| | | Purim Krapfen, | 323 |

# Q

| | PAGE. | | PAGE. |
|---|---|---|---|
| Quail on toast, | 91 | Quince cheese, | 405 |
| Pie, | 91 | Preserves, | 396 |
| Roasted, | 88 | Quinces, brandied, | 418 |
| Quark, | 252 | Canned, | 429 |

# R

|                                | PAGE. |
|--------------------------------|-------|
| Rabbit,                        | 84    |
|   Barbecued,         | 88    |
|   Broiled,           | 87    |
|   Fricasseed,        | 87    |
|   Fried,             | 87    |
|   Pie.               | 89    |
|   Ragout,            | 86, 88 |
|   Roast,             | 84    |
|   Spiced,            | 85    |
|   With caper sauce,  | 85    |
| Railroad cake,                 | 299   |
| Raisin sauce,                  | 49    |
|   Wine,              | 482   |
| Raspberry compote,             | 267   |
|   Cream,             | 261   |
|   Cream Pie,         | 201   |
|   Float,             | 267   |
|   How to serve,      | 423   |
|   Ice cream,         | 375   |
|   Ice,               | 373   |
|   Jam,               | 404   |
|   Jelly,             | 409   |
|   Preserves,         | 397   |
|   Syrup,             | 412   |
|   Vinegar,           | 466   |
| Raspberry-currant jelly,       | 410   |
| Reed birds,                    | 82    |
| Red cabbage,                   | 126   |
| Redsnapper,                    | 40    |
| Red wine spiced,               | 469   |
| Relishes, (see pickles, relishes, etc.) | |
| Rhubarb, custard pie,          | 208   |
|   How to can,        | 428   |
|   Pie,               | 207   |

|                                | PAGE. |
|--------------------------------|-------|
| Rhubarb, Pudding,              | 230   |
|   Sauce,             | 256   |
| Ribbon tart cake,              | 310   |
|   Potatoes,          | 318   |
| Rice broth,                    | 26    |
|   Custard,           | 263   |
|   Pudding,           | 228   |
|   Soup.              | 27    |
|   Strudel,           | 251   |
|   Water.             | 472   |
| Roast beef                     | 60    |
|   Beef with Yorkshire pudding. | 60 |
|   Duck,              | 82    |
|   Goose,             | 84    |
|   Lamb,              | 61    |
|   Mutton with potatoes, | 62 |
|   Quail,             | 83    |
|   Rabbit,            | 84    |
|   Sweet potatoes,    | 119, 126 |
|   Turkey,            | 83    |
|   Veal,              | 63, 64 |
|   Venison,           | 88    |
| Roasts, time-table for,        | 54    |
| Roley-poley,                   | 331   |
|   Cherry,            | 251   |
| Roll spice                     | 331   |
| Rolls, French,                 | 167, 169 |
|   Plain,             | 167   |
| Roman punch,                   | 371   |
|   Sauce,             | 244   |
| Rum sauce,                     | 242   |
| Russian punch tart,            | 306   |
|   Salad,             | 148   |

# S

PAGE.

Sago soup, 27
Salade d'orange, 422
Salads, 135
  Asparagus, 137
  Celery, 146, 147
  Chicken, 141, 148
  Chopped cabbage, 142
  Cucumber. 143
  D'Orange, 422
  Haeringsalat, 145
  Italian, 138
  Lettuce, 143, 144
  Lobster, 137
  Mayonnaise, 138,142,150
  Neapolitan, 140
  Oyster, 137
  Polish, 147
  Remarks on making, 135
  Russian, 148
  Salad dressing, 148
  Salmon, 138
  Sweetbread. 135
  Tomato, 139, 140, 150
  Unique potato, 145
  Vegetable, 140
  Salmon, 138
Salt pickles 442
Salted Almonds, 389
Salzgurken, 442
Sandwiches, 152
  Appetite silds, 154
  Boiled tongue, 153
  Cheese, 154
  Chicken, 153
  Egg, 154
  Ham toast, 154
  Ham and Chicken 153

PAGE.

Sandwiches, Ham 153
  Imitation pate de foi
    gras, 155
  Lunches, 152
  Minced tongue, 153
  Minced goose, 156
  Royal ham, 157
  Veal, 153
Saratoga chips, 117
Sardellen sauce, 50
Sauce, apple, 266
  Chand'eau 241, 477
  Cranberry, 245
  Figs, 270
  Fruit, 244. 245
  Jelly, 242
  Hard, 243
  Lemon, 244, 245
  Maitre d'hotel, 48
  Mushroom, 48
  Peach, 243
  Plum pudding, 244
  Prune, 246
  Rhubarb, 256
  Roman, 244
  Vanilla, 245
  Wine 482
Sauces, pudding, 241
Sauerbraten, 62
Sauerkraut, 444, 445
Seed cake, 285
Seder table, 475
Servants, how to treat, 8
Schalet, Matzo, 476
Schwamm Kloesse, 192
Schwaemchen, 192
Shad, baked, 38
Shavings, 251

PAGE.

Sherbet, strawberry 483
Peach, 305
Silver cake, 283
Simple cake, 299
Slippery elm water. 472
Slump, apple, 217
Smelts, fried, 42
Smoked tongue, 101
Snowballs, 187
Snowflakes, 424
Soda cream. 468
Soft shell crabs, 46
Sore throat, treatment, 510
Souffles, apple, 284
Soup, barley. 18, 19
Beef, a la Julienne, 19
Beer, 27
Beer and milk, 28
Bouillon, 21
Chicken, 14
Cherry, 26
Crouton, 24
Drop dumplings. 17
Dumplings for, 193
Farina, 22
Green Pea 17
Green Kern, 20
Gumbo, 18
Lintel, 25
Linsen, 25
Meat, 57
Mehlsuppen, 28
Milk and Flour, 27
Milk or Cream, 27
Mock Turtle 14
Mutton broth, 25
Noodle, 16
Okra, 18
Oyster, 22

PAGE.

Soup. Ox tail, 15
Pigeon, 22
Potato, 25
Rice broth, 26
Split pea, 28
Tomato, 20
Turkey, 28
Veal, 15
Wine, 26
White bean, 24
Sour beans, 131
Milk cookies, 848
Spanish onions, 131
Puffs, 176
Speckled trout, 83
Spice cake, 287
Roll, 331
Wafers, 350
Spiced apples, 458
Rabbit, 88
Red wine 481
Veal loaf, 66
Spinach, 123
Sponge batter, 253
Cake. 282, 294, 484
Pudding, 233
Split pea soup, 28
Spring chicken, fried, 77
Squabs, 70
Squirrel, broiled, 88
Steak, Hamburger, 56
Steamed chicken, 78
Stewed goose, 77
Milt, 102
Oysters, 42
Potatoes, 115, 116
Prunes, 480
Tomatoes, 121, 126
Veal, 67
Stollen, 832

PAGE.

Stove, how to clean, 11
Strawberry cream, 259
   Cream cake, 300
   Dessert, 421
   Ice, 369
   Ice cream, 377
   Jam. 404
   Jelly, 408
   Marmalade, 400
   Preserves. 398, 399
   Sherbet, 465
   Shortcake, 489
   Syrup, 467
Strawberries, how to
   serve, 426
   How to can, 427
String beans, pickled, 448
Strudel, apple. 248. 249
   Batter with prunes, 253
   Cherry, 249, 250
   Cherry roley-poley, 251
   Chocolate batter, 253
   Kraut, 254

PAGE.

Strudel, Mandel, 254
   Quark, or Dutch
     Cheese 252
   Rice 251
   Sponge batter, 253
   Aus Kalbslunge, 252
Succotash, 129
Suet, 220, 221
Sulze von Kalbsfeussen, 99
Sunfish, 40
Sunshine cake, 278
Sweetbread glace, 98
   Salad. 135
Sweetbreads, 67, 98
Sweet omelet, 109
Sweet potato pudding, 231
Sweet potatoes boiled, 119
   Fried, 119
   Roasted, 119, 126
Syrup. blackberry, 403
   Cherry, 471
   Raspberry, 404
   Strawberry, 467

# T

PAGE.

Table of measures and
   weights, 277, 520
Taffy butter, 387
Tapioca cream, 257
Tartar sauce 49
Tart cake, biscuit, 309
   Cake, 294
   Cake, filled, 310
   Cake, Ribbon, 310
   Filbert, 310
   Russian punch, 306
Tarts, chocolate, 309
Tarts, Date, 812

PAGE.

Tea, 364
   A la Russe, 464
   A la Russe, iced, 465
   Ice-cream, 365
   Iced, 465
   Stains to remove, 515
Teufelsgurken pickled, 450
Time table for roasts, 54
   Vegetables, 118
Tinware, to wash, 10
Tipsy pudding, 229
Toast, French, 174

|  | PAGE. |  | PAGE. |
|---|---|---|---|
| Toast, Ham, | 155 | Torte, Apple, | 204 |
| Milk, | 175 | Brod, | 307. 308, 309 |
| Water, | 472 | Trefa, (see valuable hints.) | |
| Toddy, apple, | 471 | Tripe, | 104 |
| Tomato catsup, | 451, 452 | Trout, | 35 |
| Preserves, | 402 | Brook, | 88 |
| Salad, | 150 | Speckled, | 83 |
| Tomatoes baked, | 129 | Turkey dressing, | 79 |
| Canned, | 434 | Roasted, | 71 |
| Escaloped, | 130 | Soup, | 23 |
| Fried, | 130 | Wild, | 88 |
| How to serve, | 422 | Tutti-frutti, | 423 |
| Pickled, | 459 | Cake, | 302 |
| Puree, | 46 | Candy, | 392 |
| Soup, | 20 | Ice, | 373 |
| Stewed, | 121, 126 | Ice-cream, | 374 |
| Tongue, boiled, | 103 | Twisted Bread, | 163 |
| Smoked, | 101 | | |

# V

|  | PAGE. |  | PAGE. |
|---|---|---|---|
| Vanilla cookies, | 358 | Vegetables, Boiled sweet | |
| Ice-cream, | 375 | potatoes, | 119 |
| Icing, | 341 | Beets, | 127 |
| Sauce, | 245 | Bohemian potato puff, | |
| Veal cutlets. | 64 | | 120 |
| Veal, Fricasseed, | 65 | Canned asparagus, | 125 |
| Loaf, spiced, | 66 | Canned corn. | 124 |
| Roasted, | 63, 64 | Canned green peas, | 130 |
| Sandwich, | 153 | Cauliflower, | 122 |
| Soup, | 15 | Carrots, | 128 |
| Stewed, | 67 | Dried beans, | 131 |
| Sweetbreads, | 67 | Egg plant, | 132 |
| Vegetable salad, | 140 | Escaloped tomatoes, | 130 |
| Vegetables, | 113 | Fried potatoes, | 117 |
| Baked potatoes, | 114. 116 | Fried sweet potatoes, | 119 |
| Baked tomatoes, | 129 | Fried tomatoes, | 130 |
| Boiled potatoes, | 114. 115 | Green corn, | 120 |

PAGE.

Vegetables,
Horseradish, 127
Imitation of cauli-
flower, 122
Kohlraben. 121
Lima beans, 129
Mashed potatoes. 115
Oyster plant, 132
Potatoes, how to pre-
pare, 113
Potato puffs, 117. 120
Potato ribbon, 118
Potato croquettes, 125
Roast sweet pota-
toes, 119, 126
Saratoga chips, 117
Spinach, 123

PAGE

Stewed potatoes, 115,116
Vegetables,
Stewed tomatoes.
121, 126
Snap beans, 127, 128
Succotash, 129
Sour beans. 131
Spanish onions, 131
Time-table 113
Tomato Puree, 133
Vinegar pie, 89
Roast, 88
Steak, 89
Vinegar pie, 209
Raspberry. 466
Vomiting, to stop, 512

# W

PAGE.

Wafers. chocolate. 361
Ginger, 356
Spice, 351
Waffles, French, 179
German. 180
Wall paper, to clean, 494
Walnut cake, 297, 298
Chocolate drops, 385
Washing dishes, 9
Water, barley, 472
Rice. 472
Slippery elm, 472
Toast. 472
Watermelon, how to
serve, 424
Rind, preserved, 401
Sherbet, 473
Wax paper, 387

PAGE.

Wedding menu, 501, 505
Weights and meas-
ures, 495
Wheat muffins. 170
Whip, 471
Whipped cream, 258
Whipped cream pie, 209
White biscuits, 168, 169
Cream cake, 300
Fish. 35, 39
Icing. 338
White Mountain cake. 296
Wiener Braten, 55
Kartoffel Kloesse, 191
Kipfel, 321
Studenten Kipfel, 322
Wild Duck, 84

|                          | PAGE. |                 | PAGE.     |
| ------------------------ | ----- | --------------- | --------- |
| Wild, Goose,             | 84    | Wine, currant,  | 467       |
| Pigeon,                  | 83    | Egg,            | 470       |
| Turkey,                  | 83    | Jelly,          | 411, 414  |
| Windbeutel,              | 328   | Raisin,         | 481, 482  |
| Windows, to clean(see    |       | Sauce,          | 482       |
| Valuable Hints.)         |       | Soup,           | 26        |

# Y

|                      | PAGE. |                  | PAGE. |
| -------------------- | ----- | ---------------- | ----- |
| Yeast,               | 160   | Yum yum pudd t,  | 234   |
| Yellow icing,        | 840   | Yum yums,        | 848   |
| Yorkshire pudding,   | 60    | Zweivel Platz,   | 165   |

# PREFACE.

IN compiling these receipts, dear reader, it never occurred to me that the public would ever lay eyes on them. I hoarded them up as treasures for my own daughters and grandchildren. I think it the duty of every woman to be the head of her household, as much as it is the duty of the man to be the head of his place of business or counting room, wherein to rule means to understand his position and duties. This same rule is applicable to the household. In order to govern and command the respect of your servants and to show them that you are not ignorant of the duties you expect them to perform, you must first learn the management of a household yourself.

The more and better educated you are the more fit you are to perform the duties of help-meet to your dear husband. It is indeed a wife's duty to see that nothing goes to waste, and food improperly prepared is a waste; and what is still more important the health of every member of the family depends on properly selected and prepared food, made palatable by seasoning, and that not too high. A young lady ignorant of housekeeping and its duties is as unfit to be married as a

man that has not the certainty of providing for
a family. A lady that is able to go into the
kitchen when necessity calls her there to perform certain duties is surely to be more respected
than the ignorant one that boasts of her edu-
cation and yet is sorely deficient in that sphere.

Many a lady may tell you that she did not
know how to make a cup of tea when she got
married, but prides herself on being an excellent
" cook and housekeeper " now. Well and good,
all honor is due her for her industry and per-
severance, but she probably never told you of
the heartaches and restless nights of worry it
caused her when Henry came home and told her
that his dear mother or father intended paying
them a visit, or that he had invited them to
dinner, on a special occasion, and wouldn't
*dear mother* see that their favorite dish was prepared for dinner? She may have had a good
plain cook, but she did not know how Henry
wanted that favorite dish prepared. " Wouln't
missus just be kind enough to explain and tell
me just how she wants it done and shure I'll try
me besht to plaise? " But, oh, dear! she didn't
know how to cook a potato, much less give the
receipt for Henry's favorite dish. Poor child—
I hope I have not worked in vain; try and learn
from me, through practicing the following receipts, and if I have succeeded in eliciting
Henry's praises about his dear wife's meals and

making you look all smiles and happy, I shall feel fully repaid for my labor.

In issuing this edition for the "household" I I must admit with thanks that I owe my success to the many encouraging letters received, through the kindness of the publishers, from intelligent housekeepers all over the country. The letters of praise and kind acknowledgments I have in my possession would alone fill a volume like this.

BABETTE.

be particular about rinsing all goblets that have contained milk in cold water before washing with hot, as the milk gives the glass a murky look if put into hot water. Wash all your china in hot, soapy water or soda and rinse in clear, boiling water. Kitchen utensils should be cleaned and scoured carefully after each meal. Every tin cover, pie-plate and kettle should be scoured with sapolio or sand and soda water after using — the rolling pin and pastry board likewise. Have a stationary covered box convenient to your kitchen sink, in which to keep chamois skin and sapolio to clean the faucets after each dish-washing.

### HOW TO PRESERVE LUNCHES.

In preparing a traveler's or a picnic lunch, lay a damp napkin, wrung out in cold water, at top and bottom of the lunch so as to envelope it entirely. This will keep it quite fresh for a good many hours

Groceries such as rice, barley, peas, beans, raisins, currants, citron, etc., should be put into covered glass jars as soon as received—Mason frut jars will answer this purpose—then arrange them on shelves in your pantry. This will help to keep your pantry clean and also save time, for you can then see at a glance what you are looking for and know when to order a fresh supply.

Stove-blacking and other like articles should be kept within easy reach, say in a covered box on the wall back of the kitchen range. See that your stove is brushed off at least once every day, and wiped off at intervals with old newspapers. Old newspapers spread on your kitchen table while working will save you considerable scrubbing.

### CLEANING CREAM.

For cleaning woolen garments of any description, especially boys' and men's clothes, dissolve four ounces of white Castile soap, cut up fine, in one quart of soft water, over the fire. When dissolved, add four quarts more of water; then add four ounces of ammonia, two ounces of ether, two ounces of alcohol, and one ounce of glycerine. Bottle and keep for use. This will keep forever.

# SOUPS.

MEAT SOUPS.

|  | Page. |  | Page. |
|---|---|---|---|
| How to make, - | 13 | Turkey, - - | 23 |
| Mock Turtle, - | 14 | Split Pea, - | 23 |
| Chicken, - - | 14 | Croutons, - - | 24 |
| Ox Tail, - - | 15 | White Bean, - | 24 |
| Veal, - - - | 15 | Linzen (Lintel), - | 25 |
| Noodle, - - | 16 | Potato, - - | 25 |
| Green Pea, - - | 17 | Mutton Broth, - | 25 |
| Drop Dumplings, | 17 | Rice Broth, - | 26 |
| Okra Gumbo, - | 18 |  |  |
| Barley, - - | 18 | COLD SUMMER SOUPS. |  |
| Beef a la Julienne, | 19 | Cherry, - - | 26 |
| Barley and Pea, | 19 | Wine, - - - | 26 |
| Tomato, - - | 20 | Beer, - - | 27 |
| Green Kern, - | 20 | Rice or Sago, - | 27 |
| Bouillon (Beef), | 21 | Milk and Flour, | 27 |
| Farina, - - | 22 | Milk or Cream, - | 27 |
| Pigeon, - - | 22 | Beer, with Milk, | 28 |
| Oyster, - - | 22 | Mehlsuppen, - | 28 |

(12)

# SOUPS.

## MEAT SOUPS

SHOULD be boiled in a closely-covered kettle, used for no other purpose; boil slowly and steadily to extract all of the meat juices. I prefer a granite soup kettle to any other, it being easily kept clean. Skim your soup as soon as it begins to boil and never add salt until your soup is strained. When strained skim off every particle of fat and save this fat in a little jar; you will find it comes in very handy for various uses, such as pie-crust and for browning flour and croutons and other purposes too numerous to mention. Root celery, parsley, onions, carrots, asparagus and potatoes are the best vegetables to add to soup stock. Never use celery leaves for beef soup. You may use celery leaves in potato soup, but sparingly, with chopped parsley leaves. Bouillon should always be thickened with yelks of eggs, beat up with a spoonful of cold water. Ordinary beef soup or tomato soup may be thickened with flour. To do this properly heat a scant spoonful of soup drippings, stir in briskly a spoonful of flour, and add a large quantity of soup to prevent it becoming lumpy.

## MOCK TURTLE SOUP.

Make a rich bouillon from three to four pounds of meat and a calf's head, which had better be boiled the day previous, add celery root, an onion, a few cloves, two bay leaves, and if you happen to have some smoked or pickled tongue, add it also. Soak one quart of turtle beans over night and boil in the soup from four to five hours. When half done add salt and pepper; and when done strain through a collander. An extra and very nice addition are a few sweetbreads boiled in the soup about half an hour and cut into squares and served with the soup. You may also cut up part of the meat that was boiled in the soup, and add. A cup of Madeira and a pint of oysters may be added, but just allow them to boil up once.

## CHICKEN SOUP.

Take an old fat hen; after cleaning and singeing let it lay in fresh water half an hour. Scald the feet, scrape off the skin, crack them in two. Set them on to boil, with the heart and gizzard. Reserve the liver to add to the soup a few minutes before serving, it not requiring more than about three minutes to cook. Boil the chicken, which should be the largest you can get, at least three hours; add some parsley root, an onion and some asparagus, cut into bits. Season with salt. Rice, barley,

noodless or dumplings are nice ingredients for
this soup. Strain and beat up the yelks of two
or more eggs with a tablespoonful of cold water,
just before pouring into the soup bowl. This
soup should not be too thin; and make use of
the chicken either for salad or stew. Season to
taste. I forgot to mention that you must skim
the soup carefully when it begins to boil, and,
after straining, skim off every particle of fat,
which will come in very handy for salads, etc.
Chicken fat takes the place of olive oil.

### OX TAIL SOUP.

Three pounds of lean beef, two ox tails,
chopped up; one large onion, celery root, parsley
and two or three carrots. Boil in one gallon of
water for four hours, slow but steady; boil until
reduced to nearly one-half. Strain; return the
pieces of ox tail and pieces of carrots cut up into
the soup and thicken with one tablespoonful of
flour, browned in a spider with a spoonful of fat.
You may add dumplings or green peas. Very
nice.

### VEAL SOUP.

Boil a piece of veal, off the neck, and a couple
of veal shanks, in two quarts of water; add parsley, an onion and asparagus, cut up into small
pieces. Strain and thicken with the yelks of
eggs. Very nice for the sick.

## NOODLE SOUP.

For six or more persons, select a piece of beef off the neck, say three or four pounds; add three quarts of water, an onion, one celery root, two carrots, a large potato, some parsley, three tomatoes and the giblets of poultry if you happen to have any. Cover up tight. It is important to cook soup in a vessel with a tight-fitting cover and put on as early as eight o'clock in the morning and boil very slow and steady if intended for twelve o'clock dinner. Remove every bit of scum that rises. Strain. Add salt and remove every particle of fat; put in noodles; boil about five minutes and serve at once. If allowed to stand it will become thick. I wish to suggest something right here: never throw away fat or drippings that you have skimmed off soup or meat gravy; save and put into refrigerator for pie-crust.

## NOODLES.

How to make. Put a large handful of flour into a bowl, sifted of course. Make a hollow in the center of the flour, break in an egg. Take the handle of a knife and stir the egg slowly, always in the same direction, until the dough is so stiff that you can not stir it any more with the knife. Flour a baking board and empty your dough upon it, and knead with the hollow of your hand, work with the hands until quite stiff. Flour your board and roll out as thin as possible. Lay

on a clean table near the kitchen fire to dry. Cut
into halves, double up, and cut as fine as possible; spread lightly to dry. If in a hurry just
cut into little squares. Tastes just as nice, the
only difference being in looks.

### GREEN PEA SOUP.

Make your soup stock as usual, adding about
a pint of pea pods to the soup. Lay all the other
vegetables used (in fact, I always save the pea-
pods) into your ice-chest and use them in any
quantity in your soups daily. Heat a tablespoonful of nice drippings in a stewpan, put in the
peas, with a little chopped parsley, cover up tight
and let them simmer on the back of the stove.
Keep adding soup stock when dry. When the
peas are tender, put into the strained soup. Season with salt, and throw in a lump of loaf sugar;
add some drop dumplings to this soup before
serving.

### DROP DUMPLINGS.

Break into a cup the whites of three eggs, fill
the cup with water or milk, put it with a cupful of sifted flour and a tablespoonful of butter or
drippings, into a spider, and let it boil until it
leaves the sides of the spider clean. Then remove from the fire, stir until cold, add the yelks
of the eggs. Keep stirring for about five minutes.
Season it with salt and nutmeg; then drop with
a teaspoon, which has been previously wet with

cold water, into the boiling soup. These little
·dumplings are called in German schwamm-
klaesse. They are very good, and may be used in
any clear soup stock.

### OKRA GUMBO SOUP (SOUTHERN).

Take two quarts of nice ripe tomatoes, stewed
in a porcelain-lined kettle, with two quarts of
okra, cut into small rings. Put this on to boil
with about three quarts of water and a nice piece
of soup meat (no bone), chop up an onion, a
carrot and some parsley and add this to the soup.
Fricassee one chicken with some rice, to be dished
up with the soup, putting a piece of chicken and
a spoonful of rice into each soup plate before adding the soup. Let the soup boil four or five
hours, slowly but steadily. Season with salt and
pepper. A little corn and Lima beans are an improvement, if you have them; they should be
cooked with the soup for several hours. Cut the
soup meat up into small squares and leave in the
soup to serve.

### BARLEY SOUP.

Put on the barley in a porcelain kettle, a very
small teacupful, with about a quart of water.
Let it boil slowly on the back of the stove. Put
on the soup meat in another kettle, with the
addition of whatever vegetables you may happen
to have. As the barley gets thick keep adding
some of the soup stock, strained of course.

Salt to taste. Put on the soup meat two hours before you do the barley.

### BEEF SOUP A LA JULIENNE.

Cook all the vegetables in a separate kettle. Use a nice piece of soup meat, about four pounds, and a large soup bone. Cut up two carrots, two turnips, quarter of a head of cabbage, two heads of celery, a few tomatoes, some beans; cut up very fine a handful of peas and a few tablespoonfuls of corn — you may use canned. When tender pour your soup stock over this. Season to taste and serve. You may add some noodles, cut into little squares, but not too many, or it will be too thick.

### BARLEY AND PEA SOUP.

Barley and peas cooked with goose, often used as soup, makes a very palatable dish. Take the backs of two geese, after being skinned and well salted with ginger and garlic. Lay the backs in the bottom of a porcelain-lined kettle, throw in a pint of whole peas, which have been previously soaked over night. Cover with water and plenty of it, add as much water as you would for soup; in an hour after throw in just as much barley. Cook slowly all the time for at least four hours. You may set it in the bake oven the last hour, in fact it improves by so doing. Add salt to taste. This is just as good warmed over.

### TOMATO SOUP.

Take a large soup bone or three pounds of soup meat, the latter preferred, one or two onions, a few potatoes, a few carrots, a turnip, soup greens and a can of tomatoes or a quart of fresh ones, and in season two ears of grated sweet corn. Season with salt and pepper. Thicken with a tablespoonful of flour, dissolved in cold water. A nice addition to this soup is a handful of noodles cut into round disks with a thimble.

### TOMATO SOUP WITHOUT MEAT.

One quart of tomatoes, one quart of water and one quart of cream or milk, salt and pepper to taste. Cook the tomatoes thoroughly in the water (and have the milk or cream scalding in another vessel), with a little parsley and celery. When cooked strain through a sieve. Put a piece of fresh butter into the soup dish before serving, also some oyster crackers or boiled rice. Add the cream just before serving. A valuable recipe for abstinence days.

### GREEN KERN SOUP.

Soak about a small teacupful of green kern in a bowl of water over night. Put on the soup meat as early as eight o'clock in the morning, half-past eight at the latest (provided you have dinner at noon); add a carrot, an onion, celery, parsley, one or two tomatoes, a potato, in fact

any vegetable you may happen to have at hand.
Cover up closely and let it boil slowly on back
of the stove until dinner time.  Put the green
kern on to boil in water slightly salted, at least
two hours before dinner, and as it boils down
keep adding soup stock from the kettle of soup
on the stove, always straining through a hair
sieve, until all has been used up.  Serve as it is
or strain through a collander and put pieces of
toasted bread into the soup.  Cut the bread into
little squares and fry in hot fat.  Another way of
using the green kern is to grind it to a powder.
Also very fine.

### BOUILLON (BEEF).

Put into the soup kettle three pounds of lean
beef (off the neck is best), two pounds of breast
of veal and an old chicken.  Add six quarts of
water (cold), place on the back of the stove,
where it will boil very slowly.  Remove every
particle of scum as it rises; boil at least three
hours or until the meat is very tender.  Remove from the fire and set in a cool place over
night.  Remove carefully all the fat from the
stock, strain and put on to boil, with the following vegetables:  One head of celery, three
carrots, a small turnip, an onion and a few
tomatoes and some parsley.  Peel and slice the
vegetables quite thin before adding.  Boil an
hour, adding salt just before straining a second
time through a sieve.  This should make a gal-

lon of soup. If less is desired use less meat. If preparing for invalids it is better to omit all the vegetables except celery. Serve in cups. Beat the yelk of one egg for a cup of bouillon. In making a quantity three yelks will be sufficient; beat up the yelks, adding a few drops of cold water before adding the boiling bouillon.

### FARINA SOUP.

When the soup stock has been strained and every particle of fat removed, return it to the kettle to boil. When it boils hard stir in carefully quarter of a teacupful of farina, do this slowly to prevent the farina from forming lumps. Stir into the soup bowl the yelks of one or two eggs, add a teaspoonful of cold water. Pour the soup into the bowl gradually and stir constantly until all the soup has been poured into the bowl. Serve at once.

### PIGEON SOUP.

Make a beef soup, and an hour before wanted throw in a pigeon. Boil slowly, with all kinds of vegetables (provided your patient is allowed to have them, for remember this is a soup intended for the convalescent). Strain, add the beaten yelk of an egg, add salt to taste.

### OYSTER SOUP.

Pour one quart of boiling water into a porcelain-lined kettle and one quart of good, rich

SOUPS.                    23

milk. Stir in one-half cup of finely rolled
cracker crumbs; as soon as this comes to a boil
add one quart of fresh oysters and a lump of
fresh butter, about the size of an egg. Let it
boil up once, then remove from the fire immediately. Dish up in a soup bowl in which
you have previously put salt and pepper. Stir
briskly while pouring in the soup.

### TURKEY SOUP.

Crack all the bones and cut up all the meat
of a cold turkey left over from a meal. Add an
onion, a carrot, a turnip, celery, parsley, in fact
any vegetable you may happen to have at hand.
Boil slowly for two or three hours. Strain and
add boiled rice or barley.

### SPLIT PEA SOUP.

Wash the peas in warm water by rubbing
them through your hands a great many times.
A better plan is to soak them in lukewarm water
over night, Use a quart of peas to a gallon of
water. Boil about two hours, with the following
vegetables: a few potatoes, a large celery root, a
little parsley and a large onion. When boiled
down to about half the quantity, take out the
vegetables and press through a collander. To
make this soup very rich add about two pounds
of beef and boil with the soup until tender, then
remove it. Boil some little sausages in this soup

after it is strained. Serve these as an entree with
your dinner. If your soup is too thin put a
piece of butter into a saucepan, with a spoonful
of flour. Let it boil, stir in part of the soup
briskly and add to the whole. Have some croutons ready in the souptureen and serve. Season
with salt and pepper to taste.

### CROUTONS.

Heat some butter or fat in a spider. Cut up
about two slices of stale bread, put them into a
spider and brown on both sides. Cut up the bread
in dice shape before throwing into the hot fat.
Brown nicely, but do not let it burn. Serve with
split pea soup, bean and potato soups.

### WHITE BEAN SOUP.

To one quart of small dried beans add as
much water as you wish to have soup. You may
add any cold scraps of roast beef, mutton, poultry, veal or meat sauce that you may happen to
have. Boil until the beans are very soft. You
may test them in this way: Take up a few in a
spoon and blow on them very hard, if the skin
separates from the beans you may press them
through a sieve, or take up the meat or scraps and
vegetables and serve without straining. Add salt
and pepper to taste. A great many prefer this
soup unstrained. The water in which has been
boiled a smoked tongue may be used for this

soup. This may be thickened like split pea soup. Excellent.

### LINTEL, OR LINZEN SOUP.

It is made just like split pea soup, without straining. Add the sausage and croutons.

### POTATO SOUP.

For two quarts of soup, boil about a dozen potatoes. After boiling a few minutes, pour off the water and add fresh water from the boiling teakettle. Add salt and fat, any drippings left from roast beef or boiled smoked tongue are particularly nice for this purpose. Celery and parsley roots and an onion should be added. When the potatoes are very soft strain through a collander. Salt and pepper to taste. Add croutons and serve. Sauce of roast beef or poultry improves this soup. This is a cheap and wholesome soup and deserves to be better known.

### MUTTON BROTH.

Cut three pounds of lean mutton into small squares; cover closely and boil with three quarts of water, slowly, for two hours; then soak one-fourth of a cupful of rice in warm water, just enough to cover it, then add the rice to the boiling soup. Cook an hour longer, slowly; watch carefully, and stir from time to time. Strain and thicken it with a little flour; salt and pepper to taste. Particularly nice for invalids.

### RICE BROTH.

May be made either of beef or mutton, adding all kinds of vegetables. Boil half a cupful of rice separately in a farina kettle. Strain the beef or mutton broth. Add the rice and boil half an hour longer, with potatoes cut into dice shape; use about two potatoes; then add the beaten yelk of an egg. Strained stock of chicken broth added to this soup makes it vey palatable and nutritious for the sick

### CHERRY SOUP.

This delicious soup is to be eaten cold, it is a summer soup. Use large, dark red or black cherries, a quart is sufficient. Take a bottle of claret, or any other red wine, and twice as much water as you have wine; half a cup of pearl sago, a few slices of lemon and some cinnamon bark or stick cinnamon, cook about one-half hour, cherries and all. If you find that the soup is too thick add more wine and water, sweeten to suit the taste, a cupful of sugar is the most 1 ever use.

Strawberry, blueberry and raspberry soups may be prepared according to above receipt.

### WINE SOUPS

Boil half wine and half water, sweeten to taste, add cinnamon, a few slices of lemon and thicken with a few yelks of eggs. Just before serving,

break in some sweet almond macaroons. This
may be eaten hot or cold; better cold.

### BEER SOUP.

Mix the beer with one-third water, boil with
sugar and the grated crust of stale rye bread,
add stick cinnamon and a little lemon juice.
Pour over small pieces of zwieback (rusk).
Some boil a handful of dried currants. When
done add both currants and juice.

### RICE, OR SAGO SOUP.

Take of rice or sago about one-quarter of a
pound, scald it and put on to boil in cold water;
add cinnamon, sugar and the grated rind of a
lemon, a handful of currants thoroughly cleaned,
not forgetting a good pinch of salt. Just before
removing from the fire add a bottle of red wine
and as much water; add more sugar if necessary.

### MILK AND FLOUR SOUPS.

An earthen milk or a porcelain-lined kettle
may be used for these soups, but a farina kettle
is preferable if you have one large enough.

### MILK, OR CREAM SOUP.

Heat a quart or more of milk or cream, add
a spoonful of sweet butter and thicken with a
spoonful of flour or corn starch, wet with cold
milk. Pour boiling over pieces of toasted bread
cut into dices; crackers may also be used.

### BEER SOUP WITH MILK.

Boil separately a quart each of beer and milk; sweeten the beer, add cinnamon, the crust of a rye loaf and the grated rind of a lemon; beat up the yelks of two eggs, add the milk gradually to the eggs, then the beer. Serve in small bowls.

### MEHLSUPPEN.

Braune Mehlsuppe (No. 1).—Heat a spoonful of butter in a spider, add a spoonful of flour, stir briskly, but do not let it get black; pour boiling water over it, add salt and carroway seeds.

Mehlsuppe—Flour Soup (No. 2).—Heat butter or fat in a spider, put in a tablespoonful of flour; mix while boiling, but do not let it brown; add as much milk as you desire; add grated nutmeg and salt to taste. Rule, one tablespoonful of flour for one plate of soup.

# FISH AND OYSTERS.

Page.

How and what to do
   with, - - 30
When to eat, - 32
Boneless, filled, - 32
Speckled Trout, - 33
Fried Perch, - 34
Baked Black Bass, 34
White or Trout (sweet
   and sour), - 35
Pike, with egg sauce, 36
Pickerel (Hecht), 37
Fish a la Brunswick, 38
Brook Trout, - 38
Baked Shad, stuffed
   with oysters, - 39
Croquettes, - 39
Fried White, - 39
  " Sea Bass, - 40
  " Sunfish, - 40

Page.

Redsnapper with
   tomato sauce, - 40
Marinirter Herring, 41
Flounders, baked, 41
Smelts, fried, - 42
Black Bass, boiled, 42
Oysters, how to serve, 42
Oysters Stewed, - 42
  " Fried, - - 43
  " Escaloped, 43
  " Dry Stew, - 44
  " Cream Stew, 44
  " Boston Fry, 44
  " Patties, - 45
  " Cream on the
     shell, - 45
Tomato Puree for
   fried Oysters, - 46
Soft-shell Crabs, 46

(29)

## FISH AND OYSTERS.

FISH, to scale readily, should be dipped in boiling water, for a second only. Clean thoroughly, not forgetting to remove the eyes and ears, but in so doing try not to destroy the shape of the head, which not only adds to the looks of the boiled fish but to its flavor as well. Salt your fish the day previous to cooking, this applies to both baked and fried fish. Heat the salt; this little extra trouble will pay you, for then the salt will penetrate through the flesh to the bone. Rub with salt inside and outside. Remember—heat the salt, this is easily done by putting the salt in a tin plate and setting in the oven a minute.

To cook fish properly is very important, as no food, perhaps, is so insipid as fish if carelessly cooked. It *must be well done and properly salted.* A good rule to cook fish by is the following: Allow ten minutes to the first pound and five minutes for each additional pound; for example: Say you have a fish weighing five pounds—boil it thirty minutes. By pulling out a fin you may ascertain whether your fish is done; if it comes out easily and the meat is an opaque white, your fish has boiled long

enough.  Nothing is so disgusting to the palate
as a piece of raw or underdone fish.  Always
set your fish on to boil in hot water, hot from
the teakettle, adding salt and a dash of vinegar
to keep the meat firm; an onion, a head of
celery and parsley roots are always an accept-
able flavor to any kind of boiled fish, no matter
what kind of sauce you intend to serve it with.
If you wish to serve the fish whole, tie it in a
napkin and lay it on an old plate at the bottom
of the kettle; if you have a regular "fish kettle"
this is not necessary.  I prefer carving, or rather
cutting up, the fish before boiling, and then ar-
ranging the fish on the platter as though it were
whole—head first and so on, it is then much
more convenient to serve.  In boiling fish this
way, always lay the head at the bottom of the
kettle.  In boiling fish, avoid adding too much
water—I have heard a great many complaints
about getting the sauce too thin, or too thick,
especially the former.  A good way to thicken
sauces, where flour is used, is an even teaspoonful of flour to a cupful of sauce, or the yelk of
one egg to a cupful of sauce.  When boiling
fish, allow the water to just reach the top, but
not to cover it.

In frying fish do not leave the fish lie in the
spider in which it has been fried, for this ab-
sorbs the fat and destroys the delicate flavor.
Be sure that the fish is done.  Fried fish should

be nicely browned, then removed at once to a platter. Persons who say they can not eat fried fish, on account of its oily, indigestible qualities, do not know that in most cases it is not the mode of cooking that is to blame, but the careless cook, who allows it to spoil after it is cooked.

### WHEN TO EAT VARIOUS KINDS OF FISH.

Fresh Salmon is best in May.

Pickerel is best from September to January.

Black Bass is best from September to January.

Pike is best from January until April.

Carp is best from October until April.

Shad is best from March until May.

Trout all the year round.

Lobster is best from May until September.

Oysters are best from September until April.

### BONELESS FISH, FILLED.

Prepare trout, pickerel, or pike in the following manner: After the fish has been scaled and thoroughly cleaned, remove all the meat that adheres to the skin, being careful not to injure the skin; take out all the meat from head to tail, cut open along the back bone, removing it also; but do not disfigure the head and tail. Still another way is to pull off the whole skin of the fish, then remove all the meat, being very careful not to have any bones mixed with it; chop the meat in a chopping bowl, then heat

about a quarter of a pound of butter in a spider,
throw in a handful of chopped parsley, and some
soaked white bread; remove from the fire and
add an onion grated, salt, pepper, pounded
almonds, three whole eggs and the yelks of two
also a very little nutmeg grated. Mix all
thoroughly and fill the skin until it looks nat-
ural. Boil in salt water, containing a piece of
butter, celery root and parsley and an onion;
when done remove from the fire and lay on a
platter. Have some almonds blanched; cut
each almond lengthwise into four strips, and
stick them into the body of the fish, until it
looks as though it were all bristles. Thicken
the fish sauce with yelks of eggs, adding a few
slices of lemon. To bake this fish first roll it in
flour, then lay it in plenty of fresh butter.

### SPECKLED TROUT.

I take it for granted that you have cleaned
and salted the trout the day previous; line a kettle with an onion cut up, also some celery root
and parsley, if you have it; tie the fish in a napkin and lay it on this bed of roots; pour in
enough water to just cover it and add a dash of
vinegar—the vinegar keeps the meat firm—then
boil over a quick fire and add more salt to the
water the fish has been boiled in. Lay your
dish on a hot platter and prepare the following
sauce: Set a cup of sweet cream in a kettle,

heat it, add a lump of fresh butter, salt and
pepper and thicken with a dessertspoonful of
flour (wet the flour with a little cold milk before
adding), stir the flour into the cream and boil
about one minute, stirring constantly; pour over
the fish. Now boil two eggs, and while they are
boiling blanche about a dozen or more almonds
and stick them into the fish, points up, now dash
the eggs into cold water, peel them, separate the
whites from the yelks, chop up each separately in
a saucer, with a knife; chop up some nice fresh
parsley. Garnish the fish, first with a row of
chopped yelks, then white, until all is used up;
lay chopped parsley all around the platter.
Eat hot.

### FRIED PERCH.

Clean well, be very particular about getting
off all the scales; remove the head, split open and
clean inside as thoroughly as out; wash and
wipe dry; sprinkle with salt inside and outside,
and dredge with flour. Have ready a frying pan
of boiling hot butter; put in the fish and fry a
nice brown, turning at the end of five minutes.
Lay on a hot platter and garnish with parsley
and slices of lemon.

### BAKED BLACK BASS.

After having carefully cleaned, salt well and
lay it in the baking pan with a small cupful of
water, and strew flakes of butter on top, also salt,

pepper and a little chopped parsley. Bake about one hour, basting often until brown. Serve on a heated platter; garnish with parsley and lemon and make a nice sauce by adding a glass of sherry and a little catsup and thicken with a teaspoonful of flour, adding this to fish gravy. Serve potatoes with fish, boiled in the usual way, making a sauce of two tablespoonfuls of butter put into a saucepan, to heat. Throw in a bunch of parsley chopped very fine and salt and pepper to taste, adding a small cup of sweet cream, thickened with a spoonful of flour. Pour over potatoes.

### WHITE OR TROUT, SWEET AND SOUR.

Salt the fish the day previous; line the kettle with slices of onions and celery root and lay the fish upon this, adding water to barely cover; add a piece of fresh butter, a few slices of lemon and a dash of vinegar, also a few cloves. Let the fish boil, uncovered, and in the meantime soak half a "lebkuchen," the finest you can get, in a very little vinegar; add a handful of raisins, also a handful of pounded almonds and some ground cinnamon; sweeten with a handful of brown sugar and a tablespoonful of syrup; add also a small crust of rye bread. By this time your fish will be ready to turn, then add the sauce and allow the fish to boil a few minutes longer. Taste, and if too sour add more sugar. Take up the fish

carefully, lay it on a platter and let the sauce
boil until it coats the spoon, then pour over the
fish. Eat warm or cold.

### PIKE WITH EGG SAUCE.

Clean the fish thoroughly, and wash it in hot
water, wipe dry and salt inside and out. If you
heat the salt it will penetrate through the meat
of the fish in less time. Now take a porcelain-
lined kettle, lay in it a piece of butter about the
size of an egg; cut up an onion, some celery root
and parsley root and a few slices of lemon, and
lay the fish in, either whole or cut up in slices;
boil in enough water to just cover the fish, and
add more salt if required, and throw in about a
dozen whole peppers, black or white; season also
with ground white pepper. Let the fish boil
quickly. In the meantime beat up the yelks
of two eggs, and pound a handful of almonds
to a paste, and add to the beaten yelks, together
with a tablespoonful of cold water. When done
remove the fish to a large platter; but to ascertain whether the fish has cooked long enough,
take hold of the fins, if they come out readily
your fish has cooked enough. Strain the sauce
through a sieve, taking out the slices of lemon
and with them garnish the top of the fish; add
the strained sauce to the beaten egg, stirring
constantly as you do so; then return the sauce
to the kettle, and stir until it boils, then remove

quickly and pour it over the fish. When it is
cold garnish with curly parsley.

### HECHT (PICKEREL).

This fish is best prepared " scharf." Clean your
fish thoroughly and salt the day previous;
wrap it in a clean towel and lay it on ice until
wanted. Line a porcelain-lined kettle with celery
and parsley roots; cut up an onion, add a lump
of fresh butter, and pack the fish in the kettle,
head first, either whole or cut up; sprinkle a
little salt and white pepper over all and add
about a dozen peppercorns; put on enough
water to just cover, and add a whole lemon cut
in slices. Do not let the fish boil quickly. Add
also about a dozen pounded almonds. By this
time the fish will be ready to turn, then beat up
the yelks of two or three eggs in a bowl, to be
added to the sauce, after the fish is boiled. Try
the fish with a fork and if the meat loosens
readily it is done. Now take up each piece
carefully, if it has been cut up, and arrange on
a large platter, head first and so on, make the
fish appear whole, and garnish with the slices
of lemon and sprigs of parsley; then mince up
some parsley and throw on top of the fish,
around the lemon slices. Now thicken the gravy
by adding the beaten yelks, add a tablespoonful
of cold water to the yelks before adding to the
boiling sauce; stir, remove from the fire at once

and pour over the fish. If you prefer the sauce strained, then strain before adding the yelks of the eggs and almonds. Give this a fair trial and you will never prepare pickerel any other way. Pike and perch may be prepared in the same manner.

### FISH A LA BRUNSWICK.

Cook any large fish in salt water—salmon is particularly nice prepared in this style—add one cup of vinegar, onions, celery root and parsley. When the fish is cooked enough, remove it from the fire, kettle and all—letting the fish remain in its sauce until the following sauce is prepared. Take two hard-boiled eggs, rub the yelks with two raw yelks; add one teaspoonful of prepared mustard, some salt, pepper, sweet butter, some vinegar and lemon juice; take parsley, green onions, capers, shallots and one large vinegar pickle and some astragon, chop all up very fine, as fine as possible; chop up the hard-boiled whites separately and then add the sauce; mix all this together thoroughly, then taste to see if seasoned to suit. This is often called fish piquant.

### BROOK TROUT.

Clean with care in order not to destroy its shape; wash in salt water, wipe perfectly dry and roll in salted flour and fry in hot butter; drain off every drop of grease; serve on a hot platter and garnish with parsley.

## BAKED SHAD, STUFFED WITH OYSTERS.

Dry the fish (which should be a large one) thoroughly after it is cleaned; rub well with salt inside and out. Make a stuffing of grated bread crumbs, flakes of butter, salt, pepper and oysters; stuff the fish and sew it up. Lay it in a baking-pan, with a cupful of water to keep it from burning; bake an hour, basting often with pieces of butter and the water in pan; bake until brown. When done lay the fish on a hot platter and cover tightly while you boil up the gravy with a spoonful of catsup; add a little more hot water and a spoonful of browned flour, which has been wet with a little cold water and the juice of part of a lemon. Serve sauce in sauceboat and garnish the fish with slices of lemon, curly parsley, or watercress.

## CROQUETTES OF FISH.

Take any kind of boiled fish, separate it from the bones carefully, chop with a little parsley and salt and pepper to taste. Beat up an egg with a teaspoonful of milk and flour. Roll the fish into balls and turn them in the beaten egg and cracker crumbs or bread. Fry a light brown. Serve with any sauce or a mayonnaise.

## FRIED WHITE FISH.

Clean and dry the fish, salt inside and out; roll in cracker flour or bread crumbs and then in beaten egg that has been seasoned with a

pinch of salt. Fry in very hot butter, a nice
brown on both sides. If the fish is very large,
split it lengthwise through the center and then
cut into pieces about three inches wide. Serve
with catsup and slices of lemon.

### FRIED SEA BASS.

Fry same as white fish, omitting the eggs;
just roll in cracker or bread crumbs — flour
slightly salted is best—and fry in very hot butter.

### SUNFISH OR SMALL FLAT FISH.

Clean, wash and wipe dry; salt and roll in
flour and fry in hot butter a nice brown on both
sides.

### REDSNAPPER WITH TOMATO SAUCE.

This delicious fish is best prepared in the following manner: Scale thoroughly, salt and pepper inside and out, and lay upon ice, wrapped
in a clean cloth over night. When ready to
cook cut up a celery or parsley root, or both,
two fine large onions, a carrot or two, and let
this come to a boil in about one quart of water,
then lay in the fish, whole or in pieces, to suit
yourself; let the water almost cover the fish;
add a lump of fresh butter and three or four
tomatoes (out of season you may use canned
tomatoes, say three or four large spoonfuls);
let the fish boil half an hour, turning it occasionally. Try it by taking hold of the fins,

if they come out readily, the fish is done. Take it up carefully, lay on a large platter and strain the sauce, then let it boil, adding a cupful of sweet cream in which you have dissolved a teaspoonful of flour; chop up a bunch of parsley and garnish the fish with this, letting a quantity mingle with the sauce. You may omit the cream and thicken with the yelks of two or three eggs. This fish is very good fried also.

### MARINIRTER (PICKLED) HERRING.

Take new Holland herring, remove the heads and scales, wash well, open them and take out the milch and lay the herring and milch in milk or water over night. Next day lay the herring in a stone jar with alternate layers of onions cut up, also lemon cut in slices, a few cloves, whole peppers and a few bay leaves, some capers and whole mustard seed. Now take the milch and rub it through a hair sieve, the more of them you have the better for the sauce; stir in a spoonful of brown sugar and vinegar and pour it over the herring. Will keep for a long time.

### BAKED FLOUNDERS.

Clean, wipe dry, add salt and pepper and lay them in a pan; put flakes of butter on top, an onion cut up, some minced celery and a few bread crumbs. A cup of hot water put into the pan will prevent burning. Baste often; bake until brown.

## FRIED SMELTS.

Clean, wipe dry, salt and roll in beaten egg and cracker flour; fry in hot butter.

## BOILED BLACK BASS.

See pickerel or pike, with egg sauce.

## OYSTERS.

In giving an oyster supper always serve raw oysters first, then stewed, fried and so on. Serve nice, white crisp celery, olives, lemons, good catsup, cold slaw and pickles, and do not forget to have two or three kinds of crackers on the table. Chili sauce is a good addition; also piccalilli.

## OYSTER STEW.

Drain off all the liquor from a quart of oysters, heat the liquor, and at the same time heat a quart of rich, sweet milk to boiling point, skim the boiling liquor, then put in the oysters. In the meantime put salt and pepper in the oyster bowl and a tablespoonful of sweet butter; when the oysters begin to ruffle, take the stew from the fire, pour it into the bowl, stirring constantly, adding the scalded milk at the same time. Serve with oyster crackers; be very careful not to let the milk burn, nor the oysters cook too long: take them up as soon as they are ruffled.

### FRIED OYSTERS.

Use none but select oysters for frying. Drain
off every drop of liquor, lay them on a clean
towel, and cover with another, pat lightly upon
the covered oysters so as to dry them, remove
the upper cloth and sprinkle the oysters with
salt and pepper. Crush some soda crackers very
fine—do this with a rolling pin—roll each oyster
into the cracker flour; beat up three or more
eggs lightly, dip each oyster into the beaten eggs;
pick up each oyster with a fork and drop carefully into a frying pan containing plenty of
butter; the butter must be very hot; test by
frying one oyster, if it browns quickly, go on
with the rest. Put on a platter garnished with
parsley. Always serve lemons, catsup, pickles
and cold slaw with fried oysters. Your oysters
will fry much nicer by using half lard and half
butter.

### ESCALOPED OYSTERS.

Roll fine a pound of soda crackers or bread
crumbs; put a layer of these in the bottom of
a deep buttered dish (a porcelain pudding dish
is preferable to any other); wet the layer of
cracker crumbs slightly with the liquor of the
oysters, then put a layer of oysters on top of
the cracker crumbs; sprinkle with fine salt and
pepper, and lay small pieces of butter here and
there over the oysters; then another layer of
crumbs, and so on until you have used up all

the oysters. Have a layer of cracker crumbs
on top; put flakes of butter over the top; pour
on milk, a cupful over all, and bake a light brown.
It is improved by adding a couple of well-beaten
eggs with the milk.

### DRY STEW.

Drain off every drop of liquor from the
oysters; set the liquor on to boil and skim it
thoroughly; put in a lump of best butter, salt
and pepper to taste; throw in the oysters and
boil about two minutes and serve with crackers.
Delicious.

### CREAM STEW.

Is made precisely like a milk stew (called
oyster stew), using cream instead of milk.

### BOSTON OYSTER FRY.

Take large select oysters and drain off every
bit of liquor; lay the oysters on a clean towel,
cover with another, and pat them lightly in
order to dry them, then remove the upper towel
and sprinkle with salt and pepper. Crush two
or three soda crackers with a rolling pin until
they are as fine as flour. Salt the rolled
cracker crumbs slightly; roll each oyster in the
cracker flour, then beat up three or more eggs
slightly, and dip in this each oyster as you take
it from the rolled crackers; pick up each oyster
with a fork and drop carefully into a frying pan,

containing plenty of butter, the butter must be very hot (use half lard and half butter); test by frying one oyster, if it browns quickly, go on with the rest; when done put them on a hot platter, and pour a puree of hot tomatoes over them and garnish with curly parsley.

### OYSTERS PATES, OR PATTIES.

Make a very rich puff paste and bake in patty-pans; bake smaller patties to be used as covers (many prefer the patties uncovered); when baked turn out on a large platter until your oyster filling is ready. Set the oysters on to boil in their own liquor, add a piece of butter, a little cream; beat up the yelks of two eggs, with a little salt and pepper. Remove the oysters from the fire, stir in the beaten egg; fill the patties and set in the oven; brush with beaten egg; bake about five minutes. Serve hot. Boil the liquor, and skim before putting in the oysters.

### CREAM OYSTERS ON THE SHELL.

In the first place get some nice clam shells and wash them, wipe them dry and butter them inside. Range these closely in a large baking pan and prop them up with pieces of coal; put one oyster in each shell, sprinkle salt and pepper over each one, and pour a spoonful of the following mixture over each oyster: Pour into a farina kettle about two cups of milk, stir in two spoonfuls of butter, a little salt and pepper.

Take from the fire as soon as boiled, and thicken
with one tablespoonful of flour wet with the
liquor of the oysters; add also the yelks of two
eggs, then stir and pour a spoonful of this mixture over each oyster and bake five minutes.
Serve on the shell.  Delicious.

### TOMATO PUREE.

Scald the tomatoes, take off the skins carefully and stew with a spoonful each of butter
and sugar; salt and pepper to taste.  When very
soft, strain through a coarse sieve, and if necessary thicken with a spoonful of flour; pour this
over the oysters hot.  This should be prepared
before you begin to fry the oysters.

### SOFT SHELL CRABS.

Take out the sandbags and pull off the spongy
substance from the sides; wash and wipe dry;
roll in beaten cracker crumbs, which have been
slightly salted, then in beaten egg.  Have ready
a deep spider, filled with seething hot butter;
fry brown.  Serve hot and garnish with parsley
and slices of lemon.

# FISH AND MEAT SAUCES.

|                          | Page. |
|--------------------------|-------|
| Mushroom,                | 48    |
| Maitre d'hotel,          | 48    |
| Onion,                   | 48    |
| Tartar,                  | 49    |
| Raisin,                  | 49    |
| Horseradish,             | 49    |
| Sauce Bordelaise,        | 50    |
| Garlic, or Knoblauch,    | 50    |
| Carroway, or Kimmel,     | 50    |
| Sardelen, or Herring,    | 50    |
| Hollandaise, or Dutch,   | 51    |
| Lemon,                   | 51    |
| Butter,                  | 51    |
| Cranberry,               | 52    |
| Mint,                    | 52    |

(47)

# FISH AND MEAT SAUCES.

## MUSHROOM SAUCE.

STEW a teacupful of mushrooms in a very little soup stock or water; add two table-spoonfuls of flour mixed with a little cold water; add nutmeg; salt and pepper to taste and stir all up with the mushrooms and pour into sauce-boat.

## MAITRE D'HOTEL SAUCE.

Take a heaping tablespoonful of nice drip-pings or goosefat, heat it in a spider, stir two teaspoonfuls of flour into this, then add grad-ually and carefully a small teacupful of hot soup or water, the former is preferable; add some chopped parsley also the juice of a lemon; salt and pepper; stir up well. May be used either with roast or boiled meats.

## ONION SAUCE.

Stew some finely-chopped onions in fat; you may add half a clove of garlic, cut extremely fine; brown a very little flour in this, season with salt and pepper and add enough soup stock to thin it.

(43)

## TARTAR SAUCE.

Brown some fat or butter in a spider, stir in a tablespoonful of flour; cut up part of an onion, a clove of garlic, a few laurel or bay leaves; grate in part of a celery root, also half a carrot, a few cloves, whole peppers; add soup stock and water. Let this boil for an hour, then strain and add capers and chopped sardellen and a few slices of lemon.

## RAISIN SAUCE.

Brown some fat or butter in a spider, stir in a tablespoonful of flour; stir until it becomes a smooth paste; then add hot soup, stirring constantly; throw in a handful of raisins, some pounded almonds, a few slices of lemon, also a tablespoonful of vinegar; brown sugar to taste: flavor with a few cloves and cinnamon, and if you choose to do so, grate in part of a stick of horseradish and the crust of a rye loaf. Very nice for fat beef.

## HORSERADISH SAUCE.

To be used with soup meat. Grate a stick of horseradish (do this over a hot stove or in the open air); take some soup stock, a spoonful of fat, half a cup of vinegar, a little salt, sugar to taste, some raisins, cinnamon and a few slices of lemon. Let this come to a boil, then stir in the horseradish. Let it boil until quite thick,

and pour while hot over the meat. This sauce
may be used with veal, tongue and very fat beef.
If the sauce is too thin grate some stale bread
and add to it. Pounded almonds are very nice
and add greatly to the flavor of the sauce.

### SAUCE BORDELAISE.

Nice for broiled steaks. Take one medium-
sized onion, chopped very fine and browned in
fat or butter; add a cup of strong beef gravy
and a cup of claret or white wine; add pepper,
salt and a trifle of finely-chopped parsley; allow
this to simmer and thicken with a little browned
flour.

### GARLIC, OR KNOBLAUCH SAUCE.

Heat a spoonful of fat or goose oil in a spider;
cut up one or two cloves of garlic very fine and
let it brown in the heated fat; add a spoonful
of flour and soup stock, or water; salt and pepper
to taste.

### CARROWAY, OR KIMMEL SAUCE.

Heat a spoonful of nice drippings in a spider;
add a little flour; stir smooth with a cupful of
soup stock, added at once, and half a teaspoonful of carroway seeds.

### SARDELLEN, OR HERRING SAUCE.

Brown a spoonful of flour in heated fat, add
a quantity of hot soup-stock and a few sardellen

chopped fine, which you have previously washed in cold water, also a finely-chopped onion. Let this boil a few minutes, add a little vinegar and sugar; strain this sauce through a wire sieve and add a few capers and a wineglassful of white wine and let it boil up once again and thicken with the yelks of one or two eggs.

## HOLLANDAISE, OR DUTCH SAUCE.

Heat flour and butter, or fat, in a spider; add soup or fish stock, a little salt, lemon juice or vinegar and a little sugar; boil about five minutes; thicken with the yelks of eggs. This sauce is used for fish, meats, cauliflower, asparagus, etc. Always use butter for fish and vegetables.

## LEMON SAUCE.

Boil some soup stock with a few slices of lemon, a little sugar and grated nutmeg; add chopped parsley; thicken with a teaspoonful of flour or yelks of eggs. Mostly used for stewed poultry.

## BUTTER SAUCE.

One tablespoonful of butter, one of flour; stir constantly and allow to boil briskly, then add quickly a cupful of boiling water, and stir constantly. This will make a rich, smooth sauce, to which may be added capers or shrimps, mustard, or whatever ingredient the sauce will take its name from. This is more of a fish sauce.

## CRANBERRY SAUCE.

Pick a quart of cranberries, wash and drain, and put on to boil in a saucepan with half a tea- cupful of water. Stew slowly, stirring often, until thick. Give them from one to two hours to cook. Then take from the fire and strain through a collander or sieve; sweeten abund- antly with white sugar; wet a mold with cold water, pour in the sauce and set away in a cold place to get firm. When firm, turn out on a glass or China salver. Eat with roast turkey, ducks, geese and game of any kind. Never sweeten while cooking; it injures the color. Better prepared the day previous to using.

## MINT SAUCE.

Chop some mint fine; boil half a teacupful of vinegar with one tablespoonful of sugar; throw in the mint and boil up once; pour in a sauce- boat and cool off a little before serving.

# MEATS.

| | Page. |
|---|---|
| Time-table for roasts, | 54 |
| Filet de Bœuf au Champignons, | 54 |
| Broiled Beefsteak, | 55 |
| Fried Beefsteak, | 56 |
| Round Beefsteak, | 56 |
| Hamburger Steak, | 56 |
| Wiener Braten, | 57 |
| Soup Meat (how to prepare), | 57 |
| Fleisch Kugel (meat-ball), | 58 |
| Brisket of Beef, | 58-59 |
| Mutton or Lamb Chops, | 59 |
| Breast of Mutton Stewed with Carrots, | 59 |
| Roast Beef with Yorkshire Pudding, | 60 |
| Roast Beef, | 60 |
| Roast Lamb, | 61 |
| Roast Mutton with Potatoes, | 62 |
| Sauerbraten, | 62 |
| Calf's Liver, | 63 |
| Roast Veal, | 63-64 |
| Veal Cutlets, | 64 |
| Fricassed Veal, | 65 |
| Calf's Liver Smothered in Onions, | 65 |
| Hashed Calf's Lung and Heart, | 66 |
| Spiced Veal Loaf, | 66 |
| Stewed Veal, | 67 |
| Veal Sweetbreads, fried, | 67 |
| Croquettes of Calf's Brains, | 68 |

(53)

# MEATS.

## TIME-TABLE FOR ROASTED MEATS.

BEEF, from ten to twenty minutes to the pound.
Mutton, ten minutes to the pound for rare and twenty minutes for well done.

Lamb, fifteen to twenty minutes to the pound.

Veal, twenty minutes to the pound.

Turkey, of eight to ten pounds' weight, not less than three hours.

Goose, of seven or eight pounds, two hours.

Chicken, from an hour to an hour and a half.

Domestic duck, an hour and a half.

Game duck, forty minutes.

## FILET DE BŒUF AU CHAMPIGNONS.

For this you must get a tenderloin roast, which you will have to order at least a day or two before you wish to use it, as butchers do not always keep them on hand. Rub the roast well with salt and pepper; make a bed of onions, celery and parsley root in the roasting pan, lay the roast upon this bed and put flakes of fat or butter here and there on top of the roast, and cut up a few tomatoes and lay on top also. Cover up the roast, air tight, and roast in a quick oven. Look after it carefully, basting when necessary and adding hot water. When done lay on a platter, strain the sauce and add the mushrooms;

(51)

thicken the sauce with a teaspoonful of flour and pour it over the roast when ready to serve. Dissolve the flour in a very little cold water before adding to the sauce. Spinach is a nice accompaniment. A very attractive looking dish may be made of this roast by putting all kinds of vegetables around it on the same platter, such as cauliflower, green peas, Lima beans, spinach and carrots; of course judgment must be used as to the harmonizing of colors; do not put more than about four tablespoonfuls of each vegetable around the roast. Serve the sauce in a sauce-boat. Slice the roast, but do not destroy its shape.

### BROILED BEEFSTEAK.

All steak should be cut at least three-quarters of an inch thick, and should never be pounded, as it affords ready escape to all the juices; do not put it in water, if you doubt its being clean scrape across it with a knife. For a family of two or three I recommend the porterhouse, for a large family the sirloin, it being equally nice and more economical. For broiling, the coals should be red hot. Heat the broiler well before putting on the steak and turn frequently, being careful not to burn and not to pierce the meat with the fork. When the steak is cooked, lay it on a heated platter, salt and pepper and lay a lump of nice fresh butter on the top; turn the steak, repeat this process again, so as to have

both sides seasoned, and decorate with parsley
and slices of lemon.

### FRIED BEEFSTEAK.

Steak fried in a spider, if done properly, is almost as good as broiled. Have the spider very
hot, cut a piece of fat off the steak and allow
this to heat just enough to grease the spider.
Lay in the steak, turning very often to keep the
juices in; salt and pepper. When done put on
a hot platter and cover up. Now cut up a piece
of onion and throw into the spider, stir up
quickly, add a few spoonfuls of water and a few
spoonfuls of canned tomatoes to make the gravy;
cover for a few minutes and pour this over the
steak and serve.

### ROUND BEEFSTEAK.

If you are compelled to live very econom-
ically, round steak prepared in above manner is
indeed very palatable; and how few know what
a delicious steak may be prepared out of a flank.
Ask your butcher, he knows, and will prepare it
ready for frying. Goose or any kind of poultry
drippings is nice to fry this steak in.

### HAMBURGER STEAK

Is made of round steak chopped extremely fine
and seasoned with salt and pepper. You may
grate in part of an onion or fry with onions.
For invalids, scrape the steak instead of chopping. Very fine indeed.

## WIENER BRATEN.

Take a large, thick piece of steak of round or
shoulder, have the bone taken out and then
pound the meat well with a mallet. Lay it in
vinegar for twenty-four hours. Heat some fat
or goose oil in a deep pan or kettle which has a
cover that fits air tight and lay the meat in the
hot fat and sprinkle the upper side with salt,
pepper and ginger. Put an onion in with the
meat; stick about half a dozen cloves in the
onion and add one bay leaf. Now turn the meat
over and sprinkle the other side with salt, pepper
and ginger. You may cut up one or two tomatoes and pour some soup stock over all, and a
dash of white wine. Cover closely and stew
very slowly for three or four hours, turning
the meat now and then; in doing so do not
pierce with the fork, as this will allow the juice
to escape. Do not add any water. Make enough
potato pancakes to serve one or two to each
person with " Wiener Braten."

## SOUP MEAT.

The meat must be cooked until very tender
then lift it out of the soup and lay upon a platter and season while hot. Heat a spoonful of
fat or drippings of roast beef in a spider, cut up
a few slices of onion in it, also half a clove of
garlic and throw in a spoonful of flour, stirring
all the time; then add soup stock or rich gravy,

lay in the soup meat, which has been seasoned
with salt, pepper and ginger. You must sprinkle the spices on both sides of the meat, and
add half a teaspoonful of carroway seed to the
sauce, and if too thick add more soup stock
and a little boiling water. Cover closely and
let it simmer about fifteen minutes. If properly
seasoned, this is very nice.

### FLEISCH KUGEL (MEAT BALL).

Two pounds of beef, chopped extremely fine
(the round is best); have half a pound of suet
chopped with it and get your butcher to chop
two onions in with the meat, as it will be mixed
better. Season with salt, pepper and half a loaf
of grated stale bread half soaked in water and
then pressed well and dried in hot fat before
adding to the meat. Break in two eggs and mix
thoroughly then mould into a huge ball and put
into a deep iron kugel form or spider, which
has been well greased and heated before putting
in the kugel. Dip a spoon in cold water to
smooth the top of the kugel, put flakes of fat on
the top and bake about two hours, basting often.

### BRISKET OF BEEF.

No. 1. Take about five pounds of fat, young
beef (you may make soup stock of it first), then
take out the bones, salt it well and lay in the
bottom of a porcelain-lined kettle and put a

quart of nice sauer kraut on top of it and let it boil slowly until tender. Add more vinegar if necessary, thicken with a grated raw potato and add a little brown sugar. Some like a few carroway seeds added.

### BRISKET OF BEEF.

No. 2. May be prepared in numerous ways. After taking it out of the soup you may prepare it with a horseradish sauce, garlic sauce, onion sauce, etc. (See Meat Sauces.)

### MUTTON OR LAMB CHOPS.

Those off the loin are best. Cut off some of the fat, throw into the spider and heat. Season the chops with salt and pepper or salt and ginger. I prefer the latter. Have the spider very hot with not too much fat in it. To be nice and tender they must fry quickly to a nice brown.

### BREAST OF MUTTON STEWED WITH CARROTS.

Salt the mutton on both sides, adding a little ground ginger; put on to boil in cold water in a porcelain-lined kettle and cover up tightly and stew slowly. In the meantime pare and cut up the carrots and add these and cover up again. Pare and cut up about half a dozen potatoes into diceshape and add them three-quarters of an hour before dinner. Cover up again, and when done, make a sauce as follows :- Skim off about two tablespoonfuls of fat from the mutton

stew, put this in a spider and heat. Brown a
tablespoonful of flour in the fat, add a heaping
tablespoonful of brown sugar, some cinnamon
and pour the gravy of the stew into the spider,
letting it boil up once, and then pour all over the
carrots and stew until ready to serve.

### ROAST BEEF WITH YORKSHIRE PUDDING.

Put a piece of beef to roast upon a grating in
a dripping pan; half an hour before it is done
mix the pudding and pour it into the pan, under
the grating; continue to roast the beef; the
dripping does not injure the pudding, as the
pudding is eaten with the beef, it taking the
place of a vegetable. When done, cut the pudding into pieces, and serve each person with
pudding and beef at the same time. Receipt
for pudding: One pint of milk or water, yelks
of five eggs, two small teaspoonfuls of flour, a
pinch of salt; beat the whites to a stiff froth
and add last; pour into the pan immediately.
You may bake this pudding separately and
serve with roast.

### ROAST BEEF.

The best roasts are sirloin, porterhouse and
rib roasts. If desired rare, allow ten minutes to
the pound; if medium, twelve to fifteen minutes;
and if very well done, twenty minutes. Cut up
a small onion, a celery root and part of a carrot
into rather small pieces and add to these two or

three sprigs of parsley and one bay leaf. Sprinkle these over the bottom of the dripping-pan and place your roast on this bed. The oven should be very hot when the roast is first put in, but when the roast is browned sufficiently to retain its juices, moderate the heat and roast more slowly until the meat is done. Do not season until the roast is browned, and then add salt and pepper. Enough juice and fat will drop from the roast to give the necessary broth for basting. Baste frequently and turn occasionally, being very careful, however, not to stick a fork into the roast. Never allow your butcher to skewer your meat, but have it tied carefully into shape and cut and remove the strings before serving. Wooden skewers invariably give an unpleasant taste to the beef, and any skewer makes a hole for the escape of the juices. If it is dusty, wring a cloth from cold water and wipe it off. Many a careless cook wastes a good proportion of the best part of the roast in a pan of water which is thrown away. I forgot to mention that if you have a patent roaster, the roast does not require turning or basting. No household ought to be without one. Add to the roast about two sliced fresh tomatoes or two tablespoonfuls of canned ones.

## ROAST LAMB.

Prepared same as roast mutton.

## ROAST MUTTON WITH POTATOES.

Take a leg or loin of mutton—must be young
and tender—wash the meat well and dry with a
clean towel. Rub well with salt, ginger and a
speck of pepper and dredge well with flour. Lay
it in a covered roasting pan. Put a few pieces
of whole mace and a few slices of onion on top;
and pour a cup of water into the pan. Cover it
up tight and set in a hot oven to roast, basting
frequently. Allow twenty minutes to the pound
for roasting mutton; it should be well done.
Add more water if necessary (always add hot
water as no not to stop the process of boiling),
skim the gravy well and serve with currant or
cranberry jelly. Pare potatoes of uniform size
and wash and salt them about three quarters of
an hour before dinner. Lay the potatoes in pan
around the roast and sprinkle them with salt
and return to the oven to roast. Let them brown
nicely. You will find the potatoes highly glazed
and they will taste delicious roasted with the
mutton.

## SAUERBRATEN.

Take a solid piece of meat, say about five or
six pounds, put it in a deep earthen jar and pour
enough boiling vinegar over it to cover it; you
may take one-third water. Add to this vinegar
when boiling four bay leaves, some whole peppercorns, cloves and whole mace. Pour this over

the meat and turn it daily. In summer three
or four days is the longest time allowed for the
meat to remain in this pickle; but in winter
eight or ten days is not too long. When ready
to boil, heat some nice poultry drippings in a
stew pan. Cut up one or two onions in it; stew
until tender and then put in the beef, salting it
on both sides before stewing. Stew closely covered and if not acid enough add some of the
brine it was pickled in. Stew about three hours
and thicken the gravy with flour.

### CALF'S LIVER.

Have your butcher slice the liver smoothly
and lay it in salt water at least one hour before
using. Then spread it on a board and sprinkle
it with salt and pepper. Heat some fat (goose
fat is decidely the best for this purpose), and
dip each piece of liver in flour and fry a nice
brown. Lay it on a heated platter, then cut up
an onion in the remaining hot fat, cover for a
few seconds, then add a little hot water to make
a gravy and pour this over the liver and it is
ready to be served.

### ROAST VEAL.

In the first place never buy veal that is not
fat and white. Veal that is lean and red is not
fit for use. The best parts for roasting are the
loin or leg. Prepare for the oven in the following manner: Wash and then dry; rub it

well with salt, and a very little ground ginger,
and dredge it well with flour. Lay in roasting
pan and put slices of onion, celery and tomato
on top, with a few spoonfuls of goose fat or drippings. If you have goose fat use it by all means.
Cover tightly and roast, allowing twenty minutes to the pound and baste frequently. Veal
must be well done. When cold it slices up as
nicely as turkey.

### BREAST OF VEAL ROASTED.

This may be roasted in same manner as above.
To be nice should be stuffed with bread crumbs,
seasoned with salt, pepper and a little onion
chopped very fine and mixed with an egg. Fill
where the butcher has prepared the pocket, and
sew up. You may sprinkle a little carroway
seed on top of roast and baste often.

### VEAL CUTLETS.

Roll out some crackers until they are like
flour. Season the cutlets with salt and ground
ginger, sprinkle them well on both sides and dip
each cutlet first in beaten egg and then in the
rolled crackers. Have some nice goose oil or
poultry drippings hot in a spider before you lay
in the cutlets (if you put the cutlets in before
the fat is hot they will stick to the spider) and
fry a nice brown. Lay on a hot platter and
garnish with parsley and slices of lemon.

### FRICASSEED VEAL WITH CAULIFLOWER.

Use the breast or shoulder for this purpose, the former being preferable, and cut it up into pieces, not to small. Sprinkle each piece slightly with fine salt and ginger. Heat a tablespoonful of goose oil or poultry drippings in a stew pan, and lay the veal in it. Cut up an onion and one or two tomatoes (a tablespoonful of canned tomatoes will do), and add to this very little water, hot if any, and stew two hours, closely covered. When done mix a teaspoonful of flour and a little water and add to the veal (you may use cream instead of water). Chop up a small handful of parsley, add it and boil up once and serve. Place the cauliflower around the platter in which you serve the veal. Boil the cauliflower in salt and water, closely covered. Put it on at the same time you put on the veal.

### FRICASSEED VEAL WITH CARROWAY SEEDS.

This cooked as above, only adding half a teaspoonful of carroway seeds instead of the parsley.

### CALF'S LIVER SMOTHERED IN ONIONS.

Soak the liver in salt water for 'an hour. Take off the thin outer skin and wipe dry. Heat some goose fat in a stew pan with a close-fitting lid. Cut up an onion in it and when the onion is of a light yellow lay it in the liver, which you

have previously sprinkled with fine salt and
pepper, and dredged with flour. Put in a bay
leaf, some whole cloves and peppercorns. Now
cover up air tight and stew. Turn the liver
occasionally, and, when required, add a very
little hot water.

### HASHED CALF'S LUNG AND HEART.

Lay the lung and heart in water for half an
hour and then put on to boil in a soup kettle
with your soup meat intended for dinner.
When soft, remove from the soup and chop up
quite fine. Heat a spoonful of goose fat or
butter in a spider; chop up an onion very fine
and add to the heated fat. When yellow, add
the hashed lung and heart, salt and pepper, and
add soup stock and thicken with flour. You
may prepare this sweet and sour by adding a
little vinegar and brown sugar, half a teaspoonful of cinnamon and a tablespoonful of molasses; boil slowly; keep covered until ready to
serve. Very nice.

### SPICED VEAL LOAF.

Chop up three pounds of veal very fine (let
your butcher chop it for you), roll six crackers
very fine, beat up three eggs light, and season
highly with salt, pepper, ginger and nutmeg.
Mix all this thoroughly, not forgetting to add a
tablespoonful of goose fat or butter. Press all
into a baking pan, about four inches high; grease

the pan well and put lumps of butter or goose
fat on top. Bake about three hours, basting
frequently. When cold, this is very nice cut
into thin slices.

### STEWED VEAL.

Wash a breast of veal, wipe it dry and sprinkle
with a mixture of fine salt and ginger. Heat
some goose fat or butter in a stew pan, cut up
an onion in it, add sliced parsley root or celery.
When hot lay in the breast of veal. Cover up
air tight and stew a few minutes. Remove the
lid and turn the veal on the other side. Now
add one or two tomatoes cut up, or a tablespoonful of canned tomatoes and a very little hot
water. Cover up tight again and stew slowly
and steadily for two hours, turning the meat
often. When done, thicken the gravy with a
teaspoonful of flour, wet in a little cold water.
Add minced parsley or carroway seed. Boil up
once and serve. Mashed potatoes and green peas
or stewed tomatoes are usually served with veal.

### VEAL SWEETBREADS (FRIED)

Wash and lay your sweetbreads in slightly
salted cold water for an hour. Pull off carefully
all the outer skin, wipe dry and sprinkle with
salt and pepper. Heat some goose fat in a spider,
lay in the sweetbreads and fry slowly on the
back of the stove, turning frequently until they

are a nice brown.　You may roll them in cracker crumbs and then in beaten egg, seasoned with salt.

### CROQUETTES OF CALF'S BRAINS.

Lay the brains in salt water for an hour, or until they look perfectly white, then take out one at a time, pat with your hands to loosen the outer skin and pull it off.　Beat or rub them to a smooth paste with a wooden spoon, season with salt and pepper and a very little mace; add a beaten egg and about half a cup of bread crumbs.　Heat some goose fat in a spider and fry large spoonfuls of this mixture in it. Spinach is a nice accompaniment.

# POULTRY.

| | Page. |
|---|---|
| Squabs, or Nest Pigeons, - - - - | 70 |
| Broiled Squabs, - - - - - | 70 |
| Roast Turkey, - - - - - - | 71 |
| Duck, - - - - - - - | 72 |
| Chicken with Rice, - - - - - | 72 |
| Roast Goose, - - - - - - | 73 |
| Gaenseklein, - - - - - - | 74 |
| Geschundene Gans, - - - - | 75 |
| Grieben, - - - - - - - | 75 |
| Minced Goose, - - - - - | 76 |
| Geraucherte Gansbrust, - - - - | 77 |
| Stewed Goose Piquant, - - - - | 77 |
| Spring Chicken, fried, - - - - | 77 |
| Chicken Fricassee, - - - - | 78 |
| Steamed Chicken, - - - - - | 78 |
| Chicken Croquettes, - - - - | 79 |
| Oyster Dressing for Turkey, - - - | 79 |
| Meat Dressing for Poultry, - - - | 79 |

# POULTRY.

## SQUABS, OR NEST PIGEONS

PICK, singe, draw, clean and season them well inside and out, with salt mixed with a little ginger and pepper, and then stuff them with well seasoned bread dressing. Pack them closely in a deep stew pan and cover with flakes of butter or goose fat, minced parsley and a little chopped onion. Cover with a lid that fits close and stew gently, adding water when necessary. Do not let them get too brown. They should be of a light yellow.

## BROILED SQUABS.

Squabs are a great delicacy, especially in the convalescent's menu, being peculiarly savory and nourishing. Clean the squabs; lay them in salt water for about ten minutes and then rub dry with a clean towel. Split them down the back and broil over a clear coal fire. Season with salt and pepper; lay them on a heated platter and butter or grease them liberally with goose fat and cover with a deep platter. Now toast a piece of bread for each pigeon, removing the crust. Dip the toast in boiling water for an instant. In serving lay a squab upon a piece of

toast. Crabapple jelly is a nice acccompani-
ment.

### ROAST TURKEY.

Select a nice, fat turkey and see that it is
young. If the breastbone yields to the touch or
pressure of your finger it is the one you want.
Singe, wash and clean thoroughly and let it lay
it salt water for a quarter of an hour. In the
meantime prepare this dressing: Soak a stale
loaf of baker's white bread. Heat some goose
fat (about a tablespoonful) in a spider and cut
up an onion quite fine and throw it into the hot
fat. Squeeze every drop of water out of the
bread, and put it in the hot fat to dry. Remove
from the fire, throw the bread into a bowl, season
with salt, pepper, ginger and a little nutmeg
and add two tablespoonfuls of canned tomatoes,
or one fresh one, and two eggs. Mix as you
would dough. After having rubbed the turkey
inside and out with salt, pepper and a very
little ground ginger, stuff it with the prepared
dressing, sew up and leave in refrigerator until
next day. If my readers will try this method
of dressing poultry the day previous to using,
they will surely try it again as it helps to season
the meat and renders it much more juicy. I
frequently have the dressing prepared before
the butcher delivers the poultry. It saves time,

## DUCK.

Singe off all the small feathers; cut off neck and wings, which may be used for soup; wash thoroughly and rub well with salt, ginger and a little pepper, inside and out. Now prepare this dressing: Take the liver, gizzard and heart and chop to a powder in chopping bowl. Grate in a little nutmeg, add a piece of celery root, half an onion and a tomato. Put all this into your chopping bowl. Soak some stale bread, squeeze out all the water and fry in a spider of hot fat. Throw this soaked bread into the bowl; add one or two eggs, salt, pepper and a speck of ginger and mix all thoroughly. Fill the duck with this and sew it up. Lay in the roasting pan with slices of onions, celery and tomatoes and specks of fat. Put some on top of fowl; roast covered up tight and baste often. Roast two hours.

### CHICKEN WITH RICE.

Joint a chicken; season with salt and ground ginger and boil in a deep porcelain-lined dish with water enough to just cover. Allow one-half pound of rice to one chicken. Boil this after chicken is tender. Serve together on a large platter. If prepared separately it will require less attention. This is a wholesome dish.

## ROAST GOOSE.

After the goose has been picked, take some old
newspapers, light them in a coal-bucket, hold
the goose over the flames in this way: Take the
neck in your left hand and the feet in your right,
swing it back and forth over the blaze until the
little hairs are all singed off, being very, very
careful that your dress or apron does not take
fire. Now wash the goose and take out all pin
feathers. Make an incision in the stomach just
large enough to insert your hand, take out the
fat and loosen the entrails with your forefinger.
When everything is removed, wash out well with
salt water and cut off the wings close to the
body, also the neck, feet and head. Separate
the gall from the liver. In doing this be very
careful not to break the gall, which has a
very thin skin. Lay the liver in salt water.
Srape all the fat off carefully that adheres to
the entrails and lay it in a separate dish of
water over night. Cut off the point and top of
the heart and cut open so as to let out all of the
congealed blood. Cut open the gizzard, clean
and pull off the skin, or inner lining, as it is
called. Lay gizzard and feet in boiling water
to scald the skin, which can then be easily
removed. Chop off nails of the feet, and if you
make use of the head, which you may in soup,
cut off the top of the bill. Split open the head
lengthwise, take out brains, eyes and tongue.

All goose meat tastes better if it is well rubbed
with salt, ginger and a very little garlic a day
or two previous to using. Now, to roast a goose,
prepare as above directed and dress with bread
dressing, or chestnuts—a dressing of apples is
also very nice. Sew up, then line a sheet iron
pan with a few slices of onion and celery and
lay the goose upon this, breast downward. Fill
up half way with water, cover closely and stew
in the oven. If it browns too quickly, cover
with greased paper. When half done, turn the
goose on its back, and when tender remove cover
and have a hot fire to brown quickly. Baste
frequently.

### GAENSEKLEIN.

Rub wings, neck, gizzard, heart and back of
goose with salt, ginger, pepper and garlic and
set on the fire in a stew pan with cold water.
Cover tightly and stew slowly but steadily for
four hours at least. When done skim off all
the fat. Now put a spider over the fire, put into
it about two or three spoonfuls of the fat that
you have just skimmed off and then add the fat
to the meat again. Cut up fine a very small piece
of garlic and throw in a heaping teaspoonful
of flour (brown). Add the hot gravy and pour
all over the goose. Cover up tightly and set on
back of stove till you wish to serve. You may
cook the whole goose in this way after it is
cut up. A great many prefer it to roast.

## GESCHUNDENE GANS.

Take only a very fat goose for this purpose. After cleaning and singeing, cut off neck, wings and feet. Lay the goose on a table, back up (for this is the proper way to begin to take off the skin or hide). Take a sharp knife, make a cut from the neck down to the tail end. Begin again at the top near the neck, take off the skin, holding it in your left hand, your knife in your right to assist you (I wish I could show you this personally, for I am afraid my young house-keepers will not understand just how). After all the skin is removed, which can easily be done, and all in one piece, throw it into cold water; separate the breast from back and cut off joints, and proceed with entrails as described in Roast Goose. Have ready in a plate a mixture of salt ginger and a very little garlic; cut up fine. Rub the joints and small pieces with this, and make a small incision in each leg and four in the breast. Put in each incision a small piece of garlic, and rub also with a prepared mixture of salt and ginger. Put away in stone jars until you wish to use.

## GRIEBEN.

Cut up the fat into two-inch squares. Put on to boil slowly for about three hours with salt but no water. You may preserve one or two breasts of geese by laying them in the hot goose oil half an hour before taking off the fire and leave them in the goose fat until spring. You may also roast the goose breasts and joints. Keep closely covered all the time, so as not to get too brown. They cut up nicely cold for sandwiches. The best way to roast a goose breast is to remove the skin from the neck and sew it over the breast (easily done), and fasten it with a few stitches under the breast. Roast covered all the time. Make it more like a pot roast.

If any of my readers object to garlic in the preparation of the above (which you will not if you are a Frenchman) you may use onions instead. I also forgot to mention that you should make an incision with a pointed knife in the breast and joints of the goose, so as to be able to insert a little garlic (or onion) in each incision, also a little salt and ginger.

### MINCED GOOSE.

Take the entire breast of a goose, chop up fine in a chopping bowl; grate in part of an onion, and season with salt, pepper and a tiny piece of garlic. Add some grated stale bread and work in a few eggs. Press this chopped meat back on to the breast bone and roast, basting very often with goose fat. This is "Hungarian," and is very nice for a change.

### GERAUCHERTE GANSBRUST.

Dried or smoked goose breast must be prepared in the following manner: Take the breast
of the fattest goose you can find; leave the skin
on; rub well with salt, pepper and saltpetre;
pack in a stone jar and let it remain pickled
thus four or five days at least. Dry well and
cover with gauze and send away to be smoked.

### STEWED GOOSE, PIQUANTE.

Cut up after being skinned and stew, after seasoning with salt, pepper, a few cloves and a very
little lemon peel. When done heat a little goose
fat in a frying pan, brown half a tablespoonful
of flour, add a little vinegar and the juice of half
a lemon.

### SPRING CHICKEN, FRIED.

After the chicken has been cleaned and singed
lay it in salt water for half an hour. Cut it up
as for fricassee and see that every piece is wiped
dry. Have ready heated in a spider some goose
fat or other poultry drippings. Season each
piece of chicken with salt and ground ginger, or
pepper (I prefer the ginger, it is also more
wholesome than pepper). Roll each piece of
chicken in sifted cracker crumbs (which you
have previously seasoned with salt). Fry in
the spider, turning often, and browning evenly.
You may cut up some parsley and add while

frying. If the chicken is quite large, it is better to steam it before frying.

### CHICKEN FRICASSEE.

After the chicken has been singed and thoroughly cleaned, cut off the wings, legs and neck. Then separate the breast from the chicken, leaving it whole. Cut the back into two pieces. Then prepare a mixture of salt, ginger and a very little pepper in a saucer and dust each piece of chicken with this mixture, and, if possible, let the chicken remain salted a whole day before using. When you are ready to cook the chicken, take all the particles of fat you have removed from it and lay in the bottom of the kettle, also a small onion, cut up, some parsley root and celery. Lay the chicken upon this, breast first, then the leg, and so on. Then lay on top one or two tomatoes, cut up, or one or two spoonfuls of canned tomatoes, and then cover up tight and let it stew slowly on the back of the stove, adding hot water when necessary. Just before serving chop up some parsley fine and rub a teaspoonful of flour in a little cold water, and add. Let it boil up once. Shake the kettle back and forth to prevent becoming lumpy.

### STEAMED CHICKEN WITH OYSTERS.

Fill the inside of a spring chicken with oysters, seasoned with salt, pepper and butter. Season the outside of the chicken as well; steam in a pan set in another one of water and boil one hour and a half. Then add half a cup of cream, one egg and sufficient butter and flour to thicken the gravy in the pan. You may add oysters to this gravy.

### CHICKEN CROQUETTES.

Cut up the white meat of one cold boiled chicken and pound it to a paste, together with a large boiled sweetbread, adding salt and pepper. Beat up one egg, with a teaspoonful of flour, and a wineglassful of rich cream. Mix all together; put in a pan and simmer just enough to absorb part of the moisture, stirring all the time. Turn it out on a flat dish and place in ice-box to cool. Then roll into small cones, dip in beaten egg, roll again in powdered bread or cracker crumbs and drop them into boiling fat until a delicate brown. This is a dainty breakfast dish.

### OYSTER DRESSING FOR TURKEY.

Grate some stale white bread, add flakes of butter, salt, pepper, a beaten egg and the oyster liquor and oysters and mix all thoroughly. Stuff the turkey the day previous to roasting with this or any other dressing,

### MEAT DRESSING FOR POULTRY.

If you can not buy sausage meat at your butcher's have him chop some for you, adding a little suet. Also mix in some veal with the beef while chopping. Season with salt, pepper, nutmeg, or thyme. Grate in a piece of celery root and a piece of garlic about the size of a bean, add a small onion, add a minced tomato and then add a quarter of a loaf of stale bread, also grated, and mix up the whole with one or two eggs. If you prefer, you may soak the bread, press out every drop of water and dry in a heated spider with fat. You will find this a very superior dressing.

# GAME.

                                                          Page.
Reed Birds,        -      -      -      -      -      -    82
Canvas Back Duck, roasted,    -      -      -    82
Quails, roasted,  -      -      -      -      -      -    83
Wild Pigeons,      -      -      -      -      -    83
      "   Turkey,      -      -      -      -      -      -    83
      "   Goose,    -      -      -      -      -      -    84
      "   Duck,       -      -      -      -      -      -    84
Rabbit,  -      -      -      -      -      -      -    84
Rabbit, roasted,       -      -      -      -      -    85
Rabbit, with Caper Sauce,    -      -      -    85
Spiced Rabbit (Hasenpfeffer),    -      -      -    85
Ragout of Rabbit,  -      -      -      -      -    86
Fricasseed Rabbit,    -      -      -      -      -    87
Fried Rabbit,       -      -      -      -      -    87
Broiled Squirrels,    -      -      -      -      -    88
Barbecued Rabbit, -      -      -      -      -    88
Rabbit Ragout, sweet and sour,      -      -    88
Venison Roast,       -      -      -      -      -    88
Venison Steak,  -      -      -      -      -      -    89
Venison and Rabbit Pie,       -      -      -    89
Prairie Chicken,      -      -      -      -      -    90
Quail on Toast,      -      -      -      -      -    91
Quail Pie,  -      -      -      -      -      -      -    91
Pigeon Pie,      -      -      -      -      -      -    91
To Keep Game Fresh,       -      -      -      -    92

# GAME.

### REED BIRDS.

AFTER the birds are wiped clean, tie them to a toaster and lay them across your roasting pan, turn and baste frequently and season them with salt and pepper. Another way is to roll them in a dumpling dough, and steam them. Still another way is to pare and hollow large potatoes, cut off one end and scoop them out, make or cut the hollow large enough to receive and hold a bird. Drop a piece of butter into each bird after seasoning with salt and pepper and put in the hollows of the potatoes. Set them in a greased deep pan, close together and upright. Be sure to grease the pan well before putting in the potatoes and add a little water. Serve in the dish they were baked in. Wrap a napkin around the dish. (Considered a great delicacy.)

### CANVAS BACK DUCK ROASTED.

After cleaning, wipe the ducks perfectly dry, rub with fat or butter inside and out, also salt and pepper and stuff the same as any other fowl. Roast about an hour and make a gravy out of the giblets and wings. Boil slowly in a saucepan, with a little water, adding a little onion and parsley. Thicken the gravy with a little flour.

### ROAST QUAILS.

Clean the quails. Wash them in soda and water, cleanse with pure water and wipe dry, both inside and out. Put two oysters inside of each bird, sew up and arrange them side by side in a baking pan. Pour a very little boiling water over them, cover and roast about half an hour and baste frequently with butter. Serve upon pieces of fried toast, laid on a hot dish. Pour a spoonful of gravy over each.

### WILD PIGEONS.

Clean and lay them in salt water for an hour, then wipe dry and salt and pepper inside and out. Stuff the birds with sausage meat, or a dressing made of bread crumbs; sew up and lay them side by side in a deep-covered stew pan, adding water enough to just barely cover them and stew until tender. Then baste with butter, chopped onion and parsley, and brown.

### WILD TURKEY.

Prepare same as you would domestic turkey, allowing twice the amount of fat or butter for basting. Stew covered at first, then sprinkle thickly with salted flour and put flakes of butter all over it and roast brown, basting often. Dress with any kind of meat or bread dressing. Serve with currant or cranberry jelly.

### WILD GOOSE.

Wild geese should not be roasted unless very young, as they are even tougher than domestic ones. Prepare same as any goose and roast covered until very tender. The safest way is to salt and pepper inside and out and pot roast it on top of the stove, adding a goblet of hot water as soon as put on, and stew closely covered. When tender put in the oven to brown.

### WILD DUCK.

Cut up the duck into joints, salt and pepper and lay in a deep earthen bowl, and pour a pint of hot vinegar over all. Before heating the vinegar add peppercorns, cloves and a bay leaf. Leave in this pickle for twenty-four hours or more, then take out and stew with an onion, adding very little vinegar. Thicken the gravy with flour. Game of any kind that you are in doubt about being young or tender should be prepared in this way.

### RABBITS.

Never attempt to skin and clean a rabbit yourself if you can get your butcher to do it for you, for it is not an easy task. Squirrels and rabbits may be prepared in numerous ways— roasted, fricasseed, fried and broiled.

### ROAST RABBIT.

After the rabbit has been thoroughly cleaned and washed, lay it in salted water for an hour or more. Stuff the rabbit with a dressing of bread crumbs and sausage meat, seasoned well with salt and pepper and mixed with a well-beaten egg. Or dress with soaked bread and add the liver and heart of the rabbit, chopped up very fine, which should be parboiled. Stuff with this and sew up. Then line a roasting pan with the following: One onion and one carrot cut up, a few cloves, whole peppercorns and one bay leaf. Rub the rabbit with salt and pepper and lay it upon this dressing, putting flakes of butter here and there over the rabbit. Sift a little flour over the top and pour about a teacupful of hot water in the bottom of the pan. Cover up air tight and roast, basting frequently. When ready to serve, put on a hot platter and garnish with slices of lemon and wine or cranberry jelly.

### RABBIT WITH CAPER SAUCE.

Roast as above, then strain the gravy, adding half a teacupful of capers and a teaspoonful of flour for thickening.

### SPICED RABBIT (HASENPFEFFER).

Cut up the rabbit after it has been thoroughly cleaned and lain in salt and water about an hour. Pour some vinegar over it and let it remain in this pickle over night. Then put a lump of fresh butter about the size of an egg into a deep stew pan. Cut up an onion in it, adding one bay leaf, about a dozen peppercorns and part of a celery root. Lay the rabbit in this and stew, adding part of the vinegar that the rabbit was pickled in, and salt each piece slightly before stewing. When tender thicken with flour that has been browned in a spider with butter. Taste, if not spiced enough, add some white pepper and a very little mace.

### RAGOUT OF RABBIT.

Cut the rabbit into small pieces; lay them in salted water one hour and then wipe each piece dry. Sprinkle slightly with salt and ginger. Cut up two onions in a porcelain-lined stew pan; add half a pound of butter and stew the onions until they are a light brown. Then add a pint of red wine, two bay leaves, a dozen peppercorns, and let the rabbit stew in this until tender. Then take up the pieces carefully, lay them on a platter and set them in a warm place until the gravy is finished. Remove every particle of fat from the gravy and let it boil hard for a few minutes. Then thicken with flour, strain through a hair sieve and pour over the ragout. Garnish with small pickled onions and curly parsley.

### FRICASSEED RABBIT.

Clean one or two young rabbits; cut into joints and lay them in salt water half an hour or more. Then wipe each piece on a clean towel, sprinkle slightly with a mixture of salt, pepper and ginger. Put into a stewpan a piece of butter, an onion, cut up, some celery and parsley root  Lay the pieces of salted rabbit upon this, pour a pint of water over all; cover and stew until tender. Then take out the pieces of rabbit and set in a dish where they will keep warm. Thicken the gravy with the yelks of two well beaten eggs, adding gradually. If the gravy has boiled down very much, add half a cup of sweet cream. Boil up once only and thicken with flour wet in cold cream. Just before serving, squeeze the juice of a lemon into the sauce, stirring all the while, and pour this over the rabbit. Serve at once. Apple compote or a compote of pears is a nice accompaniment.

### FRIED RABBIT.

Select very young rabbits, clean, cut into joints and soak in water slightly salted for an hour or more. Wipe dry, sprinkle each joint with fine salt, pepper and ginger. Roll in cracker crumbs, then in beaten egg and fry in hot butter or fat, as you would spring chickens. Fry brown and well done. Garnish with slices of lemon and sprigs of parsley. Cranberry or

currant jelly is usually served with fried or
roast rabbit. Squirrels are to be fried precisely
like rabbits.

### BROILED RABBIT OR SQUIRREL.

Clean thoroughly; lay in salt water an hour
and then wipe dry. Have a clear, hot fire.
Heat the gridiron, wipe the rabbit dry and
broil, turning often. When done, lay on a
heated platter in which you have melted a lump
of sweet butter. Season with salt and pepper,
cover with a hot platter and garnish with slices
of lemon and curly parsley. Serve at once.

### BARBECUED RABBIT.

Is prepared precisely like broiled rabbit, cutting off the head only.

### RABBIT RAGOUT (SWEET AND SOUR).

Prepare as usual. Set on to boil with one
onion, a bay leaf, a few whole peppercorns, some
cloves and stick cinnamon. Boil until tender,
not forgetting the necessary salt. Add half a
teacupful of vinegar and the crust of a rye loaf.
When tender, remove the rabbit to a heated platter. Keep covered until the gravy has boiled
down quite thick, adding brown sugar and ginger snaps to thicken the gravy.

### VENISON ROAST.

Rub the haunch well with salt and pepper
and cover the meat entirely with a layer of

butter. Have very little hot water in the roasting pan; cut up one onion and lay the haunch upon this. Your fire should be kept hot until the roast is done. Baste often, allow about twenty minutes to the pound to roast. When nearly done, add a goblet of claret and more butter and baste with this. When done, strain the gravy and thicken with flour. Spice with cloves and mace. Serve with currant jelly.

### VENISON STEAK.

Heat the gridiron over a clear, hot fire. Butter the bars slightly before putting on the steaks. Broil rapidly, turning often to keep in the juices. Have a warm platter at hand, with a piece of butter the size of an egg to dip your steaks in when done. Salt, pepper and cover to keep hot. Then heat a little claret, add a few spoonfuls of currant jelly to it and pour over the steak just before serving. You may fry the steaks as you would beef, omitting the wine. Use onions with it. Serve with slices of lemon.

### VENISON AND RABBIT PIE.

Make a paste of one pound of flour. Rub twelve ounces of butter into this and add the yelks of two eggs, a teaspoonful of salt and ice-water enough to mix lightly. Roll and line a deep pie-plate with this and fill with the meat of

venison or rabbit, which has been previously
stewed in the following manner: Cut the raw
meat from the bones into small pieces and put
them into a stew-pan with one onion. Add salt,
pepper, nutmeg, and just enough cold water to
cover, and boil until tender. Before filling this
in the pie-crust, roll some flakes of butter in flour
and put over the pie. Cover with a thick layer
of pastry, make a hole in the center of the top
crust and bake slowly. In the meantime heat
some port wine, into which you have thrown a
few cloves and blades of mace. When the pie is
nearly baked, pour this mixture into the pie
through the hole in the top crust by means of a
funnel. Brush the top of the pie with beaten
egg and return to the oven and bake a light
brown.

### PRAIRIE CHICKEN.

Clean and wash thoroughly in water in which
you have put a little soda. Rinse in clear water
several times, and if time allows, let them lay in
water half an hour or more. Then wipe dry and
fill with a good dressing. Tie down the wings
and legs with a cord and stew, closely covered,
with plenty of butter, or steam over hot water
in a steamer until tender and then place them
in a pan with a little butter, and brown. Serve
with a tart jelly and garnish with parsley.

### QUAIL ON TOAST.

Split the birds down the back and clean nicely.
Wash thoroughly, then wipe dry, salt and pepper
them and dredge with flour. Pound down the
breast bones so they will lie flat and place them
in a buttered pan, closely covered, with a very
little hot water, into a hot oven and roast until
nearly done. Then heat some butter or goose
oil in a spider, and fry each piece a nice brown.
Have the toast ready, buttered and laid upon a
platter and place a quail upon each piece of
toast. Thicken the sauce in the pan with a little
flour and pour over the quails.

### QUAIL PIE.

After the quails have been cleaned, salt and
pepper them and stuff them either with bread
crumbs or oyster dressing and stew them, closely
covered, for ten minutes at least. Line a deep
pie plate with a thick, rich puff paste. Fill them
in your pie plate, sprinkle with minced parsley
and chopped hard-boiled eggs and flakes of
butter rolled in flour. Squeeze a little lemon
juice over all and add the gravy that the birds
were stewed in; cover with puff paste and bake
slowly an hour at least.

### PIGEON PIE.

Prepare as many pigeons as you wish to bake
in your pie. Salt and pepper, then melt some
fat or butter in a stew pan, and cut up an onion

in it. When hot, place in the pigeons and stew
until tender. In the meatime line a deep pie
plate with a puff paste. Cut up the pigeons, lay
them in, with hard boiled eggs chopped up and
minced parsley. Season with salt and pepper.
Put flakes of butter rolled in flour here and there,
pour over the gravy the pigeons were stewed in
and cover with a crust. Bake slowly until done.

### TO KEEP GAME FRESH

Draw and clean thoroughly as soon as possible after it is killed, or as soon as it comes into
your possession. Wash many times in clean
water and then in salt water. Wipe dry and
salt and pepper. Put a piece of charcoal into
the cavity. Cover with a cloth and hang up in
a dark, cool place. Charcoal is a good preventive of decomposition and should always be kept
in the refrigerator and in the cellar corners.

# ENTREES.

|  | Page. |
|---|---|
| Sweetbreads, - - - - - - | 94 |
| Calf Brains, - - - - - - | 94 |
| Cod Fish Balls, - - - - - - | 95 |
| Goose Liver, - - - - - - | 96, 97 |
| Sulze von Kalbsfuessen, - - - - | 97 |
| Sweetbread Glace, - - - - - | 98 |
| Chicken Fricassee, - - - - - | 99 |
| Pressed Chicken, - - - - - | 99 |
| Paprica, - - - - - - | 100 |
| Smoked Tongue, - - - - - | 101 |
| Gefillte Milz, - - - - - - | 101 |
| Stewed Milt, - - - - - | 102 |
| Boiled Tongue, - - - - - | 103 |
| Tripe, - - - - - - | 104 |
| Aspic, - - - - - - | 104 |
| Gansleber in Sulz, - - - - | 105 |
| Gansleber Puree in Sulz, - - - - | 105 |
| Boston Baked Beans, - - - - | 105 |

# ENTREES.

## SWEETBREADS.

WASH very carefully, and remove all bits of skin and fatty matter. Cover with cold water, salt and boil for about fifteen minutes. Then remove from the boiling water and throw into cold water. Roll them in rolled cracker and beaten egg and fry a nice brown in hot fat. You may fry them without parboiling. Just sprinkle with salt and pepper, roll in cracker and egg, and fry very slowly and be sure they are well done. I recommend them either way.

## CALF'S BRAINS (SOUR).

Lay the brains in ice-water and then skin. They will skin easily by taking them up in your hands and patting them, this will help to loosen all the skin and clotted blood that adheres to them. Let them lay in cold salted water for an hour at least, then put on to boil in half vinegar and half water (a crust of rye bread improves the flavor of the sauce). Add one onion, cut up fine, some whole peppers, one bay leaf, one or two cloves and a little salt, boil all together about fifteen minutes. Serve on a platter and decorate with parsley. Eat cold. Inexpensive and nice.

### BRAINS (SWEET AND SOUR).

Clean as described above. Lay in ice-cold
salted water for an hour. Cut up an onion, a few
slices of celery root, a few whole peppers, a little
salt and a crust of rye bread. Lay the brains
upon this bed of herbs and barely cover with
vinegar and water. Boil about fifteen minutes,
then lift out the brains with a perforated skimmer, and lay upon a platter to cool. Now take
a "lebkuchen," or some ginger bread (the former
is preferable), some brown sugar, a spoonful of
molasses and half a teaspoonful of cinnamon, a
few seedless raisins and a few pounded almonds.
Moisten this with vinegar and add to the boiling
sauce. Boil the sauce ten minutes longer and
pour scalding over the brains. Eat cold and
decorate with slices of lemon. This is a very
nice dish for lunch or supper.

### CALF'S BRAINS FRIED.

Clean as described in calf brains cooked sour;
wipe dry, roll in rolled cracker flour, season
with salt and pepper and fry as you would
cutlets.

### COD FISH BALLS.

Put the fish to soak over night in lukewarm
water. Change again in the morning and wash
off all the salt. Cut into pieces and boil about
fifteen minutes, pour off this water and put on
to boil again with boiling water. Boil twenty

minutes this time, drain off every bit of water, put on a platter to cool and pick to pieces as fine as possible, removing every bit of skin and bone. When this is done, add an equal quantity of mashed potatoes, a lump of butter, a very little salt and pepper, beat up one or two eggs, a little milk if necessary and work all into a dough. Flour your hands well and form into biscuits. Fry in hot butter or drippings. You may prepare this the day before wanted and fry for breakfast

### GOOSE LIVER.

If very large (not likely to get them too large) cut in half, dry well on a clean cloth, after having lain in salted water for an hour. Season with fine salt and pepper, fry in very hot goose fat and add a few cloves. While frying cut up a little onion very fine and add. Then cover closely and smother in this way until you wish to serve. Dredge the liver with flour before frying and turn occasionally. Serve with a slice of lemon on each piece of liver.

### GOOSE LIVER WITH CHESTNUTS.

Prepare as above and garnish with glaze chestnuts which have been prepared thus: Scald until perfectly white, heat some goose fat or butter in a porcelain-lined kettle, throw in the nuts, adding a little white sugar, and glaze until a light brown.

## GOOSE LIVER WITH MUSHROOM SAUCE.

Take a large white goose liver, lay in salt water for an hour at least (this rule applies to all kinds of liver), wipe dry, salt, pepper and dredge with flour. Fry in hot goose fat. Cut up a piece of onion, add a few cloves, a few slices of celery, cut very fine, whole peppers, one bay leaf, and some mushrooms. Cover closely and stew a few minutes. Add lemon juice to sauce.

## SULZE VON KALBSFUESSEN (CALF'S FOOT JELLY).

Take one calf's head and four calf's feet, and clean carefully. Let them lay in cold water for half an hour at least. Set on to boil in a porcelain-lined kettle, with four quarts of water. Add two or three small onions, a few cloves, salt, a teaspoonful of whole peppers, two or three bay leaves, juice of a large lemon (extract the seeds) and a cupful of white wine and a little white wine vinegar (just enough to give a tart taste). Let this boil slowly for five or six hours (it must boil until it is reduced one-half). Then strain through a fine hair sieve and let it stand ten or twelve hours. Remove the meat from the bones and when cold cut into fine pieces. Add also the boiled brains (which must be taken up carefully to avoid falling to pieces). Skim off every particle of fat from the jelly and melt slowly in the porcelain-lined kettle. Add a tea-

spoonful of sugar and the whipped whites of
three eggs, and boil very fast for about fifteen
minutes, skimming well.   Taste, and if not tart
enough, add a dash of vinegar.   Strain through
a flannel bag; tie the bag on a door knob with
a bowl underneath to catch the juice or jelly.
Do not squeeze or shake it until the jelly ceases
to run freely.   Then remove the bowl and put
another under, into which you may press out
what remains in the bag (this will not be as clear,
but tastes quite as good).   Wet your mould, put
in the jelly and set in a cool place.   In order to
have a variety, wet another mould and put in
the bits of meat, cut up, and the brains and last
the jelly; set this on ice.   It must be so thick
that you can cut it into slices to serve.

### SWEETBREAD GLACE, SAUCE JARDINIERE
### WITH BAKED SPAGHETTI.

Put on some butter or poultry drippings to
heat in a deep saucepan, cut up an onion,
shredded very fine and then put in the sweetbreads, which have been picked over carefully
and lain in salt water an hour before boiling.
Salt and pepper the sweetbreads before putting
in the kettle, slice two tomatoes on top and cover
up tight and set on the back of stove to simmer
slowly.   Turn once in awhile and add a little
soup stock.   Boil a handful of string beans, half
a can of canned peas, a handful of currants, cut

up extremely fine, with a piece of butter or drippings, a little salt and ground ginger. When
the vegetables are tender, add to the simmering
sweetbreads. Thicken the sauce with a teaspoonful of flour. Boil the spaghetti in salted
water until tender. Line a pudding dish with
pie dough, after having greased, and fill in with
the boiled spaghetti. Pour over some cream,
which has been thickened with a little flour (if
you object to the cream or milk, just serve boiled
in salted water). Bake the spaghetti about ten
minutes. Have the sauce boiled down quite
thick. Serve with the sweetbreads.

### CHICKEN FRICASSEE, WITH NOODLES.

Prepare a rich chicken fricassee (receipt for
which you will find among poultry receipts; see
index), but have a little more gravy than usual.
Boil some noodles or maccaroni in salted water,
drain, let cold water run through them, shake
them well and boil up once with chicken. Serve
together on a large platter. Very nice.

### PRESSED CHICKEN.

Boil one or more chickens just as you would
for fricassee, using as little water as possible.
When tender remove all the meat from the bone
and take off all the skin. Chop as fine as possible in a chopping bowl (it ought to be chopped
as fine as powder). Add all the liquor the

chicken was boiled in, which ought to be very
little and well seasoned. Press it into the shape
of a brick between two platters, and put a heavy
weight over it so as to press hard (if pressed
properly it will ornament the table). Set away
to cool in ice-chest and garnish nicely with parsley and slices of lemon before sending to the
table. It should be placed whole upon the
table, and sliced as served. Serve pickles and
olives with it. Veal may be pressed in the same
way, some use half veal and half chicken, which
is equally nice.

### PAPRICA (HUNGARIAN HASH).

Take about two pounds of round or flank
steak, have your butcher remove every particle
of skin, and cut it up for you into small square
pieces, dice shape. Heat some fat or goose oil
in a deep stewpan; cut up half an onion very
fine and when slightly browned put in the meat.
Cover up tight, and stew on the back of the
stove. Stew about half a dozen potatoes, which
have been pared, washed and also cut dice-shape
and add to the meat. Salt to taste and add a
scant half teaspoonful of paprica (this is an
imported red pepper that grows in Hungary, it
looks like Cayenne, but taste very mild com-
pared to it, and is also of a different shade of
red); and then add half a teacupful of hot water
and boil another half hour, keeping covered

closely all the time. This is a favorite dish with most gentleman. You may find the paprica at most any first-class German grocer's

## SMOKED TONGUE.

Put on to boil in a large kettle, fill with cold water, enough to completely cover the tongue; keep adding hot water as it boils down so as to keep it covered with water until done. Keep covered with a lid while boiling and put a heavy weight on the top of the lid so as not to let the steam escape. (If you have an old flat iron use it as a weight.) It should boil very slow but steady for four hours. When tongue is cooked set it outdoors to cool in the liquor in which it was boiled; this will keep it nice. If the tongue is very dry, soak over night before boiling. In serving slice very thin and garnish with parsley.

## GEFILLTE MILZ (MILT).

Clean the milt by taking off the thin outer skin and every particle of fat that adheres to it. Then lay it on a clean board, make an incision with a knife through the center of the milt, taking care not to cut through the lower skin, and scrape the milt with the edge of a kitchen spoon, taking out all the blood you can without tearing the milt and put it into a bowl until wanted. . In the meantime dry the bread which you have previously soaked in water, in a spider in which you have heated some suet or goose oil, and cut up part of an onion in it very fine. When the bread is thoroughly dried, put it with the blood scraped from the milt. Break into it also two or three eggs, half a teaspoonful of salt, pepper, nutmeg and a very little thyme (leave out the latter if you object to the flavor), and add a speck of ground ginger instead. Now work all thoroughly with your hands and fill in the milt. The way to do this is to fill it lengthwise all through the center and sew it up; when done prick it with a fork in several places to prevent its bursting while boiling. You may parboil it after it is filled, in the soup you are to have for dinner, then take it up carefully and brown slightly in a spider of heated fat; or, you may form the mixture into a huge ball and bake it in the oven with flakes of fat put here and there, basting often. Bake until a hard crust is formed over it. You may add the skin of the milt to your soup. It will add to its richness and flavor

### STEWED MILT.

Clean the milt thoroughly and boil with your soup meat. Set to boil with cold water and let it boil about two hours. Then take it out and cut into finger lengths and prepare the following sauce. Heat a spoonful of nice drippings in a spider. When hot cut up a clove of garlic very fine and brown slightly in the fat. Add a

spoonful of flour, stirring briskly, pepper and
salt to taste and thin with soup stock. Throw
in the pieces of milt and let it simmer slowly.
If the sauce is too thick add more water or soup
stock. Some add a few carroway seeds instead
of the garlic, which is a matter of taste. This
is one of the cheapest meat dishes made and is
very palatable.

### BOILED TONGUE, (SWEET AND SOUR.)

Lay the fresh tongue in cold water for a couple
of hours and then put it on to boil in enough
water to barely cover it, adding salt. Boil until
tender. To ascertain when tender run a fork
through the thickest part. A good rule is to boil
it, closely covered, from three to four hours
steadily. Pare off the thick skin which covers
the tongue, cut into nice even slices, sprinkle a
little fine salt over each piece and then prepare
the following sauce: Put a spoonful of nice
drippings in a porcelain-lined kettle or spider
(goose fat is very good). Cut up an onion in it,
add a tablespoonful of flour and stir, adding
gradually about a pint of the liquor the tongue
was boiled in. Cut up a lemon in slices, remove
the seeds, and add a handful of raisins, a few
pounded almonds, a stick of cinnamon and a
few cloves. Sweeten with two heaping tablespoonfuls of brown sugar, in which you have put
half a teaspoonful of ground cinnamon, a table-

spoonful of molasses and two tablespoonfuls of vinegar. Let this boil, lay in the slices of tongue and boil up for a few minutes. Taste, and if too sweet, add more vinegar; if too sour, more sugar.

### TRIPE.

Take tripe that has been boiled tender, but not prickled and clean several times in water. Cut into strips about two or three inches long and a quarter of an inch in width. Make a sauce as follows: Put a spoonful of fat in a spider, add a spoonful of flour, salt and pepper and a speck of ginger. Cut up a clove of garlic as fine as possible and add to the heated fat before adding the flour. Add hot water and pour over the tripe and boil slowly for a couple of hours. Boil the tripe in salted water before adding the sauce. The oftener this is warmed over the better.

### ASPIC (SULZ).

Set on to boil six calf's feet, chopped up, two or three pounds of beef and one calf's head with three quarts of water and one bottle of white wine. Add two celery roots, three or four small onions, a bunch of parsley, one dozen whole peppercorns, half a dozen cloves, two bay leaves and a tablespoonful of fine salt. Boil steadily for eight hours and then pour through a fine hair sieve. When cold remove every particle of fat and set on to boil again, skimming until clear.

Then break three or four eggs, shells and all, into a deep bowl, beat them up with a pint of vinegar, pour some of the soup stock into this and set all back on the stove to boil up once, stirring all the while. Then remove from the fire and pour through a jelly-bag as you would jelly. Fasten the bag to a doorknob and put bowl under it; pour into cups or one large mould. Set on ice.

### GANSLEBER IN SULZ.

Fry a large goose liver in goose fat. Season with salt, pepper, a few whole cloves and a very little onion. Cut it up in slices and mix with the sulz and the whites of hard-boiled eggs. Cut into fanciful shapes.

### GANSLEBER PUREE IN SULZ.

After the liver is fried, rub it through a sieve or collander and mix with sulz.

### BOSTON BAKED BEANS.

Soak the beans in water over night. In the morning change water and parboil them gently for two hours. Then rinse them in fresh water and put them in a pot with a good-sized piece of salt pork, with a streak of lean in it. Then bake the beans slowly all day in the oven, taking care to have plenty of water in the pot while cooking. They are better warmed over next day.

## EGGS.

| | Page. |
|---|---|
| Boiled Eggs, - - - - - - 107 |
| Omelet, plain, - - - - 107, 108 |
| Baked Omelet, - - - - - - 108 |
| Sweet Omelet, - - - - - 109 |
| Herb Omelet, - - - - - - 109 |
| Baked Eggs, - - - - - 110 |
| Eggs Piquant, - - - - - - 110 |
| Poached Eggs, - - - - - 111 |
| Egg Barley, - - - - · - - 111 |

(106)

# EGGS.

## BOILED EGGS.

BE sure the eggs are fresh before you attempt to boil them. Have ready a stew-pan of boiling water; put in the eggs carefully with a tablespoon, so as not to crack them. If you want them soft, boil steadily for three minutes; if hard, eight or ten minutes. Another way is to put them in a dish and pour boiling water over them; cover up, and in fifteen minutes they are ready to be served. Still another way to boil eggs is to put the eggs on in cold water and let them just come to a boil. Hard-boiled eggs should be thrown into cold water as soon as they are taken from the fire, as that will prevent the yellow from turning color.

## OMELET.

One egg, one teaspoonful of corn starch, four tablespoonfuls of milk and a pinch of salt. Separate the yelk from the white and beat the yelk. Wet the corn-starch with the milk and add the milk to the beaten yelk, and add a pinch of salt. Beat the white of the egg with a fork until it is perfectly stiff. Heat butter in griddle

(107)

and pour in the omelet and bake.  When done
on both sides sprinkle well with powdered sugar;
roll and serve immediately.  You may pour a
tablespoonful of brandy over it and light it.
Send to the table in flames.

### OMELET FOR ENTIRE FAMILY.

Take from four to six eggs, whites separate,
allow a tablespoonful of corn-starch for each egg,
and a cup of milk for every two eggs, not forgetting the salt.

### BAKED OMELET.

Six eggs, two tablespoonfuls of flour, a pinch
of salt, one cup of cold milk.  Wet the flour
with a little of the milk, then add the rest of the
milk and the yelks of the eggs.  Beat the whites
of the eggs to a stiff froth and pour into the
flour, milk and yelks.  Put a piece of butter
into a spider and let it get hot, but not so hot
that the butter will burn.  Then pour the mixture in and put in a moderate oven to bake in
the spider.  It takes about ten minutes to bake.
Then slip a knife under it and loosen it and
slip off on a large plate.  Sift powdered sugar
on top and serve with a slice of lemon.

### OMELET FOR ONE.

One egg, beat white separately, one teaspoonful
of corn-starch dissolved in four tablespoonfuls

of cold sweet milk, a pinch of salt. You may brown on both sides or roll, spread with compote, or sprinkle powdered sugar thickly over it. Serve at once.

### SWEET OMELET.

Take six eggs, beat whites and yelks well, add a pinch of salt and a teaspoonful of brandy. Fry in a spider quickly and spread with a compote of huckleberries or any other fruit. Roll up the omelet, pour a very small wineglassful of rum over it, light it and serve at once. You may omit the fruit and just use pulverized sugar over and between.

### HERB OMELET.

Take six eggs, and beat well in a bowl. Add two tablespoonfuls of cold water and a quarter of a teaspoonful of salt, a pinch of pepper, a teaspoonful of chopped parsley a quarter of a teaspoonful of grated onion and a teaspoonful of fine butter, shaved in little pieces. Mix well with a wooden spoon. Dissolve in the spider two ounces of butter and add at once the beaten eggs, etc., inclining the spider to the handle for an instant and then shaking the omelet into the center and turn up the right edge, then the left and fry briskly five minutes and serve.

### SWEET OMELET.

Beat up the whites of four eggs and the yelks of six and add salt. Heat a lump of butter in a spider and as soon as hot pour in the mixture. As soon as it has set spread with preserves of any kind and fold. Serve with powdered sugar.

### EGGS BAKED.

Butter a shallow baking-dish and break the eggs on it, one at a time being careful not to break the yelks. Put on each egg a bit of butter, a little pepper and salt. Bake in the oven from four to six minutes.

### EGGS PIQUANT.

Set to boil the following mixture in a porcelain-lined kettle: Pour into the kettle water to the depth of about one inch, adding a little salt and half a cup of vinegar. When this boils, break in as many fresh eggs, one at a time, as you desire to have. Do this carefully so as not to break the yelks. As soon as the whites of the eggs are boiled, take up carefully with a perforated skimmer and lay in cold water. Then remove to a large platter and pour over the following sauce: Strain the sauce the eggs were boiled in, and set away until you have rubbed or grated two hard-boiled eggs, yelks only. Add a tablespoonful of butter, rubbed very hard and add also some sugar and part of the strained sauce. Boil up once and pour over the eggs. Garnish with parsley.

### POACHED EGGS.

Heat water in a deep, clean frying-pan. When the water boils, break the eggs, one at a time, in a saucer and slip into the boiling water. Salt the water and pour the boiling water over the eggs. Boil about four minutes. Take up with a perforated skimmer, drain and lay upon nicely buttered toast, sprinkle with salt and pepper. Put two eggs on each piece of toast, unless you have cut the toast into round pieces, then one egg will answer.

### GEROESTETE FERVELCHEN (EIRGRAUPEN) EGG BARLEY.

Make just as you would a noodle dough, only stiffer, by adding and working in as much flour as possible and then grate on a coarse grater. Spread on a large platter to dry; boil in salt water or milk, which must boil before you put in the egg barley and boil until thick. Serve with melted butter poured over them. A simpler and much quicker way is to sift a few handfuls of flour on a board; break in two or more eggs, and work the dough by rubbing it through your hands until it is as fine as barley grains

# VEGETABLES.

|  | Page. |  | Page. |
| --- | --- | --- | --- |
| Time-table, | - 113 | Kohlraben, - | 121 |
| Potatoes, how to | | Cauliflower, | - 122 |
| prepare, - | 113 | Imitation Caul- | |
| Boiled Potatoes, | | iflower, - | 122 |
| - - - | 114, 115 | Spinach, - | 123 |
| Baked Potatoes, | | Canned Corn, | - 124 |
| - - - | 114, 116 | Potato Croquettes, | 125 |
| Mashed Potatoes, | 115 | Canned Aspara- | |
| Stewed Potatoes, | | gus, - - | 125 |
| - - - | 115, 116 | Red Cabbage, | - 126 |
| Fried Potatoes, - | 117 | Beets, - - | 127 |
| Saratoga Chips, | 117 | Horseradish, | 127 |
| Potato Puffs, | 117, 120 | Snap Beans, | 127, 128 |
| Imitation New | | Carrots, - | 128 |
| Potatoes, - | 118 | Succotash, - | 129 |
| Potato Ribbon, | 118 | Lima Beans, | 129 |
| Roast Sweet Po- | | Baked Tomatoes, | 129 |
| tatoes, - | 119, 126 | Fried Tomatoes, | 130 |
| Boiled Sweet Po- | | Escaloped Toma- | |
| tatoes, - | - 119 | toes, - - | 130 |
| Fried Sweet Po- | | Canned Green Peas, | 130 |
| tatoes, - | 119 | Sour Beans, - | 131 |
| Bohemian Potato | | Dried Beans, | 131 |
| Puff, - - | 120 | Spanish Onions, | 131 |
| Green Corn, - | 120 | Oyster Plant, | 132 |
| Stewed Toma- | | Egg Plant, - | 132 |
| toes, - | 121, 126 | Tomato Poiree, | 133 |

# VEGETABLES.

PEAS, potatoes, asparagus, corn, summer squash, tomatoes, rice, spinach, half an hour.

Young beets, young turnips, young carrots and parsnips, baked potatoes (sweet and Irish), also string beans, three quarters of an hour.

New onion, new cabbage, winter squash, oyster plant, cauliflower, shelled beans, shelled peas one hour.

Winter carrots, onions, cabbage, turnips, beets and mushrooms, two hours.

Always have your vegetables as fresh as possible. Before putting on to boil pick over carefully and lay them, when peeled, in cold water and let them remain there for half an hour before cooking. Put on to boil in salted water. Be sure that they are thoroughly done and always serve steaming hot.

## POTATOES.

No vegetable, perhaps, is, as a rule, more carelessly cooked than the potato. This is to be regretted, as it is one of the most valuable of vegetable foods, and no dinner is complete without it. The most economical method is to cook them in their "jackets," as the waste caused by paring is at least fourteen per cent., while when cooked in the skin, it is but five per cent. The salts, moreover, which add flavor to the potato, lie next to the skin, and they are largely lost when peeled. Potatoes should be put on to boil in hot water, allowing half an hour to boil. When done, pour off the water and set them on the back of the stove to dry before serving. Don't forget to salt—about a tablespoonful.

### POTATOES WITHOUT THE SKIN.

Pare very thin and lay in cold water for half an hour. Have ready a pot of boiling water, salted, of course, drop in the potatoes and keep them at a quick boil until tender. Drain off the water, sprinkle with a little fine salt and put a lump of butter over them. Shake the pot and add a little chopped parsley or chives and serve immediately, as potatoes spoil if kept standing too long.

### BAKED POTATOES.

Select fine, smooth potatoes and boil them about twenty minutes. Drain off the water, remove the skins and pack in a buttered dish. Lay a small piece of butter on each potato, sprinkle with salt and pepper and sprinkle fine bread crumbs over all, with a few tablespoonfuls of cream. Bake until a nice light brown. Serve in the same dish. Garnish with parsley

### MASHED POTATOES.

Old potatoes may be used (in fact it is the only way that old potatoes should be sent to the table). Pare and let them lie in cold water until time to cook. Boil in salt water, drain thoroughly when done and mash them in the pot with a potato masher, working in a large tablespoonful of nice butter and enough milk to make them resemble dough, and be sure not to allow any lumps to form in your dish. Garnish with parsley.

### NEW POTATOES (HOW TO BOIL).

Scrape off all the skins and boil for half an hour in salted water, drain, salt and dry for a few minutes and then pour melted butter over them and sprinkle with parsley.

### STEWED POTATOES.

Pare and quarter, soak in cold water and put on to boil. When almost done drain off the water, add a cupful of milk, a tablespoonful of butter, a little chopped parsley and cook awhile longer. Thicken with a little flour (wet with cold water or milk), stir, and take from the fire. You may use soup stock in place of milk as some prefer it.

### STEWED POTATOES.

Put a tablespoonful of drippings or butter in a porcelain-lined kettle, and when it is hot cut up an onion fine and throw it in the hot fat, and cover closely. Then put in your potatoes, which have been previously pared, washed, quartered and well salted. Cover them tight and stew slowly until soft, stirring them occasionally. Then heat in a spider a very little butter or drippings. Brown in this a spoonful of flour and add some soup stock, vinegar and chopped parsley. Pour this over the potatoes, boil up once and serve.

### BAKED POTATOES.

Wash large potatoes (Prince Alberts are best) and bake in a quick oven until soft, which will take about three quarters of an hour (to be eaten with butter and salt). This is the most wholesome way of cooking potatoes, and the only way that invalids should ever eat them.

### STEWED POTATOES WITH ONIONS.

Take small potatoes, pare and wash them very clean, use one onion to about ten potatoes, add butter or goose-oil (in fact any kind of drippings from roast meat will answer) and put them in a pot or spider. When hot cut up an onion very fine and throw in the boiling fat. Then add the potatoes. Salt and pepper to taste. Pour some water over all (not too much),

cover up tight and let them simmer for about
three quarters of an hour. These are very nice.
If you like them sour, you may add a little
vinegar, which is also very nice.

### FRIED POTATOES.

Cut up some raw potatoes quite thin, salt
and pepper and throw in boiling fat in a spider.
Cover up at first, to soften them. Turn them
frequently to prevent burning and then remove
the cover to brown slightly.

### SARATOGA CHIPS.

Get a spider made for this purpose, and proceed as above; but do not cover and do not take
as many potatoes at one time.

### FRIED POTATOES.

Take potatoes left from the day before or
some that you have just cooked in their
"jackets," pare, slice, add more salt,if necessary
and add a very little pepper. Heat some butter
or fat in a spider, and if you like, add some
chopped onion before you put in the potatoes.
Fry, turning frequently and carefully so as not
to burn or break up the slices. Add more butter
if necessary.

### POTATO PUFFS.

Take mashed potatoes and season with nutmeg, pepper and salt. Add one or two eggs,
well beaten, and mix together well and make

into balls. After having floured your hands
well. turn the puffs over in cracker or bread
crumbs and fry in hot fat. This is a nice way
to use up cold mashed potatoes left over from
the day before, and make a nice side dish,
especially for breakfast.

### IMITATION NEW POTATOES.

This is rather a troublesome dish, and requires considerable time and patience to prepare, as they are to represent "new potatoes."
Of course this is only done when new ones are
not to be had or are too expensive. Well, to begin: First buy a potato cutter at a first-class
hardware store, and with it cut the potatoes to
the size of a hickory nut, and then fry or steam
them. When cooked they look just like new potatoes. They are especially nice to garnish meats.
You may also parboil and brown in fat, or boil
and add parsley as you would with new potatoes.
The remainder of the raw potatoes may be
boiled and mashed or fried into ribbons; for
there is a good deal of waste in cutting with
this little instrument.

### POTATO RIBBON.

Pare and lay in cold water (ice-water is best)
for half an hour. Select the largest potatoes,
then cut round and round in one continuous
curl-like strip (there is also an instrument for
this purpose, which costs but a trifle); handle

with care and fry a few at a time for fear of en-
tanglement. Arrange nicely on a platter and
serve. Use plenty of fat, as they must swim in
it. They garnish meats handsomely.

### ROAST SWEET POTATOES.

These are commonly called "baked" sweet
potatoes. Select those of uniform size; wash,
and roast in the oven until done, which you can
easily tell by pressing the potatoes. If done
they will leave an impression when touched.
It usually requires three-quarters of an hour.
Serve in their "jackets;" Eat with nice butter.

### BOILED SWEET POTATOES.

Put on in cold water, without any salt, and
boil until a fork will easily pierce the largest.
Drain off the water and dry.

### FRIED SWEET POTATOES.

Boil, peel and cut lengthwise into slices a
quarter of an inch thick. Fry in sweet drippings
or butter (cold boiled potatoes may also be fried
in this way). When I roast fowl or meat of any
kind, I take either sweet or Irish potatoes, or
both, pare, wash, salt them and lay them around
the meat and let them roast for about an hour
(three quarters of an hour will do). Turn them
about once, so as to have them nicely browned.
They are best cooked this simple way, and, being
in the oven, require less room.

## BOHEMIAN POTATO PUFF.

Pare, wash and boil potatoes until soft enough
to mash well. Drain off nearly all the water,
leaving just a little, add a small handful of salt
and return to the stove. It is better to boil the
potatoes in salt water and add more salt if necessary after mashing. Sift half a cupful of flour
into the potatoes after returning to the fire and
keep covered closely for about five minutes.
Then remove from the stove and mash them as
hard as you can, so as not to have any lumps.
They must be of the consistency of dough and
smooth as velvet. Now put about two large
spoonfuls of goosefat in a spider, chop up some
onions very fine and heat them until they become a light brown, take a tablespoon and dip
it in the hot fat. and then cut a spoonful of the
potato dough with the same spoon and put it in
the spider, and so on until you have used it all
up. Be careful to dip your spoon in the hot fat
every time you cut a puff. Let them brown
slightly. If you have ever tried this you will
always have this dish at least once a week during the winter, as old potatoes are always palatable prepared in this way.

## GREEN CORN.

Select young, evergreen sugar corn, fullgrown.
Test by pressing it with your finger nail and
if good, the milk will escape readily. Strip off

the outer leaves, turn back the inner ones, pick off every thread of silk, and re-cover the ear with the thin husk nearest it. Put into boiling ` salt water and boil closely covered from twenty to thirty minutes. When done, cut off the stalks close to the cob and rub off the remaining husks with a napkin. Send to the table steaming hot. Eat with butter, salt and pepper.

### STEWED TOMATOES.

Pour boiling water over ripe tomatoes and skin them. Then cut them up and put them into an earthern or porcelain-lined stew-pan, and let them cook slowly a few minutes. Season with salt, pepper and a lump of fresh butter and a heaping tablespoonful of brown sugar. Do not allow them to cook but a few minutes longer, or their flavor will be spoiled. If the sauce is too thin thicken with a scant teaspoonful of corn starch, wet with a little cold water, before adding. Eat cold or hot.

### KOHLRABEN.

Strip off the young leaves and boil in salt water. Then peel the heads thickly, cut into round, thin slices, and lay in cold water for an hour. Put on to boil a breast of mutton or lamb, which has been previously well salted, and spice with a little ground ginger. When the mutton has boiled half an hour add the sliced kohlraben and boil covered. In the meantime,

drain all the water from the leaves, which you
have boiled separately, and chop them, but
not too fine, and add them also to the mutton.
When done thicken with flour, season with
pepper and more salt if needed.  You may omit
the leaves if you are not fond of them.

### CAULIFLOWER.

Pick off the leaves and cut the stalk close to the
bottom of the flower, being careful not to break
the bunch.  Lay it in cold salt water for half
an hour and examine carefully for fear of
worms lurking among the flowers.  Tie the cauliflower in a napkin or some coarse net and put
it in hot water to boil, adding salt, of course.
Boil about fifteen minutes steady; then lift the
cauliflower up carefully, lay in a hot vegetable
dish and cover until the following sauce has
been prepared:  Heat a cupful of cream; beat
the yelks of two eggs light, wet a teaspoonful of
corn starch with a little cold milk, and add a
little grated nutmeg.  Add all of this to the
heated cream, boil up once, pour over the cauliflower and serve immediately.  It darkens with
standing.  You may omit the eggs if you prefer,
and use half a cupful of the water the cauliflower was boiled in, and add a lump of butter.

### IMITATION CAULIFLOWER.

Boil a head of cabbage as directed below.
When it is cold, chop up quite fine and beat up

a couple of eggs, a tablespoonful of butter and half a cup of sweet cream. Add salt, pepper and nutmeg to taste. Stir up well, mix thoroughly with the cabbage and bake in a buttered dish. Eat hot.

## WHITE CABBAGE.

Reject the outer green leaves, cut the cabbage in quarters and lay for an hour in cold water. Then put it on to boil in hot water for fifteen minutes. Pour off this water and fill up again with boiling water; add salt and boil until tender. Always boil cabbage in two waters. Three quarters of an hour will be all the time required to cook a good-sized head of cabbage when young. Drain well, heat some nice drippings or butter in a spider, throw in a tablespoonful of flour, stir slowly, add some soup stock gravy from roast beef, or cream; season with white pepper and salt and pour over the cabbage. You may boil some potatoes with the cabbage. Cut them into dice shape.

## SPINACH.

I can't help but stop to laugh at a "young housekeeper," a very dear friend of mine, who once bought a quart of spinach for a company dinner of six. You may imagine her surprise and chagrin when the spinach was served in a saucer, for the maid-of-all-work could not serve it in a vegetable dish; as there was no spinach to be seen, for the eggs completely covered it. I have written this for your benefit, " House-keeper." Spinach is very deceptive as regards quantity — it shrinks dreadfully after being boiled. A peck of spinach for a family of five or six is not too much. Pick it over carefully, break off all the stems, using the leaves only and wash in several waters, shaking it well in last washing. Set to boil in boiling water, adding salt, of course. Boil about fifteen minutes, drain thoroughly through a sieve and chop extremely fine. Indeed, I consider this as important as the seasoning. You must chop the spinach so fine that it will resemble a smooth batter. Now heat some drippings or butter in a saucepan, rub a teaspoonful of flour in it, add salt and pepper and a little nutmeg to taste, grate in a small onion and add some soup stock to the whole, or some meat gravy left over from roast beef, or any other meat gravy that you may be fortunate enough to have on hand. Put the spinach in the sauce, and just before serving beat up two or more eggs and stir through the spinach. Garnish with hard-boiled eggs or use only the hard-boiled whites for the decoration, and rub the yelks to a powder and mix through the spinach.

### CANNED CORN.

Heat with milk and add a piece of nice butter, pepper and salt. Serve hot, in individual dishes.

### VELVET POTATO PUFFS.

Pare potatoes, put on to boil as usual, with
salt. When done throw off almost all the water,
leaving just a little. Then set back on the
fire and sift on them about half a cupful of
flour; cover them up and let them steam for
about five minutes. Now take them off and
mash them with a potato-beetle as hard as you
can, until they are a perfectly smooth dough;
taste, and be sure you have them well salted.
Now brown some onion, cut up very fine, in
goose fat (enough of it), dip a tablespoon in the
heated fat and cut out puffs with it from your
potato dough, lay each puff in the spider with
the heated fat and onion until all is used up.
Serve hot. You may use butter in place of fat
if you so prefer.

### POTATO CROQUETTES.

Work into two cups of mashed potatoes a
tablespoonful of melted butter—work until
smooth and soft; then add two eggs beaten to a
froth, and beat all together with a wooden spoon.
Season with salt and nutmeg, and roll into balls,
with floured hands. Roll each in beaten egg
and cracker crumbs; fry in hot butter or fat.
As soon as fried, drain perfectly dry.

### CANNED ASPARAGUS.

Heat the asparagus and pour over it the following sauce: Take a cupful of the sauce off

the asparagus, providing it is not bitter (if it is, do not use it), or a cupful of soup stock or water; add a tablespoonful of flour, three tablespoonfuls of sweet cream, grated nutmeg, a lump of butter and pour over the asparagus. Then remove from the fire, or it will curdle. For a large family you may double the quantity.

### CANNED TOMATOES, STEWED.

Salt, pepper; add a lump of butter the size of an egg and add a tablespoonful of sugar. Thicken with a teaspoonful of corn starch wet with a tablespoonful of cold water, stir into the tomatoes and boil up once.

### ROAST SWEET POTATOES.

Pare, cut lengthwise, salt and put them around roast meats or poultry of any kind. Roast about three-quarters of an hour, or until brown.

### RED CABBAGE.

Cut fine on slaw-cutter; salt, mix well and cut up a sour apple with it. Now take a porcelain-lined kettle; heat in it about a tablespoonful of goose oil or drippings; cut up an onion very fine, throw it in the cabbage and stew slowly, covered up. Add a little hot water after it has boiled about five minutes. When tender put in a little vinegar, a few cloves, some brown sugar and a little cinnamon; taste, if necessary add more sugar.

### BEETS.

Clean them nicely, but do not pare them.
Leave on a short piece of the stalk so as to keep
them a nice red. Put on to boil, well covered
with water. Young beets will cook tender in an
hour; old ones require several hour's boiling.
When done, skin quickly while hot, and slice
them into a bowl. Put on salt, pepper and a
tablespoonful of brown sugar, some carawy
seed, and pour vinegar over all. Another way
to prepare beets is to grate them and mix with
equal parts of grated horseradish. .Very nice.

### HORSERADISH.

Pare and grate over a hot stove or where there
is a draught of air (do this to prevent shedding
too many tears). Use white wine vinegar and
add a tablespoonful of sugar. Keep air-tight.

### STRING OR GREEN SNAP BEANS.

Cut off the tops and bottoms and "string"
carefully; break the beans in pieces about an
inch long and lay them in cold water, with
a little salt, for ten or fifteen minutes. Heat
some drippings or butter in a stew-pan, in which
you have cut up part of an onion and some parsley; cover this and stew about ten minutes.
In the meantime, drain the beans, put into the
stew-pan and stew until tender, adding a little
soup stock now and then. Sift in a spoonful

of flour and season with salt and pepper; add
meat gravy or soup stock—this will improve
them. You may pare about half a dozen potatoes, cut into dice shape, and add to the beans.
If you prefer, you may add cream or milk instead of soup stock.

### CARROTS BOILED WITH CABBAGE.

Pare the carrots and cut them into finger
lengths, in thin strips. Put a breast of lamb or
mutton on to boil, having previously salted it
well. When boiling, throw in the carrots and
cover closely. Prepare the cabbage as usual and
lay in with the mutton and carrots; boil two
hours at least; when all has boiled tender, skim
off some of the fat and put it into a spider.
Add to this a spoonful of flour, a spoonful of
brown sugar and half a teaspoonful of cinnamon.
Keep adding gravy from the mutton until well
mixed, and pour all over the mutton and vegetables. Serve together on a platter. Very fine;
even better warmed over. In salting the mutton add a little ground ginger. You will find it
improves the flavor of the stew very much.

### STRING BEANS WITH TOMATOES.

Cut off both ends of the beans, string them
carefully and break into pieces about an inch in
length and boil in salt water. When tender
drain off this brine and add fresh water (boiling
from the kettle). Add a piece of butter, three

or four large potatoes cut into squares, also four large tomatoes, cut up and season with salt and pepper. Now melt a tablespoonful of butter in a spider, stir into it a spoonful of flour, thin with soup stock, meat gravy or milk, and add this to the beans.

## SUCCOTASH.

Cut from the cob enough green corn to fill a pint measure; then take two-thirds of a pint of Lima beans and let them stew in just enough water or milk to cover them. When tender season with butter, pepper and salt; if too thin, thicken with a teaspoonful of flour.

## LIMA BEANS.

Shell and put into cold water and let them remain in it for half an hour before boiling. Drain and put into boiling water and cook until tender. Pour off the water, add a little cream and butter, and season with pepper and salt. Let them simmer in this dressing for a few minutes before serving. You may boil a few tomatoes with the beans if you like; very nice for a change. Dried Lima beans should be soaked over night and allowed two hours to cook.

## BAKED TOMATOES.

Select large, smooth tomatoes; wash, wipe and cut in halves. Place them in a baking tin, skin side down Season with salt and pepper,

and place in a hot oven. When done take up
carefully, place in the dish you intend to
serve them in, putting flakes of butter over
each one.

### FRIED TOMATOES.

Cut large, sound tomatoes in halves and flour
the insides thickly. Season with a little salt
and pepper. Allow the butter to get very hot
before putting in the tomatoes. When brown
on one side, turn and when done serve with hot
cream or thicken some milk and pour over the
tomatoes hot.

### ESCALOPED TOMATOES.

Scald the tomatoes and pare off all the skin.
Line an earthen baking dish, well buttered, with
a layer of cracker crumbs and small bits of butter. Then put in a layer of tomatoes with a
very little brown sugar sprinkled over them;
then another layer of cracker crumbs, seasoned
with butter, pepper and salt, and then another
layer of tomatoes, until your dish is filled; let
the last layer be cracker crumbs; put flakes of
butter here and there over this. Bake half an
hour. One or two tablespoonfuls of rich cream
poured over the top layer is an improvement.

### CANNED GREEN PEAS.

Use the imported canned peas for " extra occasions." Heat, add a tablespoonful of sugar,
some minced parsely and a teaspoonful of flour

wet with cold water to thicken. A piece of fresh butter improves them. You may prepare them in sweet cream, which is also very nice. Use about half a cupful with a teaspoonful of flour.

### SOUR BEANS.

If you use canned string beans, heat some fat in a spider and put in a spoonful of flour; brown slightly; add a handful of brown sugar, a pinch of salt, some cinnamon and vinegar to taste; then add the beans and let them simmer on the back of the stove, but do not let them burn. The juice of pickled peaches or pears is delicious in preparing sweet and sour beans.

### DRIED BEANS.

Must be soaked over night, then boiled in salted water until tender; drain and prepare same as sour beans, or with salt and pepper, and thicken by heating some butter or drippings in a spider. Stir in a spoonful of flour and some soup stock. Pour this over the beans and boil for a few minutes.

### SPANISH ONIONS.

Pare and throw into hot salted water and boil. After boiling half an hour change the water, renewing the water three times, using boiling water each time. Fifteen minutes before time to serve, heat in a saucepan a little sweet cream (half a teacupful), adding a spoon-

ful of butter, and stir all the time until the
butter is melted. Season with salt and pepper.
Drain the onions out of the water and boil them
up once in this hot cream.

### OYSTER PLANT, OR SALSIFY.

Scrape the roots thoroughly and drop each
into cold water as soon as cleaned. Cut in pieces
an inch long; put into a stew-pan with enough
hot salted water to just cover them, and stew
until tender. Then pour off most all the water,
add about a pint of milk and boil ten minutes
longer. Add a piece of butter, pepper and salt
and thicken with flour.

### FRIED OYSTER PLANT.

Scrape the roots and drop each into cold water
as soon as it is cleaned, and leave them in the
water about fifteen minutes. Boil whole until
tender. Drain when cold and mash with a potato beetle, picking out all the fibres. Mix with
a little milk, about a tablespoonful of butter,
salt, pepper and two eggs; beat the eggs light
before adding. Make into round cakes, dip in
hot flour and fry in hot butter a light brown.

### FRIED EGG PLANT.

Cut the egg plant into very thick slices; pare
carefully and lay them in salt water for half an
hour; then wipe each piece dry and dip in beaten

egg and cracker crumbs; fry in hot butter until nice brown.

### TOMATO POIREE.

Scald the tomatoes cut into quarters and put on to boil with a lump of butter about the size of a walnut, Add a punch of salt, pepper and two tablespoonfuls of sugar. Boil until soft— then strain and thicken with a teaspoonful of corn starch. Serve either hot or cold. This is a nice accompaniment to any kind of meat chops.

# SALADS.

| | Page. |
|---|---|
| Remarks, | 135 |
| Sweetbread, | 135 |
| Mayonnaise, | 136 |
| Oyster, | 137 |
| Asparagus, | 137 |
| Lobster, | 137 |
| Salmon, | 138 |
| Italian, | 138 |
| Tomato, | 139, 140 |
| Vegetable, | 140 |
| Neapolitan, | 140 |
| Chicken, | 141 |
| Mayonnaise, | 142 |
| Chopped Cabbage, | 142 |
| Cucumber, | 143 |
| Lettuce, | 143, 144 |
| Unique Potato, | 145 |
| Haeringsalat, | 145 |
| Celery, | 146, 147 |
| Polish, | 147 |
| Salad Dressing, | 148 |
| Russian, | 148 |
| Chicken Salad for Forty or More. | 148 |
| Mayonnaise of Tomatoes—Whole. | 150 |
| Stuffed Tomatoes—Southern Favorite. | 150 |
| Stuffed Tomatoes with Mayonnaisse of chicken, | 150 |

# SALADS.

SALADS are becoming so popular that scarcely a meal can be called complete without some kind of salad. In fact, at receptions and lunch parties all that is required is a good salad accompanied by " cheese sticks," coffee, hot rolls and dessert, of course, such as creams, ices, etc. Cheese sticks are made of French puff paste, cut into strips about five inches long with a jagging iron, with grated cheese on top of each stick and baked a light brown; they must be very flaky. Parmesan cheese is the best, the flavor being delicate. It is expensive, but a little of it goes a great way.

## SWEETBREAD SALAD

The most delicious of all salads is sweetbread. Lay the sweetbread in cold salted water for an hour before cooking, then boil, changing the water twice. Then throw into cold water immediately after they are done, which will be in about twenty minutes. Remove every particle of skin before chopping, and do not chop too fine. In season, chop up some nice white crisp celery, say about one-third as much as you have

(135)

of sweetbreads.  You may also mix some French
peas with this salad—looks pretty and tastes
nice.  Line a salad bowl with lettuce leaves,
and put in the salad, which has been previously
mixed with the following mayonnaise (you may
add a small quantity of cold roast veal, if you
happen to have it, in fact, for economy's sake,
you may add it to almost any salad, and it is as
nice).

### MAYONNAISE FOR SALADS.

(No. 1.)  Take the yelks of three hard-boiled
eggs and the yelk of one raw egg, stir to a cream,
with two teaspoonfuls of prepared mustard, one
teaspoonful of grated onion, some white pepper,
as much as the point of a knife will hold; a
tablespoonful of sugar, the juice of a lemon,
and about two tablespoonfuls of white wine
vinegar.  Stir until smooth, then drop in gradually three teaspoonfuls of oil, one drop at a
time.  Grind hard and stir very energetically
so as to get it thoroughly mixed.  You may
add capers and chopped parsley to this mayonnaise, but omit both for the sweetbread salad.

### MAYONNAISE FOR SALADS.

(No. 2.)  The yelks of two hard-boiled eggs,
rubbed to a powder, add a teaspoonful of salt,
one of oil (add the oil a drop at a time, stirring
continually), one teaspoonful of prepared

mustard, one of pepper and two of sugar.
Then whip up a raw egg to a froth, beat this
into the dressing and pour in the vinegar, spoonful at a time, using half a cupful altogether.
Pour this dressing over the salad and mix well
with two forks. I forgot to mention that
cooked peas and beans are fine mixed with the
sweetbread salad.

### OYSTER SALAD.

Cook the oysters in their own liquor, allowing
them to boil up but once, then spread upon a
platter. Leave until ice cold, and cut them up
into small pieces (do not chop). Cut up bits of
crisp celery and mix up half a cup of capers
with the salad. Serve on lettuce with the above
mayonnaise.

### ASPARAGUS SALAD.

Boil the asparagus in salted water, being very
careful not to break the caps; drain, and pour
over it when cold a mayonnaise dressing, with
some chopped parsley. Serve each person with
three or four stems on a plate, with a little
mayonnaise dressing. Do not use a fork; take
the stems in the fingers and dip in the dressing.

### LOBSTER SALAD.

Boil the lobster, and when cold pick it to
pieces, or use canned lobster; then line the salad
bowl with lettuce, put in the lobster and set
it away in the ice-chest until wanted. Do not

put the dressing over it until ready to serve.
Dressing: Beat up the yelks of two eggs, one
teaspoonful of salt, one tablespoonful of sugar,
two teaspoonfuls of prepared mustard, a pinch
of white pepper, two tablespoonfuls of oil and
four tablespoonfuls of white vinegar; stir long
and thoroughly. If you wish to have it extra
nice mix in last a cupful of whipped cream;
this will make it truly delicious. If any of my
readers object to oil, use butter, it is equally
good and certainly preferable to inferior oil.

### SALMON SALAD (CANNED OR FRESH).

Is as good as lobster salad, and is prepared
in the same manner as above, as is also

### SHRIMP SALAD.

This makes a delightful change for the table.
I wish to call attention to one thing right here,
that is, when you intend to use canned fish of
any kind always open the can, and put its contents into the salad bowl at least one hour
before time to serve, in order that the close
smell which is always present in canned fish
may escape.

### ITALIAN SALAD.

Soak two herrings in milk over night, then
take off every particle of skin, being careful to
remove every bit of bone and cut up very fine.
Cut up six boiled potatoes, also a handful of
little vinegar pickles and two boiled beets; then

take one or two pounds of cold roast veal, the same amount of cold boiled smoked tongue, two apples, pared, seeded, cored, then chopped; three carrots and one large celery root which have also been cooked, pared and chopped; mix all thoroughly and pour a mayonnaise dressing over all. Serve in a large bowl; garnish the top with chopped hard-boiled eggs and the sides with alternate layers of the yelks and whites, also some capers, olives and beets and outside of this edge lay curly parsley. In the center of the salad put a little basket made of a hard-boiled egg and filled with capers.

### TOMATO SALAD.

(No. 1.) Skin the tomatoes, and slice; sprinkle each layer with salt, sugar and pepper; cover with vinegar. The tomatoes should be set on ice before serving. You may add one or two yelks of eggs to the dressing if you like.

### TOMATO SALAD.

(No. 2.) Scald the tomatoes thoroughly; drain and peel, and slice evenly and then set on ice. When time to send to table, put in your salad bowl a layer of tomatoes and sprinkle with salt, pepper and an even tablespoonful of powdered sugar, then another layer and so on until all are used up; then pour enough white wine vinegar over them to barely cover. If the vinegar is too strong, dilute it with water.

## WHOLE TOMATO SALAD.

Select tomatoes of uniform size, scald and skin, and set on ice until wanted. Then line your salad bowl with lettuce leaves and pile your tomatoes in it like a mound; serve on individual plates with a mayonnaise dressing. This is a pretty dish and very much relished.

## VEGETABLE SALAD.

Take cold vegetables left from dinner, such as potatoes, string beans, peas, beets, Lima beans, cauliflower, asparagus, cabbage, etc., and set them on ice. You may use a mayonnaise or any other salad dressing.

## NEAPOLITAN SALAD.

Take some white meat of a turkey, cut up fine, cut up a few pickles the same way, also a few beets, one or two carrots, a few potatoes (the carrots and potatoes must be parboiled, say in the soup for dinner), also a few stalks of asparagus; chop up a bunch of nice, crisp, white celery; also a whole celery root (parboiled) and sprinkle all with fine salt and pour a mayonnaise dressing over it. Then line the salad bowl with lettuce leaves or nice white cabbage leaves. Add a few hard-boiled eggs and capers; garnish very prettily, also sprigs of fresh parsley.

### CHICKEN SALAD.

Take the white meat of one or more boiled chickens, a few stalks of nice celery, chopped separately, but not too fine (I prefer to cut it with a knife; it is not so apt to become mushy); put in a large bowl, sprinkle with a little salt and set away in a cool place until you prepare the following mayonnaise: Rub the yelks of two hard-boiled eggs as fine as possible, add a small teaspoonful of salt, then add, a drop at a time, a teaspoonful of the finest olive oil. Now stir harder than ever; add a teaspoonful of prepared mustard and white pepper, and two teaspoonfuls of white sugar; whip the white of an egg to a froth and add to the dressing; add vinegar last, a spoonful at a time, stirring constantly (use about half a cupful). Put the salad into the dressing carefully, using two silver forks; line the salad bowl with lettuce leaves, and garnish the top with the whites of hard-boiled eggs, chopped up, or cut into half-moons. The white meat of a turkey makes even a better tasting salad. If you wish your salad particularly nice, add a cupful of whipped cream just before serving. A pretty way to garnish this salad is with the chopped yelks and whites of hard-boiled eggs, being careful to have the whites and yelks separate. A few olives and capers will add to the decoration.

### MAYONNAISE OF CHICKEN.

Take the white meat of a boiled chicken, stalks
of nice, crisp celery, and chop up separately;
put in a salad bowl, sprinkle with a little salt
and put in a cool place until you have prepared
the following: Rub the yelks of two hard-
boiled eggs as fine as possible, add a small teaspoonful of salt and a teaspoonful of finest olive
oil, and stir harder than ever. Then add a
teaspoonful of prepared mustard and white pepper, and two teaspoonfuls of sugar. Whip the
white of an egg to a froth and add to the
dressing; add vinegar last, a spoonful at a time,
stirring constantly, use about half a cupful.
Put the salad into the dressing carefully, using
two silver forks. Line the bowl with lettuce
leaves and garnish the top of salad with the
whites of hard-boiled eggs, chopped up or cut
into half-moons. The white meat of a turkey
is even better for this salad.

### CHOPPED CABBAGE SALAD.

Chop up a head of white cabbage; salt and
pepper; heat some vinegar in a spider, adding
a teaspoonful of prepared mustard; beat up the
yelks of two eggs with a tablespoonful of sugar,
and add the hot vinegar gradually to the beaten
eggs; pour all over the cabbage. This makes a
nice salad.

## CUCUMBER SALAD.

Pare thickly, from end to end, and lay in ice-water one hour; wipe them and slice thin, and slice an onion equally thin. Strew salt over them, shake up a few times, cover and let them remain in this brine for another hour. Then squeeze or press out every drop of water which has been extracted from the cucumbers. Put into a salad bowl, sprinkle with white pepper and scatter bits of parsley over them; add enough vinegar to just cover. You may slice up an equal quantity of white or black radishes and mix with this salad, which is very good.

## LETTUCE SALAD.

(No 1.) If you use head lettuce, break off the outer leaves, using the inner ones only, tear out the hard vein and cut up into bits. Wash thoroughly, and drain in a collander but do not press with the hands, Just before sending to the table mix with a teaspoonful of best salad oil, adding some salt, sugar and vinegar.

## LETTUCE SALAD.

(No. 2.) Dress the lettuce as decribed above, mixing it well with a spoonful of best salad oil and pour the following dressing over it: Beat up the yelks of two eggs; cut up part of an onion, very fine, add half a teaspoonful of salt, and two tablespoonfuls of white sugar; stir this

well, adding about four or five tablespoonfuls
of vinegar, and pour over lettuce.

### LETTUCE SALAD.

(No. 3.) The French style of making lettuce
salad is as follows:  After dressing the salad,
mix it in a tablespoonful of oil, then take only
two tablespoonfuls of white wine vinegar, mixed
with a very little pepper and salt, and just turn
the lettuce over and over in this mixture; the
idea is not to have any sauce.

### LETTUCE SALAD.

(No. 4.) After the lettuce has been carefully
picked, washed and drained, pour the following
sauce over it, and mix up well with two silver
forks.  Rub the yelks of two hard-boiled eggs
to a paste, adding a teaspoonful of best salad
oil or melted butter, being careful to add only a
few drops at a time.  Add half a teaspoonful of
salt, half a teaspoonful of prepared mustard,
very little pepper, two tablespoonfuls of white
sugar.  Stir very vigorously, then pour in gradually half a teacup full of vinegar.  If there is
more sauce than required, put in the refrigerator; it will keep two or three days.

### LETTUCE SALAD.

(No. 5.) Wash, cut out all the hard stems,
make a dressing of the yelk of one egg, beaten
light, adding salt, a little onion cut very fine

and two tablespoonfuls of white sugar, adding vinegar gradually and pour over lettuce just before serving.

### UNIQUE POTATO SALAD.

Boil potatoes in their jackets. When done, peel and cut them in squares. While still hot put on a tablespoonful of butter or drippings of poultry, and add two or more hard-boiled eggs, cut into squares; sprinkle salt and pepper over potatoes and eggs. You may add an onion if you like the flavor. Boil enough vinegar to just cover the salad and add two teaspoonfuls of prepared mustard; beat up the yelks of one or two eggs light, and add the boiling vinegar to the beaten eggs gradually. When thorougly mixed pour over the potatoes. Serve in a salad bowl; garnish with chopped parsley. Eat cold.

### HAERINGSALAT.

Take six fine milch herrings, remove the heads and the skin, and take out the milch, which much be reserved for sauce. Remove every bit of meat from the bones of the herrings, and soak it and the milch in milk over night (you may use water, but milk is better). Chop up the herrings not too fine, and chop an equal quantity of nice cold roast veal, which ought to be tender and white. Chop also a few pickles and about four nice, large sour apples.

Boil about ten eggs hard, reserving four of these
for decoration.  Add a few pieces of preserved
or candied ginger, and a small cup of capers,
also a few olives.  Chop everything separately,
but not too fine, and put all these ingredients
into a porcelain bowl and pour the following
sauce over it:   Rub the milch of the herrings to
a cream, then rub it through a fine wire sieve;
rub the yelks of two hard-boiled eggs to a cream
add a grated onion (a very small one), a spoonful of prepared mustard, a little white wine and
vinegar, a pinch of salt, two tablespoonfuls of
brown sugar and pour over the salad.  Next
day, before decorating, mix up well.  For
decorating, chop up the yelks and whites of
eggs separately and line each dish with a lettuce
leaf (for I think it the most practical to serve
individual dishes of salads).  Put a layer of
white, then a layer of yellow chopped eggs on
each dish.  To accomplish this easily, take a
piece of pasteboard or the blade of a knife in
your left hand, and hold in line as you would a
ruler, putting an olive in the center of each dish.
This salad may be improved by adding all kinds
of nuts chopped up.

### CELERY SALAD.

Chop up white crisp celery, sprinkle with fine
salt.  Line your salad bowl with lettuce leaves,
pile up the chopped celery in the center and

pour a mayonnaise dressing over it. Garnish
with hard-boiled eggs, cut into fanciful shapes

### BOILED CELERY ROOT SALAD.

Pare and wash the celery roots (they should
be the size of large potatoes), put on to boil in a
little salted water, and when tender remove
from the water and set away until cool. Cut
in slices about an eighth of an inch thick;
sprinkle each slice with fine salt, sugar and
white pepper; pour enough white wine vinegar
over the salad to cover. A few large raisins
boiled will add to the appearance of this salad.
Serve cold in a salad bowl, lined with fresh
lettuce leaves.

### POLISH SALAD, OR SALAD PIQUANT.

Lay half a dozen or more large salt pickles
in water for about six hours, then drain off all
the water. Chop up two sour apple, sone large
onion or two small ones, chop the pickles and
mix all thoroughly in a bowl and sprinkle over
them a scant half teaspoonful of pepper (white
is preferable) and a heaping tablespoonful of
sugar (either white or brown), adding a pinch
of salt if necessary. Pour enough white wine
vinegar over all to just cover. Do not make
more at a time than you can use up in a week,
as it will not keep longer. Try this. Makes a
nice change.

### SALAD DRESSING.

Beat up two raw eggs, one tablespoonful of chicken fat or butter, one half teaspoonful of mustard and six tablespoonfuls of vinegar and one of sugar. Set this over a bowl or teakettle of boiling water and stir until it becomes thick like cream; pepper and salt to taste. Add also a tablespoonful of sugar.

### RUSSIAN SALAD.

Cut up all kinds of pickled cucumbers, small and large, sweet and sour, also (senf) mustard pickles, into very small lengths, also pickled beans and capers. Add six herrings, which you have soaked in water for twenty-four hours; skin and take out every bone, cut up as you did the pickles. Add half a pound of smoked salmon, also cut into lengths, and six large apples chopped very fine, and one onion grated. Add as much cold roast veal, chicken or turkey as you desire; mix all thoroughly and pour a rich mayonnaise dressing over all. Next day line a salad bowl with lettuce leaves, fill in the salad and garnish with hard-boiled eggs, nuts, capers and fancy figures cut out of aspic.

### CHICKEN SALAD FOR A COMPANY OF FORTY.

Dress four chickens, cut off the wings, legs and backs of the chickens and set away to use as a fricassee. Boil the four breasts in enough

water to just cover them, add salt while boiling;
when very tender remove from the fire and allow
the chicken to cool in the liquor it was boiled
in; when cold skim off every particle of fat,
and reserve it to use instead of oil. If possible
boil the chickens the day previous to using.
Now cut the chickens up into small bits (do
not chop), cut up one whole dozen stalks of fine
white crisp celery and sprinkle with fine salt,
mixing the chicken and celery, using two silver
forks to do this. Rub the yelks of twelve hard-
boiled eggs as fine as possible, add two teaspoonfuls of salt, two scant teaspoonfuls of
white pepper, four teaspoonfuls of chicken fat,
or best olive oil, adding one at a time (I prefer
chicken or goose oil to olive oil), stirring harder
than ever, add three tablespoonfuls of best prepared mustard and two tablespoonfuls of white
sugar; add gradually, stirring constantly, two
cupfuls of white wine vinegar. Pour this
dressing over the chicken and celery and toss
lightly with the silver forks. Line a large
salad bowl with lettuce leaves, pour in the salad
and garnish the top with the chopped whites of
the twelve hard-boiled eggs; pour a pint of very
thick cream over the salad about an hour before
serving, (whipped cream is preferable). A neat
way is to serve the salad in individual salad
dishes, lining each dish with a lettuce leaf, garnish the salad with an olive stuck up in the

center, and four or five candied cherries around it, putting the whites of the chopped eggs around the sides.

### MAYONNAISE OF TOMATOES, (WHOLE).

Select tomatoes that are of uniform size, round, smooth and spotless, scald and take off outer skin, set away on ice, until ready to serve. Serve on individual dishes, putting each on a lettuce leaf and pour a heaping tablespoonful of mayonnaise dressing over each tomato. This makes a pretty center decoration for a lunch table, if heaped on a round platter into a mound.

### STUFFED TOMATOES.

No. 1. Select round, very firm and even sized tomatoes, cut off the top (reserve to use as a cover) scrape out the inside, being very careful to not break the tomato. Fill each tomato with some finely prepared "cold slaw," cover with the top of the tomato, lay them on lettuce leaves and pour a mayonnaise dressing over each. You may lay them en masse on a decorated platter heaping them in the shape of a mound, or serve individually.

### STUFFED TOMATOES.

No. 2. With mayonnaise of chicken and served as above, makes a course at fashionable luncheons. Prepare as you would stuffed tomatoes. Either are suitable courses at luncheons.

# SANDWICHES.

| | Page. |
|---|---|
| Appetite Silds, - - - - - - 154 |
| Boiled Tongue, - - - - - 153 |
| Cheese, - - - - - - - 154 |
| Chicken, - - - - - - 153 |
| Egg, - - - - - - - 154 |
| Ham, - - - - - - - 153 |
| Ham and Chicken, - - - - - 154 |
| Ham Toast, - - - - - - 155 |
| Imitation Pate de Foi Gras, - - - 155 |
| Lunches, Remarks on, - - - - 152 |
| Minced Goose, - - - - - - 156 |
| Minced Tongue, - - - - - 153 |
| Royal Ham Sandwiches, - - - - 157 |
| Sandwich Cheese or Koch-Kaese, - - 156 |
| Veal, - - - - - - - 153 |

# SANDWICHES.

## PORTABLE LUNCHES.

COLD corned beef, nicely sliced, bread, butter, pickles and fruit, and carry sugar and
salt in separate envelopes. Cold veal, radishes
sliced and salted, and hard-boiled eggs. Sandwiches of cold boiled ham or corned beef, smoked
beef, boiled, pickled or smoked tongue. Chick-
en salad, pressed meats, cold roast beef, sardines,
salmon (smoked or canned), herring, sardellen,
olives, summer sausages. Cold steak is nice if
cooked rare; cold chicken or any other fowl.
Cake in variety, also pies and cheese.

## SANDWICHES.

Sandwiches are almost indispensable at
luncheons, "kettledrums," teas and evening card
parties, and require some taste and dainty handling in serving. Nice, sweet bread is the first
requisite, then comes variety, which has been
aptly termed "the spice of life." The defini-
tion of the word sandwich is literally two pieces
of bread and butter, with a thin slice of ham
or other salt meat between them; said to have
been a favorite dish of the Earl of Sandwich.

### CHICKEN SANDWICHES.

Mince some cold roast or boiled chicken in a chopping bowl, then mix the gravy with it, adding a few hard-boiled eggs, which have been minced to a powder, and add salt and pepper if necessary. Mix all into a soft paste. Then cut some shapely slices of bread, butter them and spread the chicken between the slices (if desired you may add a little mustard); and press the pieces gently together, then spread a fringed napkin on a salver and arrange your sandwiches on it.

### VEAL SANDWICHES.

May be prepared as above, or slice the veal in thin slices and spread with mustard.

### BOILED, SMOKED, OR PICKLED TONGUE.

This also makes a very nice sandwich, as follows: Remove the crust from the slice of bread (unless it is very soft), butter them and place the slices of tongue (cut very thin) between the slices; roll lengthwise, tie with a fancy narrow ribbon, and pile in a basket or plate, lined either with watercresses or green curly parsley.

### MINCED TONGUE SANDWICHES.

This makes a delicious sandwich. You may mince a few pickles with it.

### HAM SANDWICHES.

These are made according to above receipts.

### HAM AND CHICKEN SANDWICHES.

Ham and chicken minced together make a delicious sandwich.

### CHEESE SANDWICHES.

Cut the bread round with the cover of a tea-kettle, butter one side and spread mustard on the other. Grate cheese thickly on the buttered side and press the one with mustard over the other. A slice each of rye and wheat bread is preferable for this sandwich.

### SANDWICHES OF APPETITE SILDS, OR SARDINES.

These are best prepared as follows: Slice a piece of fresh rye bread and a piece of fresh wheat bread, butter both, lay the silds, sardines or sardellen between them. Serve with olives or pickles. Nice with beer.

### EGG SANDWICHES.

Boil the eggs very hard and throw them immediately into cold water. When cold, remove the shells carefully and cut the eggs in half lengthwise and butter slightly. Lay one or two sardellen or appetite silds on one-half of the egg and press the one-half gently on the other half which has the sardellen. The egg must appear whole. Now tie lengthwise and across with the narrowest, various colored ribbons you can find,

finishing up with a pretty little bow. Make a
nice decoration piled up in a fancy basket, and
are often used in place of a salad.

### IMITATION PATE DE FOI GRAS.

Take as many livers and gizzards of any kind
of fowl as you may have on hand; add to these
three tablespoonfuls of melted butter, a finely
chopped onion, one tablespoonful of pungent
sauce, and salt and white pepper to taste. Boil
the livers until quite done and drain; when
cold, rub to a smooth paste. Take some butter
and chopped onion and simmer together slowly
for ten minutes. Strain through a thin muslin
bag, pressing the bag tightly, turn into a bowl
and mix with the seasoning; work all together
for a long time, then butter a bowl or cups and
press this mixture into them; when soft cut up
the gizzards into bits and lay between the mixture. You may season this highly, or to suit
taste; spread between buttered bread for sandwiches, or serve in cups.

### HAM TOAST.

Take a quarter of a pound of lean ham, finely
chopped; the yelks of three eggs well beaten,
half an ounce of butter, two tablespoonfuls of
cream and a little red pepper, stir together over
the fire until it becomes thick. Spread this over
thin slices of buttered toast and garnish with
parsley.

### SANDWICH CHEESE, OR KOCH KAESE.

Press one quart of fine cottage cheese through a coarse sieve or collander, and set it away in a cool place for a week, stirring it once or twice during that time; when it has become quite strong, stir it smooth with a wooden or silver spoon; add a saltspoonful of salt and one-fourth as much of carroway seed, yelks of two eggs and an even tablespoonful of flour, which has been previously dissolved in about one-half a cupful of cold milk; stir the flour and milk until it is a smooth paste, adding a lump of butter, about the size of an egg; add all to the cheese. Now put on the cheese to boil in a double farina kettle, boil until quite thick, stirring occasionally; boil altogether about one-half hour, stirring constantly the last ten minutes; the cheese must look smooth as velvet. Pour it into a porcelain dish, which has been previously rinsed in cold water. Set it away in a cool place; if you wish to keep it any length of time, cover it with a clean cloth, which has been dipped in and wrung out of beer. This cheese is excellent for rye bread sandwiches.

### MINCED GOOSE SANDWICHES.

Take either boiled or roast goose (which has been highly seasoned) and mince in a chopping bowl, add one or two pickles, according to quantity, or a teaspoonful of catsup. Spread thin

slices of bread or nice fresh rolls, with a thin
coating of butter or goose oil, slightly salted,
then spread the minced goose and cover with a
layer of bread which has been previously spread
with butter.  Delicious.

### ROYAL HAM SANDWICHES.

Chop up some boiled ham and the yelks
of three or four hard-boiled eggs, according
to quantity required.  Press all through a
collander, then cream a tablespoonful of best
butter and mix with the ham and eggs; a teaspoonful of prepared mustard is a nice additional
flavor; spread between thin slices of bread and
cut around or fold up as you desire.  An empty
baking powder can will do to use as a cutter.

**MEMORANDUM.**

.

# BREAD.

BREAD, ROLLS, BISCUITS, MUFFINS, YEAST.

| | Page. |
|---|---|
| Angel Food Bread, - - - - - | 166 |
| Bread, Hints on Making, - - - | 159 |
| Buns, - - - - - - - | 171 |
| Boston Brown Bread, - - - - | 166 |
| Butterbarches, - - - - - - | 162 |
| Chicago Brown Bread, - - - | 171, 172 |
| Corn Bread, - - - - - - | 171 |
| Corn·Muffins, - - - - - | 170 |
| Family Bread, white, - - - - | 160 |
| Family Graham Bread, - - - - | 165 |
| French Rolls, - - - - - | 167, 169 |
| Graham Gems, - - - - - - | 169 |
| Graham Biscuits, - - - - - | 169 |
| Graham Muffins, - - - - - | 170 |
| Individual Loaves, - - - - | 162 |
| Kinsley's Muffins, - - - - | 171 |
| Plain Rolls, - - - - - | 167 |
| Rye Bread, - - ·· - - - | 164 |
| Twisted Bread, - - - - - | 163 |
| White Biscuits, - - - - | 168, 169 |
| Wheat Muffins, - - - - - | 170 |
| Yeast, - - - - - - | 160 |
| Zviebel Platz, - - - - - | -165 |

**MEMORANDUM.**

# BREAD.

BREAD, ROLLS, BISCUITS, MUFFINS, YEAST.

SOMEWHERE in the book of Genesis we
read: "In the sweat of thy face shalt thou
eat bread." Now, I think it should read:
"In the sweat of thy face shalt thou knead
bread." For it is almost impossible to make
bread without experiencing the sweat of the
brow and an aching back.

The three important requisites to the making
of good bread are: good flour, good fresh yeast,
and strength and endurance to knead or work it
well. Try the yeast always by setting to rise in
a cup of lukewarm water or milk; adding salt
and sugar, providing you use compressed yeast.
If it rises in the course of ten or fifteen minutes
the yeast is fit to use. In making bread always
sift your flour. Set a sponge with warm milk
or water, keeping it in a warm place until very
light, then mold this sponge, by adding flour,
into one large ball and kneading well and
steadily for half an hour. Set to rise again,
and, when sufficiently, light, mold into small
loaves, or one large one, and let it raise again.
Take care not to get the dough too stiff with
flour. It should be as soft as can be kneaded

well. Bake slowly (unless you brush with beaten egg). Wet the top with water before baking. Bread should bake an hour, if the loaves are large, and when taken from the oven it should be wrapped in a clean towel wrung out of warm water, and stood up slanting, leaning against something; the wet towel will prevent the crust from becoming hard.

### GOOD HOME-MADE YEAST.

Grate six large raw potatoes, have ready a gallon of water in which you have boiled three handfuls of hops. Strain through a fine hair sieve, boiling hot, over the potatoes, stirring well, or the mixture will thicken like starch. Add a small cup of sugar and half a cup of salt. When cold, add a cup of fresh yeast. Let it stand until a thick foam rises on the top. Bottle in a couple of days. If kept in a cool place this yeast will last a long time. Use one cupful of yeast for one large baking. In making it, from time to time, use a bowl of the same to raise the new yeast with.

### FAMILY BREAD (WHITE).

Set your dough at night and bake early in the morning; or, set in the morning and bake in the afternoon. First set your yeast in a cup of lukewarm milk or water, adding a teaspoonful of salt and a tablespoonful of brown sugar. Let this rise, but if it fails to do so there is no

use in mixing your bread. It must rise to show
that the yeast is fresh and good. Now sift
about two quarts of flour into a deep bread bowl
and strew a few teaspoonfuls of fine salt over it.
(I like bread salty.) Make a hole in the center
of the flour, pour in the risen yeast and two
cups of milk or water; and in winter be sure
your bowl, flour, milk, in fact everything, has
been thoroughly warmed before mixing. Now
mix the dough slowly with the handle of a
knife; when so thick that you can work it in
this way no longer, begin to.work it with the
palm of your hand. Sprinkle some flour on the
baking board and put your ball of dough on it
and work it for half an hour by the clock,
steadily. Work with the palm of your hand,
always kneading toward center of ball (the
dough must rebound like a rubber ball); put
into a deep bowl, cover up and let it raise.
When through kneading, it should leave your
hands and board perfectly clean. When risen,
work again for fifteen minutes, form into loaves
to suit yourself, either twisted or in small bread
pans. In cutting fresh bread or cake heat the
knife or it will be doughy. Bake slowly for
one hour in a moderate oven. Your fire should
be just right, so as not to have to add fuel while
baking, or shake the stove. You may have a
pan of biscuits made out of this dough for
breakfast.

### INDIVIDUAL LOAVES.

These are made according to the above receipt.
Work small pieces of dough into strands a
finger long and take three strands for each loaf.
Make small as possible; brush with beaten egg
or sweetened water and sprinkle with poppy
seed (mohn). Allow them to raise before setting in the oven. These are called "Vienna
loaves," and are used at weddings, parties, etc.

### BUTTERBARCHES.

Dissolve two cents' worth of compressed yeast
in half a cup of lukewarm milk, add a teaspoonful of salt and a tablespoonful of sugar and let
it raise. Then make a soft dough of two quarts
of flour and as much milk as is required to work
it—say about two cupfuls—add the yeast, one
quarter of a pound of sugar, one quarter of a
pound of butter dissolved in the warm milk, the
sugar also and the grated peel of a lemon, a
small handful of raisins, seeded, and two eggs,
well beaten. Work this dough perfectly smooth
with the palm of your hand, adding more flour
if necessary. It is hardly possible to tell the
exact quantity of flour to use; experience will
teach you when you have added enough. Different brands of flour vary, some containing
more gluten than others. It is always safe, however, to sift more than the receipt calls for, so
as to have it ready. Don't knead, as it will

make the dough heavy and firm. Work the
dough at least half an hour, always toward the
center of the ball of dough. Let the dough
raise until it is twice again as high as the
original piece of dough. Then work the dough
again for fifteen minutes (takes elbow grease, I
know), and divide the dough into two parts, and
divide each of the pieces of dough into three
parts. Work the six pieces of dough thoroughly
and then roll each piece into a long strand—
three of which are to be longer than the other
three. Braid the three long strands into one
braid (should be thicker in the center than at
the end), and braid the three shorter strands
into one braid and lay it on top of the long
braid, pressing the ends together. Butter a
long baking pan, lift the barches into the pan
and set in a very warm place to raise again—
say half an hour. Then brush the top with
beaten egg and sprinkle (mohn) poppy seed all
over the top. Bake in a moderate oven one
hour at least, thoroughly.

### TWISTED BREAD (BARCHES).

This is to be used with meat and made in the
same manner, omitting the milk and butter;
use water, and a little shortening of nice drippings or rendered suet, and grate a handful of
blanched almonds and add. Beat up two eggs
and add half a cup of sugar, salt, raisins and

the grated peel of one lemon. Work just as
you would butter barches. Bake for an hour,.
slowly. Wrap in a damp, clean towel as soon
as baked to prevent the crust from becoming
too hard.

## RYE BREAD.

Get a piece of sour dough from a baker, about
as large as an apple; mix the dough in a deep
pan, say about four pounds of flour and one
quart of lukewarm water (buttermilk is better,
if you can get it), a handful of salt and some
carroway seed. Make a soft sponge and let it
rise all night. In the morning work in the rest
of the flour and make a. pretty stiff dough.
You may use a little wheat flour on your baking
board in kneading it in the morning. Work the
mass of dough into a ball, your hands having
been well floured; knead hard, always toward
the center of the ball which should be repeatedly turned over and around that every
portion may be manipulated. The longer you
knead the finer the pores of your bread will be.
No matter if you do feel fatigued, the exercise
is beneficial to your arms and chest. Now work
the dough into shapely loaves and let it rise
again for an hour, then wet, or rather brush,
the top of the loaves with water and bake slowly
for almost two hours. Break off a piece of
dough and keep for next baking; and if you

find at any time that your dough has not risen properly, add some yeast in the morning.

### ZWIEBEL PLATZ.

Take a piece of rye bread dough. After it has raised sufficiently roll out quite thin, butter a long cake pan and put in the rolled dough. Brush with melted butter; chop some onions very fine, strew thickly on top of cake, sprinkle with salt and put flakes of butter here and there. Another way is to chop up parsley and use in place of the onions. Then called " Petersilien Platz."

### FAMILY GRAHAM BREAD.

Make a sponge of three boiled potatoes, mashed fine while hot, a piece of compressed yeast, one tablespoonful of sugar, one tablespoonful of butter, a pint of warm water and a cup and a half of wheat flour. Make a sponge of this and let it raise all night. In the morning take as much Graham flour as you used white in your sponge, a tablespoonful of salt and a handful of Indian meal. Wet this all up with the sponge, and when mixed add a quarter of a tablespoonful of molasses; the dough should be quite soft. If there is not enough sponge to reduce it to the desired consistency, add a little more warm water, for the dough must be very soft. Knead it for a long time, as it does not raise as quickly as white flour, therefore should

be allowed a much longer time to rise. Make
into loaves, kneading again and set in a warm
place to rise. Bake slowly, as it will take longer to bake than white bread.

### BOSTON BROWN BREAD.

Three and one-half cups of Graham flour,
two of cornmeal, three of sour milk, one-half
cup of molasses, one and a half teaspoonful of
soda; steam two and one-half hours, then bake
fifteen minutes.

### ANGEL FOOD BREAD

Sift two quarts of the finest patent flour into
your bread bowl (which should be slightly
warm); soak a piece of yeast in a cup of lukewarm milk, add a spoonful of sugar and a
spoonful of salt, and let it raise. Now sift the
flour again, mixing another teaspoonful of fine
salt into it. Make a hole in the center of the
flour, stir in the yeast and a quart of lukewarm
milk, deducting the cup you have previously
added to the yeast; stir well (like a cake batter), then beat with the hollow of the hand half
an hour at least and let it raise all night. In
the morning flour a baking board and work
well; do not knead the dough, but work lightly
with the palm of your hand, always toward you.
Grease your bread pans well, put in your loaves
and let them raise again; butter or grease the

loaves on top before putting in the oven. If properly made the bread will be very white and flaky. Bake one hour.

### FRENCH ROLLS.

Prepare the yeast as you would for bread, and work just the same; add one-quarter of a pound of butter, one-quarter of a pound of sugar, four eggs, beaten light; work until it leaves your hands perfectly clean, then form into rolls; raise and then brush with beaten egg and bake.

### PLAIN ROLLS.

Put two quarts of flour into a deep bowl, sift and rub a large spoonful of butter into the flour as you would for biscuit; then make a hole in the center of the flour and stir in half a teacup of milk in which you have dissolved a piece of yeast, a teaspoonful of sugar and half a tea-spoonful of salt and a pint of milk, mix well. Let it rise over night; or reverse, and mix in the morning and let it rise all day. Bake so as to have fresh rolls for six o'clock dinner. Roll out about an inch thick, after having worked the dough on a baking board, using more flour if necessary, cut with a large cutter, rub over with melted butter and lap like turnovers. Let them rise one hour after putting in the pan. Bake twenty minutes.

## BISCUITS.

Sift one quart of flour, adding two heaping teaspoonfuls of baking powder, two large tablespoonfuls of butter, a saltspoonful of salt. Sift the flour and baking powder together two or three times; rub the butter into the flour until it looks and feels like sand. Wet with very cold milk. Do this quickly and make as soft a dough as can possibly be handled. Roll about an inch thick, cut with a biscuit cutter or top of a spice box and bake in a hot oven. In making biscuits let every movement be as quick as possible and do not let the dough stand a moment after it is ready for the oven. Time required for baking is fifteen to twenty minutes, allowing yourself thirty minutes in all from the time you begin to mix.

### RAISED BISCUITS.

Make a sponge of one pint of milk, a little salt and half a cake of compressed yeast. When light take a piece of butter the size of an egg, one quarter of a cup of sugar, one egg and a little salt. Beat all up together and stir into the sponge, adding flour enough to make a stiff batter. Stir it well and leave to raise; then take of the light dough with a spoon just enough for each biscuit, and work softly into shape, lay upon buttered pans to raise; then bake.

## WHITE BISCUITS.

Two heaping teaspoonfuls of baking powder sifted with one quart of flour; one tablespoonful of butter, rubbed well together; mix with cold water or milk and stir quickly with a knife; when well mixed roll up on a thickly-floured board, roll out about an inch thick, cut with a tumbler or biscuit cutter, place on a buttered pan and bake quickly in a well-heated oven. If mixed properly they will be as light and white as foam.

## FRENCH ROLLS.

Prepare the yeast as you would for bread and work the same. Add one-quarter of a pound of butter, one-quarter of a pound of sugar and four eggs beaten light. Work until it leaves your hands perfectly clean and form into rolls; raise and then brush with beaten egg and bake.

## GRAHAM BISCUITS.

One quart of Graham flour, three and one-half heaping teaspoonfuls baking powder, one teaspoonful of salt and one of butter; make into a soft dough with milk, and bake.

## GRAHAM GEMS.

To one quart of water add three eggs, one teaspoonful of salt, one tablespoonful of sugar, and two teaspoonfuls of baking powder; add enough Graham flour to make a stiff batter. Beat all very hard. Bake in a hot oven.

### WHEAT MUFFINS.

Take one tablespoonful of butter, two of sugar,
two eggs and stir all together well. Add one
cup of sweet milk, three teaspoonfuls of baking
powder, and flour enough to make a thick batter.
Bake twenty minutes in a quick oven.

### GRAHAM MUFFINS.

(No. 1.)  Two cups Graham flour and one cup
wheat flour, two eggs, well beaten; mix with
sweet milk to make quite a thin batter. Mix
with the flour a heaping teaspoonful of baking
powder and add salt. Bake in hot muffin-irons,
then set on the upper grating to brown.

### GRAHAM MUFFINS.

(No. 2.)  One egg, butter half the size of an
egg, three cups Graham flour, three teaspoonfuls
baking powder, some salt, one large cup of milk
and half a cup of water. Make as thick as ordinary cake batter. Bake in a hot oven.

### CORN MUFFINS.

One cup of Indian meal, and half a cupful of
flour, in which you have sifted two teaspoonfuls
of baking powder. Wet this with two cups of
sweet milk, add one teaspoonful of butter, one
teaspoonful of salt and one of sugar. Beat the
yelks of two eggs light and add, and last the
stiff-beaten whites; bake in muffin rings. Eat
cold.

### KINSLEY'S MUFFINS.

Mix one pint of milk with six well-beaten eggs, a good pinch of salt, one tablespoonful of sugar, one quart of flour with three teaspoonfuls of baking powder; sift flour and baking powder together twice; bake in a quick oven. Eat hot.

### CORN BREAD.

One pint of Indian meal, one pint of buttermilk, two eggs, whites and yelks beaten separately, whites to be put in the last thing; two tablespoonfuls of sugar; one tablespoonful of melted butter, a little salt and a teaspoonful of baking powder.

### HOT BUNS.

Dissolve one piece, or two cents' worth of yeast in half a cupful of lukewarm milk, add a pinch of salt and a little sugar; let this raise. Mix a dough (soft dough) with three cups of milk and sufficient flour to make it just thick enough to roll. Next morning roll, cut round or mold into half-moons. You may add half a cup of butter and sugar, if you wish them extra nice. Let them raise again, about half an hour after putting them in the pan, and when half baked brush them with beaten egg.

### CHICAGO BROWN BREAD.

Take one quart of rye flour and one quart of Graham flour and one quart of wheat flour; mix

one teaspoonful of salt and two cents' worth of
yeast in one quart of warm water, add to this
one scant cupful of molasses. Now stir and
work this into the flour—beat hard and then
work with the hand as you would other bread.
Let it raise from ten to twelve hours—longer
raising will not injure it, on the contrary it will
be all the lighter. Mould into loaves into iron
bread pans and raise again before baking. Eat
fresh. This will make three loaves.

## TOAST, FRITTERS, DOUGHNUTS, WAFFLES, MUSH, AND MILK, ETC.

|                          |          | Page. |
|--------------------------|----------|-------|
| Boiled Fritters,         | -  -  -  -  - | 175 |
| Bread Pancakes,          | -  -  -  -  - | 179 |
| Boiled Hominy,           | -  -  -  -  - | 184 |
| Crullers,                | -  -  -  -  | 177, 178 |
| Delicious Fritters,      | -  -  -  -  - | 175 |
| Doughnuts, -             | -  -  -  -  | 177 |
| Erbsen Lievanzen,        | -  -  -  -  - | 175 |
| French Toast,            | -  -  -  -  | 174 |
| French Waffles,          | -  -  -  -  - | 179 |
| Farina Mush,             | -  -  -  -  | 184 |
| German Waffles,          | -  -  -  -  - | 180 |
| Indian Meal Mush,        | -  -  -  -  | 184 |
| Kaese Kraepfli,          | -  -  -  -  - | 182 |
| Lemon Fritters, -        | -  -  -  -  | 176 |
| Milk Toast,              | -  -  -  -  - | 175 |
| Mush and Milk, -         | -  -  -  -  | 183 |
| Noodles with Cheese,     | -  -  -  -  | 181 |
| Orange Fritters, -       | -  -  -  -  | 176 |
| Oysters with Noodles,    | -  -  -  -  | 180 |
| Oat Meal Mush, -         | -  -  -  -  | 184 |
| Oat Meal Gruel,          | -  -  -  -  | 184 |
| Potato Pancakes, -       | -  -  -  -  | 178 |
| Potato Cakes, -          | -  -  -  -  | 179 |
| Pineapple Fritters,      | -  -  -  -  | 185 |
| Peach Fritters,          | -  -  -  -  | 185 |
| Spanish Puffs,           | -  -  -  -  | 176 |

## TOAST, FRITTERS, DOUGHNUTS, WAF-
## FLES, MUSH, AND MILK, ETC.

### FRENCH TOAST (ARME RITTER).

TAKE thin, even slices of stale bread, dip them in milk; have ready in a bowl some beaten eggs, fry quickly in hot butter. Sprinkle with sugar and cinnamon as soon as the toast is a light brown on both sides. This is nice for convalescents. Use wine sauce.

### FRENCH TOAST.

Take shapely slices of stale bread, soak in milk, for one minute only. Beat up some eggs in a bowl or deep plate, add a pinch of salt (can not give you exact number of eggs to be used, depends upon the quantity of bread used. Begin with three eggs, if more are necessary add one at a time); have the butter hot in the griddle, dip each piece of bread (that has been soaked in milk) in the beaten egg, and drop in the hot butter. Fry a light brown and when brown on one side, turn over and fry on the other. When done place on a warm platter and sprinkle well with powdered sugar in which you have previously grated the peel of a lemon, or mix with

(174)

cinnamon. You may serve with sweet sauces or preserves, compote, etc.

### MILK TOAST.

Toast the bread quickly, dip each piece of toast into hot water, butter it well, lay in a deep covered bowl and cover it with hot milk.

### ERBSEN LIEVANZEN (DRIED PEA FRITTERS).

Boil one pint of dried peas, pass through a hair sieve, pour into a bowl, add four ounces of butter rubbed to a cream, add also some soaked bread (soaked in milk), stir all into a smooth paste. Add salt, a tablespoonful of sugar, two yelks and two whole eggs, two ounces of blanched and pounded almonds. If too thick add more egg, if too thin more bread. Fry a nice brown.

### BOILED FRITTERS.

Boil one quart of water, butter the size of an egg, boil a few minutes, add salt, stir in flour until as thick as mashed potatoes. Pour this into a bowl and beat six eggs into it, adding a little nutmeg and sugar. Fry in hot butter. Try half the receipt.

### DELICIOUS FRITTERS.

One quart of water and a tablespoonful of butter, boil together for a few minutes, then stir in enough sifted flour to make it as thick as mashed potatoes. Pour this into a bowl and stir until almost cold. Beat in six eggs, one at a time, and add salt and nutmeg. Fry in hot butter or fat, using plenty of it. Eat with fruit sauce.

### LEMON FRITTERS.

Beat up the yelks of five eggs, with half a cup of pulverized sugar, add a pinch of salt, and the grated peel of a lemon, a little grated nutmeg and a pinch of ground cinnamon. Add gradually half a cup of sweet cream and two cups of flour, in which you have sifted a teaspoonful of baking powder; sift all again before stirring into the batter, add last the stiff beaten whites. Work altogether quickly and lightly into a soft dough, just stiff enough to roll out, pass the rollingpin over it until it is about half an inch thick, then cut into small, round cakes with a tumbler and fry in hot butter. Eat warm with lemon sauce.

### ORANGE FRITTERS.

Yelks of four eggs beaten with four tablespoonfuls of sugar, stir into this the juice of half a lemon, and just enough flour to thicken like a batter; add the beaten whites, and dip in one slice of orange at a time, take up with a large kitchen spoon and lay in the hot butter and fry a nice brown. Sprinkle pulverized sugar on top.

### SPANISH PUFFS.

Put into a saucepan a teacupful of water, one tablespoonful of powdered sugar, half a tea-

spoonful of salt, and two ounces of butter; while
it is boiling add sufficient sifted flour. Stir in,
one at a time, the yelks of four eggs. Drop a
teaspoonful at a time of this mixture into boiling fat or butter and fry a light brown. Sift
powdered sugar over them or eat with sweet
sauce.

### DOUGHNUTS.

Mix one scant cup of butter, one cupful and
a half of sugar, four eggs, two cups of milk, one
whole nutmeg grated, sifted flour enough to make
as stiff as biscuit dough, and put a large teaspoonful of baking powder in the sifted flour. Flour
your board well, roll out about half an inch thick,
and cut into pieces three inches long and one inch
wide. Cut a slit about an inch long in the center
of each strip, and pull one end through this slit.
Fry quickly in hot butter. Sprinkle powdered
sugar on top.

### CRULLERS.

(No. 1.) Take half a pound of butter, three-
quarters of a pound of sugar, sifted, and six eggs.
Flavor with nutmeg or mace, or a little of both;
flour enough to roll out stiff. Roll out on a
large baking board; cut into fanciful shapes,
and fry in plenty of hot butter; test the heat
first by dropping in one; it should rise instantly to the surface. Fry a nice yellow. If
the crullers brown too quickly, take the kettle

from the fire for a few moments. Cut them all
out before you begin to fry them, if you under-
take the task alone. You may make double
this quantity, for they are better the second day
than the first. Sift a heaping teaspoonful of
baking powder in with the flour.

### CRULLERS.

(No. 2.) Take four teaspoonfuls of melted
butter, eight heaping teaspoonfuls of sugar and
rub to a cream. Add four eggs and two tablespoonfuls of milk, and two of wine (or four of
milk) and a pinch of soda dissolved in hot water; flour enough to roll quite stiff; fry in hot
butter. Sprinkle powdered sugar over them
while hot.

### CRULLERS.

(No. 3.) One cup of butter, two of sugar,
three eggs, one cup of sweet milk, and three teaspoonfuls of baking powder; sift in the flour,
use flour enough to roll out stiff; spice with
nutmeg and brandy.

### POTATO PANCAKES.

Pare large potatoes, the night previous, if you
intend them for breakfast, and lay them in
cold water over night. Grate them in the morning and pour off all the water you can. Salt
liberally, add a large spoonful of flour and a few
eggs, beaten together. Heat butter in griddle,

bake a nice brown and have the cakes as thin as possible. Eat with tomato preserves. In cold weather have all the breakfast plates heated. When eggs are very high in price your potato cakes will taste almost as good without.

## BREAD PANCAKES.

Soak stale bread over night in sour milk, mash up fine with your hands in the morning, put in salt, three eggs, and two teaspoonfuls of baking soda, dissolved in hot water, and thicken with finely sifted flour. Delicious.

## POTATO CAKES.

Is made just as the pancakes, only baked in the oven in a long cake pan with plenty of butter or drippings under and above. Nice with meat sauce.

## FRENCH WAFFLES.

Half a pound of sweet butter, a teacupful of powdered sugar, rubbed to a cream, yelks of seven eggs, one pint of milk, one tablespoonful of brandy and the grated peel of a lemon or half a teaspoonful of mace. Make a soft dough of three-quarters of a pound of flour and two cents' worth of compressed yeast; add the creamed butter, sugar and eggs, the whites last, beaten to a froth. Beat the dough until it throws blisters, then let it raise for three hours at least. Bake the same as German waffles.

### GERMAN WAFFLES.

(No. 1.) One-quarter of a pound of sweet butter, rubbed to a cream, with eight tablespoonfuls of powdered sugar; add to this the yelks of eight eggs, one at a time, half a cup of milk, and half a pound of flour, sifted with two even teaspoonfuls of baking powder, and a pinch of salt, the grated peel of a lemon, also the beaten whites of the eggs added last. Grease the waffle-iron thoroughly with some butter tied in a cloth. Bake a nice yellow, and sprinkle over them sugar mixed with cinnamon and the grated peel of a lemon.

### GERMAN WAFFLES.

(No. 2.) Half a pound of sweet butter, teacupful of powdered sugar, rubbed to a cream; yelks of seven eggs, one pint of milk, one tablespoonful of brandy and the grated peel of a lemon, or half a tablespoonful of mace. Make a soft dough of three-quarters of a pound of flour and two cents' worth of compressed yeast, add the creamed butter, sugar and eggs, whites beaten to a froth. Beat the dough until it throws blisters, then let it rise for three hours at least. Bake same as No. 1.

### ESCALOPED OYSTERS WITH NOODLES.

Cut the noodles as you would for pudding; boil in salt water, drain, pour cold water over them and stir with a spoon while water runs through them and drain thoroughly. Lay on a platter until you are ready to use them. Now butter a pudding dish, put in a layer of noodles, then a layer of oysters, sprinkle salt and pepper over them, and flakes of butter here and there, then another layer of noodles, then oysters again and last another layer of noodles. Pour the liquor of the oysters over all and a scant half cup of cream. Bake about half an hour. This is a palatable dish and deserves to be better known. You may use the maccaroni bought at the grocer's, but it is not so nice. A nice supper dish.

## NOODLE DESSERT WITH CHEESE.

If you make the noodles at home, use two eggs for the dough; if you buy maccaroni use one-quarter of a pound, cut up and boil in salt water; boil about fifteen minutes; drain off the water and let cold water run through them; grate a cupful of Parmesan cheese; melt a piece of fresh butter, about the size of an egg, in a saucepan, stir in a heaping tablespoonful of flour, add gradually to this a pint of rich milk, stirring constantly; take from the fire as it thickens. Butter a pudding dish, lay in a layer of noodles, then cheese, then sauce, then begin with noodles again until all is used up. Sprinkle cheese on

top, a few cracker crumbs and flakes of butter
here and there.  Bake until brown.

## KAESE KRAEPFLI.

Make a dough of one or two eggs, with a
tablespoonful of water; add a pinch of salt;
work this just as you would noodle dough, quite
stiff.  Sift the flour in a bowl, make a hole in
the center, break in the eggs, add the salt and
water, mix slowly by stirring with the handle
of a knife, stirring in the same direction all the
time.  When this dough is so stiff that you can
not work it with the knife, flour your noodle
board and work it with the hollow of your
hands, always toward you, until the dough is
perfectly smooth; roll out as thin as paper and
cut into squares three inches in diameter.
Fill with "Dutch cheese," or schmierkaese, as
the Germans call it, which has been prepared
in the following manner:  Stir up a piece of
butter the size of an egg, adding two or three
eggs, sugar, cinnamon, grated peel of a lemon
and a pinch of salt; a little rich cream and
pounded almonds which improve it; fill the
kraepfli with a teaspoonful, wet the edges with
beaten egg, fold into triangles, pressing the
edges firmly together; boil in boiling milk;
when done they will swim to the top.  Eat with
melted butter or cream.  A nice supper dish.

## MUSH AND MILK.

Oh, the flavor, sweet and rare
Of the simple farmer fare—
Mush and milk, the wholesome diet
Of the life so pure and quiet.

Clear the realm of table show!
Get thee hence, Delmonico!
Out, ye modern viands flat,
A la this and A la that.

Give me now a table bright—
With its bowl so clean and white—
Glittering spoons in hands so manful,
Milk so luscious, by the panful.

Oh, the fields of golden maize!
Oh, the halcyon autumn days!
Nibblers pale in russet silk,
What know ye of mush and milk?

Once again in foreign lands
O'er my bowl I clasp my hands;
Giving thanks that, as of yore,
Mush and milk I taste once more.

Oh, the rosy cheeks it gave!
Oh, the arms so strong and brave!
Mush and milk has raised the latest
Of the nations and the greatest.

*—Brooklyn Standard Union.*

## INDIAN MEAL MUSH.

Set a quart of water to boil, add a lump of fresh butter and salt to taste. When boiling hard sift in three-fourths of a cup of Indian meal, stirring all the while; or wet the meal with cold milk before adding. Boil on the back of the stove slowly until thick. You may boil in milk instead of water. Serve with milk or cream and sugar. This is an excellent breakfast dish for those suffering from constipation.

## FARINA MUSH.

Boil one quart of milk; while boiling, stir in half a cup of farina, stirring constantly while pouring in the farina. Do this very slowly to prevent lumbs from being formed; add a lump of butter, and salt. Serve with cream and sugar.

## OAT MEAL MUSH.

Soak over night one cupful of oatmeal in one quart of water; put on to boil in the morning add more water if necessary, salt, and add a piece of fresh butter; cook slowly in a farina kettle. Serve with sweet cream and sugar.

## OAT MEAL GRUEL.

This is made in the same way. You may boil it in water and serve with cream.

## BOILED HOMINY.

Soak the hominy in warm water over night and boil until quite thick; stir almost con-

stantly, add salt and butter to the water while
boiling. Eat with sugar and cream.

Any of the above receipts for mush when
cold—left over from breakfast—may be sliced
and fried in hot butter. Fry a light brown on
both sides and eat with syrup.

### PINEAPPLE FRITTERS.

Pare and core a pineapple and slice it into
large, even, round slices. Sprinkle each piece
with pulverized sugar, then prepare your batter.
Break four or five eggs into a deep dish, yelks
and whites separate, add a pinch of salt to each
dish of eggs, and a tablespoonful of sugar to
the yelks. Add a cupful of sweet milk and
enough sifted flour to the beaten yelks to make
a thin batter, about a tablespoonful of flour to
each egg; beat very smooth, add a teaspoonful of
baking powder and last add the stiff-beaten
whites of the eggs. Before you begin to fry the
fritters, see that the butter or lard is very hot.
Dip each piece of pineapple in the batter and
fry a golden brown. Lay the fritters on a hot
platter and sprinkle each one with pulverized
sugar. Another way is to steam the pineapple
first; and it is a very wise plan. And still another way is to stew the sliced fruit in sweetened
wine or brandy before putting into the batter.

### PEACH FRITTER.

Made according to the pineapple receipt; and
eat with brandy sauce. Makes a delicious entree.

**MEMORANDUM.**

# DUMPLINGS.

|                                              | Page. |
| --- | --- |
| Apple with Rice, - - - - - | 194 |
| Baked Apple Dumplings, - - - | 187 |
| Bairische Dampfnudeln, - - - 188, | 189 |
| Boiled Rice with Pineapple, - - | 194 |
| Boiled Rice with Apples, - - - - | 195 |
| Dumplings for Soups, - - - - | 193 |
| Kartoffelkloesse, .. - - - - | 191 |
| Leberknadel (Calf Liver Dumplings), - | 193 |
| Peach Dumplings, - - - - - | 189 |
| Potato Dumplings, - - - - | 190 |
| Rice Dumplings, - - - - - | 191 |
| Snow Balls, - - - - - - | 187 |
| Schwaemchen or Schwamm-Kloesse, - | 192 |
| Spaetzlen, or Spatzen, - - - - | 195 |
| Sour Spaetzlen, - - - - - | 196 |
| Wiener Kartoffel Kloesse, - - - | 193 |

(186)

**MEMORANDUM.**

# DUMPLINGS.

## BAKED APPLE DUMPLINGS.

TAKE one quart of flour and two tablespoonfuls of butter and rub the butter into the flour with your hands till it looks like sand. Add two heaping teaspoonfuls of baking powder into the flour, wet with two cups of cold milk and work up quickly, just stiff enough to roll into a paste less than half an inch thick. Cut into squares, and lay in the center of each a tart apple, pared and cored; fill up the place that was cored with brown sugar, a clove and some cinnamon and take the corners of the square and pinch them together neatly. Lay in a buttered baking pan and bake until brown. Then brush them over with beaten egg and put back in the oven to glaze, say for two or three minutes. Eat hot, with brandy sauce.

## SNOWBALLS.

Pare and core nice large baking apples, fill the holes with some nice preserves or jam, roll the apples in sugar, and cover with a rich pie-crust and bake. When done, cover with a nice boiled icing, and set back in the oven, leaving both doors open, to let the icing dry.

## BAIRISCHE DAMPFNUDELN.

(No. 1. ) Soak two cents' worth of compressed yeast in a cupful of lukewarm milk, with a teaspoonful of sugar and a teaspoonful of salt, and sift a pint of flour in a bowl, in which you may also stir a small cupful of milk and two eggs (one egg will answer when they are scarce). Pour in the yeast and work all thoroughly, adding more flour, but guarding against getting the dough too stiff. Cover up the bowl of dough and let it raise until it is as high again, which will take at least four hours. Then flour a baking board and mold small biscuits out of your dough, and let them raise at least half an hour. Then butter a large, round, deep pan, and set in your dumplings, spreading or rather brushing each with melted butter as you do so. When all are in, pour in enough milk to reach just half way up to the dumplings. Set in the oven on a brick, and let them bake until a light brown. Eat hot, with vanilla sauce.

## BAIRISCHE DAMPFNUDELN.

(No. 2.) Make the dough just as you would in the above receipt, adding a tablespoonful of butter, and after they have risen steam instead of baking them. If you have no steamer improvise one in this way: Put on a kettle of boiling water, set a collander on top of the kettle and lay in your dumplings, but do not crowd them; cover with a close-fitting lid and put a weight on top of it to keep in the steam; when done they will be as large again as when first put in. Serve with vanilla or prune sauce.

## BAIRISCHE DAMPFNUDELN.

(No. 3.) Made as above. Set on the fire a kettle of boiling salt water and when it boils very hard put in the noodles, but do not crowd them, as they require plenty of room to spread and raise. Take up one at first to try whether it is done by tearing open with two forks. If you have more than enough for your family, bake a pan of biscuits out of the remaining dough.

## PEACH DUMPLINGS.

Make a dough of a quart of flour and a pint of milk, or water, a tablespoonful of shortening, a pinch of salt, one egg and a spoonful of sugar; add a piece of compressed yeast, which has previously been dissolved in water. Let the dough raise for three hours. In the meantime make a compote of peaches by stewing them with sugar and spices, such as cinnamon and cloves. Stew enough to answer for both sauce and filling. When raised, flour your baking board and roll out the dough half an inch thick. Cut cakes out of it with a tumbler, brush the edges with white of egg, put a teaspoonful of peach compote in the center of a cake and cover it with another layer of cake and press the edges firmly together. Steam over boiling water and serve with peach sauce. A delicious dessert may also be made by letting the dough rise another half hour after being rolled out, and before cutting.

### POTATO DUMPLINGS.

Boil as many large potatoes as you wish dumplings (to twelve dumplings, twelve potatoes). It is better to boil the potatoes the day before using. Boil them in their jackets, pare and grate them then add half a loaf of grated stale bread, a tablespoonful of melted butter or suet, a teaspoonful of salt, two tablespoonfuls of flour, half of a grated nutmeg, and part of the grated peel of a lemon, three or four eggs and a saucerful of bread which has been cut in the smallest dice shape possible and browned in butter or fat. Mix all thoroughly and form into round dumplings. Put them into boiling salt water and let them boil until done. As soon as they raise to the top of the water, take up one and try it, if cooked through the center remove them all. Serve with a fruit sauce, or heated fat, with an onion cut up very fine and browned in it. A sweet and sour is also very nice, made as follows: Boil vinegar and water together in equal parts and sweeten to taste. Melt a piece of butter in a spider, throw in a

spoonful of flour, mix rapidly, then add a pinch
of salt, and also add the boiling vinegar gradually to this, also some ground cinnamon and a
pinch of ground cloves

### RICE DUMPLINGS.

Wash and scald two cups of rice, and put on
to boil in a farina kettle with a pint of milk and
as much water. Let it boil until tender, not
omitting the required salt. Spread the rice
upon dishes to cool. Blanche two ounces of
sweet almonds and one ounce of bitter almonds
and pound to a paste in a mortar. Grate the
peel of a lemon into a quarter of a cup of butter,
rub the butter to a cream, with three-quarters
of a cup of pulverized sugar, and add the yelks
of four eggs, one at a time. Add the boiled rice
gradually, a spoonful at a time, and about half
a cupful of grated stale bread. When all is
thoroughly mixed add the beaten whites of two
eggs and form into flat dumplings. Turn each
one into rolled cracker crumbs and then into
beaten egg and fry in hot butter a nice brown.
Serve with fruit or wine sauce. If you wish to
serve them with meat, boil the rice in water
and fry in fat.

### KARTOFFELKLOESSE.

Take large potatoes, say half a dozen, that
have been cooked the day previous to using,
grate a soup plateful, add about one-third as

much of grated bread and cut up the crusts of
the bread into dice shape and brown in heated
fat; add salt, grated nutmeg or mace, about an
ounce of fat, one tablespoonful of flour, a large
tablespoonful of farina, and three or four eggs,
whites beaten separate. Mix all up well and
form into "kloesse." Flour them and put into
boiling water that has been salted, boil for about
fifteen minutes uncovered. Fry one, and if done
it will be perfectly dry inside. Heat some fat
and cut up a piece of onion in it. Brown and
pour over dumplings. You may roll these out
on a floured baking board and fill with bread
crumbs which have been browned in heated fat
and onion. Roll up, cut into lengths of about
three inches, close the ends and boil.

### SCHWAEMCHEN OR SCHWAMM-KLOESSE.

Take the whites of three eggs, put them in an
ordinary teacup, fill up the remaining space of
the cup with milk or water and pour this into a
small stew pan. Add a small cup of flour and
two teaspoonfuls of butter or fat. Stir this
over the fire until it is a thick mass of dough
and remove from the fire to cool. When perfectly cold beat in the yelks of the eggs lightly,
add salt and a little nutmeg or mace. Drop
into boiling soup with a teaspoon, and cook
about ten minutes covered. These dumplings
may be cooked in with green peas or soups.

### DUMPLINGS FOR SOUPS.

Scald some flour in a small tincup either
with milk or water, mix in a small piece of
butter and salt, and boil until thick. When
cool beat in one or two yelks of eggs, and if too
stiff add the beaten whites.

### EGG DUMPLINGS FOR SOUPS.

Rub the yelks of two hard-boiled eggs to a
smooth paste, add a little salt and graded nutmeg and a speck of butter. Add the beaten
whites of two eggs and just enough flour to be
able to mold the dough into little marbles.
Guard against making too stiff, and put in boiling soup one minute.

### LEBERKNADEL (CALF LIVER DUMPLINGS).

Chop and pass through a collander one-half
pound of calf's liver; rub to a cream four ounces
of marrow, add the liver and stir hard. Then
add a little thyme, one clove of garlic grated,
pepper, salt and a little grated lemon peel, the
yelks of two eggs and one whole egg. Then add
enough grated bread crumbs or rolled crackers
to this mixture to permit its being formed into
little marbles.

### WIENER KARTOFEL KLOESSE.

Boil as many potatoes as you want kloesse.
When they are very soft drain off every drop of
water, lay them on a clean baking board and

mash them while hot, with a rolling pin, adding
about two handfuls of flour.  When thoroughly
mashed break in three or four eggs, salt to taste,
and flavor with grated nutmeg.  Now flour the
board thickly and roll out this potato dough
about as thick as your little finger and spread
with the following:  Heat some fresh goose fat
in a spider, cut up part of an onion very fine,
add it to the hot fat together with a plateful of
grated bread-crumbs.  When brown spread over
the dough and roll just as you would a jelly-roll.
Cut into desired lengths (about three or four
inches), put them in boiling water, slightly
salted, and boil uncovered for about fifteen
minutes.  Pour over them some hot goose fat,
in which has been browned part of an onion.
Serve with sauer kraut, sauer braten or compote
of any kind.

### APPLES WITH RICE.

Boil rice in water or milk in a farina kettle;
rub the kettle all over with a piece of butter before putting in the rice, say a cupful, season
with salt and add a lump of butter.  When
cooked, add about six apples, pared, quartered
and cored, sugar and cinnamon.  This makes a
nice side dish, or dessert, served with cream.

### BOILED RICE WITH PINEAPPLE.

Pick the rice over carefully, pour boiling
water over as much as you wish to boil, say a

large coffee cupful—let it remain in the boiling water at least five minutes; pour it away and set the rice on to boil in a farina kettle, with a lump of butter, a teaspoonful of salt and a pint of milk or water, when done slice up the pine-apple and add, with as much sugar as is required to sweeten to your taste; you may add a little ground cinnamon also.

### BOILED RICE WITH APPLES.
Cook according to above receipt.

### SPAETZLEN OR SPATZEN.
Sift one pound of flour into a bowl and make a hollow in the center of the flour and break into it two or three eggs, add a saltspoonful of salt and enough water or milk to form a smooth stiff dough. Set on some water to boil, and salt the water and when the water boils drop the spaetzle into it, one at a time. Do this with the spoon with which you cut the dough, or roll it on a board into a round roll and cut them with a knife. When the spaetzle is done, they will rise to the surface, take them out with a per-forated skimmer and lay them on a platter. Now heat a fourth of a pound of butter and add bread crumbs, let them brown for a minute and pour all over the spaetzle. If you prefer you may put the spaetzle right into the spider in which you have heated the butter. Another way to prepare them is after you have taken

them out of the water is to heat some butter in
a spider, and put in the spaetzle and then scram-
ble about a dozen fresh eggs over all, stirring
eggs and spaetzlen together.  Serve hot.

## SOUR SPAETZLEN.

Make a sauce of one tablespoonful of butter,
into which you put three tablespoonfuls of flour.
Brown the flour with the butter in a spider, add
part of an onion finely chopped, then cover up
the spider and let the onion smother for a little
while, do this on the back of the stove, so there
will be no danger of the onion getting too brown.
Add vinegar and soup stock and a lump of sugar.   Let this boil until the sauce is of the right
consistency.  Serve with spaetzlen made according to the foregoing receipt.  You may
pour the sauce over the spaetzlen before serving.
If you desire the sauce sweet and sour, add more
sugar.

# PIES.

| | Page. |
|---|---|
| Apple, - - - - - - - - - | 200 |
| Apple Torte, - - - - - - - | 204 |
| Apple Meringue, - - - - - - | 205 |
| Apple Custard, - - - - - - | 210 |
| Aunt Babette's Favorite Mince, - - - - | 211 |
| Cocoanut, - - - - - - - - | 200 |
| Cherry, - - - - - - - - | 204 |
| Cheese, - - - - - - - | 208 |
| Cheese Straws, - - - - - - | 209 |
| Cream, - - - - - - - - | 209 |
| Custard, - - - - - - - | 210 |
| French Puff Paste, - - - - - | 199 |
| Grated Apple, - - - - - - | 205 |
| Grape, - - - - - - - - | 210 |
| Lemon, - - - - - - - | 206 |
| Mince, - - - - - - - | 201, 202 |
| Pie Crust, - - - - - - - | 198 |
| Plum, - - - - - - - - | 200 |
| Peach Cream, - - - - - - | 208 |
| Peach, - - - - - - 203, 204, 212 |
| Pumpkin, - - - - - - - | 206 |
| Pineapple, - - - - - - - | 212 |
| Raspberry Cream, - - - - - | 201 |
| Rhubarb, - - - - - - - | 207 |
| Rhubarb Custard, - - - - - | 208 |
| Vinegar, - - - - - - - | 209 |
| Whipped Cream, - - - - - - | 209 |
| Wine, or Mirror Pie, - - - - - | 213 |

# PIES.

## FAMILY PIE-CRUST.

TAKE one cup of nice drippings and mix with goose, duck or chicken fat. In the fall and winter, when poultry is plentiful and fat, you should save all drippings for pie-crust. If you have neither of the above, use rendered meat fat (I do not mean suet—that is horrid!—but genuine meat fat); use half butter; if you consider this "Trefa" use all fat. Take one cupful of fat, and stir to a cream; add a salt-spoonful of salt, four cups of sifted flour and rub creamed fat and flour between your hands until it looks like sand. Make a hole in the center, pour in a cupful of ice-water and mix lightly; do not knead and it will be flaky. This will make four pies. You may keep the dough in your refrigerator for a week. Bake pies fresh every day, as they are quickly made when the dough is ready.

## PIE-CRUST.

Take a small cup of butter, nice rendered suet, or both, and rub to a cream, add a pinch of salt, also a little brown sugar and sift into this mass a pound of flour. Rub the flour and butter (or fat) with your hand, until it looks like sand, then take the yelk of an egg, a wineglassful of brandy and half a cup of ice-water, and work it into the flour lightly. Knead as little as possible and roll out thin. If the dough is of the right consistency, no flour will be required to roll it out. If you are compelled to use flour use as little as possible. The pie-plates should be well greased; I use perforated tin pie-plates. Pie-crust being so simple a thing to make it is strange that so few know how to make it well. Pie-crust should be handled as little as possible, and baked in a hot oven. All pies should be removed, while hot, to the plates they are to be served on.

### FRENCH PUFF PASTE.

Take half a cup of nice drippings or butter, and rub into a pound of sifted flour. Stir the yelk of an egg into a scant cup of ice-water and work the flour and water into dough. Roll out very thin, baste the dough with another half a cup or more of butter, and fold closely. Roll out again, and so on until you have used up all the fat, say about a cupful and a half. Set away for an hour at least in a very cold place (on top of ice in summer) before rolling out. You may use a wineglassful of brandy when mixing the dough, as it improves it very much; add salt also.

## PLUM PIE.

Select large purple plums, about fifteen plums for a good-sized pie; cut them in halves, remove the kernels and dip each half in cornstarch or flour. Line your pie-tin with a rich paste and lay in the plums, close together, and sprinkle thickly with a whole cup of sugar. Lay strips of paste across the top, into bars, and also a strip around the rim, and press all around the edge with a pointed knife or fork, which will make a fancy border. Sift powdered sugar on top. Damson pie is made in the same way. Eat cold.

## PLAIN APPLE PIE.

Cut the apples very thin, and mix them up well with sugar and cinnamon. See that your apples are tart and juicy, lay them upon your pie crust (fill it up), adding more sugar. Put flakes of butter here and there, add about two tablespoonfuls of water and cover it with a sheet of rich pie-crust. Bake half an hour in a hot oven.

## COCOANUT PIE.

Line a pie-plate with a rich puff paste. Grate up a cocoanut, reserving the milk. Rub a quarter of a pound of butter to a cream, add half a pound of powdered sugar and the beaten yelks of four eggs, the grated peel of a lemon, a wineglassful of brandy and the milk of the cocoanut, and then add the grated nut to this mixture.

This will make two pies. Bake in open shells.
Now make a meringue of the whites with pulverized sugar and spread on top. After the pie
is baked and set back in the oven for a minute,
you may beat up the whites to a stiff froth and
mix with the cocoanut and bake at once.

### RED RASPBERRY CREAM PIE.

Line a pie-plate with a rich crust, and fill
with raspberries and powdered sugar and cover
with a layer of pie-crust, but do not press down
the edges. When the pie is baked lift up the
top crust and pour over the fruit the following
mixture: Boil a cup of cream, stir the yelks of
three or four eggs with three tablespoonfuls of
sugar and one teaspoonful of cornstarch and
pour into the hot cream. When perfectly cold
spread over the pie, put the top crust on again
and sprinkle with powdered sugar. If you prefer this cream white, use the whites of the eggs
instead of the yelks, using one egg less, and
proceed just as you would with the yelks.

### MINCEMEAT.

Chop fine three pounds of boiled beef, scrape
fine one pound of suet, chop up four pounds of
apples, two pounds of raisins, seeded and
chopped, two pounds of currants (wash the
currants about half a dozen times and carefully
at that); pick over carefully one pound of
sultana raisins; chop up one pound of citron,

add two pounds of brown sugar, one tablespoonful of salt, one of allspice, one of cloves, two teaspoonfuls of grated nutmeg, one of mace, four of ground cinnamon, one quart of sherry or other wine, one pint of good brandy and one pint of boiled cider. This quantity fills a two-gallon stone jar and will keep all winter. Tie up the jar with a clean cloth and another covering of paper and keep it in a cool place. It will be ready to use twenty-four hours after it is prepared. All this seems a great deal of trouble, and so it is; but when once made it is so handy to use and very good. When using the mincemeat always take from the bottom, as the juice naturally settles there. Tie up carefully before putting away. I prepare a large jarful every winter and am always sorry when it is gone. I also use mock mincemeat, as follows:

### MOCK MINCE PIE.

Line a plate with a rich puff paste, and fill with the following: Beat up two eggs with one cup and a quarter of sugar, one cupful of bread which has been soaked in warm water, one-half cup of molasses, half a cup of vinegar, half a cup of water, one cup of raisins, a pinch of salt, half a teaspoonful of ground cloves, one teaspoonful of cinnamon and pinch of pepper. This quantity will make two pies. Cover with strips of crust and bake half an hour.

### PEACH CREAM PIE.

Line a pie-plate with a rich crust and bake, then fill with a layer of sweetened grated peaches which have had a few pounded peach kernels added to them. Then whip one cupful of rich cream, sweeten and flavor and spread over the peaches. Set in ice-chest until wanted.

### PEACH PIE.

(No. 1.) Line a pie-plate with a rich pie-crust, cover thickly with peaches, that have been pared and sliced fine (canned peaches may be used when others are not to be had), adding sugar and cover with strips of dough and bake quickly. If you do not mind the expense, spread over the peaches a meringue made by whipping the whites of three eggs to a stiff froth and sweetening with a tablespoonful of pulverized sugar for each egg. Add half a teaspoonful cream tartar to the meringue; flavor with vanilla and set back in the oven until the meringue begins to color. Take out carefully. Eat cold. Delicious served with cream.

### PEACH PIE.

(No. 2.) Pare, stone and slice the peaches. Line a deep pie-plate with a rich paste, sprinkle a very little cornstarch over the bottom crust and lay in your fruit, sprinkle sugar liberally over them in proportion to their sweetness.

Add a few peach kernels, pounded fine, to each
pie and bake with crossbars of paste across the
top.  If you want it extra fine, whip the whites
of three eggs to a stiff froth and sweeten with
about four tablespoonfuls of pulverized sugar,
adding a teaspoonful cream tartar and spread
over the pie and return to the oven until the
meringue is set.  Eat cold.

### CHERRY PIE.

Line a pie-plate with rich paste, sprinkle
cornstarch lightly over the bottom crust and fill
with cherries and regulate the quantity of sugar
you scatter over them by their sweetness.  Bake
with an upper crust, secure the edges well, by
spreading the white of an egg all around and
pinching firmly together.  Eat cold.

### APPLE TORTE PIE.

Grate about two cups of stale rye oread, mix
it with a little sugar and cinnamon and grated
lemon peel.  Butter a deep pie-plate (must be
well greased), and line it with the bread crumbs.
Cut up very thin, five or six tart apples, mix
these well with sugar, cinnamon, raisins or
currants, and a little citron cut up fine.  Put
the apples on your crumbs, which have been
seasoned, adding a little more sugar, and cover
with the remaining crumbs, put flakes of butter
on top and sprinkle with about a wineglassful

of wine, either red or white. Bake for about twenty minutes.

### APPLE MERINGUE PIES.

Line a deep pie-plate with a rich pie-crust, grate four or five large apples, add the grated peel of a lemon and sweeten to taste, you may add a few pounded almonds (not necessary though, just as good without), add raisins or currants, the latter must be carefully cleaned and free from all stems. Beat up the yelks of three or four eggs, and stir well into the apples. Fill your crust and bake. Spread over the pie a thick meringue, made of the whites of the eggs, whipped stiff, and add about three table-spoonfuls of pulverized sugar, and half a tea-spoonful of cream tartar. Flavor with rose-water or vanilla; set back in the oven until the meringue is of a light brown. Eat cold. Very fine.

### GRATED APPLE PIE.

Line a pie-plate with a rich puff paste. Pare and grate four or five large tart apples into a bowl into which you have stirred the yelks of two or three eggs with about half a cup of sugar. Add a few raisins, a few currants, a few pounded almonds, a pinch of ground cinnamon, and the grated peel of a lemon. Have no top crust. Bake in a quick oven. In the meantime, make a meringue of the whites of the eggs by beating

them to a very stiff froth, and add about three
tablespoonfuls of pulverized sugar. Spread
this over the pie when baked and set back in
the oven until brown. Eat cold.

### PUMPKIN PIE.

Press through a sieve one pint of stewed
pumpkin and add four eggs and a scant cup of
sugar. Beat yelks and sugar together until very
thick and add one pint of milk to the beaten
eggs. Then add the pressed pumpkin, one-half
teaspoonful cinnamon, less than half a teaspoonful of mace and the sauce of grated nutmeg. Stir the stiff-beaten whites in last.
Bake in a very rich crust without cover.

### LEMON PIE.

Line a deep pie-plate with a rich puff paste,
and bake a light brown. Remove from the
oven until the filling is prepared. Take a large
juicy lemon, grate the peel and squeeze out
every drop of juice. Now take the lemon and
put it into a cup of boiling water to extract
every particle of juice. Put the cup of water
on to boil with the lemon juice and grated peel,
and a cup of sugar; beat up the yelks of four
eggs very light and add to this gradually the
boiling lemon juice. Return to the kettle and
boil. Then wet a teaspoonful of cornstarch
with a very little cold water, and add also a tea-

spoonful of butter and when the boiling mixture
has thickened remove from the fire and let it
cool. Beat up the whites of the eggs to a very
stiff froth, add half of the froth to the lemon
mixture and reserve the other half for the top of
the pie. Now bake the lemon cream in the
baked pie-crust. Add a few tablespoonfuls of
powdered sugar and half a teaspoonful cream
tartar to the remaining beaten whites. If you
desire to have the meringue extra thick, add
the whites of one or more eggs. When the pie
is baked take from the oven just long enough
to spread the meringue over the top, and set
back for two or three minutes, leaving the oven
doors open just the least bit, so as not to have
it brown too quickly.

### RHUBARB PIE.

Strip the skin from the stalks of rhubarb,
more commonly called pie-plant, then cut them
in pieces about an inch long, pour boiling water
over them and let them remain in it until you
prepare the pie-crust. Drain the pie-plant,
line your pie-plates with a rich pie or puff paste,
sprinkle cornstarch over the paste and then
sugar. Now lay in the pie-plant, sprinkle
heavily with sugar, and put flakes of butter over
them (you may omit the butter if you object.)
Cover with a rich paste and retain the juice by
moistening the edge of the under crust with
white of egg, and pressing the upper one upon

it. Spread beaten egg over the top crust also. Use perforated pie-plates and remove from the plates as soon as taken from the oven, to prevent them from sticking.

### RHUBARB CUSTARD PIE.

Strip the skin carefully from the stalk of the pie-plant and cut it into small pieces. Scald with boiling water, then drain and press out every drop of water with your hands. Now set over the fire to stew, with as little water as possible. When done, press through a collander or wire sieve, sweeten to taste and flavor with grated nutmeg or lemon. Bake with strips of dough put across the top. I forgot to add: Beat up two eggs for each pie, after mixing the sugar. You may put in the yelks alone and use the whites for a meringue. If you do this, bake the paste first, then the custard.

### CHEESE PIE.

Take a quart of Dutch cheese, rub smooth with a silver or wooden spoon, then rub a piece of butter the size of an egg to a cream, add half a cup of sugar and the yelks of four eggs gradually, a pinch of salt, grate in the peel of a lemon, wash half a cupful of currants, and add also a little citron, cut up very fine. Line two pie-plates with some rich pie-crust, and fill with above mixture, not forgetting to add the beaten whites.

## CHEESE STRAWS.

Take a quarter of a pound of puff paste and half an ounce of Parmesan cheese, grated very fine, and a little salt. Sprinkle the cheese and salt over the paste and roll it two or three times. Cut it into narrow strips about five inches long. Bake in a slow oven and send to the table hot.

## VINEGAR PIE.

Line a pie-plate with a rich crust and fill with the following mixture: One cup of vinegar, two of water and two cups of sugar, boil; add a lump of butter and enough cornstarch to thicken; flavor with lemon essence and put in a shell and bake.

## WHIPPED CREAM PIE.

This is so simple and nice that it deserves to be better known. Make a crust as rich as possible and line a deep tin. Bake quickly in a hot oven and spread it with a layer of jelly or jam. Next whip one teacupful of sweet cream until it is thick. Set the cream in a bowl of ice while whipping. Sweeten slightly and flavor with vanilla, spread this over the pie and put in a cool place until wanted.

## CREAM PIE.

First line a pie-plate with puff paste and bake, and then make a cream of the yelks of four eggs, a little more than a pint of milk, one tablespoonful of cornstarch and four tablespoonfuls of sugar, and flavor with two teaspoonfuls of vanilla. Pour one rust and bake; beat up the whites with two tablespoonfuls of powdered sugar and half a teaspoonful of cream tartar. Spread on top of pie and set back in the oven until baked a light brown.

### APPLE CUSTARD PIE.

Line your pie-plate with a rich crust. Slice apples thin, half fill your plates, and pour over them a custard made of four eggs and two cups of milk, sweetened and seasoned to taste.

### CUSTARD PIE.

Line your pie-plate with a rich crust. Beat up five eggs light with one-half cup of sugar, a pinch of salt, one pint of milk and grated nutmeg or grated lemon peel, and pour in shell and bake.

### GRAPE PIE.

Squeeze out the pulps and put them in one vessel, the skins into another. Then simmer the pulp a little and press it through a collander to separate the seeds. Then put the skins and pulps together and they are ready for the pies. To make these pies truly delicious, beat up two eggs with half a cup of sugar for each pie; pour over the grapes and bake without a cover. .

AUNT BABETTE'S FAVORITE MINCE MEAT.

Chop up four pounds of tender boiled beef, which you have picked over carefully; scrape very fine one pound of beef suet; pare, core and chop up six pounds of tart apples; seed and cut in halves two pounds of raisins, two pounds of currants, carefully washed and picked over, also two pounds of sultanas, carefully picked; chop or cut up very fine one pound of citron, one pound of figs, one pound of dates, one piece of candied lemon peel, half a piece of candied orange peel, two pounds of brown sugar, one large tablespoonful of salt, one tablespoonful of new allspice, one teaspoonful of freshly ground cloves, two teaspoonfuls of grated nutmeg, one of mace, two tablespoonfuls of ground cinnamon, one quart of sherry, one pint of best brandy, and one of boiled cider. To this you may add any quantity of " Melange," the French fruit preserves, if you are fortunate enough to have any. Your mince meat will be good without the melange, but, its addition is a great improvement. This quantity will fill a three-gallon jar. Keeps all winter. Add more wine or brandy if too dry. When using the " mince meat " always take up from the bottom, as the juice naturally sinks leaving the top quite dry. Cover with a plate, then tie up with several thicknesses of strong paper and set in a cool place. It is ready for use in twenty-four hours after it is prepared. When boiling the meat for mince, season with salt, and boil until very tender. Allow it to cool in the liquor it was boiled in, which keeps the meat juicy. You may add a large cupful of the liquor to the mince meat.

### PINEAPPLE PIE.

(No. 1.) Line your pie-plate with a rich paste, slice pineapples as thin as possible, sprinkle sugar over them abundantly and put flakes of sugar here and there. Cover and bake.

You may make pineapple pies according to any of the plain apple pie recipes.

### PINEAPPLE PIE.

(No. 2.) Pare and core the pineapple and cut into small slices and sprinkle abundantly with sugar and set it away in a covered dish to draw enough juice to stew.the pineapple in. Bake two shells on perforated pie-plates of a rich pie dough. When the pineapple is stewed soft enough to mash, mash it and set it away to cool. When the crust is baked and cool whip half a pint of sweet cream and mix with the pineapple and fill in the baked shell. Delicious.

### PEACH PIE.

Made according to above recipe. Are also very fine.

### WINE OR MIRROR PIE.

Bake a rich pie-crust in a deep pie-plate, and fill in with wine jelly. Allow the jelly to cool a little before pouring it into the pie-shell. Then set away in a cool place to harden. Patties made the same way are delicious. Serve with whipped cream.

**MEMORANDUM.**

# PUDDINGS.

|  | Page. |
|---|---|
| Apfel Charlotte, | 217 |
| Apple Slump, | 217 |
| Apple, | 218, 219, 220 |
| Almond Roley-Poley, | 237 |
| Bread, | 225 |
| Cherry, | 226 |
| Children's Favorite, | 227 |
| Custard, | 231 |
| Cranberry, | 232 |
| Chocolate, | 232, 233 |
| Corn-Starch, | 236 |
| Corn-Starch Meringue, | 237 |
| Fig, | 216 |
| Farina, | 227 |
| Graham, | 217 |
| Grimslich, | 221 |
| Kraut, | 231 |
| Metropolitan Apple, | 235 |
| Noodle, | 224 |
| Peach, | 215, 216 |
| Plum, | 221, 222, 223 |
| Potato, | 223 |
| Prince Albert, | 230 |
| Queen of Plum Puddings, | 238 |
| Rice, | 228 |
| Rhubarb, | 230 |
| Suet Pudding, | 220, 221 |
| Sweet Potato, | 231 |
| Sponge, | 233 |
| Tipsy, | 229 |
| Yum-Yums, | 234 |

**MEMORANDUM.**

# PUDDINGS.

## PEACH PUDDING.

LINE the bottom of a pudding dish with stale sponge or cup cake and shave enough peaches to cover thickly (you may use preserves or compote instead). Sprinkle a cupful of pulverized sugar over the fruit. Now let a pint of milk get boiling hot by setting it in a pot of boiling water. Add the yelks of three eggs, well beaten, one tablespoonful of cornstarch, made smooth with a little cold milk, and stir it all the time. As soon as thickened, pour over the fruit. Beat the whites to a stiff froth, adding a tablespoonful of sugar, and spread over the top for frosting. Set it in the oven for a few minutes to harden. Eat cold, with or without cream.

## PEACH PUDDING.

Pare and cut in halves nice freestone peaches and blanch a few of the kernels. Use about one quart of peaches and stew them in a little wine and sugar. Now, beat the yelks of nine or ten eggs with half a pound of pulverized sugar and the peel and juice of half a lemon. Line your pudding dish with macaroons; put in the stewed peaches, then the beaten eggs, and set it

(215)

in the oven until slightly browned. Beat the whites to a stiff froth and sweeten to taste, spread over the pudding, and set it in the oven until it is of a light brown color. Use half of the whites in the pudding and half on top. Eat cold with cream.

### PEACH CREAM TARTS.

One cup of butter, one cup of nice drippings and a little salt; cut through just enough flour to thoroughly mix (say about a pound of flour), a cup of ice-water, one whole egg, and the yelks of two eggs mixed with a tablespoonful of brown sugar. Add to the flour in which you have previously sifted two teaspoonfuls of baking powder. Handle the dough as little as possible in mixing. Bake in round rings in a hot oven until a light brown. When baked, sift pulverized sugar over the top and fill the hollow center with a compote of peaches. Heap whipped cream or ice-cream on top of each one, the latter being preferable.

### FIG PUDDING.

Chop up very fine one pound of figs and shave one pound of beef suet to a powder, one pound of bread crumbs, one pound of brown sugar and five eggs, yelks and whites beaten separately. Boil three hours in a mold. Eat with hard butter sauce.

### GRAHAM PUDDING.

Take one cup and a half of Graham flour, half a cup of sweet milk, half a cup of molasses, one teaspoonful of soda beaten in molasses, a little salt, one and one-half cups of seeded raisins and one-half cup of currants. Add spices to taste, such as allspice, cloves, cinnamon, etc. Bake. Serve with sauce.

### APFEL CHARLOTTE.

Line an iron pudding dish with a rich puff paste, greasing it well before you do so. Chop up some apples quite fine, put on the crust, also some raisins (seeded), sugar and cinnamon, then put another layer of pie and another layer of chopped apples, and so on until filled, say about three layers, the last being crust. Bake slowly and long until a nice dark brown.

### APPLE SLUMP (DIMPUS DAMPUS).

One quart of sifted flour, in which you have sifted two teaspoonfuls of baking powder and rubbed in a little shortening. Mix with cold milk or water, the same as for biscuit, but not quite as stiff. Mix with this dough two quarts of finely-sliced apples, then line a baking-pan with hot fat or butter, pour in your slump, about half an inch thick, put flakes of fat or butter on top. Bake in a quick oven. Do not forget to add salt. You may add to this sugar and eggs.

Make it as rich as you please, but the majority prefer it plain.

### APPLE PUDDING.

(No. 1.) Pare four or five large tart apples and cut off the top of each apple to use as a cover. Now scrape out all the inside, being careful not to break the apples; mix scrapings with sugar, cinnamon, raisins, a few pounded almonds and add a little white wine and the grated peel of one lemon. Fill up the apples with this mixture and put back the top of each apple, so as to cover each apple well. Grease a deep dish, set in the apples and stew a few minutes. In the meantime make a sponge cake batter of four eggs, one cup of pulverized sugar, one cup of flour and pour over the apples and bake. Eat warm or cold, with or without sauce.

### APPLE PUDDING.

(No. 2.) Line a deep pudding dish with a pie-crust, fill with stewed apples and sweeten with sugar to taste; add a little cinnamon, a few flakes of butter and some cracker or cake crumbs. Pour over this the yelks of four eggs, the grated peel of a lemon and a cup of sugar, beaten until as thick as batter. Pour over the apples and bake. In the meantime beat the whites to a meringue with sugar. Spread over the pudding as soon as baked. Strew some blanched almonds over the top and set in the oven until slightly browned.

### APPLE CRACKER PUDDING.

Cut and pare about five or six apples, according to size. Stew them with sugar just enough to sweeten and add raisins and cinnamon. When tender, set away to cool. Now beat the yelks of six eggs and one cup of sugar until thick like a batter. Add the grated peel of one lemon and four crackers rolled very fine and add last the stiff-beaten whites. Then grease a pudding dish and pour in the apples, then the custard and bake. Eat cold with whipped cream.

### APPLE SUET PUDDING.

Soak half a loaf of bread, shave a cupful of suet very fine and cut up some tart apples in thin slices. Add sugar, raisins, cinnamon, about a handful of pounded almonds and the yelks of six eggs. Mix all thoroughly. Add whites beaten to a stiff froth last. Bake one hour

### APPLE TAPIOCA PUDDING.

Pour three cups of lukewarm water over one cup of tapioca, and soak over night, or soak in the morning, so as to have your pudding for five o'clock dinner. Pare and core about five or six large apples, pack the apples in a deep dish and add a cup of water. Cover closely and steam in a moderate oven until soft, turning them occasionally. Sweeten the apples, adding a little cinnamon and a few whole cloves. Pour the

tapioca over the apples and bake one hour.   Eat
warm with or without sauce.

### GRATED APPLE PUDDING.

Grate seven large tart apples, beat the yelks
of eight eggs with two cups of pulverized sugar
until thick like a batter and add the grated apples.   One dozen lady fingers, grated, the grated
peel of one lemon and the stiff-beaten whites of
the eggs.   Strew blanched almonds on top.   Bake
in a well greased spring form.   Eat with cream.

### SUET PUDDING BOILED IN PRUNES AND · DRIED APPLES.

Soak about half a loaf of bread, press out
every drop of water, add salt, ginger, cinnamon
and cloves, about half a teaspoonful of each.
Add four eggs and about one cup of flour in
which you have sifted a teaspoonful of baking
powder; work all together thoroughly.   Form
into a large ball, place in the center of a large porcelain-lined kettle, which you have lined with
prunes and dried apples, and pour a spoonful of
molasses and some brown sugar over the prunes
and dried apples, also a few slices of lemon and
some stick cinnamon.   Bake for three hours.
Warms over nicely.

### SUET PUDDING WITH PEARS.

Take half a pound of very nice suet and scrape
it to a powder.   Soak a loaf of stale bread, squeeze

out the water and add to the suet. Work bread
and suet well with your hands and add two eggs,
a cup of sugar, a teaspoonful of salt, allspice,
cloves and cinnamon and grated peel of a lemon.
Add flour enough to work into a huge ball; sift
two teaspoonfuls of baking powder in flour. Pare
about half a peck of cooking pears and cut in
halves, leaving the stems on. Lay half the pears
in a large porcelain-lined kettle, put the pudding in center of the pears, and lay the rest of
the pears all around. Add sugar, sliced lemon,
a few cloves, some cinnamon bark and three
spoonfuls of syrup. Fill up and boil half an
hour on top of stove. Then put in the oven for
at least three hours, adding water if needed. This
is a delicious pudding and worth the trouble
of trying. Must be eaten hot and is even better
warmed over.

### GRIMSLICH.

Half a loaf of bread, which has been soaked
and pressed, four eggs, one cup of sugar, raisins,
cinnamon, almonds pounded fine. Beat whites
to a froth and add last. Fry in hot fat.

### PLUM PUDDING.

(No. 1.) Take one-half pound stoned raisins
and one-half pound of currants, a quarter of a
pound of citron, half a pound of sugar, half a
pound of bread crumbs, half a pound of suet,
scraped very fine, and three or four ounces of

almonds pounded in a mortar, two apples chopped
fine and the grated peel of a lemon.  Prepare
the fruit the day previous, put in a bowl and
pour a wineglassful of brandy over it.   Next day
add the suet, bread crumbs, salt, a pinch of
pounded cloves and four eggs and mix well.
Butter a mold, fill it with the mixture and see
that the mold is secure.  Place a plate at the
bottom of a kettle, three-fourths full of boiling
water.  Put the pudding in and boil for three
or four hours, keeping the pot replenished
with boiling water.  Turn out the pudding on a
hot dish, sprinkle sugar over it, pour over it a
wineglassful of warm brandy, and light it when
ready to send to the table.  Sauce made of jelly
thinned with a little water and brandy, and a
little more sugar added, or serve with a
chand'eau sauce.

### PLUM PUDDING.

(No. 2.)  Take half a pound of scraped suet,
half a pound of seeded raisins, half a pound of
currants (washed about a dozen times and then
laid on a cloth to dry), a quarter of a pound of
citron, half a pound of sugar, half a pound of
bread crumbs, two apples cut into small dice, a
handful of almonds, pounded or grated, and the
grated peel of one lemon.  Mix the whole in a
deep bowl, add a pinch each of salt, ground
cloves and cinnamon, five well-beaten eggs and

a wineglassful of brandy. Butter a pudding mold, fill in the mixture, cover up tight and put on to boil in a deep kettle, placing a plate at the bottom, and keep the kettle replenished with boiling water, so that it will reach almost to the top of the mold. Boil three hours steadily. Turn out the pudding on a hot dish, sprinkle sugar over it, then pour a small teacupful of brandy over it, light it, and send to the table immediately. Of course this is done merely for looks. Prepare the fruit the day previous, and soak the fruit in brandy over night. Serve hot with "Roman sauce." This pudding is just as nice warmed over, which should be done by steaming over boiling water.

### PLUM PUDDING.

(No. 3.) Soak a small loaf of bread, press out every drop of water, work into this one cup of suet, shaved very fine, the yelks of six eggs, one cup of currants, one cup of raisins, seeded, half a teaspoonful of ground cloves, some pepper, a teaspoonful of cinnamon, the grated peel of one lemon, one glass of cognac, two cups of sifted flour, adding the stiff-beaten whites last. Boil four hours. Eat hot, with sauce.

### POTATO PUDDING.

Peel and grate six or eight potatoes, pass them through a sieve and salt well. Add a spoonful of hot fat; stir a handful of flour through the

potatoes and four well-beaten eggs. Pour this
in an iron pudding form, in which you have
heated a large spoonful of nice drippings. Bake
brown. Eat hot.

### NOODLE PUDDING.

Sift about one pint of flour into a bowl, make
a cavity in the center of the flour, break four
eggs into it, and add a pinch of salt and two
tablespoonfuls of water. Now take the handle
of a knife and commence to stir the eggs slowly,
and in one direction, doing so until you can not
work it any more in this way, then flour a baking board and put the contents of your bowl on
it and work the dough with the palm of your
hands, always kneading toward you. Work a
long time until perfectly smooth, then divide
the dough into four equal parts and work each
piece separately. Now roll out as thin as possible and lay on a table to dry. When dry cut
into stripes half an inch wide. Have a kettle of
boiling water on the stove ready to receive the
noodles; add salt, and let them boil about five
minutes, stirring occasionally to prevent the
noodles from sticking to one another. Then
put them into a collander and let cold water
run through them. When all the water has
been drained off, beat up eight or ten eggs and
stir the noodles into the beaten egg. Now line
a flat-bottomed iron kettle (one that is about

one foot high with some drippings to grease it, put in a layer of the noodles, then sprinkle with a handful of sugar and some pounded almonds, the grated peel of one lemon and a few raisins, sprinkle some melted fat over this, then add another layer of noodles, some sugar and proceed as you did before until all are used up. Bake two hours. This makes a very large pudding, but if you choose you can make half the recipe calls for. You ought to have a kugelhopf for this noodle pudding. You may make this pudding out of very fine sweet noodles, which make it still better.

## BREAD PUDDING.

Soak two teacupfuls of bread crumbs in a quart of sweet milk for half an hour; separate the whites and yolks of four eggs, setting the whites in a cool place until needed. Beat the yolks with a small cupful of pulverized sugar, add the grated peel of one lemon and stir into the bread crumbs. Put in some raisins and pour into a greased pudding dish and bake in a moderate oven about half an hour. Beat the whites of the eggs to a stiff froth, adding half a cup of powdered sugar; and spread this on top of pudding and return to the oven and brown delicately. May be eaten hot or cold with jelly sauce or whipped cream. Stale cake of any kind may be used instead of bread; and gingerbread also is particularly nice, adding raisins and citron, and spreading a layer of jelly on the pudding before putting on the icing.

### CHERRY PUDDING.

(No. 1.)   Scald a pint of crackers or bread crumbs in a quart of boiling milk; add a piece of butter the size of an egg, a good pinch of salt, four eggs, a cup and a half of sugar, a little ground cinnamon and a quart of stoned cherries. Bake quickly.

### CHERRY PUDDING.

(No. 2.)   Soak three stale rolls in milk, blanch a few ounces of almonds, pound them in a mortar, stir a piece of butter the size of an egg to a cream, add half a pound of pulverized sugar, the almonds, four ounces of citron cut up very fine, a pinch of cinnamon; and the yelks of eight eggs, beaten light.  Press out the rolls, stir all well and last add the beaten whites of the eggs, and a pound of stoned cherries.  Bake in a buttered pudding dish.  Eat with a sauce made of cherries.

### CHERRY PUDDING.

(No. 3.)   Grate one pound of stale rye bread and wet this with a wineglassful of red wine. Pound one-quarter of a pound of almonds, stir the yelks of eight eggs with a cup of pulverized sugar, flavor with cinnamon, and add the grated bread and almonds.  Stone one pound of sweet

and one pound of sour cherries. Mix all
thoroughly with the beaten whites of four eggs,
added last. Do not take the juice of the cherries. Butter the pudding mold well before you
put in the mixture. Eat cold.

### FARINA PUDDING WITH PEACHES.

To one quart of milk add half a cup of farina,
salt, and a small piece of butter. Boil in a
farina kettle until thick. Beat the yelks of
four eggs with four heaping tablespoonfuls of
white sugar, and add this just before taking off
the fire. Stir it thoroughly, but don't let it
boil any more. Flavor with vanilla. Beat the
whites of the eggs to a stiff froth with pulverized sugar. After the eggs have been whipped,
butter a pudding dish, put in part of the custard, in which you have mixed the whites (if
you have any extra whites of eggs beat and use
them also) then a layer of stewed or canned
peaches; cover with the remaining custard and
bake. Eat with rum sauce.

### CHILDREN'S FAVORITE DESSERT.

Take one dozen lady fingers, put jelly between
each and line a pudding dish with them. Take
one pint of rich, sweet cream; and sweeten to
taste. Boil slowly in a farina kettle, stirring
constantly. Stir in two teaspoonfuls of cornstarch, previously wet with cold milk, beat the
yelks of five eggs very light, and stir them into

the cream.  After this is cool, flavor with vanilla
and pour over the cakes.  Have the whites
beaten to a stiff froth, sweeten, cover the pudding smoothly with this meringue, set in oven
to brown.  Eat cold with whipped cream.

### RICE PUDDING.

(No. 1.)  Boil about one-half pound of rice
in milk until thick, then let it cool.  In the
meantime rub a tablespoonful of butter to a
cream; add a small teacupful of pulverized
sugar, a little cinnamon, the grated peel of one
lemon, the yelks of five or six eggs, adding one
at a time, half a cupful of raisins, seeded, then
add the cold rice, and last the well-beaten whites
of the eggs.  A handful of pounded almonds,
mixed with a few bitter ones, improves this
pudding.  Serve with a nice pudding sauce,
either wine or brandy.  This pudding may be
eaten hot or cold, in fact a great many prefer it
cold, and may be either baked or boiled.  Time
to bake, one hour; to boil, two hours; keeping
the water boiling steadily.  You may use cold
rice that has been left over; it is not necessary
to measure it accurately, and where I have used
butter you may use fat and boil the rice in water
if you so prefer.

### RICE PUDDING.

(No. 2.)  Soak one-half cupful of rice in hot
water, drain and let it steam in three cupfuls of

milk until soft, then add a piece of butter, half a cupful of sweet cream and the yelks of three eggs, well beaten with six tablespoonfuls of sugar. Mix thoroughly and pour in a well-buttered pudding dish and bake. When done, whip the whites of the eggs, sweeten and flavor, spread on top and bake a light brown. Eat hot or cold, with fruit sauce.

## TIPSY PUDDING.

(No. 1.) Cut stale sponge cake into thin slices, spread with jelly or preserves, put two pieces together like sandwiches and lay each slice or sandwich on the plate it is to be served on. Wet each piece with wine, then pour or spread a large tablespoonful of rich custard over each piece of pudding, and then frost each piece with a nice frosting and put in a moderate oven for a few minutes. Eat cold.

## TIPSY PUDDING.

(No. 2.) Cut stale sponge cake into thin slices, moisten each slice with brandy or wine, then spread with jelly or compote, lay two pieces together like a sandwich and put each piece on a dessert plate. Make a custard of one quart of milk and five or six eggs, leaving out the whites of four. Sweeten to taste and flavor. Beat the whites to a stiff froth, adding enough pulverized sugar to sweeten. Put a heaping tablespoonful on each piece of pudding and put in the oven until set having previously covered each piece with the custard. You may ornament each piece with a spoonful of jelly or a piece of candied fruit. Eat cold.

### PRINCE ALBERT PUDDING.

Rub to a cream half a pound of sweet butter and half a pound of sifted powdered sugar, add the yelks of six eggs, one at a time, and the grated peel of one lemon. Stone half a pound of raisins, and add also a little citron, cut very fine. Now add gradually half a pound of the finest flour, sifted three or four times, and the stiff-beaten whites of the eggs. Pour this mixture into a well-buttered mold, into which you have strewn some blanched and pounded almonds. Boil fully three hours. Serve with sweet brandy or fruit sauce.

### RHUBARB PUDDING.

Prepare the stalks just as you would for pies, cover the bottom of a buttered pudding dish with slices of bread, cover with the pie-plant; sprinkle with brown sugar, enough of it, then another layer of bread, and so on until your dish is filled. Beat up three or four eggs with some pulverized sugar, pour over the pudding and bake; covered at first, then remove the cover to brown. Flavor with lemon or nutmeg.

## CUSTARD.

Beat the yelks of five eggs and one cup of sugar until very light and stir into one pint of hot milk, return to farina kettle and heat until it reaches boiling point; remove from the fire and flavor with one teaspoonful of vanilla. A handful of blanched and pounded almonds improves the custard very much.

## KRAUT KUGEL.

Chop up cabbage and let stew in fat slowly until quite brown. Do this the day previous to using. Next day mix in with the stewed cabbage, a quarter of a loaf of soaked bread, squeezing all the water out of it, a large handful of flour, a handful of brown sugar, a handful of raisins, some finely-chopped citron, a handful of almonds (mixed with bitter), half a teaspoonful of salt, some cinnamon and allspice, juice and peel of one lemon and six eggs. Mix all thoroughly and bake in the oven. Grease the kugel form well. Bake slowly.

## SWEET POTATO PUDDING.

Boil one pound of sweet potatoes, let them get perfectly cold before grating them. In the meantime cream a heaping tablespoonful of butter and two tablespoonfuls of sugar, add gradually the yelks of four eggs, the grated peel of a lemon, a teaspoonful of cinnamon, a little grated nutmeg and one cup of sweet milk; add the

beaten whites last.  Then grease a pudding dish,
line with a rich crust and fill in the custard.   To
make it still richer, add a wineglassful of brandy
to the sweet potatoes.   Eat cold, with or without sauce.

### CRANBERRY PUDDING.

Boil a quart of cranberries till soft and add a
pound of sugar.   When cold proceed just as with
Apple Cracker Pudding.   Very nice.

### CHOCOLATE SOUFFLE.

Rub about two ounces of butter with three
ounces of sugar to a cream.   Add the yelks of six
eggs, well beaten ; three ounces grated chocolate,
one teaspoonful of vanilla, six ounces of bread,
which has been previously soaked in milk (press
every drop of milk out of it), and rub the bread
very smooth before adding to the mixture.   Add
last the stiff-beaten whites of eggs.   Bake three-
quarters of an hour.   Serve in the dish it was
baked in.   Pin a napkin around the dish and
serve.

### CHOCOLATE PUDDING.

(No. 1.)   Dry and grate two cupfuls of bread,
mix with this twelve tablespoonfuls of chocolate,
grated.   Heat to boiling one quart of rich milk,
and pour this over the chocolate and bread.
When cooled, add the beaten yelks of five eggs
and one cup of sugar, flavor with vanilla.   Bake

in a pudding dish for one hour. When baked spread with meringue of the whites of the eggs, not forgetting to add sugar. If you wish it extra fine spread with a layer of jelly or marmalade before frosting.

### CHOCOLATE PUDDING.

(No. 2.) Boil six sticks of chocolate in milk or water, when boiled add a loaf of soaked bread, enough pulverized sugar to sweeten and a lump of butter. Stir this until cold, then add seven eggs, yelks and whites beaten separately, adding one yelk at a time. Add last the beaten whites. Bake slowly from one to two hours.

### ORANGE PUDDING.

Line the bottom of a pudding dish with lady fingers; slice over them five oranges (extract the seeds), pour over them a cup of sugar, and pour over all a custard made of one quart of milk and six eggs, sweeten to taste. Leave out the whites of four, beat these whites to a stiff froth, adding sugar, put on top of pudding, set in the oven to brown. Berries or peaches may be substituted. Eat cold.

### SPONGE PUDDING.

Set one quart of milk to boil. Beat the yelks of five eggs light with three tablespoonfuls of sugar, three of butter and three of flour. Beat

to a light batter. When the milk begins to boil,
stir in this batter, take from the fire, add the
stiff-beaten whites and set in the oven and bake
a light brown. Bake and set in another dish of
hot water. You may use any flavor desired and
serve with any kind of pudding sauce.

## YUM-YUM.

Make a rich puff paste, with half a pound of
butter rubbed to a cream; rub into this half a
pound of sifted flour, a tablespoonful of brandy,
half a cup of ice-water with the yelk of an egg
beaten up into the ice-water and a pinch of salt.
Mix all lightly, handling as little as possible.
Butter a pudding dish, roll out enough of this
dough to just line the rim of the pudding dish—
no more and put the remainder of paste on ice,
until wanted for pies. Now for the pudding:
Take a very large juicy lemon, half a pound of
powdered sugar and a small cup of the best butter. Grate the peel of the lemon into the sugar,
rub the butter to a cream, add the sugar, and
squeeze every drop of juice out of the lemon into
the butter and sugar through a strainer, so as to
avoid having any seeds in it. Stir this mixture
until it is a very light cream, using a silver
spoon. Beat six eggs, until like batter, mix all
gently, and fill in your pudding dish, and set it
immediately into the oven. Bake half an hour
and serve in the dish it was baked in.

## METROPOLITAN APPLE PUDDING,
### (APFEL SCHALET.)

Take one pound of fresh beef heart fat, shave it as fine as possible with a knife. Sift one quart of flour into a deep bowl, add two tumblerfuls of ice-cold water, one tablespoonful of brown sugar, a saltspoonful of salt and then add the shaved heart fat and work well into the sifted flour. Then put it on a pie board and work as you would bread dough, with the palm of your hand, until it looks smooth enough to roll. Do not work it too long, not over five minutes. Now take half of this dough, flour your pie-board slightly and roll out as you would pie dough, about once as thick. Butter a deep pudding dish (an iron one is best), one that is smaller at the bottom than the top, grease it well, line the pudding dish, bottom and sides, clear to the top, fill this one-third full with chopped tart apples, raisins, part of a grated lemon peel, citron cut quite fine, pounded almonds and flakes of butter here and there. Sprinkle thickly with sugar, half brown and half white, and a little ground cinnamon. Moisten each layer with half a wineglassful of wine. Now put another layer of dough, rolling out half of the remaining dough and reserving the other half for the top covering, fill again with apples, raisins, etc., until full, then put on top layer. Press the dough firmly together all round the edge, using a beaten egg to make sure of its sticking. Roll the side dough over the top with a knife and pour a whole goblet of water over the pudding before setting it in the oven. Time for baking two hours. If the top browns too quickly, cover. The advantage of this pudding is, it may be baked the day previous to using, in fact it is better the oftener it is warmed over—always adding a small goblet of water before setting it in the oven. The crust should be the color of varnished cherry wood, and sticky as molasses candy, to be nice. Before serving, dump the pudding carefully on a large platter, pour a wineglassful of brandy which has been slightly sweetened over the pudding and light it, carry to the table in flames. A novice had better try this pudding plain omitting the wine, brandy, almonds and citron, moistening with water instead of wine, before baking. Almost as nice and very good for ordinary use. Some apples require more water than others, the cook having to use her own judgment regarding the amount required.

## CORN-STARCH PUDDING.

Heat one quart of milk to boiling point in a farina kettle, leave out just enough cold milk to dissolve three tablespoonfuls of corn-starch. When the milk begins to boil, stir in the corn-starch, add a pinch of salt and a piece of butter about the size of a walnut. When thickly boiled take off the fire and stir until quite cool, then add the yelks of three or four eggs and a scant teacupful of pulverized sugar and flavor with lemon or vanilla. Add the stiff-beaten whites of the eggs last, and bake in a porcelain pudding dish. Eat with jelly sauce.

### CORN-STARCH MERINGUE PUDDING.

Heat one quart of rich milk in a farnia kettle, leave out just enough cold milk to dissolve three tablespoonfuls of corn-starch. When the milk begins to boil stir in the dissolved starch, add a pinch of salt and a lump of butter, about the size of an egg. When thickly boiled remove from the fire and stir occasionally until cold. Add the yelks of four or five eggs, and a cupful of pulverized sugar, flavor with vanilla, add half of the stiff-beaten whites, reserving the other half for the top of pudding. When the pudding is baked, spread a layer of jelly or fruit preserves on top, then cover with the stiff-beaten whites, which you must sweeten with two tablespoonfuls of finely pulverized sugar. Set in the oven for one or two minutes. Eat cold with plain sweet or whipped cream.

### ALMOND ROLEY POLEY (STRUDEL).

Mix a dough of one large cupful of flour and half a cupful of warm water, slightly salted. Set it away in a warm place, covered up to keep warm. Now stir to a cream one-half a cupful

of best butter, with a cupful of pulverized sugar, add the grated peel of a lemon,
stir in gradually, one at a time, the yelks of
six eggs, stir all thoroughly, then add a cupful
of almonds, blanched and pounded in a mortar,
or roll them (measure the almonds before
pounding), add last the stiff-beaten whites of
the eggs. Now roll out the dough as thin as
possible on a kitchen table, which has been
previously covered with a table-cloth and slightly
sprinkled with sifted flour, when through rolling
the dough (which must be done quickly) pull it
gently and deftly with your fingers until it is
as thin as paper; then brush it quickly with
melted butter, covering every particle of the
dough, and fill the dough with the almond mixture, covering the center of the rolled dough.
Now roll it all up securely, take hold of the
cloth with both hands, one at each end, and roll
in that way, not touching the dough with your
fingers at all. Butter a long pan, and slip the
roley-poley on it, brush it over the top with
butter, bake in a quick oven until brown. Eat
warm or cold. A half teaspoonful of rose water,
added to the filling, greatly improves it.

### THE QUEEN OF PLUM PUDDINGS.

One-half pound of cracker crumbs, one-half
pound of finely-shaved suet, one-half pound of
sugar, one-half pound of seeded and chopped

raisins, one-half pound of candied fruits and
stuffed prunes mixed, also one-half pound of
citron, and candied orange and lemon peel
mixed. One-half pound of dried currants, half
a dozen eggs, a wineglassful of brandy, nutmeg,
allspice, cinnamon, half a teaspoonful of each,
sift very little flour over the fruit and mix it
to prevent the fruit from sinking to the bottom.
Boil as you would other plum puddings, when
ready to serve, stick blanched almonds all over
the pudding and pour a little sugared brandy
over all and send to the table lighted (to do this
just touch a burning match to the pudding, it
will flame instantly). Serve with wine or
brandy sauce.

**MEMORANDUM.**

# PUDDING SAUCES.

|  |  | Page. |
|---|---|---|
| Chand'eau, | - - - - - - | 241 |
| Cranberry, | - - - - - | 245 |
| Fruit, | - - - - - - | 244, 245 |
| Hard Sauce, - | - - - - - | 243 |
| Jelly, | - - - - - - | 242 |
| Lemon, - | - - - - - | 242, 243 |
| Peach, | - - - - - - | 243 |
| Plum Pudding, | - - - - - | 244 |
| Prune, | - - - - - - | 246 |
| Rum, | - - - - - - | 242 |
| Roman, | - - - - - - | 244 |

(240)

**MEMORANDUM.**

# PUDDING SAUCES.

## CHAND'EAU SAUCE.

TAKE the yelks of six eggs, one cup of sugar, one tumblerful of Madeira and the grated peel of one lemon and stir over the fire until the spoon becomes coated. Serve in a sauce-boat. You may make this sauce of brandy, using half water.

## WINE SAUCE.

(No. 1.) Take a cupful of white wine, half a cup of water, a few slices of lemon, a little cinnamon, and sweeten to taste, then boil. Then wet a teaspoonful of cornstarch or potato flour and add, stirring constantly. Beat up the yelks of four eggs, and add the boiling wine gradually to the beaten egg. Return to the kettle stirring constantly. Then add part of the beaten whites of the eggs, and put the remaining on top of the sauce, sweetening the whites also.

## WINE SAUCE.

(No. 2.) Take a small teacupful of white wine, put on to boil in a farina kettle or porcelain-lined kettle, and in the meantime beat up the yelks of two eggs. Beat them very light, with two teaspoonfuls of white sugar, add some

grated nutmeg or the grated peel of half a lemon
and add a teaspoonful of flour to this gradually.
When perfectly smooth add the boiling wine,
pouring very little at a time and stirring constantly.    Return to farina kettle and stir until
the spoon is coated.

## WINE SAUCE.

(No. 3.)   One cup of wine, a little water, one
cup of sugar, the grated peel of a lemon and a
little of the juice, and the yelks of four or five
eggs, stir until this comes to a boil, then add
the stiff-beaten whites and remove from the fire
at once.

## JELLY SAUCE.

Take thin jelly, add a little water and brandy
or wine, add a little more sugar and thicken
with egg or cornstarch.

## RUM SAUCE.

Boil one cup of milk with one cup of sugar,
and wet a teaspoonful of arrowroot or cornstarch
with a little cold milk, and add.   Just before
removing from the fire add a teaspoonful of rum.
Serve hot.

## LEMON SAUCE.

(No. 1.)   Boil the strained juice of two lemons
and grated peel of one, with a heaping cupful of
sugar and one glassful of white wine or water.
When boiled to a syrup add the yelks of three

eggs well-beaten, also half of the whites beaten
to a froth. Use the other half of the stiff-beaten
whites to decorate the sauce. When in the sauce-
boat, sweeten with pulverized sugar. Serve immediately.

### LEMON SAUCE.

(No. 2.) Juice of two lemons, and half a
teacup of water. Add the grated peel of one
lemon, one or two cups of sugar, and sweeten
to taste. Let this come to a boil after adding
the yelks of five eggs; stir constantly, and add
last the beaten whites. Remove from the fire
as soon as you have added the whipped whites.

### HARD SAUCE FOR PUDDINGS.

Take one cup of sugar, one-half cup of butter
(wash the butter in cold water to extract the
salt, it will also cream easier), and stir to a cream.
Flavor with grated lemon peel or essence of
lemon. Make into any shape desired and
serve.

### PEACH SYRUP.

This is very nice for all kinds of griddle cakes,
and is more economical than maple syrup, for
the material does not cost you anything except
the sugar. Use the peelings of your peaches
when you are through canning and preserving.
Add one-third of the peach kernels, and put all
on to boil in a stone jar on the back of the stove,
with a little water. When soft, strain through

a jelly-bag by letting it drip all night. In the
morning add the juice of two or three lemons
and boil as you would jelly. Set a pint of juice
on to boil and boil for five minutes. Add a
pound of sugar and boil five minutes more, but
it must boil very hard. Bottle in wide-mouthed
bottles or jars. Seal.

### PLUM PUDDING SAUCE.

Take one cup of water, a liquor glassful of
brandy, two cups of sugar, juice of half a lemon.
Boil all in a farina kettle. Beat the yelks of
three eggs light, and add the boiling sauce gradually to them, stirring constantly until thick.

### ROMAN SAUCE.

One-half pint of brandy, quarter of a pound
of sugar. Heat until it comes to a boil; then
add the well-beaten yelks of six eggs, stir until
the spoon is coated, then remove from the fire,
grate in the peel of one lemon and pour in sauce-
boat. You may use sherry instead of brandy,
adding water if too strong.

### FRUIT SAUCES.

(No. 1.) These sauces may be made of either
fresh or dried fruits. Boil the fruit with spices,
whole cinnamon, lemon peel and a few cloves.
When very soft press through a coarse sieve or
collander. Sweeten to taste, add a glass of wine
or rum and set on to boil again, and thicken

with a teaspoonful of cornstarch or flour, which
has been dissolved in a quarter of a cup of
water. If the sauce is very thin, do not add any
water, but dissolve the cornstarch in the wine
or brandy. Potato flour is also very excellent
for thickening sauces.

### FRUIT SAUCES.

(No. 2.) Take the juice of any fruit, either by
boiling or pressing through a sieve, or both;
sweeten to taste, adding wine or lemon juice, and
thicken with a little cornstarch or flour. Out
of season you may use the juice of canned fruit.

### CRANBERRY SAUCE.

Wash cranberries, pick carefully, put on to
boil in a porcelain-lined kettle, and cook with
very little water. They should boil fast and be
covered closely. Add a pound of white sugar to
a quart of berries, strain, then dip a mold in
cold water and fill with cranberry sauce and
put on ice until time to serve.

### VANILLA SAUCE.

Set on to boil just as much milk as you desire sauce. When it boils, sweeten to taste. In
the meantime, beat the yelks of two or more
eggs light, adding the boiling milk to the yelks
gradually, a spoonful at a time. You may use
cornstarch instead of the egg, say about a des-

sertaspoonful, or both. When cold flavor with
two teaspoonfuls of vanilla.

### PRUNE SAUCE.

Take about one pound of Turkish prunes, wash
them in hot water, and put on to boil in cold
water. Boil until they are very soft. Now remove
the pits or kernels, and strain over them the
water they were boiled in, and sweeten to taste.
Flavor with ground cinnamon, then mash them
with your hands until a soft mush. If too thick,
add the juice of an orange.

# STRUDELS.

|                              |       |       |       |       |       | Page.    |
|------------------------------|-------|-------|-------|-------|-------|----------|
| Apple Strudel,               | -     | -     | -     | -     |       | 248, 249 |
| Batter with Prunes, -        | -     | -     | -     | -     |       | 253      |
| Cherry, -                    | -     | -     | -     | -     |       | 249, 250 |
| Cherry, Roley-Poley,         | -     | -     | -     | -     |       | 251      |
| Chocolate Batter, -          | -     | -     | -     |       |       | 253      |
| Kraut,                       | -     | -     | -     | -     | -     | 254      |
| Mandel,                      | -     | -     | -     | -     | -     | 254      |
| Quark, or Dutch Cheese, -    | -     | -     | -     |       |       | 252      |
| Rice,                        | -     | -     | -     | -     | -     | 251      |
| Strudel aus Kalbslunge,      | -     | -     | -     |       |       | 252      |
| Sponge,                      | -     | -     | -     | -     | -     | 253      |

# STRUDELS.

### APPLE STRUDEL (ROLEY-POLEY).

TAKE about one pint of flour, sift it into a bowl, make a hole in the center of the flour, pour in it gradually one cup of lukewarm water, a pinch of salt and a spoonful of butter or goose-fat. Stir this slowly, making a nice smooth dough of it and adding a little more flour if necessary. Cover up the dough and set it in a warm place until you have pared half a peck of apples, and cut them very fine in the following manner: Pare, quarter and take out cores and seeds, and cut or rather shave them very fine. Now cover your kitchen table with a clean tablecloth, sift flour all over it and roll out your dough as thin as possible. Now use your hands, placing them under the rolled dough and stretch it gently, very gently, so as not to tear it, walking all around the table as you do this, to get it even and thin as tissue paper. Pour a few tablespoonfuls of melted butter or goose oil over the dough; next the apples, brown sugar, cinnamon and raisins. Now take hold of the tablecloth with both hands, about a yard apart, and begin to roll the strudel (it will roll itself almost—just lift the cloth high enough). Now butter or grease a large cake-pan, hold it up to the edge of the table and dump in the strudel. Bake a nice brown, basting often with butter or goose oil.

### APPLE STRUDEL.

(No. 2.) Take a pint of flour, sift it into a bowl, make a hole in the center of the flour, pour in half a cup of lukewarm water, four ounces of butter, two whole eggs and two yelks and a pinch of salt. Stir as you would noodle dough. Spread a tablecloth over the kitchen table, roll out the dough as thin as possible, then stretch it as described above. Pour over this the melted butter, then the shaved apples, sugar, cinnamon, seeded raisins and a little citron, cut very fine. Roll and bake. Butter the pan well, and also put flakes of butter on top of the strudel. When half baked pour a cup of cream over it and finish baking. Bake about half an hour.

### CHERRY STRUDEL.

Make a dough of one pint of flour, a pinch of salt and a little lukewarm water; do not make it too stiff, but smooth. Slap the dough on the table back and forth. To do this take the dough in your right hand and hit the table with a vengeance as hard as you can. Do this repeatedly for about fifteen minutes. Now put the dough in a warm, covered bowl and set it in a warm place and let it rest for half an hour. In the

meantime stem and pit two quarts of sour cherries. Grate into them some stale bread (about
a plateful); also the peel of half a lemon, and
mix. Add half a pound or more of sugar, some
ground cinnamon and about four ounces of
pounded sweet almonds, and mix all thoroughly.
Now cover your kitchen table with a clean tablecloth, one that is large enough to cover it entirely, and sift flour over the whole of it. Roll
out the dough as thin as possible, lay aside the
rolling pin and pull, or rather stretch the dough
as thin as tissue paper. In doing this you will
have to walk all around the table, for when well
stretched it will cover more than the size of an
ordinary table. Pull off all of the thick edge,
for it must be very thin to be good (save the
pieces for another strudel). Pour a little melted
goose oil or butter over this, and sprinkle the
bread, sugar, almonds, cherries, etc., over it; roll
the strudel together into a long roll. To do this
properly, take hold of the cloth with both hands
and roll up carefully; have ready a long baking
pan well greased with either butter or goose fat;
fold the strudel into the shape of a pretzel, pull
the cloth to the edge of the table, dump the
strudel into the pan as quickly as possible,
securing the edges well so as not to have the
juice escape, butter the top also and bake a
light brown; baste often while baking. Eat
warm.

## CHERRY ROLEY-POLEY.

Make a rich baking powder biscuit dough, and roll it out until it is about two-thirds of an inch thick. Pit and stew enough cherries to make a thick layer of fruit and add sugar to taste. Spread them over the dough thickly; and roll it up, taking care to keep the cherries from falling out. Wrap a cloth around it, and sew it up loosely with coarse thread, which is easily pulled out. Allow plenty of room for the dough to rise. Lay the roley-poley on a plate, set it in a steamer and stew for an hour and a half steady. Serve in slices, with cream or sauce.

## RICE STRUDEL.

Prepare the dough same as for apple strudel. Leave it in a warm place covered, until you have prepared the rice thus: Wash a quarter of a pound of rice in hot water—about three times—then boil it in milk until very soft and thick. Let it cool, and then add two ounces of butter, the yelks of four eggs, four ounces of sugar and one teaspoonful of vanilla, some salt and the beaten whites of two eggs, and mix thoroughly. When your dough has been rolled out and pulled as thin as possible, spread the rice over it and roll. You may add pounded almonds and raisins if you choose. Put in a greased pan and bake until brown, basting with sweet cream or butter.

## QUARK STRUDEL (DUTCH CHEESE).

Make a strudel or roley-poley dough and let
it rest until you have prepared the cheese. Take
half a pound of cheese, rub it through a coarse
sieve or collander, add salt, the yelks of two
eggs and one whole egg, and sweeten to taste.
Add the grated peel of one lemon, two ounces of
sweet almonds, and about four bitter ones,
blanched and pounded, four ounces of sultana
raisins and a little citron chopped finely. Now
roll out as thin as possible, spread in the cheese,
roll and bake, basting with sweet cream.

## STRUDEL AUS KALBSLUNGE.

Wash the lung and heart thoroughly in salt
water, and put on to boil in cold water, adding
salt, one onion, a few bay leaves and cook until
very tender. Make the dough precisely the
same as any other strudel. Take the boiled
lung and heart, chop them as fine as possible
and stew in a saucepan with some butter or fat,
adding chopped parsley, a little salt, pepper
and mace, or nutmeg, and the grated peel of half
a lemon and a little wine. Add the beaten yelks
of four eggs to thicken, and remove from the
fire to cool. Roll out the dough as thin as possible, fill in the mixture and lay the strudel in
a well greased pan; put flakes of butter or fat
on top and baste often. Eat hot.

## SPONGE STRUDEL.

Make a pancake batter of four whole eggs and the yelks of two, one pint of milk, some salt, and flour enough to make it the consistency of a pancake batter. Bake quite thin in pie-tins, spread on the following mixture when baked, and roll immediately or it will be liable to break. Now pound four ounces of almonds to a powder, stir in the yelks of four eggs and add the beaten whites, the grated peel of a lemon and four ounces of sugar. Mix all thoroughly and spread on the baked dough and roll immediately. Cut each one through the center, roll in beaten egg and cracker and fry a light brown. Strew powdered sugar over them and serve.

### BATTER STRUDEL WITH PRUNES.

Boil the prunes until very soft, take out the kernels, and mash them. Add sugar, cinnamon, the grated peel of a lemon and mix thoroughly. Now make a batter like in the receipt above. When baked spread with the prunes, roll and lay in a buttered pan, put in the oven a few minutes with flakes of butter on top. Serve with powdered sugar.

### CHOCOLATE BATTER STRUDEL.

Boil a pint of cream with one-quarter of a pound of chocolate (grated), adding four ounces of sugar. Beat the yelks of six eggs with a lit-

tle cold cream and add to the boiling chocolate
and stir until thick and set away to cool. Prepare the batter thus: Break four whole eggs
into a bowl, the yolks of two, one pint of
milk and flour enough to make a light batter.
Bake like large, thin pancakes, and fill with the
chocolate. When all are baked and filled set
in a buttered dish in the oven and bake. Before
setting in the oven pour a little cream and flakes
of butter over the top. Sprinkle powdered
sugar over all when serving.

### MANDEL STRUDEL.

Prepare the dough as for Apple Strudel.
Blanch a pound of almonds, pound in a mortar,
when dried beat the yolks of six eggs light, with
one-quarter of a pound of sugar, add the grated
peel of a lemon and mix in the almonds. Spread
over the dough and roll. Bake with flakes of
butter and baste very often.

### KRAUT STRUDEL.

Prepare the cabbage the day previous. Cut
or chop the cabbage very fine, and stew in fat
until very tender, salt and pepper to taste. Cut
up half an onion in the fat before adding the
cabbage. Thicken with flour and fill in the
strudel dough and bake. Dough is made like in
Apple Strudel.

# CREAMS, CUSTARDS, ETC.

| | Page |
|---|---|
| Apple Souffles, | 264 |
| Apple Compote, | 264 |
| Apple Sauce, | 266 |
| Apple Sauce Victoria, | 271 |
| Baked Apples, | 265 |
| Cherry Blanc-Mange, | 256 |
| Compote of Pears, | 262 |
| Compote of Peaches, | 262 |
| Compote of Raspberries, | 267 |
| Compote of Pineapple, | 270 |
| Charlotte Russe, | 271, 272 |
| Danish Grits, | 262 |
| Escaloped Peaches, | 269 |
| Floating Island, | 268 |
| Fig Sauce, | 270 |
| Gooseberry Fool. | 257 |
| Gooseberry Cream, | 270 |
| Huckleberry Compote, | 257 |
| Jellied Apples, | 266, 269 |
| Neapolitan Blanc-Mange | 259, 260, 261 |
| Orange Custard, | 258 |
| Peach Custard. | 256 |
| Peach Compote, | 268 |
| Pistachio Cream, | 268 |
| Prunes, | 267 |
| Pineapple Cream, | 269 |
| Rhubarb Sauce, | 256 |
| Red Raspberry Cream, | 261 |
| Rice Custard, | 263 |
| Red Raspberry or Currant Float, | 267 |
| Strawberry Cream, | 259 |
| Tapioca Cream, | 257 |
| Whipped Cream, | 258 |

# CREAMS, CUSTARDS, ETC.

## PEACH CUSTARD.

TAKE a can, or one quart of peaches, pare and stone them. Blanch also a few of the kernels, stew all in half a cupful of wine and add sugar to taste. Beat up the yelks of nine or ten eggs with two small cups of sugar (beat same as for cake), grate the peel of half a lemon, and beat the whites of the eggs to a stiff froth, and add half of the stiff froth to the beaten yelks. Take the peaches off the fire and pour into a pudding dish. Pour the batter over the peaches and bake until brown. Then cover all with the remaining whipped whites of the eggs, sweetened with powdered sugar, and brown slightly. To be eaten cold, with cream. You may line your pudding dish with macaroons or lady fingers, though not necessary. In summer set in ice-chest. This makes a delicious dessert.

## CHERRY BLANC-MANGE.

Take a one-quart can of cherries, and one-half box of gelatine. Soak the gelatine in one-half glass of sherry wine; then heat the cherries and gelatine together, and sugar to taste. Flavor with a few drops of lemon juice and some of the peel. Pour it into a mold, which has been previously rinsed in cold water. When cold, serve with whipped cream and fruit cake.

### TAPIOCA CREAM.

Soak four tablespoonfuls of topioca over night in one quart of sweet milk. In the morning beat the yelks of three eggs very light, and add to them a scant teacupful of sugar. Put the milk and tapioca on to boil in a double farina kettle, adding a pinch of salt. When it comes to a boil stir in the eggs and sugar. Beat the whites to a stiff froth, and stir quickly and delicately into the hot mixture. Flavor with vanilla. Eat cold.

### GOOSEBERRY FOOL.

Stew a quart of gooseberries with a cup and a half of sugar, and when soft rub them through a sieve to remove the skins. Add a tablespoonful of fresh butter and the well-beaten yelks of six eggs. Serve in a glass dish, or in small glasses if you so prefer, and spread a meringue of the whipped whites of the eggs on top. Sweeten and flavor to taste.

### HUCKLEBERRY COMPOTE.

Pick over a quart of huckleberries or blueberries, wash them and set over to boil in a porcelain-lined kettle or earthen bowl. Do not add any water to them. Sweeten with half a

cup of sugar, and spice with half a teaspoonful
of cinnamon. Just before removing from the
fire, add a teaspoonful of cornstarch which has
been wet with a little cold water. Do this
thoroughly in a cup and stir with a teaspoon so
as not to have any lumps in it. Pour into a
glass bowl. Eat cold.

### WHIPPED CREAM.

Whip the cream to a stiff froth in a syllabub
churn. Lay the whipped cream on a hair sieve
or napkin and when all is whipped sweeten and
flavor to taste. Then line the edges of a mold
or large glass dish with lady fingers and fill up
with the whipped cream. Ornament with macaroons and candied fruit. Set on ice until
wanted. In the summer set the cream on ice
before whipping. A good plan is to set the bowl
in another one filled with ice while whipping.

### ORANGE CUSTARD.

Juice of ten oranges, one teacupful and a half
of sugar, yelks of ten eggs, and one pint of cream.
Put the juice and sugar on to boil in a farina
kettle, and when boiling skim it carefully and
set aside to cool. Beat the yelks very light and
add to the juice of the oranges. Beat the cream
also to a froth; then return the orange juice
and beaten yelks to the fire and heat slowly,
stirring until thick. Add cream, and pour into
cups. Serve cold. If you prefer, beat the

whites of the eggs very stiff with a cup of pulverized sugar, and heap this on top of each cup of custard.

### STRAWBERRY CREAM.

(No. 1.)  Stir together for about ten minutes the yelks of ten eggs, three-quarters of a pound of pulverized sugar and a wineglassful of red wine, then add a pint of strawberry juice (this is obtained by pressing about a quart of very ripe strawberries through a sieve or jelly press). Set this over the fire and stir until it boils. Then beat the whites of the eggs to a very stiff froth, and stir through the cream    Fill in glasses and serve cold.

### STRAWBERRY CREAM.

(No. 2.)  Whip half a pint of whipping cream, add half a pint of strawberry juice, sweeten to taste, and add the grated peel of a lemon.  Serve in glasses.

### RHUBARB SAUCE.

Strip the skin off the stalks with care, cut them into small pieces, put into a saucepan with very little water, and stew slowly until soft. Sweeten while hot, but do not boil the sugar with the fruit.  Eat cold.  Very wholesome.

### NEAPOLITAN BLANC-MANGE.

(No. 1.)  One quart of rich milk.  Heat it all except one cup, in which soak one ounce of gelatine.  When the milk is scalding hot, stir in the

soaked gelatine, add also five cents' worth of
almonds, which have been blanched and pounded
in a mortar.  Stir well and boil about five minutes, then add a small teacupful of sugar.  See
that the gelatine is thoroughly dissolved.  I forgot to mention that you should boil this blanc-
mange in a double farina kettle.  Pour this mixture into four cups.  Put a heaping teaspoonful
of grated chocolate into one cup, beat the yelk
of an egg light to color the other cup and a teaspoonful of cochineal (which you have previously
put in warm water over night) for the third cup,
which should be pink.  If you haven't any fruit
coloring, use currant jelly.  Wet a mold with cold
water and pour the white into the mold and set
on ice.  When cold and quite stiff, pour in the
pink, next the yellow and last the chocolate.
Wait long enough for each color to stiffen in the
mold.  Loosen when firm by dipping the mold
for a second in warm water or by placing it on a
platter and wrapping a hot cloth around it for a
minute, having previously loosened the edges.
This makes a very pretty dish to look at and
tastes delicious.

### NEAPOLITAN BLANC-MANGE.

(No. 2.)  Take one quart of milk, heat all of
it in a farina kettle, except one cup, in which soak
one ounce of gelatine.  When the milk is scalding hot stir in the gelatine, adding also a quarter

of a pound of almonds, which have been blanched
and pounded in a mortar.  Stir well, boil about
five minutes, and then add a small teacupful of
sugar.  See that the gelatine is thoroughly dissolved.  Pour this mixture into four cups.
Put a heaping tablespoonful of grated chocolate
into one cup, beat the yelk of an egg light to
color the other cup, a great teaspoonful of Dr.
Price's fruit coloring for the third cup, which is
intended to be pink.  If you haven't the fruit
coloring, color it with currant jelly.  Wet a
mold with cold water, pour the white into the
mold, throw in a spoonful of shaved citron or
candied cherries and set it on the ice.  When
cold and quite stiff, pour in the pink, next the
yellow, in which you may throw some fine raisins or figs chopped up fine, and last the chocolate.  Wait long enough for each color to stiffen
in the mold.  When firm loosen by dipping the
mold for a second in warm water, or by laying
the mold on a platter and wrapping a hot cloth
around it for a minute, having previously
loosened the edges.  This is a very pretty tea
dish.

### RED RASPBERRY CREAM.

Squeeze the juice out of two pounds of red
raspberries (do this through a coarse cloth).
Then stir the yelks of a dozen eggs, with three-
quarters of a pound of sugar; add to this a cupful of red wine or two teaspoonfuls of arrac and

the raspberry juice. Now stir this over the fire
in a farina kettle until it comes to a boil. Wash
out your cups with cold water, and pour in your
boiling cream. When cold, set it on ice until
ready to serve. Bake an angel food cake out of
the whites of the eggs, to be eaten with the
cream.

### COMPOTE OF PEARS.

It is not necessary to take a fine quality of
pears for this purpose. Pare the fruit, leaving
on the stems, and stew in sugar and a very little
water. Flavor with stick cinnamon and a few
cloves (take out the head of each clove) and
when soft place each pear carefully on a platter
until cold. Then arrange them nicely in a glass
bowl or flat glass dish, the stems all on the outer
rim. Pour over them the sauce, which should
be boiled thick like syrup. Eat cold.

### DANISH GRITS.

Take the juice of currants, sufficiently sweetened, and a pinch of salt. Let this boil and add
to it enough rice meal to render it moderately
thick and then boil again for ten minutes. It
should be eaten cold with cream. This is the
national dish of the Danes.

### COMPOTE OF PEACHES.

Pare the fruit, leaving it whole, and put on to
boil in a porcelain-lined kettle, with a little

sweetened water. Add a few cloves (remove the heads), also a stick of cinnamon bark. Boil the peaches until tender and then take up with a perforated skimmer and lay them in your fruit dish. Boil the syrup until thick, then pour over the peaches. You may add a wineglassful of wine in cooking the fruit. Eat cold. The commonest variety of peaches make a nice dessert, cooked in this way; clings, especially, which can not be used to cut up.

## RICE CUSTARD.

To one quart of milk, add half a cup of rice, which you have previously scalded with hot water. Boil in a farina kettle until quite soft. Beat the yelks of four eggs with four tablespoonfuls of white sugar, and add this just before taking it off the fire. Stir it thoroughly, but do not let it boil any more. Add salt to the rice while boiling, and flavor with vanilla, Beat the whites of the eggs with powdered sugar to a stiff froth, and after putting the custard into the pudding dish you wish to serve it in, spread with the beaten whites and let it brown slightly in the oven.

## PISTACHIO CREAM.

Take out the kernels of half a pound of pistach nuts and pound them in a mortar with a spoonful of brandy. Put them into a farina

kettle, with a pint of rich cream, and add
gradually the yelks of three well-beaten eggs.
Stir over the fire until it thickens, and then
pour carefully into a nice China or glass
bowl, stirring it as you do so and being very
careful not to crack the bowl. (Put a silver
spoon into the bowl before pouring in the
cream, as this will prevent it from cracking).
When cold, stick pieces of the nuts over the top
of the cream and serve.

### APPLE SOUFFLES.

Take about six large apples, pare and core
them and stew as for sauce. Beat them very
smooth with a potato masher (do this while hot).
Now rub a tablespoonful of butter with six tablespoonfuls of sugar to a cream and add the yelks
of seven eggs and beaten whites separately.
Add the beaten yelks to the creamed butter, then
beat all into the mashed apples. Flavor with
vanilla or rosewater, the latter being the finest.
Add last the stiff-beaten whites. Butter a deep
dish, pour in the mixture and bake in a moderately hot oven, the heat should be greater at the
top than at the bottom. Eat while hot.

### APPLE COMPOTE.

Take twelve apples (" Greenings," "Baldwins"
or " Bellflowers"), pare, quarter and core them
and lay them in cold water as soon as pared.
Then take the parings and seeds, put in a dish

with a pint of water and a pint of white wine, and boil for about fifteen minutes. Strain through a fine sieve, then put on to boil again, and add half a pound of white sugar and the peel of half a lemon. Then put in the apples and let them stew for fifteen minutes longer. When the apples are tender, take up each piece carefully with a silver spoon aad lay on a platter to cool. Let the syrup boil down to about half the quantity you had after removing the apples, and add to it the juice of half a lemon. Now lay your apples in a fruit dish, pyramid shape, pour the syrup over them, serve.

## BAKED APPLES.

Take nice, large, juicy apples, wash and core them well, fill each place that you have cored with brown sugar, cinnamon and raisins, and put a clove in each apple. Lay them in a deep dish, pour a teacupful of water in the dish, and put a little sugar on top of each apple. When well done the apples will be broken. Then remove them carefully to the dish they are to be served in and pour the syrup over them. To be eaten cold. If you wish them extra nice, glaze them with the beaten whites of three eggs and half a cupful of pulverized sugar and serve with whipped cream. I forgot to mention that after the apples are glazed, you must return them to the oven for a few minutes.

## APPLE SAUCE.

Pare, quarter and core nice tart apples and lay them in cold water until all are pared. Put on to boil with very little water, cover closely and boil very quickly. When soft mash with a potato masher, pass through a hair sieve and sweeten to taste. They should boil quickly, so as to remain white, and do not add sugar until strained.

## JELLIED APPLES.

Soak half a box of gelatine in half a cup of water for about one hour, or longer if convenient. Take two cups of sugar, one pint of water and half a cup of wine, the juice and grated peel of one lemon, and boil about five minutes. Pare, core and slice about eight nice, large, sweet apples, boil until tender in the wine and water, and then take out the apples carefully. Lay on a platter until the rest of the apples are boiled, for you must not crowd them all in at one time. When the last of the fruit has been taken up, remove from the fire and put the gelatine into it. Stir until the gelatine is dissolved. Then place the stewpan in a basin of cold ice-water and stir until cold. Put in the apples and mix gently. Turn into a mold which has been previously wet with cold water and set in a cold place to harden. Turn on a platter and serve with whipped cream and sugar.

## PRUNES.

Wash them two or three times in warm water; put on to boil in cold water and let them boil slowly and long, and tightly covered. If you have enough room in the oven they are far superior cooked in it. Sweeten to taste, season with a few slices of lemon and cinnamon (the juice of an orange flavors them richly) and thicken with a teaspoonful of cornstarch (wet the cornstarch with cold water before adding). As the water boils down, add a cupful of hot water (you may have to add water two or three times). They should boil at least an hour and a half.

## COMPOTE OF RASPBERRIES.

Make a syrup of half a pound of sugar and half a cup of water, put in to it one quart of berries which have been carefully picked and washed. Boil up once. Serve cold.

## RED RASPBERRY OR CURRANT FLOAT.

Take a tumblerful of red raspberry or currant juice, and mix with it a gill of sugar. Beat the whites of four eggs to a very stiff froth, and add gradually a gill of powdered sugar. Press the raspberries through a strainer, to avoid seeds, and by degrees beat the juice with the sugar and egg until so stiff that it stands in peaks. Chill it thoroughly on ice and serve in a glass dish, half filled with cold cream. Heap on the mix-

ture by the spoonful, in peaks, like floating
island. The currant juice requires a pint of
sugar. Eight large tablespoonfuls are equal to
one gill.

### PEACH COMPOTE.

Pare the fruit, leave it whole and put on to
boil in a porcelain-lined kettle, with sweetened
water. Add a few cloves (remove the heads)
also a stick of cinnamon bark. Boil the peaches
until tender, then take up with a perforated
skimmer and lay them in your fruit dish. Boil
the syrup until thick, then pour over the peaches.
You may add a wineglassful of wine in cooking
the fruit. Eat cold with sweet cream. Common cheap peaches make a very nice dessert,
cooked in the above manner, clings especially,
which can not be used to cut up.

### FLOATING ISLAND.

Beat light the yelks of six eggs with half a
cup of sugar. Boil a quart of milk, beat up the
whites of six eggs very stiff, and put them into
the boiling milk, a spoonful at a time. Take
out the boiled whites and lay them on a platter,
now pour the hot milk gradually on the beaten
yelks, when thoroughly mixed return to the fire
to boil. When it begins to thicken, remove.
When cool flavor with vanilla or bitter almond.
Pour into a deep glass dish; put the whites on
top, and garnish with jelly or candied fruit.
Eat cold.

## PINEAPPLE CREAM.

Line a deep fruit dish with lady fingers or
macaroons; then fill up the dish with a grated
pineapple and sweeten to taste (canned pineapple is equal to fresh for this purpose). Set
this on ice, and whip enough sweet cream to
cover the dish thickly; ornament with candied
fruits.

## ESCALOPED PEACHES.

Pare a number of peaches and put them whole
into a baking tin, together with layers of bread
crumbs and sugar, and add a few cloves. Bake
until the top is brown. Serve with hot butter
sauce or cream.

## JELLIED APPLES.

Soak half a box of gelatine in half a cup of
water for two hours. Use two quarts of nice,
tart apples, peeled, quartered and cored. Boil
two cupfuls of sugar with the juice of one lemon
and a pint of water. Boil hard for ten minutes
and then put in as many apples as may be
cooked without crowding. Cook gently until so
tender that they may be pierced with a broom-
straw. Then take up with a skimmer and spread
on a platter. Put in more apples, until all are
cooked. Then remove the pan from the fire and
stir the gelatine into it, until dissolved, stir until nearly cold, to do this quickly set the pan in
snow or ice-water. Then put in the apples, and

mix gently, and then put into a mold and set on
ice to harden. Serve with sugar and whipped
cream.

### GOOSEBERRY CREAM.

Boil a quart or more of ripe gooseberries with
a little wine, cinnamon and the peel of one lemon,
and then press through a hair sieve. Beat the
yolks of six eggs light with three-quarters of a
pound of pulverized sugar and an additional
wineglassful of wine and a pint of gooseberry
juice. Stir all of this over the fire in a farina
kettle until it boils. Then stir in quickly the
stiff-beaten whites of the eggs. Fill in glasses
and set on ice until ready to serve.

### FIG SAUCE.

Stew figs slowy for two hours, until soft;
sweeten with loaf sugar, about two tablespoonfuls to a pound of fruit; add a glass of port or
other wine and a little lemon juice. Serve when
cold.

### COMPOTE OF PINEAPPLE.

Cut off the rind of a pine core and trim out
all the eyes. Cut into desired slices, but not
too thin. Set on to boil with half a pound of
sugar, and the juice of one or two tart oranges.
When the pineapple is tender and clear, put
into a compote dish and boil the syrup until
clear. Pour over all and cool. The addition of
a wineglassful of brandy improves this compote
very much. *Chacun a son gout.*

### APPLE SAUCE VICTORIA.

Pare, quarter and core the apples. Set on to boil in cold water, and boil them over a very brisk fire; when they are soft mash with a potato masher and pass the mashed apples through a sieve. Sweeten to taste and flavor with a teaspoonful of vanilla. This way of seasoning apples is highly recommended, especially if they are tasteless.

### CHARLOTTE RUSSE. .

(No. 1.) Whip one pint of rich cream to a stiff froth, and drain on a fine wire sieve. To one small teacupful of milk add three eggs, beaten very light; sweeten and flavor with vanilla. Boil the milk set over a kettle of hot water with the beaten eggs until it forms a thick custard. Soak half an ounce of Cox's gelatine in a very little milk, by warming it over hot water. When the custard is quite cold, beat in gently the strained gelatine and then the whipped cream. Line the bottom of a mold with buttered paper, the sides with lady fingers or macaroons, fastened together with the white of an egg. Fill with the cream and set it in a cool place. To turn out, dip the mold for a second in hot water.

### CHARLOTTE RUSSE.

(No. 2.) To one pint of rich, sweet cream use one large tablespoonful of sherry, the white of one egg, beaten to a stiff froth, one teaspoonful of pulverized sugar and a quarter of a box of gelatine dissolved in one quarter of a cupful of sweet milk; flavor with vanilla; beat the cream until thick, then add the wine, then the egg, then the sugar, and last the vanilla and strained gelatine.   Fill in mold as in recept No. 1.

# CAKE.

| | Page. |
|---|---|
| Angel Food, | 279 |
| Chocolate, | 280 |
| Cup, | 281 |
| Coffee Fruit, | 282 |
| Cheap Black, | 284 |
| Date, | 282 |
| English Coffee Cake, | 289 |
| Eggless Gingerbread, | 291 |
| Fruit, | 288, 289 |
| General Hints on Baking, | 274 |
| Garfield, | 281 |
| Gold, | 283 |
| Gingerbread, | 291 |
| Huckleberry, | 285 |
| Hickorynut, | 286 |
| Loaf Cocoanut, | 286 |
| Lemon, | 287 |
| Lady, | 287 |
| Marble, | 287 |
| One Egg, | 284 |
| Pound Plum, | 284 |
| Pound, | 285 |
| Quickly-made Sponge, | 281 |
| Rules, | 275 |
| Sunshine, | 278 |
| Sponge, | 282 |
| Silver, | 283 |
| Seed, | 285 |
| Spice, | 287 |
| Time-Table for Baking, | 276 |
| Table of Weights and Measures, | 277 |
| Walnut Torte, | 290 |
| Watermelon, | 291 |
| Wine or Mirror, | 299 |

# CAKE

## GENERAL HINTS ON BAKING CAKE.

IN making cake use none but the best materials; in fact, everything you buy to cook with ought to be of the best. We ought to be just as particular about what kind of food we eat as we are about what kind of medicine we swallow. Remember, none but the best. And then the mixing and the baking of cake are both very important elements in the final result. What is worth doing at all is worth doing well, so never hurry, but take your time in baking and you will be well rewarded. And pray don't get discouraged if your first attempt is a failure, but try and try again, and never be ashamed to ask your neighbor, or any friend, to show you how to mix a cake, as this is the most important part, and upon this mainly depends success. Two persons may each take exactly the same materials, and one produce a light, delicate cake, while the other will produce an ugly, heavy-looking loaf, neither nice to look at nor good to eat. The first has properly mixed the ingredients and attended carefully to the temperature of the oven, while the second has put the ingredients together in a careless

(274)

manner. Now, if my directions are carefully followed every recipe for cake I have given you will turn out to be successful. Each one has been tested many times. And now I wil lay down some rules for you, which I hope you will remember.

RULES.

Gather together all materials and utensils that are needed. Grease the tins carefully, but not too much, and line with buttered paper. For cakes that are large and rich use spring forms, wich can be bought or made to order. Sift flour twice at least and measure after sifting. Measure or weigh the sugar, butter, milk and flour. Break the eggs, each separately, into a saucer or cup, always separating the yelks from the whites. Rub the butter to a cream with the sugar, which should be done with a wooden spoon, in a deep bowl, sifting the sugar into the butter is the easiest way. In winter set the bowl over hot water for a few minutes, as the butter will then cream more easily. Always add the yelks one at a time to creamed butter and sugar. Mix the baking powder in the last cup of sifted flour and add flour and milk alternately, until both are stirred thoroughly into the mixture. Beat the whites of the eggs to a stiff froth, so stiff that you can turn the dish upside down without spilling the eggs. Always add beaten whites of eggs last to the dough and then set in the oven immediately.

Keep your box of baking powder covered so that the powder will not lose is strength. Use a common kitchen cup for measuring and always use the same size cup for measuring milk, sugar, butter and flour. Be sure that the oven is right before the cakes are set in, for you must never shake the stove or put in coal after your cake is in, and if possible have no water on the stove. Never look after your cake until it has been in the oven over ten minutes. All cake requires a moderate oven, for if put into a hot oven it will crust over before it is perfectly risen, and then as it rises the dough will force its way through the crust, making an ugly shaped loaf. When you think your cake is baked, open the oven door carefully so as not to jar the cake; take a straw from the broom and run it through the thickest part of the cake, and if the straw comes out perfectly clean and dry your cake is done, otherwise it is not done. When done take it out and set it where no draught of air will strike it, and in ten minutes turn it out on a flat plate or board. Don't put it in the cake-box until perfectly cold. If you wish to frost your cake do so while hot.

TIME-TABLE FOR BAKING CAKES.

Sponge cake, three-quarters of an hour.

Pound cake, one hour.

Fruit cake, three and four hours, depending upon size.

Cookies, from ten to fifteen minutes  Watch carefully.

Cup cakes, a full half hour.

### TABLE OF WEIGHTS AND MEASURES.

An ordinary cup holds half a pint.

One quart of sifted flour is one pound

Two cups of butter are one pound.

Ten eggs are equal to one pound.

A wineglassful is half a gill.

Eight even tablespoonfuls are a gill.

Use two teaspoonfuls of baking powder to one quart of flour.

Let me, my dear readers, try to describe to you a "spring form." It is almost indispensable in baking tart cakes and large fruit pies. It is a high, round cake form, the rim of which is held in place by a key made of wire, the rim fitting in the flat bottom. When the cake is baked you simply draw out the key and the rim comes off, allowing all the steam to escape, which prevents the cake from falling, which is the great danger in baking light biscuit tarts, such as almond, chocolate, bread, sponge and others too numerous to mention. After removing the rim of the spring form, it is best to leave it on the plate it was baked on, unless you wish to frost it, when you may turn the cake upside down upon a flat board and loosen the bottom plate upon which it was baked by running a knife under it. If

baked on paper remove it carefully. I don't see
how any one manages to get along without a
spring form. I could not. I use them for layer
cakes and rich pies also, and when once you have
them they last a lifetime. In ordering spring
forms, I would advise you to have two bottoms
made for each one, or have them made double
in thickness, for cakes burn very easily in them
if too thin.

### SUNSHINE CAKE.

This delicious cake is simply perfect, if you
follow my directions carefully, and is made almost like "angel food," and is particularly nice
for invalids. Take one cupful of pulverized sugar, sifted five or six times, and one cupful of
flour, sifted about seven times. Sift one teaspoonful of baking powder in last, sifting and
measuring again and using an even cupful. Beat
up on a platter the whites of eleven eggs to a
stiff froth, stir the yelks of six eggs and the sugar
about a quarter of an hour, grate the peel of one
orange in this, adding the juice also. Add part
of the flour and part of the beaten whites, and
so on until all has been used up. Set in a very
moderately hot oven and bake from fifty to sixty
minutes; then hold the cake to your ear, if you
can not hear it "siz," it is done. Or try it with
a clean, dry broom-straw, by sticking it into the
cake, and if it comes out clean and dry it is a
sure sign that it has baked enough. Bake this

cake in an angel food pan, and do not grease
the form or pan. Set a dish of water in the
oven while baking, and do not open the oven
more than is necessary. If it browns too quickly
cover the cake with thick paper. Ice the cake
with boiled icing, flavored with orange juice. If
you desire to have the icing yellow, grate the peel
of the orange into the juice and press it through
a thin piece of muslin. You may use yellow
confectioner's sugar instead.

### ANGEL FOOD.

Take whites of eleven eggs, one tumbler and a
half of pulverized sugar, one tumbler of sifted
flour, one teaspoonful of extract of vanilla and
one teaspoonful of cream tartar. Sift the flour
four times, then add cream tartar and sift again,
and then measure so as to have exactly one tumblerful after the last sifting. Sift the sugar and
measure again in the same way. Beat the eggs
to a stiff froth, add the sugar lightly, then the
flour, mixing very gently and then the vanilla.
Do not stop beating until you have put all into
the pan. Bake in a very moderate oven ; try with
a broom-straw, and if the cake does not stick to
the straw it is done. Turn the pans upside down
and leave them until the cake is cool. When cool,
loosen the sides with a knife and take out. Use
a pan that has never been greased before and the
cake-pan solely for this cake. The tumbler for
measuring must hold two and three-fourth gills.

Beat the eggs on a large platter, and mix the batter on the same platter. Have the pan made with short legs, to raise it a little from the bottom of the oven. You can buy an angel cakepan in any first-class hardware store. Be sure that you follow these directions minutely, and I assure you of success. You must beat on a platter, a deep dish will not do. Remember this.

### CHOCOLATE CAKE.

Take half a pound of the best vanilla chocolate, grated, half a pound of grated almonds, half a pound of pulverized sugar, thirteen eggs and a pinch of pulverized ammonia, or one teaspoonful of baking powder. Stir the yelks of eleven eggs and the sifted sugar about a quarter of an hour, add the whole of the two remaining eggs and then the grated almonds. Beat five minutes longer and add the grated chocolate and stir ten minutes more. Mix the ammonia or baking powder in with the stiff-beaten whites of the eggs, and stir in gently with the cake mixture. Bake a full hour in a moderately hot oven. Frost the cake with a pink frosting, you may use pink confectioner's sugar, or color with Dr. Price's fruit coloring. If you can not get either, use cochineal, which you can get at any druggist's. Soak a little of it in water over night, say a teaspoonful in two tablespoonfuls of water; strain, add a cupful of sugar and boil until the consistency of very thick syrup; beat the white of one egg to a very stiff froth and add the boiling syrup, stirring constantly until cold, then spread over the cake. Set in a warm place until dry.

### GARFIELD CAKE.

Take one cup of butter, two cups of pulverized sugar, rubbed to a cream, one cupful of sweet milk, six eggs (yelks added one at a time, whites whipped in last), three cups of flour (measure after sifting), two teaspoonfuls of baking powder, one cup of chopped walnuts and hickorynuts mixed, one cupful of seeded and chopped raisins and thin slices of citron. Sift the flour three times, and in last sifting add baking powder. Whip the whites very stiff. This makes quite a large cake. Ice with boiled icing.

### CUP CAKE.

Cream one cup of butter with two cups of sugar and add gradually the yelks of four eggs, one at a time. Sift three cups of flour, measure again after sifting, and add a teaspoonful of baking powder in last sifting. Add alternately the sifted flour and a cup of sweet milk. Add last the stiff-beaten whites of the eggs. Flavor to taste. Bake in a loaf or in jelly-tins.

### QUICKLY-MADE SPONGE CAKE.

Take four eggs and one cup of pulverized sugar and beat them together until you can not possibly beat any longer, say half an hour at least. Take one scant cupful of flour, sifted many times,

stir in gradually and lightly. Add a pinch of
salt and the grated peel of a lemon or any other
flavoring. Never fails.

### DATE CAKE.

Take twelve eggs and one pound of pulverized
sugar. Beat yelks and whites separately. Then
add one-half pound of nice dates, cut very fine,
one teaspoonful and a half of allspice, the same
quantity of cinnamon, two cakes of chocolate,
grated fine, and seven soda crackers rolled to a
fine powder and flavor with vanilla. Bake in a
spring form very slowly. Cover with chocolate
icing.

### COFFEE FRUIT CAKE.

Take one cup of butter, two cups of sugar, four
eggs, one-half cup milk, one-half cup cold coffee,
two teaspoonfuls cream tartar, one teaspoonful
of soda, one-quarter of a pound of currants, one-
quarter of a pound of citron and one pound of
raisins. Chop all the fruit together and take
all kinds of spices. Rub butter and sugar to a
cream, dissolve soda in milk and sift cream tartar in flour. Take three cups of flour, measure
after sifting and add more if necessary.

### SPONGE CAKE.

Beat the yelks of twelve eggs very light, add
one pound of powdered sugar and beat again
until quite thick. Grate in the peel of a lemon,
adding the juice also, and add three small cups
of sifted flour (sift three times and measure after

sifting). Stir the flour in lightly. Beat the whites to a stiff froth, and add a pinch of salt before you begin to beat. Beat until the eggs are so stiff that you can turn the bowl upside down with safety. Then add and bake in a moderately hot oven, covering with paper when you first put it in the oven. This makes a large cake, and a very fine one if properly made. Butter your cake form and line with buttered paper; a spring form is the best. A jelly roll may be made of this by baking in a large pan. Have the jelly at hand and spread as soon as taken from the oven, and roll while hot.

### SILVER CAKE.

Take one pound of pulverized sugar, one-half pound of best butter, rubbed to a cream, three-quarters of a cupful of sweet milk, whites of ten eggs, whipped very stiff, three quarters of a pound of flour, with a teaspoonful of baking powder sifted in with the flour, which ought to be sifted twice at least. Flavor with a teaspoonful of essence of bitter almonds, and flavor the icing of silver cake with rosewater. Make a gold cake on the same day, so as to use up the yelks of the eggs.

### GOLD CAKE.

Take one pound of powdered sugar, half a pound of butter rubbed to a cream, yelks of eight or ten eggs and stir until very light. Then add one pound of flour with a teaspoonful of

baking powder sifted in well (sift the flour two
or three times). Grate in the peel of a lemon
or an orange, add the juice also, and add a cup
of sweet cream or milk.

## MARBLE CAKE.

Take one cup of butter, two cups of pulverized
sugar, three cups of flour, four eggs, one cup of
sweet milk and two teaspoonfuls of baking powder. When the cake is mixed, take out about a
soupplateful of the batter, and stir into this
about two heaping tablespoonfuls of grated
chocolate (which you must grate before you
begin to mix the cake). Fill your cake mold
about two inches deep with yellow batter and
then drop in the brown in three or four places.
Do this a spoonful at a time, and then pour in
more yellow batter, and so on until all is used up.

## CHEAP BLACK CAKE.

Take one cup brown sugar, one cup butter, one
cup cold coffee, one scant cup of molasses, one
cup raisins, one cup currants, one cup citron,
one teaspoonful allspice, one of cloves, cinnamon, two eggs, four cups flour and two teaspoonfuls of baking powder.

## POUND PLUM CAKE.

Take one pound of butter and rub it to a cream,
add one pound of sifted powdered sugar, nine
eggs, yolks added to the creamed butter and
sugar, a wineglassful of brandy, peel of a lemon,

and add by degrees a pound and a quarter of flour one pound of seeded raisins and currants, which, have been thoroughly cleaned, half a pound of citron, sliced very thin and a little orange and lemon peel shaved fine. The best plan is to soak the fruit in the brandy on the previous day. Bake very slowly.

### SEED CAKE.

Rub one pound of butter and a pound of sifted powdered sugar to a cream and add the yelks of eight eggs, one at a time, one ounce of carroway seed, one nutmeg grated, and a teaspoonful of cinnamon. Stir in one pound and a quarter of sifted flour and the stiff-beaten whites of eggs alternately. Bake slowly.

### POUND CAKE.

Rub one pound of butter and one pound of powdered sugar to a cream and add the grated peel of a lemon, a glass of brandy and the yelks of nine eggs, added one at a time, and last one pound and a quarter of sifted flour and the beaten whites of the eggs. Bake slowly,

### HUCKLEBERRY CAKE.

Stir to a cream one cup of butter and two cups of powdered sugar and add gradually the yelks of four eggs. Sift into this three cups of flour, adding two teaspoonfuls of baking powder in the last sifting and add a cup of sweet milk alternately with the flour to the creamed butter, sugar and yelks. Spice with a teaspoonful of cinnamon and add the stiff-beaten whites of the eggs. Last, stir in two cups of huckleberries which have been carefully picked over and well dredged with flour. Be careful in stirring in the huckleberries that you do not bruise them. You will find a wooden spoon the best for this purpose, the edges not being so sharp. Bake in a moderately hot oven; try with a straw, if it comes out clean, your cake is baked. This will keep fresh for a long while.

### HICKORYNUT CAKE.

Rub to a cream one cup of butter and two cups of sugar and add gradually the yelks of four eggs, one at a time, also one cup of cold water or milk and three cups of flour. Put two teaspoonfuls of baking powder in the last cup of sifted flour, and sift again before adding to the cake-batter. Have the whites beaten very stiff. Before adding stir in two cups of the kernels of hickorynuts, carefully picked out and add last of all.

### LOAF COCOANUT CAKE.

Rub one cup of butter and two cups of sugar to a cream. Add one cup of milk, whites of four eggs, three cups of flour (measure after sifting) and two teaspoonfuls of baking powder added in last sifting. Add a grated cocoanut and last the stiff-beaten whites. Bake in a loaf. Line tin with buttered paper.

### SPICE CAKE.

Cream two cups of sugar and one-half cup of butter, the usual way. Add two eggs, one cup of sour milk, one cup of chopped raisins, three cups of flour, two teaspoonfuls of baking powder, one teaspoonful of cinnamon, half a teaspoonful of cloves and nutmeg, and a wineglassful of port wine.

### ONE-EGG CAKE.

Rub half a cup of butter and one cup of sugar to a cream, add half a cup of sweet milk, one egg, two cups of flour, sifted with two teaspoonfuls of baking powder, the grated rind of a lemon, and a few drops of the juice.

### LADY CAKE.

Wash the salt out of one-half pound of butter, and rub it to a cream with one pound of powdered sugar. Have ready one pound of flour, sifted fully five times with two heaping teaspoonfuls of baking powder, and add the stiff-beaten whites of fifteen eggs, alternately, with the flour. Flavor with bitter almonds and ice with boiled icing.

### LEMON CAKE.

Rub to a cream one cup of butter with three cups of pulverized sugar and add gradually the yelks of five eggs, one at a time, and one cup of sweet milk. Sift four cups of flour with two teaspoonfuls of baking powder, add alternately with

the milk and the stiff-beaten whites of five eggs.
Add the grated peel of one lemon and the juice
of two. This is a delicious cake.

### FRUIT CAKE.

(No. 1.) Take one pound of butter and one
pound of sugar rubbed to a cream, yelks of twelve
eggs, one tablespoonful of cinnamon, one teaspoonful of allspice, half teaspoonful of mace,
half teaspoonful of cloves, one-fourth of a pound
of almonds (pounded), two ponds of raisins
(seeded and chopped), three pounds of currants
(carefully cleaned), one pound of citron (shredded very fine), and one-quarter of a pound of
orange peel (chopped very fine). Soak all this
prepared fruit in one pint of brandy over night.
Add all to the dough and put in the stiff-beaten
whites last. Bake in a very slow oven for several hours, and line your cake-pans with buttered paper. When cold wrap in cloths dipped
in brandy and put in earthen jars. If you wet
these cloths every month you may keep this
cake moist for years.

### FRUIT CAKE

(No. 2.) Wash one pound of butter, then work
in two or three tablespoonfuls of rosewater, one
pound of sugar, cream butter and sugar until
it will stand, one pound of citron, orange and
lemon peel in equal proportions, candied of
course, three pounds of currants, one pound of
sultana raisins, three-quarters of a pound of

grated almonds, the grated peel of two oranges, a gill of sherry, one of brandy, yelks of twelve eggs and whites of six, one pound of flour (very dry warmed and sifted), a teaspoonful of cinnamon, grated nutmeg and cloves. If possible, prepare the fruit the day previous, and pour over it the brandy and sherry. When the cake is ready to bake, line a large, round pan or spring form with three thicknesses of buttered paper at the bottom, two around the sides and pour the batter into it. This cake will be quite large if baked in one, and should bake from four to five hours in a very moderate oven. The oven should be quite cool at first, and never get very hot. For the first two hours cover with thick cardboard, the object being to give long baking without burning. When cold wrap in cloth dampened with brandy, and put in an earthen jar, covered.

### ENGLISH COFFEE CAKE.

One cup of butter rubbed to a cream, with two cups of the very darkest brown sugar; add four eggs, one at a time, stirring each one well; then add a cupful of black molasses and one cup of hot, strong coffee in which you have previously dissolved one even teaspoonful of soda. (Strain before adding to the batter.) Sift four and one-half cups of flour, twice, adding two teaspoonfuls of cream tartar in last, half a cupful of flour, sifting again before adding. Add the following spices: nutmeg, mace, allspice and

cloves, half a teaspoonful of each, one large cupful of raisins, seeded, and half a cupful of finely-
cut or chopped citron, dredge the raisins with
flour, using some of which you have already
sifted, not using more than four and a half cups
in all. Butter your cake tins and seed your
fruit before beginning to make the cake; whole
spices freshly pounded in a mortar are preferable to ground spices. This quantity makes
one good-sized cake and twelve gems, which if
iced prettily makes quite a display.

### WALNUT CAKE. (TORTE.)

Separate the yelks and whites of nine eggs,
being very careful not to get a particle of the
yelks into the whites. Sift half a pound of pulverized sugar into the yelks and beat until the
consistency of batter. Add a pinch of salt to
the whites and beat until very stiff. Have ready
a pound of walnuts, shelled carefully (weigh
before shelling), reserve some of the whole ones
for decorating the top of cake. Pound the rest
in a mortar or with a rolling pin, and add to the
beaten yelks, add also two heaping tablespoonfuls of grated stale sponge cake or lady fingers,
last add the stiff-beaten whites. Bake in a moderate oven three quarters of an hour in a spring
form, when done remove the key and allow it to
cool off a little before icing.

## GINGERBREAD.

To one cup of molasses add one cup of milk, sour or sweet, dissolve one teaspoonful of soda in the milk, one tablespoonful of butter, one or two eggs, one teaspoonful of ginger and one of ground cinnamon, add enough sifted flour to make a light batter. Bake in a shallow pan, you may strew a few blanched almonds on top if you desire to have it extra nice.

### EGGLESS GINGERBREAD.

Mix one cup of molasses, one cup of brown sugar, one tablespoonful of butter, and add the following spices: one and one-half teaspoonfuls of ginger, the same of cinnamon. Stir this mixture well for about ten minutes, then add gradually one cup of milk and five cups of flour into which you have previously sifted two teaspoonfuls of baking powder. Bake in a broad, shallow pan and eat warm.

### WATERMELON CAKE.

Rub half a cup of butter to a cream with one and one-half cups of pulverized sugar, add gradually one-half cup of milk, with three cups of sifted flour, add one cup at a time, and add two teaspoonfuls of baking powder in last cup and sift again before adding. Add the beaten whites of seven eggs. Reserve one cupful of this white dough for the top and color the rest with three teaspoonfuls of fruit coloring and flavor with one teaspoonful of strawberry flavoring; now add one cupful of sultanas, which have been carefully picked, and add to the pink dough. Fill dough in a well greased cake mold and spread the reserved cupful of white dough on top of cake; last cover with finely-shaved citron. Bake one hour in a moderate oven.

Make a gold cake of the yelks, using the same amount of butter, milk, flour, etc. Flavor with lemon.

### WINE OR MIRROR CAKE.

Make a rich cake of any kind and bake it in a deep jelly cake mold; and when cold, scoop out enough of the cake to leave a good deep rim, say about an inch in depth all through. Then fill in the cavity with white wine jelly, which you have prepared before you began to bake your cake. This cake may be served as a pudding with the addition of whipped cream. Either spread the cream on top or serve separately—the latter being preferable.

# LAYER AND TART CAKES.

| | Page. |
|---|---|
| Apple Jelly Cake, | 803 |
| Almond Cake, or Mandel Torte, | 307 |
| Burnt Almond Cake, | 295 |
| Brod Torte, | 307, 308, 809 |
| Biscuit Tart Cake, | 309 |
| Cream Cake, | 300 |
| Cocoanut Cake, | 301, 302 |
| Chocolate Cake, | 302 |
| Caramel Cake, | 303, 304 |
| Chocolate Cream Cake, | 305 |
| Chocolate Tart, | 809 |
| Chocolate (Iced) Layer Cake, | 313 |
| Date Tart Cake, | 312 |
| Filbert Tart Cake, | 810 |
| Filled Filbert Cake, | 810 |
| Ice-Cream Cake, | 800 |
| Jelly Roll or Layer, | 295 |
| Layer Pound Cake, | 297 |
| Love Cake, | 808 |
| Lemon Jelly for Layer Cake, | 808 |
| Marbled Biscuit Tart, | 811 |
| Mohntorte, | 311, 312 |
| Orange Cake, | 299 |
| Pink Cream Cake, | 294 |
| Peach Short Cake, | 305 |
| Pineapple Layer Cake, | 314 |
| Railroad Cake, | 299 |
| Russian Punch Tart, | 306 |
| Ribbon Tart Cake, | 310 |
| Simple Cake, | 299 |
| Strawberry Cake, | 306 |
| Spiced Cream Layer Cake, | 313 |
| Tutti-Frutti Cake, | 302 |
| White Cream Cake, | 294 |
| White Mountain Cake, | 296 |
| Walnut Cake, | 297, 298 |
| Walnut Layer, | 812 |
| Wine Cake, | 314 |

# LAYER AND TART CAKES.

## WHITE CREAM CAKE.

TAKE the whites of ten eggs, one goblet of flour, one goblet and a half of pulverized sugar, and one teaspoonful of cream tartar. Sift the flour five times, then sift the sugar and flour together and beat the whites on a platter to a very stiff froth. Stir into them when stiff the sugar and flour, and last the cream tartar and bake immediately in three or four jelly cake tins. Make the following filling: Take one pint of very cold, sweet cream (pour the cream in a bowl and set it inside another bowl containing ice or snow), add to it two tablespoonfuls of powdered sugar and a dessertspoonful of vanilla. Whip to a stiff froth, and when the cakes are cold spread it between the layers, also on top of cake. This is a delicious cake and must be used the same day it is baked.

## PINK CREAM CAKE.

Take three eggs and one cup of pulverized sugar. Beat the eggs and sugar to the consistency of batter and then add half a cup of cold water, two cups of flour and two teaspoonfuls of baking

powder, sifted twice. Color with fruit coloing.
Bake in three layers and fill with whipped cream,
sweetend to taste and flavored. Must be eaten
the same day. Keep in ice-chest. Use about a
teaspoonful of Dr. Price's fruit coloring, and
if not sufficiently colored, add more. Color
the dough only.

### JELLY ROLL OR LAYER.

Take eight eggs, two cups of sugar and beat for
half an hour. Then add two cups of flour and
one-half teaspoonful of baking powder, sifted
in flour. Add also two tablespoonfuls of water.
Bake in large tin, spread with jelly while hot,
and roll or bake in jelly-tins and spread. Cover
with boiled icing.

### BURNT ALMOND CAKE.

Beat up four eggs with one cup of sifted powdered sugar. Beat until it looks like a heavy
batter. (Use elbow-grease and enough of it.)
When you think you can not possibly beat any
longer stir one cup of sifted flour with half a teaspoonful of baking powder. Stir it into batter
gradually and lightly, adding three tablespoonfuls of water. Bake in jelly tins. Filling: Scald
one-quarter of a pound of almonds (by pouring
boiling water over them), remove skins, put them
on a pieplate and set them in the oven to brown
slightly. Meanwhile, melt three tablespoonfuls
of white sugar, without adding water, in a farina

kettle, stirring it all the while. Stir up the
almonds in this, then remove them from the fire
and lay on a platter separately to cool. Make
an icing of the whites of three eggs, beaten very
stiff, with one pound of pulverized sugar, and
flavor with rosewater. Spread this upon layers
and cover each layer with almonds. When finished frost the whole cake, decorating with
almonds.

### WHITE MOUNTAIN CAKE.

Rub one cup of butter and three small cups of
pulverized sugar to a cream and add gradually
one scant cup of milk and one pound of sifted
flour (add two teaspoonfuls of baking powder in
last sifting). Whip the whites of eight eggs to a
very stiff froth and stir them lightly into the
batter and flavor with bitter almonds. Bake in
jelly tins. Use the following filling: To the
beaten whites of three eggs allow one pound of
pulverized sugar and beat stiff as for icing. Take
out enough to cover the top of the cake and set
aside. Grate a fresh cocoanut, reserving part of
it for the top of the cake. Add the milk of the
cocoanut to that which you intend to spread
between cake. Now spread the icing on each
layer and sprinkle the cocoanut over each layer
until the mountain is made. Add a little more
sugar to the icing for top layer, also a few drops
of lemon juice, and mix two or three tablespoonfuls of sugar with the reserved cocoanut for top

layer of all. Remember, spread the icing first,
then strew the cocoanut. A delicious cake.

## LAYER POUND CAKE.

Beat the yelks of twelve eggs with a pound
of sugar; grate the peel of two lemons and add
the juice of one; add the beaten whites of eight
eggs and half a pound of sifted flour. Bake in
jelly-tins. To the whites of four eggs add a pound
and a half of confectioner's sugar, beat stiff, as
for icing, and reserve enough of it for the top of
the cake. Add to the rest the grated peel of half
a large orange and all of its juice. When the
cake is cool spread this between the layers. Beat
into the icing reserved for the top a little lemon
juice, and, if needed, add more sugar. This should
be thicker than that spread between the cake.
Decorate with slices of orange, which have been
dipped in boiled sugar and dried.

## WALNUT CAKE.

(No. 1.) Grate eight ounces of walnuts and
eight ounces of blanched almonds. Beat light
the yelks of twelve eggs and three-quarters of a
pound of sugar. Add the grated nuts and one-
quarter of a pound of sifted flour. Beat the whites
to a stiff froth and add a pinch of pulverized ammonia. Bake in layers and fill with sweetend
whipped cream, into which you may put eight
ounces of pounded walnuts and eight ounces of
pounded almonds.

### WALNUT CAKE.

(No. 2.) Make a rich cup cake dough and bake in layers. Filling: To the beaten whites of four eggs allow one pound of pulverized sugar. Beat stiff as for icing, take out enough to cover the top of the cake, and set aside. Spread the icing between each layer and lay walnuts on top as close as you wish to have them. When done ice the top of the cake and ornament with walnuts. If you prefer you may pound the walnuts first for the layers, but leave them whole for the top of the cake.

### LOVE CAKE.

Beat on a platter the whites of ten eggs to a stiff froth. Stir into them one and one-half goblet of sifted pulverized sugar and add gradually one goblet of flour, sifted six times, adding a teaspoonful of cream tartar in last sifting. Bake immediately in three large jelly cake tins. Use only two of these, and reserve the other for a strawberry or any other kind of fruit cake. For filling take one pint of very rich cream, add to it two tablespoonfuls of pulverized sugar and a teaspoonful of vanilla. Whip to a stiff froth and color pink with Dr. Price's fruit coloring. When the cakes are cold spread between the layers and pile also on top of the cake. Before you begin to whip the cream see that it is very cold. It should be set in a bowl of ice while whipping, especially in the summer.

### SIMPLE CAKE.

Take butter the size of an egg, stirred to a cream with one cup of sugar. Add gradually the yelks of three eggs and one cup of flour, in which you have sifted a teaspoonful of baking powder. Add a tablespoonful of water and the stiff-beaten whites of the eggs. Bake in jelly cake tins, and when cold spread with fruit jelly.

### ORANGE CAKE.

Beat light the yelks of five eggs with two cups of pulverized sugar, add juice of a large orange and part of the peel grated, and half a cupful of cold water and two cups of flour, sifted three times. Add a teaspoonful of baking powder in last sifting and add last the stiff-beaten whites of three eggs. Bake in layers, and spread the following icing between and on top: Beat the whites of three eggs stiff, add the juice and peel of one orange and sugar enough to stiffen. Very nice.

### RAILROAD CAKE.

Make a mandeltort batter and divide into two equal parts. Take half a pound of sweet and two ounces of bitter almonds, blanch, dry and grate them. Beat the yelks of ten eggs with three-quarters of a pound of pulverized sugar. Then beat the whites to a stiff froth adding one-quarter of a pound of sifted flour. Mix all thoroughly and divide into two parts. Add grated chocolate to the one, with a teaspoonful of ground cinnamon and half a teaspoonful of cloves and allspice. When baked spread with raspberry marmalade or jelly. Frost with lemon or almond frosting.

### ICE-CREAM CAKE.

Take one cup of butter (wash out the salt) and two cups of pulverized sugar rubbed to a cream. Then add gradually one cup of milk and three cups of sifted flour, with two teaspoonfuls of baking powder sifted into the flour and last the stiff-beaten whites of eight eggs. Bake in layers. Use the following filling: Four cups of powdered sugar, one small cup of boiling water. Boil until clear and thick like syrup and then pour on the beaten whites of four eggs, beating as you pour in the syrup, and stir until cold. Then add one teaspoonful of citric acid (pulverized, of course). Flavor with vanilla and spread between layers and on top. This quantity will make about five layers, and there will be enough frosting left to frost a gold cake, which you might make at the same time in order to use up the yelks.

### CREAM CAKE.

Rub one cup of butter and two scant cups of sugar to a cream; add gradually one cup of milk and three cups of flour. Measure flour after sifting, and add two teaspoonfuls of baking powder in last sifting. Before adding flour, add

the yelks of four eggs, put whites in last. Bake
in layers as for jelly cake. When cold, spread
with the following mixture: Wet two tablespoonfuls of cornstarch with enough cold milk to
work it into a paste. Boil half a pint of milk
with half a cup of sugar and a pinch of salt.
Beat the yelks of two eggs, light; add the cornstarch to this, and as soon as the milk boils pour
in the mixture gradually, stirring constantly
until thick. Drop in a teaspoonful of sweet
butter, and when this is mixed in, set away until
cool. Spread between layers.

### COCOANUT CAKE.

(No. 1.) Rub to a cream half a cup of butter
and a cup and a half of pulverized sugar. Add
gradually four eggs, half a cup of milk and two
cups of flour, adding one teaspoonful of baking
powder in last sifting. Bake in layers, Filling:
One grated cocoanut and all of its milk, to half
of which add the beaten whites of three eggs
and one cup of powdered sugar. Lay this between the layers. Mix with the other half of
the grated cocoanut five tablespoonfuls of powdered sugar and strew thickly on top of cake,
which has been previously iced.

### COCOANUT CAKE.

(No. 2.) Take whites of ten eggs, one goblet of
flour, a goblet and a half of pulverized sugar and
one teaspoonful of cream tartar. Sift the flour

five times, then sift the sugar and flour together.
Beat the whites to a very stiff froth. Stir into
them when stiff the sugar and flour, and last the
· cream tartar. Bake immediately in three or four
layers. Use same filling as in No. 1.

### CHOCOLATE CAKE.

Take one cup of butter, two cups of sugar, one
cup of sweet milk, the yelks of six eggs and the
whites of four, three cups of flour sifted several
times, adding two teaspoonfuls of baking powder
in last sifting, and the grated peel of one lemon.
Bake in jelly-tins. Icing: Set one-third of a
cake of chocolate in a small tincup on the back
of the stove to melt. Make a stiff icing with the
whites of four eggs and sugar. Add the melted
chocolate and flavor with vanilla. Spread on
the layers and on top of cake. Delicious.

### TUTTI–FRUTTI CAKE.

Rub to a cream two cups of sugar and three
quarters of a cup of butter. Add one cup of
sweet milk, three cups of flour and two teaspoonfuls of baking powder. Bake in layers. Filling:
Two cupfuls of granulated sugar and about three
tablespoonfuls of boiling water. Boil until it
stands alone when poured from the spoon. Pour
this slowly over the whipped whites of two eggs,
·stirring until cool. Mix with this one cupful of
small seedless raisins and one cupful of English
walnuts, chopped to the size of the raisins. Spread

between the layers and on top of cake. If you prefer you may reserve enough plain icing for the top and sides.

### LEMON JELLY FOR LAYER CAKE.

Take one pound of sugar, yelks of eight eggs with two whole ones, the juice of five large lemons and the grated peel of two and one-quarter pound of butter. Put the sugar, lemon and butter into a saucepan and melt over a gentle fire. When all is dissolved, stir in the eggs which have been well beaten, stir rapidly until it is thick as honey, and spread this between the layers of cake. Pack the remainder in jelly glasses.

### APPLE JELLY CAKE.

Rub one cup of butter and two cups of sugar to a cream and add four eggs, whites beaten separately, one cup of milk, two teaspoonfuls of baking powder and three cups and a half of flour. Bake in layers. Filling: Pare and grate three large apples ("Greenings" preferred), the juice and peel of a lemon, one cup of sugar and one well-beaten egg. Put the ingredients together in a tin vessel and boil, stirring constantly until thick. Cool and fill in cake.

### CARAMEL CAKE.

(No. 1.) Rub to a cream one cup of butter and two cups of sugar. Add gradually the yelks of five eggs, one at a time, and one cup of sweet milk. Add three cups of flour, sifted two or three times, adding two teaspoonfuls of baking powder in last sifting. Bake in jelly-tins and spread with the following mixture: Boil four cups of brown sugar, one cup of milk and a teaspoonful of butter. Mix together well and boil like you would for candy. Try a little in cold water; if it hardens, it is ready to spread between the layers. Get the medium brown sugar, it must be neither too dark nor too light.

## CARAMEL CAKE.

(No. 2.) Rub one cup of butter and two cups of sugar to a cream, add one cup of sweet milk and three cups of flour, two teaspoonfuls of baking powder put in last sifting. Add last the stiff-beaten whites of five eggs. Bake in jelly cake tins. Filling: One cup of brown sugar, a scant half-cup of milk, three tablespoonfuls of molasses, one teaspoonful of butter and about three ounces of grated chocolate; add to the boiling mixture. Boil all together about five minutes, stirring constantly; it should be the consistency of thick custard. Add a pinch of soda just as you are about to remove it from the fire. When cold, flavor with vanilla, and spread between layers; you may cover the top and sides also. Dry in a warm oven, or in a very warm place back of the range.

## PEACH SHORT CAKE.

(No. 1.) Make a sponge cake batter of four
eggs, a teacupful of pulverized sugar, a pinch
of salt and a teacupful of flour. Beat the eggs
with the sugar until very light. Beat until the
consistency of dough and add the grated peel of a
lemon, and last the sifted flour. No baking
powder necessary. Bake in jelly-tins. Shave
the peaches quite fine and sugar bountifully.
Put between layers. Eat with cream.

## PEACH SHORT CAKE.

(No. 2.) Make a good biscuit crust and bake
in jelly-tins. Roll out about half an inch thick.
As you place the crust in your tins spread over
melted butter, and then roll out another crust
and place on top of this. Set in the oven and
bake. As you take out of the oven separate the
crust and fill with peaches which have been
sliced and well sugared. Eat with rich cream.

## CHOCOLATE CREAM CAKE.

Rub one cup of butter and two cups of sugar
to a cream and add gradually one scant cup
of milk and three cups of flour, with two teaspoonfuls of baking powder put in last sifting.
Whip the whites of five or six eggs to a very stiff
froth. Stir in lightly. Bake in jelly-tins. Whip
a cup of cream as you would for Charlotte Russe,
sweeten and add half a cup of grated chocolate.
Spread between layers and ice the whole cake

with a chocolate icing made of sweet chocolate melted and mixed with the beaten white of an egg.

### STRAWBERRY CAKE.

Bake two layers of sponge or cup cake and fill with strawberries. Cut and sugar it, and spread either with whipped cream or beaten white of egg, sweetened.

### RUSSIAN PUNCH TART.

Bake three layers of sponge cake dough or three layers of almond tart (according to my receipt), which is still better, and flavor it with a wineglassful of arrack. When baked, scrape part of the cake out of the thickest layer, not disturbing the rim, and reserve these crumbs to add to the following filling: Boil half a pound of sugar in a quarter of a cup of water until it stands. Add to this syrup a wineglassful of rum and the crumbs, and spread over the layers, piling one on top of the other. Frost the cake with a nice icing, flavored with rum. Another way to fill this cake is to take some crab-apple jelly or apple marmalade and thin it with a little brandy. If you haven't either make a filling of the following: Grate a large tart apple, add the grated peel of a lemon, one egg and one cup of sugar. Let this boil five minutes steadily, stirring all the time, and flavor with rum. Spread between layers, and frost with boiled icing, flavored with rum.

## ALMOND CAKE, OR MANDEL TORTE.

(No. 1.) Take one-half pound of almonds and
blanch by pouring boiling water over them, and
pound in a mortar or grate on grater (the latter
is best). Add eight eggs, one cup of sugar, one-
half lemon, grated peel and juice, a tablespoonful
of brandy, and four lady-fingers, grated. Beat
the eggs and sugar with all your might. You
may add a pinch of lump ammonia, pulverized.

## ALMOND CAKE, OR MANDEL TORTE.

(No. 2.) Take one pound of sweet almonds and
half an ounce of bitter ones mixed. Blanch them
the day previous to using and then grate or pound
them as fine as powder. Beat until light the
yelks of fourteen eggs with three-quarters of a
pound of sifted powdered sugar. Add the grated
peel of a lemon and half a teaspoonful of mace.
Beat long and steadily (stir if you prefer doing
so). Add the grated almonds and continue the
stirring in one direction. Add the juice of the
lemon to the stiff-beaten whites. Grate six stale
lady-fingers and add and bake slowly for one
hour at least.

## BROD TORTE.

(No. 1.) Take one plate of finely-grated rye
bread, sifted (the bread should be dried in the
oven the day before), eight eggs, one cup of sugar,
one-quarter of a pound of almonds, nutmeg,
one small piece of chocolate, grated, one lemon
peel and juice, a wineglassful of brandy and

wine. Add white of eggs last—in fact, in all
cakes. You may spice this cake with cinnamon
and cloves (I shall give you different recipes for
these torten, and you will find them all reliable).
Cut this through the center and fill with jelly,
and you have it still finer. All cakes called torten
may be used as puddings, with wine sauce.

## BROD TORTE.

(No. 2.) Take ten eggs, two cups of sugar and
two cups of rye bread crumbs. Prepare thus:
Take about half a loaf of rye bread that has been
dried in the oven the day previous and grate or
pound in a mortar and sift as you would flour.
Add ten cents' worth of almonds, a few bitter
mixed, grated or pounded to powder, juice of one
orange and one lemon and the peel, one tablespoonful cinnamon, one teaspoonful allspice and
half a teaspoonful of cloves, a wineglassful of
brandy and a piece of citron shredded very fine
Add last the whites of eggs, beaten very stiff.
Bake slowly in spring form.

## BROD TORTE.

(No. 3.) Separate the yelks and whites of
twelve eggs. Beat the yelks with two cups of pulverized sugar. When thick add two cups of rye
bread crumbs (prepared as above), half a pound
of sweet almonds, also some bitter ones, grated
or powdered as fine as possible, quarter of a
pound of citron, shredded fine, one-quarter of a

cake of chocolate, grated, the grated peel of a
lemon, the juice of one orange and one lemon,
one tablespoonful of cinnamon, one teaspoonful
of allspice and half a teaspoonful of cloves, and
a wineglassful of brandy. Bake very slowly in
a paper-lined spring form which has been thoroughly buttered. Frost with a chocolate icing
made a follows: Put a small piece of chocolate
in a tin-cup on the back of the stove to melt.
Beat the white of an egg stiff with a small cup
of sugar, and stir into the melted chocolate and
spread with a knife.

### CHOCOLATE TART.

Take nine eggs, one-half pound of pulverized
sugar, one-half pound of almonds, half cut and
grated; half a pound of finest vanilla chocolate,
grated; one half pound raisins, cut and seeded;
seven soda crackers, rolled to a powder; one teaspoonful of baking powder, juice and peel of a
lemon, some cinnamon, quite a large piece of
citron, cut very fine and a glass of brandy or wine
Beat whites of eggs to a stiff froth and stir in
last. Beat yelks with sugar until very light;
then add chocolate, and so on.

### BISCUIT TART CAKE.

Beat the yelks of fifteen eggs with half a
pound of sifted sugar, until thick. Add the
grated peel of a lemon. Beat the whites very
stiff, so stiff that you can, with safety, hold the

dish upside down, then sift half a pound of flour (four times at least) and mix with the beaten whites and add to the beaten yelks. Bake in a large spring form lined with buttered paper. Bake slowly in a moderate oven. A pinch of pulverized ammonia added to the beaten whites will make all of these torten lighter.

### FILBERT TART CAKE.

Blanch half a pound of filberts and pound very fine in a mortar. Beat until thick the yelks of fifteen eggs with half a pound of sifted powdered sugar. Then add the pounded nuts and the grated peel of a lemon. Beat the whites to a very stiff froth, adding four ounces of sifted flour, and bake in a well-buttered paper-lined form. Ice and garnish with filberts.

### FILLED FILBERT CAKE.

Prepare the same as above. Bake in layers in three jelly-tins, lined with buttered or waxed paper. In the meantime, prepare a cream made of the filberts. Grate about eight ounces of filberts, mix with six ounces of sugar and a pint of whipped cream, or the whites of four or five eggs with half a pound of sugar. Frost and decorate with nuts and candied fruits.

### RIBBON TART CAKE.

Blanch half a pound of almonds, grate the peel of a lemon, beat until thick the yelks of twelve eggs with half a pound of sifted powdered sugar and mix with the grated almonds. Beat the whites to a very stiff froth and sift four ounces of flour and mix with the beaten whites. Divide into three equal parts, color one with cochineal or Dr. Price's fruit coloring and the other with grated chocolate. Bake in paper-lined jelly tins. Spread each layer, one with peach marmalade, the other with raspberry or apple jelly. Frost the top and sides with vanilla frosting.

### MARBLED BISCUIT TART.

Make a biscuit batter, like that for Biscuit Tart Cake. Divide it into five equal parts. Color one with cochineal, the other with chocolate and the third mix with a quarter of a pound of pistachio nuts, pounded very fine, leaving two parts their original color. Butter well a high cake form, pour in part of the uncolored batter, now fill in the chocolate, next the pistachio, then the uncolored again, and last the pink. Bake in a slow oven. Frost pink.

### MOHNTORTE.

(No. 1.) Line a deep pie-plate or a spring form, which is still better, with a very rich paste, and fill it with the following: Grind a cupful of mohn (poppy seed), stir the yelks of six eggs with three-fourths of a cup of sugar for about ten minutes. Add the grated peel of a lemon, a handful of pounded almonds, sweet and bitter mixed. You may add a few raisins and some finely-shredded citron to the mixture, which is very fine, also a tablespoonful of rose water. Beat the whites to a froth and stir through the mixture. Fill in the pie-plates and bake. Delicious.

### MOHNTORTE.

(No. 2.) Line a form with a rich puff paste, fill with half a pound of white mohn (poppy seed) which has been previously soaked in milk and then ground. Add a quarter of a pound of sugar and the yelks of six eggs; stir all together in one direction until quite thick. Then stir the beaten whites, to which you must add two ounces of sifted flour and a quarter of a pound of melted butter. Fill and bake. When done, frost either with vanilla or rose frosting.

### DATE TART CAKE.

Beat one pound of pulverized sugar with the yelks of twelve large eggs. Beat long and steadily until a thick batter. Add half a pound of dates, cut very fine, one and one-half teaspoonfuls of all-spice, one and one-half teaspoonfuls of ground cinnamon, two sticks of chocolate, grated, juice and peel of a lemon and eight soda crackers, rolled to a fine powder, and last the stiff-beaten whites. Bake in a spring form.

### WALNUT LAYER.

Separate the yelks and whites of nine eggs, being very careful not to get a particle of the yelks into the whites. Sift half a pound of pulverized sugar into the yelks and beat until thick

like batter. Add a pinch of salt to the whites
and beat very stiff. Have ready a pound of
walnuts, shelled and pounded (weigh before
shelling), reserving the whole pieces for decorating the top of cake. Add the pounded nuts
to the beaten yelks, and two tablespoonfuls of
grated lady fingers or stale sponge cake. Last
add the stiff-beaten whites of the eggs. Bake
in layers and fill with almond or plain icing.

### CHOCOLATE (ICED) LAYER CAKE.

Stir one scant half cupful of butter to a cream
with one and one half cups of brown sugar.
Add alternately one-half cup of sweet milk,
yelks of four eggs which you have previously
beaten until quite light, add whites of two (and
reserve the other two for the icing) and one-half
cup of sifted flour. Make a custard of one-half
cup of milk, set on to boil, with one cupful of
grated chocolate, one-half cupful of granulated
sugar; boil until thick, then remove from the
fire; stir until cool, add this to the cake batter,
add also one and one-half cups of sifted flour,
two even teaspoonfuls of baking powder and
one of vanilla flavoring. Bake in layers and ice
between and on top with plain white icing
flavored to taste. You may substitute almond
or colored icing, to suite your fancy. Delicious.

### SPICED CREAM LAYER CAKE.

Rub to a cream two tablespoonfuls of butter
with one teacupful and a half of pulverized

sugar, add the yelks of three eggs, stirring in
one at a time, one teacupful of milk, two cups
of flour in which you have sifted two teaspoonfuls of baking powder, add also two tablespoonfuls of grated chocolate, one teaspoonful of
ground cinnamon, one of allspice and cloves and
half a teaspoonful of mace.  Bake in two layers
and put whipped cream between and on top.
To be eaten while fresh.

### PINEAPPLE LAYER CAKE.

Make the layers either of gold or silver cake
recipes and fill with the following mixture:
Pare and core a pineapple and cut it into small
slices and sugar, set it away in a covered dish
till sufficient juice is drawn out to stew the
fruit in.  Stew the pineapple in the sugar and
juice till quite soft, then mash it to a marmalade with a spoon, and set it away to cool.
When cool, mix the pineapple with half a pint of
whipped cream, and fill in cake.  Ice the cake
with plain icing, ornament with candied pineapple if you wish it elaborate.  Canned grated
pineapple may be substituted for the fresh.

### WINE CAKE.

Make any kind of layer cake, white is the
best, and put wine-jelly between the layers and
on top, of course the jelly must be prepared the
day previous to using.  Put a rich icing over
the jellied top and sides if you so desire.
Delicious.

# COFFEE CAKES.

|                                              | Page.          |
| -------------------------------------------- | -------------- |
| Abgeruehrter Gugelhopf,                       | 325            |
| Apple Cake,                                  | 328            |
| Baba a la Parisienne,                        | 320            |
| Berliner Pfannkuchen (Purim Krapfen),        | 323            |
| Cheese Cake,                                 | 327            |
| Cherry Cake,                                 | 330            |
| Cottage Cheese Cake,                         | 333            |
| Chocolate Coffee Cake,                       | 336            |
| French Coffee Cake,                          | 320            |
| French Puffs (Windbeutel),                   | 322            |
| German Fruit Cake,                           | 335            |
| German Coffee Cake                           | 336            |
| Huckleberry Kuchen,                          | 330, 335       |
| Hints on Making,                             | 316, 317, 318  |
| Kaffee Kuchen,                               | 329            |
| Kreugel,                                     | 332            |
| Mohn Kuchen,                                 | 328            |
| Mohntorts,                                   | 330            |
| Mohn Wachteln,                               | 334            |
| Plain Bund, or Napf Kuchen,                  | 326            |
| Prune Cake,                                  | 327            |
| Peach Kuchen,                                | 333            |
| Roley–Poley,                                 | 331            |
| Spice Roll,                                  | 331            |
| Stollen,                                     | 332            |
| Wiener Kipfel,                               | 321            |
| Wiener Studenten Kipfel,                     | 322            |

## COFFEE CAKES·

MY DEAR LADIES:—To begin with, you must have nice rendered butter for baking purposes. I always buy enough butter in June to last all winter, for then it is cheap, say ten cents per pound, which is less than one-third what it is in winter, and it is not the "fresh May butter" you get then, either. I use the clarified butter for making omelets, frying griddle cakes, buckwheat flapjacks, and for French toast, doughnuts, fritters, greasing cake-pans and numerous other purposes. For the benefit of new housekeepers who are not supplied with last spring's butter, I must give a receipt for calrifying or rendering butter for your French and German "kuchen": Put the butter in a porcelain-lined or brass kettle, set it on the fire and let boil very slowly, until it becomes quite clear; when you can see the reflection of your spoon in the butter, like a mirror, and you can not hear the butter boil, it is done. Don't let it boil too long, or it will get too brown, and be very careful not to let it run over, and do not stir it with a spoon, nor skim it, else all of the salt will settle at the bottom of the kettle. But every time it rises, which will be about three times, lift it carefully from the stove and when it sinks put it on again to boil. It will not rise as high the second time, and still less the third. Take from the fire, set away for about fifteen minutes or more (being careful where you put it, especially if there are children about), then strain through a clean kitchen towel into a clean stone jar. When cold tie a paper over it and prick holes with a pin through the paper. If you do this and keep the butter in a dry, cool place, it will keep fresh for a year.

I must again call your attention to something quite important before we begin to bake, that is to have the dishes and pans, bowl, flour, butter, sugar, in fact everything you are going to use, with the yeast cake or bread, slightly warmed before you begin to work, with the exception of the white of the egg, which must be cold, in order to beat up nicely. In winter sift your flour and set in a warm place at least an hour before mixing your dough. Prepare the yeast by dissolving it in a very small quantity of lukewarm water or milk, add a tablespoonful of brown sugar and a good pinch of salt. If the yeast is fresh it will raise very soon, and you may feel confident of success. Do not mix your dough with yeast that does not rise, for your cake will not be fit for the table. Never lay your yeast on top of the ice. Remember this.

Try your oven before you set in the cake and

test it in this way:  Lay a sheet of white paper
in the oven, if it turns yellow soon after you may
put in your cake to bake, but should the paper
turn black, open both doors wide and wait until
the oven cools off.  If not hot enough, add more
fuel, but first test the oven again as above.  To
ascertain whether your cake is done, try it by
sticking a clean broom straw into it, and if it
comes out dry it is done.  You can also tell by the
sound.  If you hold the cake up to your ear and
you still hear a sizzing sound, as of cooking,
your cake is not done, but if there is no sound
you may take it from the oven.   Let your cake
stand about ten minutes before you take it out of
the form, being careful not to put it near a
draught of air. If a " Bund Kuchen," turn it over
on a flat plate; if a spring form, loosen the outer
rim and leave it on the tin it was baked in ; and if
a fruit cake, leave it in the large, flat tin it was
baked in, it will cut easier and may be freshened
up by setting in the oven a few minutes; this
makes the cake equal to fresh after it has become stale.  In frosting a cake always frost the
under side, as it is always level.

### MAKING DOUGH.

In the first place see that the yeast you are
going to use is strictly fresh. Dissolve two cents'
worth of compressed yeast in a cup half filled
with lukewarm milk, add a tablespoonful of sugar and a pinch of salt to the yeast, and set it in

a warm place to raise. Sift about two pounds of
flour and warm it slightly, in fact warm everything you intend to use for the yeast cake, except eggs, or your dough 'will not raise, especially in winter. Warm one quart of milk, put a
quarter of a pound of fresh butter into it, also a
quarter of a pound of nice rendered butter, a
scant cupful of sugar, a teaspoonful of cinnamon
and the grated peel of a lemon. Let all this dissolve in the milk, stirring the sugar up from the
bottom, so as to have it all well mixed. Make a
hole in the center of the flour, put in the cup of
raised yeast, and stir in gradually the contents of
your milk bowl. Stir slowly, add three eggs well
beaten and the cup of yeast. When all is mixed,
take your hand and work the dough, but do not
knead it. Beat it with the hollow of your hand
until it throws blisters and makes a cracking
noise. You may have to add more flour, but
guard against making it too stiff. Make it just
stiff enough to be rolled out on a thickly-floured
baking board. Work your dough until it leaves
both your hands and the dish perfectly clean or
free from dough. Cover with a clean cloth, set
in a moderately warm place until the next morning. Then take your baking board, which should
be a large one, flour it well, roll out a sugar, or
more commonly called, "kaffee kuchen;" roll
out another, which may be of any kind of fruit or
cheese, and roll out another for "Roley-Poley,"

and so on.   Roll all intended for fruit very thin,
and let them raise in the pans before baking.

### FRENCH COFFEE CAKE.

Soak two cents' worth of compressed yeast
in a very little lukewarm water or milk.   The
best way to do this is to put the yeast in a cup,
add two tablespoonfuls of lukewarm water, a
pinch of salt and a tablespoonful of sugar, stir it
up well with a spoon and set back of the stove to
rise.   Now rub a cupful of butter to a cream, add
three-fourths of a cup of powdered sugar, and
stir constantly in one direction.   Add the yelks
of five or six eggs, one at a time, and the grated
peel of a lemon.   Sift two cups of flour into a
bowl, make a hole in the center of the flour, pour
in the yeast and a cup of lukewarm milk.   Stir
and make a light batter of th's.   Now add the
creamed butter and eggs, stir until it forms blisters and leaves the bowl clean, and add a handful
of sultanas, some pounded almonds and a little
citron, cut up very fine, and last the stiff-beaten
whites of the eggs.   Now fill your cake form,
which has been well greased, set it in a warm
place to raise and bake slowly, covered at first.

### BABA A LA PARISIENNE.

Prepare the yeast as above; cream a scant
cup of butter with four tablespoonfuls of sugar,
the grated peel of a lemon, add seven eggs, one
at a time, stirring each egg a few minutes before

you add the next. Have ready two cups of sifted flour, and add two spoonfuls between each egg, until all is used up. Make a soft dough of the yeast, a small cupful of lukewarm milk and a cupful of flour. Let it rise for fifteen minutes. Now mix all well, rub the form well with butter, and blanch a handful of almonds, cut into long strips, and strew all over the form. Fill in the mixture or cake batter, let it rise two hours and bake very slowly.

### WIENER KIPFEL.

Dissolve four cents' worth of yeast in half a cup of lukewarm milk, a pinch of salt and a tablespoonful of sugar, set away in a warm place to rise. Sift a pound of flour into a deep bowl and make a dough of one cup of lukewarm milk and the yeast. Set it away until you have prepared the following: Rub a quarter of a pound of butter and four ounces of sugar to a cream, adding yelks of three eggs and one whole egg. Add this to the dough and work well. Let it rise about one hour, then roll out on a well-floured board, just as you would for cookies, and let it raise again for at least half an hour. Spread with beaten whites of eggs, raisins, almonds and citron and cut into triangles. Pinch the edges together. Lay them in well-buttered pans about two inches apart and let them raise again. Then spread again with stiff-beaten whites of eggs, and lay a few pounded almonds on each one.   Bake a nice yellow.

### WIENER STUDENTEN KIPFEL.

Make dough same as for Wiener Kipfel. Roll it out quite thin on a well-floured board and let it rise.   Cut also into triangles (before you cut them, spread with melted butter).   Mix one pound of nice fresh walnuts with one pound of brown sugar and fill the triangles with the mixture.   Take up the three corners and pinch together tightly.  Set in well-buttered pans and let them raise again and spread or brush each one with melted butter.  Bake a nice brown.  Truly delicious.

### FRENCH PUFFS (WINDBEUTEL).

Put one pound of water and one-half pound of butter on to boil.   When it begins to boil stir in half a pound of sifted flour.  Stir until it leaves the kettle clean, take off the fire and stir until say milk-warm, then stir in eight eggs, one at a time, stirring until all are used up.  Now put on some rendered butter, and plenty of it, in a porcelain-lined kettle.   When the butter is hot dip a large teaspoon in cold water and cut pieces of dough with it as large as a walnut, and drop into the hot butter.  Try one first to see whether the butter is hot enough.  Do not crowd—they want plenty of room to raise. Dip the hot butter over them with a spoon, fry a deep yellow and sprinkle powdered sugar over them. I forgot to tell you to flavor the dough either with nutmeg or the peel of a lemon. You may bake half of these in the oven on large tins, well floured and set far apart, and you will have delicious cream puffs. Make an incision with a sharp knife, and fill with whipped cream or marmalade, or cream made of boiled milk, eggs, sugar and cornstarch, flavored with vanilla. You may also use beer instead of milk in mixing the dough, and add a heaping teaspoonful of baking powder to the dough when cooled. I have never tried the beer, but they say it is very nice; you can not taste it in the dough.

## BERLINER PFANNKUCHEN.
### (PURIM KRAPFEN.)

To these superfine "doughnuts" take one pound of the best flour, sifted into a deep bowl, a heaping cup of lukewarm milk, and two cents' worth of compressed yeast, which you have dissolved in a little warm water and sugar, as described above. Stir into a nice dough and cover with a towel and set away in a warm place to rise. In the meantime, take a tablespoonful of rendered butter, one tablespoonful of fresh butter and two tablespoonfuls of powdered sugar, also a litle salt, and rub to a cream. Add the yelks of five eggs, one at a time, breaking each egg in a saucer (this is the safest way to prevent spoiling all, which only a part of a bad

egg would certainly do). Now add another whole
egg, stir all well and add to the rising dough.
Add also the grated peel of a lemon. Stir all the
dough till it blisters and leaves the dish perfectly
clean at the sides. Let the dough rise slowly
for about two hours (all yeast dough is better
if it rises slowly). Take a large baking-board,
flour well and roll out your dough on it as thin
as a double thickness of pasteboard. When it
is all rolled out, cut out with a round cutter the
size of a tumbler. When all the dough has
been cut out, beat up an egg. Spread the beaten
egg on the edge of each cake (spread only a few
at a time, for they would get too dry if all were
done at once). Then put half a teaspoonful of
some nice marmalade, jam or jelly on the cake.
Put another cake on top of one already spread,
and cut it again with a cutter a little bit smaller
than the one you used in the first place. This
makes them stick better, and prevents the preserves coming out while cooking. Now, I hope
you understand me. Spread the edges with egg,
then preserves, placing one that is not spread on
top of the other, and cut again. Set all away on
a floured board or pan about two inches apart.
Spread the top of each cake with melted butter,
and let them rise from one to two hours. When
ready to fry heat at least two pounds of butter
(three is still better; take nice rendered butter);
put it in a wide porcelain-lined kettle. You must

have plenty of butter to fry the cake in. None
is wasted, as it may be used again, and the kettle
must be large so as to prevent the butter from
cooking or boiling over. Try the butter with a
small piece of dough, If it rises immediately
it is right. Put in the doughnuts. In putting
them in, place the side that is up on the board
down in the hot butter. Do not crowd them in the
kettle, as they require room to rise and spread.
Cover them with a lid. In a few seconds uncover. If they are a nice light brown, turn them
over on the other side; but do not cover them
again. When done they will have a white stripe
around the center. Take them up with a perforated skimmer; lay on a large platter; sprinkle
with pulverized sugar, and so on, until all are
baked. If the butter gets too hot take from the
fire a minute. These are best eaten fresh.

### ABGERUEHRTER GUGELHOPF.

Soak two cents' worth of compressed yeast in
a very little lukewarm milk, add a pinch of salt
and a tablespoonful of sugar, stir it up smooth
and set back of the stove to rise. In the meantime rub a scant cupful of butter and a scant
cupful of powdered sugar to a cream, add gradually the yelks of four or five eggs, one at a time
and add also the grated peel of a lemon. Sift two
cups of flour into a bowl, make a hole in the
center of the flour, pour in the yeast and a cup
of lukewarm milk, and make a light batter of

this. Now add the creamed butter and eggs and stir until it forms blisters and leaves the bowl clean. Stem a handful of sultanas and cut up some citron very fine. If you have not the sultanas use cooking raisins, but seed them. Dredge flour over them before adding, and, if necessary, add more flour to the dough, which should be of the consistency of cup cake. Last add the stiff-beaten whites of the eggs. Now fill your cake form, which has been well greased, set in a warm place to raise, and bake slowly.

### PLAIN BUND, OR NAPF KUCHEN.

Take two cents' worth of compressed yeast, put it in a common kitchen cup, adding a pinch of salt, a tablespoonful of sugar and about two tablespoonfuls of lukewarm water. Stir the yeast until it is a smooth paste and set it in a warm place to rise. Now sift two cups and a half of flour (use the same size cup for measuring everything you are going to use in your cake), make a cavity in the flour, stir in the yeast and a scant cupful of lukewarm milk, make a nice batter, and let it rise until you have prepared the following: Rub three-quarters of a cup of butter and three-quarters of a cup of powdered sugar to a cream, just as you would for cup cake, then add gradually one egg at a time, using from four to five altogether, and stirring all the time in one direction. Work in your risen batter, a couple of spoonfuls at a time, between each egg. Grate

in the peel of a lemon or an orange. Butter the
form well that the cake is to be baked in (do this
always before you begin to work). Put in your
dough, set it in a warm place and let it rise for
an hour and a half or two hours. Bake in a
moderate oven one full hour, covered at first.

### CHEESE CAKE.

Take a quart of "Dutch cheese," rub smooth
with a silver or wooden spoon, then rub a piece
of sweet butter, the size of an egg, to a cream,
add gradually half a cup of sugar and the yelks
of three eggs, a pinch of salt, grate in the peel
of a lemon, wash half a cupful of currants and
add also a little citron, cut up very fine. Line
two pie-plates with some nice kuchen dough, roll
it out quite thin, butter the pie-plates quite heavily, and let the dough in them rise at least a
quarter of an hour before putting in the cheese
mixture, for it must be baked immediately after
the cheese is put in; and just before you put the
cheese into the plates whip up the whites of the
eggs to a very stiff froth, and stir through the
cheese mixture. You may make "cheese pies"
with a rich puff paste; nice either way. Eat
fresh.

### PRUNE CAKE (KUCHEN).

Line one or two plates with a thin roll of
kuchen dough, and let it raise again in the pans,
which have been heavily greased. Have some
prunes boiled very soft, take out the kernels,

mash up the prunes well (this you must do with
your hands or a potato masher, as a spoon will
not do it satisfactorily), mash them until like
mush; sweeten to taste, add cinnamon and
grated peel of a lemon, put in the lined pie-
plates and bake immediately.

### APPLE CAKE (KUCHEN).

After the pan is heavily greased with nice
butter, roll out a piece of dough quite thin, lift
it up with the aid of the rolling pin and lay it
in the pan, press a rim out of the dough all
around the pan and let it raise for about ten
minutes. Then lay on the apples in rows.
Pare the apples, core and quarter them, dipping
each piece in melted butter, before laying on the
cake, sprinkle bountifully with sugar (brown
being preferable to white for this purpose) and
cinnamon. See that you have nice tart apples.
Leave the cake in the pans and cut out the
pieces just as you would want to serve them. If
they stick to the pan, set the pan on top of the
hot stove for a minute and the cake will then
come out all right.

### MOHN KUCHEN (POPPY SEED).

Roll out a piece of dough large enough to
cover your whole baking board, roll quite thin,
but be sure to flour the board well before you
attempt it. Let it rise until you have prepared the filling: grind a coffee-mill full of
mohn (poppy seed), set the mill as tight as

possible and clean it well, throw away the first
bit you grind so as not to have the coffee taste,
put it on to boil with a cupful of milk, add a
lump of butter, a handful of seeded raisins, a
handful of almonds, chopped up fine, two tablespoonfuls of molasses or syrup, and a little
citron, cut up fine.  When thick, set it away to
cool, and if not sweet enough add more sugar
and flavor with vanilla.  Spread on the dough
when cold, which has raised by this time.  Take
up one corner and roll it up into a long roll,
like a jelly roll, put in a greased pan and let it
raise an hour at least, and longer if convenient,
then spread butter on top and bake very slowly.
Let it get quite brown, so as to bake through
thoroughly.  When cold cut up in slices, as
many as you are going to use at one time only.

## KAFFEE KUCHEN.

Butter your long and broad cake-pans thoroughly, roll out enough dough to cover them,
and let it raise about half an hour before baking, then brush it well with melted butter.
Sprinkle sugar and cinnamon on top and some
chopped almonds.  You may take a lump of
butter, a very little flour, some sugar and cinnamon and rub it between your hands until it
is like lumps of almonds, then strew on top of
cakes.  You may mix a few pounded almonds
with it.  Very nice.

### HUCKLEBERRY KUCHEN.

Line your cake-pans, which should be long
and narrow, with a rich kuchen dough, having
previously greased them well.   Now make a
pap of cornstarch, say a cup of milk, a tablespoonful of butter and a teaspoonful of cornstarch wet with cold milk.   Boil until thick,
sweeten and flavor with vanilla and spread on
top of the cake dough, and then sprinkle thickly
with huckleberries, which have been carefully
picked, sugared and sprinkled with ground
cinnamon.   Bake in a quick oven.

### CHERRY CAKE.

Line a cake-pan, which has been well buttered, with a thin layer of kuchen dough.   Stone
two or three pounds of cherries and lay them
on a sieve, with a dish underneath to catch the
juice.   Sprinkle cornstarch or bread crumbs
on the layer of dough after it has raised sufficiently, spread the cherries on evenly and
sprinkle sugar over them and bake.   In the
meantime beat up four or five eggs with a teacupful of sugar, beat until light and add the
cherry juice.   Draw the kuchen to the oven
door, pour this mixture over it and bake.   If
you have cream use it with the eggs, which is
also very fine.

### MOHNTORTS.

Line a deep pie-plate, or a spring form, which
is still better, with a thin sheet of kuchen

dough, let it raise about half an hour, then fill
with the following: Grind a cupful of poppy
seed; stir the yelks of six eggs with three-fourths
of a cup of sugar for about ten minutes, add the
grated peel of a lemon, a handful of powdered
almonds, sweet and bitter mixed; you may add
also a few raisins, some shredded citron and
a tablespoonful of rosewater or vanilla. Beat
the whites to a froth and stir through the
mixture. Fill in the pie-plates and bake. Very
nice indeed.

### SPICE ROLL.

Roll out the dough quite thin and let it raise
half an hour, brush with melted butter and
make a filling of the following: Grate some
leb-kuchen or plain gingerbread; shred some
citron, pound some almonds or nuts, seed a cupful of raisins and wash a cupful of currants.
Strew these all over the dough together with
some brown sugar and a little syrup. Spice
with cinnamon and roll. Spread with butter
and let it rise for an hour. Bake brown.

### ROLEY-POLEY.

Roll out quite thin, spread with melted butter (a brush is best for this purpose, such as
used by varnishers, and should be used for
nothing else). Let it raise a little while, then
sprinkle well with sugar, and add cinnamon
and currants, which have been carefully washed
and dried. Now cut into strips about an inch

wide and four inches long; roll and put in a
well-buttered pan to rise, leaving enough space
between each, and brush with butter. Bake
brown.

### STOLLEN.

Sift two pounds of flour into a bowl and set a
sponge in it with two cents' worth of compressed
yeast, a teaspoonful of salt, a pint of lukewarm
milk and a tablespoonful of sugar. When this
has risen, add half a pound of creamed butter, a
quarter of a pound of seeded raisins and one
quarter of a pound of sugar, yelks of four eggs,
four ounces of powdered almonds and the grated
peel of a lemon. Work all well, beating with
the hands, not kneading. Let this dough rise
at least three hours, then form into one or two
long loaves, narrower at the end, like a stolle.
Brush the top with melted butter and bake over
half an hour in a moderate oven.

### KREUGEL.

Take two pounds of flour, three quarters of a
pound of butter, one-half pound of sugar, five
eggs, one-quarter of an ounce of cinnamon,
one cup of milk, some compressed yeast and
half a pound of currants. Set a sponge with
half the flour and milk and eggs and let it
raise, then add half the sugar and enough flour
to work into a nice dough, adding the creamed
butter (gradually) and the remaining flour.
After it has risen roll out the dough quite thick,

strew the currants (which have previously been thoroughly cleaned) over the dough with the remaining sugar. Then roll it up carefully, form into a half-moon and let it raise again and then brush with melted butter and bake from half to three-quarters of an hour. You may take half of this dough and braid it and form into a wreath. Just before baking brush with beaten egg and sugar and pounded almonds.

### PEACH KUCHEN.

Grease your cake-pans thoroughly with good clarified butter, then line them with a rich coffee cake dough, which has been rolled as thin as possible, and set in a warm place to rise. Then pare and quarter enough peaches to cover the dough. Lay the peaches in rows and sweeten and set in oven to bake. Now make a meringue quickly as possible and pour over the cakes and bake a light brown. The meringue is made as follows: Beat the whites of eight eggs to a stiff froth with ten ounces of almonds, which have been blanched and pounded.

### COTTAGE CHEESE CAKE.

Line deep cake-pans or pie-plates with a very thin layer of rich coffee cake dough, and let it rise in a warm place until you have prepared the cheese. Add a cup of sweet cream to the cheese, after you have rubbed it quite smooth with a wooden spoon through a collander or a coarse sieve. Then add half a cup of melted butter, a pinch of salt, a cup of sugar, the grated peel of a lemon, the yelks of four eggs and half a cup of blanched almonds, pounded in a mortar. Whip the white of the eggs to a very stiff froth, and add last one pound of cottage cheese. Make two large, round pie-platefuls of cake, or use a large spring form. Eat while warm.

### MOHN WACHTELN.

Dissolve four cents' worth of yeast in a cupful of lukewarm milk, a pinch of salt and a tablespoonful of sugar. Set it away in a warm place to rise. Sift a pound of flour into a deep bowl and make a dough of one cup of lukewarm milk and the yeast. Set it away until you have prepared the following: Rub to a cream a quarter of a pound of butter and four ounces of sugar, add the yelks of three eggs and one whole egg to the dough and work well. Let it rise about one hour, then roll out on a baking board, which has been well floured, just as you would for cookies. Let the dough rise again for at least an hour, and spread with the following mixture, after cutting into squares, fold into triangles and pinch the edges together. Lay in well buttered pans, about two inches apart, and let them rise again, and spread with beaten egg and bake: Take half a pound of poppy seed (mohn), which have previously been soaked in milk and then ground, add a quarter of a pound of sugar and the yelks of six eggs. Stir this all together in one direction until quite thick and then stir in the beaten whites, to which you must add two ounces of sifted flour and a quarter of a pound of melted butter. Fill the tartlets and bake.

### HUCKLEBERRY KUCHEN.

Line your cake-pans, which should be long and narrow, with a rich kuchen dough, having previously greased them well. Now make a pap of cornstarch, say about a cup of milk, a teaspoonful of butter and a teaspoonful of cornstarch wet with cold milk. Boil until thick, sweeten and flavor with vanilla. Spread this on top of cake dough, then sprinkle thickly with huckleberries, which have been carefully picked; sugar them well, mixing a little ground cinnamon with the sugar. Bake in a quick oven.

### GERMAN FRUIT CAKE.

A nice variety of cakes may be made as follows: Take some very rich kuchen dough, roll it out quite thin, and cut it into squares. Fill it with any kind of compote, that of prunes being particularly nice for this purpose. Stone the prunes, mash to a pulp, sweeten, add the grated peel of a lemon, some cinnamon, etc., and put a teaspoonful of this into each. Take up the corners, fasten them firmly, also pinch all along the edges, and lay in a buttered pan and let them raise half an hour before baking.

Spread them with melted butter, by means of a feather or brush, and bake a nice brown. You may fill these small cakes with mohn, cheese, prunes or any compote at hand. They help to give you a variety, and are delicious if properly made.

### CHOCOLATE COFFEE CAKE.

Pour a bunt kuchen dough into long, well-buttered tins, and when baked remove from the oven and cover thickly with boiled chocolate icing. Very nice indeed.

### GERMAN COFFEE CAKE.

Dissolve two cents' worth of compressed yeast in a cupful of lukewarm milk, add a pinch of salt and a tablespoonful of brown sugar. Sift a cupful of flour into a small bowl, add the milk and yeast, stir all into a smooth batter and set it away in a warm place to raise. In the meantime, rub a scant three-quarters of a cup of butter and three quarters of a cup of pulverized sugar to a cream, add four whole eggs and the yelks of three, and two cups of flour in the following manner: Sift flour into the cups, and add two tablespoonfuls at a time alternately with the eggs and risen batter. Commence with adding one whole egg, stirring until it disappears, then add the yelk of another egg, and two tablespoonfuls of flour and stir again until it disappears, and then add two spoonfuls of

batter, and so on until you have used up four
whole eggs and the three yelks, two cups of flour
and all of the batter. Add a handful of pounded
or grated almonds, a tablespoonful of finely-
sliced citron and a handful of seeded raisins,
and dredge the latter with flour before adding.
Have a deep cake form richly greased with butter, fill it in with the batter, and let it raise in
a warm place for three hours or more. Bake in
a moderate oven about one hour. Cover the
cake when first set in the oven; bake covered
fifteen minutes, then uncover.

**MEMORANDUM.**

# ICING FOR CAKES.

| | Page. |
|---|---|
| Almond Icing, - - - - - - 339 | |
| Boiled Icing, - - - - - - 339 | |
| Chocolate Icing, - - - - 340, 341, 342 | |
| Caramel Icing, - - - - - 343 | |
| Cocoanut Icing, - - - - - 343 | |
| Lemon Extract, - - - - - 341 | |
| Lemon Peel, - - - - - - 342 | |
| Maple Sugar Icing, - - - - 343 | |
| Nut Icing, - - - - - - 343 | |
| Plain White Icing, - - - - 340 | |
| Pink Icing, - - - - - - 340 | |
| Unboiled Icing, - - - - - 342 | |
| Vanilla Extract, - - - - - 341 | |
| Yellow Icing, - - - - - 340 | |
| Yellow or Golden Icing, - - - - 342 | |

# MEMORANDUM.

# ICING FOR CAKES.

## BOILED ICING.

TAKE one cup of sugar to the beaten white of one egg. Put the sugar on to boil with two tablespoonfuls of water. When this has boiled clear pour on the beaten white of the egg, stirring constantly until cold. Flavor with rosewater and vanilla mixed.

## ALMOND ICING.

Take the whites of two eggs and half a pound of sweet almonds, with a few bitter mixed, which should be blanched, dried and grated, or pounded to a paste. Beat the whites of the eggs, add half a pound of confectioner's sugar, a handful at a time, until all is used up, and then add the almonds and a few spoonfuls of rosewater. Spread between or on top of cake. Put on thick, and when nearly dry cover with a plain icing. If the cakes are well dredged with a little flour after baking, and then carefully wiped before the icing is put on, it will not run, and can be spread more smoothly. Put the frosting in the center of the cake, dip a knife in cold water, and spread from the center toward the edge.

### PLAIN WHITE ICING.

Beat up the white of an egg with one-quarter of a pound of pulverized sugar until thick; half a pound for two whites, and so on. Set in a very warm place to dry.

### PINK ICING.

This icing is made as above, or like boiled icing, using pink confectioner's sugar or color with cochineal or prepared fruit coloring, which you may procure at any first-class grocery.

### YELLOW ICING.

Grate the peel of one or more oranges; put the peel in a fine batiste rag; tie it up and boil in a few spoonfuls of water. Squeeze it to extract the color, and boil with as much sugar as you want for icing — say two whites of eggs, juice of one orange and two cups of sugar. You may use the orange juice in place of the water.

### CHOCOLATE ICING.

Make a stiff icing by beating the whites of four eggs, and adding gradually one pound of sifted powdered sugar. Add gradually one-third of a cake of bitter chocolate, which you have previously melted in a tin-cup on the back of the stove. Mix with icing and flavor with vanilla. This quantity is enough to ice the layers and top of a large cake

## CHOCOLATE ICING WITHOUT EGGS.

Boil chocolate with very little water and sugar until thick. It must harden on the spoon when cool. Flavor with vanilla and spread. Set in a very warm place to harden.

## CHOCOLATE ICING, UNBOILED.

Beat the whites of three eggs and one and one-half cups of pulverized sugar, added gradually while beating. Beat until very thick, then add four heaping tablespoonfuls of grated chocolate and two teaspoonfuls of vanilla. Frosting for a strawberry cake should not be set in the oven, and it should not be frosted longer than half an hour before serving, and then set in the ice-chest immediately. Try this, you will never do otherwise. Tastes like whipped cream. You may flavor with vanilla or strawberry juice.

## VANILLA EXTRACT.

Take two ounces of vanilla bean and one of tonka. Soak the tonka in warm water until the skin can be rubbed off; then cut or chop in small pieces and put in two wine bottles. Fill with half alcohol and half water, and cork and seal and in a week's time will be ready for use.

## LEMON EXTRACT.

Take the peel of half a dozen lemons, and put in alcohol the same as for vanilla. I prefer the grated peel of a lemon for flavoring cakes. Use as little flavoring as possible, as most persons, especially gentlemen, object to too strong flavoring.

### LEMON PEEL.

Keep a wide-mouthed bottle of brandy in which to throw lemon peel. Often you will have use for the juice of lemons only. Then it will be economical to put the lemon peel in the bottle to use for flavoring. A teaspoonful of this is sufficient for the largest cake.

### UNBOILED ICING.

Take the white of one egg, and add to it the same quantity of water (measure in an egg shell). Stir into this as much confectioner's sugar to make it of the right consistency to spread upon the cake. Flavor with any flavoring desired. You may color it pink as you would boiled frosting by adding fruit coloring.

### CHOCOLATE ICING.

Prepare the above unboiled icing, add as much grated chocolate as you desire and flavor with vanilla.

### YELLOW OR GOLDEN ICING.

Is made just as you would the white unboiled icing, substituting the yelk of the egg instead of the white, flavor with orange juice, and if you wish a deeper yellow, grate the orange peel into the juice of the orange, and strain through a fine piece of cheese cloth before adding to the yellow icing.

## COCOANUT ICING.

Mix cocoanut with the unboiled icing. If you desire to spread it between the cakes, scatter more cocoanut over and between the layers.

## NUT ICING.

Mix any quantity of finely chopped nuts into any quantity of cream icing (unboiled) as in the foregoing receipts. Ice the top of cake with plain icing, and lay the halves of walnuts on top.

## MAPLE SUGAR ICING.

Boil two cupfuls of maple sugar, with half a cupful of boiling water until it threads from the spoon. Pour it upon the beaten whites of two eggs and beat until cold. Spread between and on top of cake. A pretty effect is made by sprinkling dessicated cocoanut on top of cake.

## CARAMEL ICING.

Two cupfuls of granulated sugar, a piece of best butter the size of an egg, and one scant cupful of sweet milk. Boil very briskly for ten minutes, being careful not to burn. Flavor with vanilla. Stir until cold.

**MEMORANDUM.**

# COOKIES, ETC.

|                              |          | Page.     |
|------------------------------|----------|-----------|
| Almond Macaroons,            |          | 353, 354  |
| Aniseseed Cakes,             |          | 358       |
| Baseler Leckerlein, -        |          | 362       |
| Chocolate Wafers,            |          | 351       |
| Cup Cookies,  -              |          | 347       |
| Caraway Seed Cookies,        |          | 347       |
| Clove Cookies,               |          | 347       |
| Citron Cookies,  -           |          | 348       |
| Cardamom Cookies,            |          | 349, 350  |
| Chocolate Wafers,            |          | 361       |
| Chocolate Puffs, -           |          | 355       |
| Currant Gems,                |          | 355       |
| Cream Cakes,                 |          | 357       |
| Chocolate Eclaires,          |          | 357       |
| Dominoes,                    |          | 356       |
| English Gems,                |          | 359       |
| Ginger Cookies               |          | 347       |
| Ginger Wafers,  -            |          | 356       |
| German Lebkuchen,            |          | 360       |
| Ginger Gems,                 |          | 360, 361  |
| Honey Cakes,                 |          | 351       |
| How to Begin,  -             |          | 345       |
| Hickorynut Macaroons, -      |          | 355, 362  |
| Mother's Delicious Cookies,  |          | 345       |
| Mohn Maultaschen,            |          | 352       |
| Molasses Cookies,            |          | 358       |
| Nutmeg Cakes,                |          | 359       |
| Poppy Seed Cookies, -        |          | 353       |
| Sour Milk Cookies, -         |          | 348       |
| Spice Wafers,                |          | 350       |
| Shavings,                    |          | 351       |
| Strawberry Smacks, -         |          | 363       |
| Vanilla Cookies,  -          |          | 358       |
| Yum-Yums,                    |          | 348       |

(344)

**MEMORANDUM.**

# COOKIES, ETC.

IN baking small cakes and cookies, grease the
pans with wax or butter. If the pans get
cool before you can take them off, set them on
top of the stove for a few seconds. The cakes
will then slip off easily. Sponge, drop cake,
anise, lady fingers, etc., are better baked on
floured pans. Sift, or rather sprinkle, the flour
lightly in the pans.

## MOTHER'S DELICIOUS COOKIES.

Take ten boiled eggs and two raw ones, one
pound of best butter, half a pound of almonds,
one lemon, some cinnamon, one wineglass of
brandy, one pound of pulverized sugar and about
one pound and a half of flour. This quantity
makes one hundred cookies, and, like fruit cake,
age improves them, in other words, the older the
better. Now to begin with: Set a dish of boiling water on the stove, when it boils hard break
the eggs carefully, one at a time, dropping the
whites in a deep porcelain dish, and set away in
a cool place. Take each yelk as you break the
egg and put it in a half shell, and lay it in the

boiling water until you have ten boiling. When
boiled hard take them up and lay them on a plate
to cool. In the meantime wash the salt out of
the butter, cream it with a pound of pulverized
sugar, add the grated peel of a lemon, a teaspoonful of cinnamon and half of the almonds, which
have been blanched and pounded or grated (reserve the other half for the top of the cookies,
which should not be grated, but pounded). Now
add the hard-boiled yolks, which must be grated,
and the two raw eggs, sift in the flour, and don't
forget the brandy. Beat up the whites of the
twelve eggs very stiff, add half to the dough, reserving the other half, but do not make the dough
stiff, as it should be so rich that you can hardly
handle it. Flour the baking-board well, roll
out about an eighth of an inch thick. Now
spread with the reserved whites of eggs, reserving
half again, as you will have to roll out at least
twice on a large baking-board. Sprinkle well
with the pounded almonds after you have
spread the beaten whites of the eggs on top,
also with sugar and cinnamon. Cut with a
cooky-cutter. Have at least five large pans
greased ready to receive them. See that you
have a good fire. Time to bake, five to ten
minutes. Pack them away when cold in a
stone jar or tin cake-box. These cookies will
keep a long time—if locked up.

## CUP COOKIES.

Rub to a cream three-quarters of a cup of butter and one cup of sugar; add four eggs, one at a time, and the grated peel of a lemon. Then dissolve a lump of ammonia, about the size of a bean, in a quarter of a pound of lukewarm milk; add this and just enough sifted flour to enable you to roll out on the baking-board. Roll quite thin. Beat up an egg and brush over the cookies, sprinkle with sugar, cinnamon and pounded almonds. These are very nice. Be careful not to add too much flour. Omit the almonds if you are not fond of them.

## CARAWAY SEED COOKIES.

Take one cup of butter, two cups of sugar, one cup of milk, three teaspoonfuls of baking powder, three to five eggs and two teaspoonfuls of caraway seed. Flour enough to roll. Don't get it too stiff.

## CLOVE COOKIES.

Take two cups of butter, two of sugar, one of milk; quarter of a pound of almonds, five cents' worth of oil of cloves; flour enough to roll and two teaspoonfuls of baking powder.

## GINGER COOKIES.

Take one cupful of sugar, two of molasses, one of butter; one teaspoonful of soda, dissolved in a cup of boiling water; one tablespoonful of ginger, and flour enough to mix, and roll out soft.

## SOUR MILK COOKIES.

Take one cupful of butter, one of sugar, two or three eggs, and two-thirds of a cupful of sour milk. Dissolve a teaspoonful of soda in a little hot water; add part of it at a time to the milk until it foams as you stir it. Be careful not to get in too much. Mix up soft, only using flour sufficient to roll out thin. A teaspoonful of cardamom seed may be sprinkled into the dough.

## CITRON COOKIES.

Take one-half cup of butter and one cup and a half of sugar, and rub to a cream. Add two eggs, three-quarters of a cup of milk, one-half cup of citron, cut up very fine, one teaspoonful of allspice and one of cloves. Take whole spices and pound them in a mortar, and flour to thicken. Make stiffer than ordinary cup cake dough; flavor to suit taste, and drop on large tins with a teaspoon. Grease the pans, and bake in a quick oven. The best plan is to try one on a plate. If the dough runs too much add more flour. Sift one heaping teaspoonful of baking powder in with the flour.

## YUM-YUMS.

Beat the whites of two eggs to a stiff froth, adding gradually one cup of confectioner's sugar and one heaping cupful of dessicated cocoanut, and two heaping teaspoonfuls of arrowroot. Drop from the teaspoon upon buttered paper in a large baking pan. Drop an inch apart. Bake in a moderate oven fifteen minutes.

## CARDAMOM COOKIES.

(No. 1.) Rub to a cream half a pound of best butter and add half a pound of pulverized sugar, the grated peel of a lemon, a tablespoonful of brandy, and the grated yelks of six hardboiled eggs, a teaspoonful of cardamom seed pounded fine, a tablespoonful of rosewater, and as much pulverized ammonia as you can put on the end of a knife. Work this into a soft dough, with just enough flour to roll out. Don't get your dough too stiff, flour your board thickly and roll out thin. Spread with the beaten whites of the eggs and pounded almonds. Bake in a quick oven for about ten minutes. Prepare the eggs same as for " Mother's Delicious Cookies," by breaking each egg carefully, putting the whites in a deep bowl and setting on ice until wanted, and put each yelk into a half shell (do this as you break each egg, leaving the yelk in the same egg shell) and set in boiling water and boil until hard, then take them out and set in a cool place, and do not attempt to grate them until perfectly cold. It would be much easier to boil the whole egg, but then you would waste the whites.

## CARDAMOM COOKIES.

(No. 2.) Boil six eggs hard. When cold
shell and grate the yolks (reserve the whites for
salads or to garnish vegetables), add half a pound
of sugar, the grated peel of a lemon and half a
wineglassful of brandy. Stir in half a pound of
butter which has been worked to a cream (unless
your butter is sweet, you had better wash it
through several waters before rubbing it). Sift
in as much flour as you think will allow you to
roll out the dough; take as little as possible, a
little over half a pound, and flour the board
very thick. Put in about two cents' worth of
cardamom seed and very little rosewater. Cut
out with a fancy cake cutter and brush with
beaten egg. Sprinkle pounded almonds and
sugar on top. If you add half a teaspoonful of
pulverized ammonia it will make the cookies
very light. It should be sifted with the flour.

## SPICE WAFERS.

Take one pound of flour, one pound of sugar,
seven eggs, the grated peel of a lemon, a piece of
citron, also grated, a tablespoonful of ground
cinnamon, a teaspoonful of cardamom seed,
pounded fine, and half a teaspoonful of ground
cloves. Stir the eggs, sugar and spices about
half an hour, add the sifted flour gradually; cut
the wafers with a teaspoon and bake in pans
upon buttered or waxed paper.

## CHOCOLATE WAFERS.

Take one-quarter of a pound of the best vanilla chocolate, grated, one-quarter of a pound of confectioner's sugar, one-quarter of a pound of grated almonds (a few bitter ones mixed), and the stiff-beaten whites of six eggs. Stir the sugar and beaten whites, then add the chocolate and almonds, and drop upon waxed paper with a teaspoon, about two inches apart.

### BASELER LŒKERLEIN (HONEY CAKES).

Take half a pound of strained honey, half a pound of sifted powdered sugar, half a pound of almonds (cut in half lengthwise), half a pound of finest flour, one ounce of citron (cut or chopped extremely fine), peel of a lemon, a little grated nutmeg, also a pinch of ground cloves and a wineglassful of brandy. Set the honey and sugar over the fire together, put in the almonds, stir all up thoroughly. Next put in the spices and work into a dough. Put away in a cold place for a week, then roll out about as thick as a finger. Bake in a quick oven and cut into strips with a sharp knife after they are baked (do this while hot), cut a finger long and two fingers wide.

### SHAVINGS.

Sift about a pint of flour in a bowl, make a hole in the center of the flour, break in five eggs, a pinch of salt, a teaspoonful of best ground cinnamon and a tablespoonful of pulverized sugar.

Mix this as you would a noodle dough, though not quite as stiff. Roll out very thin, and cut into long strips with a jagging iron. Heat some clarified butter, and fry a light yellow. Roll on a round stick as soon as taken up from the fat or butter, sprinkle with sugar and cinnamon or grated peel of a lemon. Mix both thoroughly. Do not let the butter get too brown; if the fire is too strong take off a few minutes. Called Kraus-gebackenes. Nice with wine.

### MOHN MAULTASCHEN (TARTLETS).

Grind a cupful of mohn (poppy seed), stir in the yelks of six eggs with three-fourths of a cup of sugar for about ten minutes, add the grated peel of a lemon, a handful of pounded almonds, sweet and bitter mixed. You may add a few raisins and some citron, shredded very fine, to the mixture, also a tablespoonful of rosewater. Beat the whites to a stiff froth and stir through the mixture. It is then ready to fill in the tarts. Bake a very light brown. Puff paste for these tarts is made as follows: Take one pound of the finest flour, and sift on the baking board. Make a hollow in the center, put in a piece of butter, a good pinch of salt and a tumbler of ice-water. Mix a dough of this with your hands and work it until it leaves your hands and the board perfectly clean. Now take a pound of fresh butter, wash the salt out of it and lay in ice-water, flatten the butter to a

finger in thickness, roll out the dough, place
the butter on it and cover securely with the
dough, then let the dough rest. This dough
should be made a day or two previous to using.
Roll out quite thin, cut into squares and add a
heaping teaspoonful of the poppy seed mixture
to each square, fold the points together to form
a triangle; spread with beaten egg and bake in
a quick oven.

POPPY SEED COOKIES (MOHN PLAETZCHEN).

Take an equal quantity of flour, sugar and
butter, and mix it well by rubbing with the hollow of the hands until small grains are formed.
Then add a cupful of poppy seed, two or more
eggs, and enough Rhine wine to hold the dough
together. Roll out the dough on a well floured
board, about half a finger in thickness, cut into
any shape desired. If you dissolve in the wine
a pinch of lump ammonia or a little warm milk,
it will help make the cookies light.

ALMOND MACAROONS.

(No. 1.) Blanch half a pound of almonds,
pound in mortar to a smooth paste, add one
pound of pulverized sugar and the beaten whites
of three eggs, and work the paste well together
with the back of a spoon. Dip your hands in
water and roll the mixture into balls the size of
a hickory nut, and lay on buttered or waxed paper an inch apart. When done, dip your hands in

water and pass gently over the macaroons, making the surface smooth and shiny. Set in a cool oven three-quarters of an hour.

### ALMOND MACAROONS.

(No. 2.)  Prepare the almonds by blanching them in boiling water. Strip them of the skins and lay them on a clean towel to dry. Grate or pound one-half pound of almonds, beat the whites of five or six eggs to a stiff, very stiff froth, stir in gradually three-quarters of a pound of pulverized sugar (use confectioner's sugar if you can get it) and then add the pounded almonds, to which add a tablespoonful of rose water or a teaspoonful of essence of bitter almonds. Line a broad baking-pan with buttered or waxed paper and drop upon this half a teaspoonful of the mixture at a time, allowing them room enough to prevent their running together. Sift powdered sugar over them and bake in a quick oven to a delicate brown. If the mixture has been well beaten they will not run. Try one on a piece of paper before you venture to bake them all. If it runs add a little more sugar.

### ALMOND MACAROONS.

(No. 3.)  Blanch the almonds in boiling water, say half a pound, and when perfectly cold pound them in a mortar, a few at a time. Beat the whites of six eggs to a very stiff froth, add three-quarters of a pound of pulverized sugar, stir in the pounded almonds, and bake in a pan lined with waxed or buttered paper, laying two inches apart. Try the mixture first, to see whether it is of the right consistency, and if the macaroons run into each other, beat in more sugar. Bake a light brown.

### CHOCOLATE PUFFS.

Beat to a stiff froth the whites of two eggs, stirring into them very gradually two teacups of powdered sugar and two tablespoonfuls of corn-starch, into which you have grated two ounces of chocolate. Bake on buttered tins fifteen minutes in a warm oven and drop with a dessert spoon one inch apart.

### HICKORY NUT MACAROONS.

Take meat of hickory nuts, pound fine and add mixed ground spices and nutmeg. Take whites of three eggs, beat in gradually one pound of confectioner's sugar, work the paste well with a spoon, and add nuts to this. Butter your hands and make the mixture into balls the size of nut-megs. Lay them in buttered tins an inch apart and bake in a very hot oven.

### CURRANT GEMS.

Rub one cup of butter to a cream, with two cups of sugar. Add the yelks of four eggs and one cup of milk, three cups of flour with two tea-spoonfuls of baking powder, sifted thoroughly. Half a pound of currants, carefully washed and dried between cloths, and then sift flour over and through them. Add the beaten whites of the eggs last and flour with nutmeg. Bake in small gem pans.

### GINGER WAFERS.

Take one cup of butter, one cup of sugar, one cup of molasses, half a cup of cold coffee, with two teaspoonfuls of soda, one tablespoonful of ginger, and flour enough to make a dough stiff enough to roll out thin. Cut with cookey-cutter and bake in quick oven.

### DOMINOES.

Make a sponge cake batter, and bake in long tins, not too large. The batter should not exceed the depth of one-fourth of an inch, spread it evenly and bake it in a quick oven (line the tins with buttered paper). As each cake is taken from the oven, turn it upside down on a clean board or paper. Spread with a thin layer of currant or cranberry jelly, and lay the other cake on top of it. Cut it with a hot, sharp knife into strips like dominoes; push them with the knife about an inch apart, and ice them with ordinary white icing, putting a tablespoonful on each piece, the heat of the cake will soften it, and with little assistance the edges and sides may be smoothly covered. Set the cakes in a warm place, where the frosting will dry. Make a horn of stiff white paper with just a small opening at the lower end. Put in a spoonful of dark choco-late icing and close the horn at the top, and by

pressing out the icing from the small opening,
draw a line of it across the center of each cake,
and then make dots like those on dominoes.
Keep the horn supplied with the icing.

### CREAM CAKES.

Boil one pint of water in a porcelain-lined
vessel, add half a pound of butter, and stir in
three-fourths of a pound of sifted flour. Let it
boil one minute, stirring constantly. Take from
the fire and let it cool. Stir into the batter the
yelks of eight eggs, one at a time, and then add
the stiff-beaten whites. Drop on buttered paper
in large baking pans, a spoonful at a time, and
bake from ten to fifteen minutes. Cream for
filling: Take one quart of milk and reserve
enough of this to wet two tablespoonfuls of cornstarch. Set the milk on to boil in a farina kettle.
Beat the yelks of four eggs with two small cups
of sugar, add the cornstarch and the milk and
stir all gradually into the boiling milk. When
thick remove from the fire, flavor with vanilla.
Pass a sharp knife lightly around the puffs,
open and fill.

### CHOCOLATE ECLAIRES.

Make same as Cream Puffs, but in long tins,
and cover with a chocolate caramel icing, as follows: Boil two cups of brown sugar with one
cup of molasses, one tablespoonful of butter and
three tablespoonfuls of flour. Boil half an hour;
then stir in half a pound of grated chocolate,

wet in half a cup of sweet milk, and boil until
it hardens on the spoon. Flavor with vanilla.
Spread this upon the Eclaires.

### MOLASSES COOKIES.

Take one cup of white sugar, one cup of
molasses, one cup of butter, one teaspoonful of
soda dissolved in a little milk, two tablespoonfuls of ginger and a little allspice, cloves and
nutmeg. Flour enough to roll.

### VANILLA COOKIES.

Rub one cup of butter and two cups of sugar
to a cream, add the yelks of four eggs and one
whole one and one teaspoonful of soda dissolved
in one tablespoonful of sweet milk. Flavor with
vanilla, roll very thin in baking, spread with
beaten white of egg and sugar.

### ANISESEED CAKES.

Take half a pound of sugar and half a pound
of flour (sift both many times), six eggs and
one teaspoonful of aniseseed. Beat the yelks
and the sugar until very thick, then add the
sifted flour and aniseseed and last the stiff-
beaten whites, which must be beaten very stiff.
Drop with a teaspoon upon waxed paper or flour
strewn upon baking-pans and bake with a very
slow fire. It improves the cakes wonderfully to
add a pinch of pulverized ammonia to the stiff-
beaten whites, and to take half potato flour and
half wheat.

### NUTMEG CAKES (PFEFFERNEUSSE).

Sift one pound of flour and one pound of pulverized sugar into a large bowl, four or five eggs, a piece of citron grated or chopped very fine, also the peel of a lemon, one whole nutmeg, grated, one tablespoonful of best ground cinnamon, one half teaspoonful of ground cloves, and half a teaspoonful of allspice. Mix all thoroughly in a deep bowl. Sift a heaping teaspoonful of baking powder in with the flour. Work into little balls as large as hickory nuts with buttered or floured hands. Bake on waxed or buttered tins, an inch apart. Very good.

### ENGLISH GEMS.

Rub one cup of butter to a cream, with two cups of dark brown sugar, add four eggs, one at a time, stirring each one well, and then add a cupful of black molasses and one cupful of hot, strong coffee in which you have previously dissolved one even teaspoonful of soda (strain before adding to the batter). Sift four and one-half cups of flour, twice, adding two teaspoonfuls of cream tartar in last half cupful of flour, and sift again before adding. Add the following spices: Nutmeg, mace, allspice and cloves; half teaspoonful of each; one cupful of sultanas, carefully picked, and one cupful of currants, carefully washed, dried and dredged with flour, also half a cupful of finely-cut or chopped citron. Now fill in small gem pans

which have been previously well greased. Fill
the gems about half to give enough room to rise.
When all are baked ice prettily, and when dry
pack away in a tin cake box. They are best
eaten fresh.

### GERMAN LEBKUCHEN.

Mix two pounds of brown sugar with eight
eggs, one nutmeg grated, two tablespoonfuls of
ground cinnamon, two teaspoonfuls of ground
cloves, one teaspoonful of mace, one-half pound
of almonds cut lengthwise, and one-half pound
of citron, shaved fine. Add sufficient flour to
make the dough stiff enough to roll. Add two
teaspoonfuls of baking soda dissolved in a very
little hot water before adding the flour. Make
the dough, roll and cut the cakes, put in buttered or floured tins and bake next day, allowing them to stand twenty four hours before
baking. You may ice after baking if so desired.
They are also very nice brushed with sweetened
water, just before baking. Bake about fifteen
minutes.

### GINGER GEMS.

(No. 1.) Take two tablespoonfuls of molasses, one cup of brown sugar, two eggs, one
teaspoonful of ground ginger, one teaspoonful
of ground cinnamon, and one-half teaspoonful
of ground cloves. Two and one-half cups of
sifted flour, to which you must add two tea-

spoonfuls of baking powder and one cupful of
sweet milk. Bake in well greased gem pans.

### GINGER GEMS.

(No. 2.) Take two tablespoonfuls of butter,
one cup of molasses, one cup of brown sugar,
two eggs, two and one-half cups of flour and
one cup of sour milk in which you have dissolved one teaspoonful of baking soda. Spice
with one heaping teaspoonful of ground ginger,
one teaspoonful of ground cinnamon and one-
half teaspoonful of ground cloves. Bake at
once in well greased gems.

### EGGLESS GINGER GEMS.

Mix one cup of molasses, one cup of sugar,
one tablespoonful of butter, and warm slightly,
beat up well and stir at least ten minutes.
Add following spices: One or two teaspoonfuls
of ginger and one teaspoonful of cinnamon; add
gradually one cup of milk, and five cups of
sifted flour in which you have sifted two teaspoonfuls of baking powder. You may add a
handful of currants or chopped raisins. Bake
in well greased gem pans and eat warm for
lunch or tea.

### CHOCOLATE WAFERS.

Make a chocolate custard of one heaping cupful of grated chocolate, one half cupful of granulated sugar, one half cupful of milk, and boil
until it begins to thicken a little. Beat until

cold, flavor with a teaspoonful of vanilla and
add it to the following batter: Stir one and
one-half cups of brown sugar with a scant half
cup of butter, then add the yelks of four eggs
and beaten whites of two, which stir in last, and
two cups of flour in which you have sifted two
teaspoonfuls of baking powder.

### HICKORY NUT MACAROONS.

Take one cupful of pulverized sugar and one
cupful of finely-pounded hickory nut meats,
the unbeaten whites of two eggs, two heaping
teaspoonfuls of flour, and one scant teaspoonful
of baking powder. Mix these ingredients together and drop from a teaspoon which you
have previously dipped in cold water upon buttered paper. Do not put them too near each
other, for they always spread a great deal.
Bake about fifteen minutes. You may double
the quantity, as this will not make very many.

### BASELER LECKERLEIN.

Take one pound of sifted sugar, one pound of
honey, one pound of almonds cut lengthwise,
one pound of best flour sifted, and three ounces
of finely-shaved citron, the grated rind of a
lemon, and half of a nutmeg grated, one teaspoonful of ground cloves, and one tablespoonful of ground cinnamon and half of a wineglassful of arrack. Warm the honey over a slow
fire and add all the ingredients gradually.

Then take it off the stove and work it into a dough, which you can keep covered up for several days before rolling out and baking. Add half an ounce of pottache just before working the dough. Cut into desired slices while still warm.

### STRAWBERRY SMACKS.

Make some puffs, according to "cream cake" recipes, and fill in with whipped cream and fresh stawberries which have been liberally sugared with pulverized sugar.

**MEMORANDUM.**

# ICE-CREAMS, ETC.

## ICE-CREAMS.

| | Page. | | | Page. |
|---|---|---|---|---|
| Apricot, - - - | 373 | Nesselrode, - - | 326 |
| Bergamot, - - | 378 | Orange, - - | 372 |
| Banana, - - - | 372 | Peach, - - - | 369 |
| Chocolate, - - | 368 | Pineapple, - - | 869 |
| Coffee, - - - | 370 | Pistache, - - | 374 |
| Caramel, - - | 328 | Raspberry, - - | 375 |
| General Instructions, | 365 | Strawberry, - - | 377 |
| Hazelnut, - - | 874 | Tea, - - - | 370 |
| Lemon, - - | 870 | Tutti-Frutti, - - | 874 |
| New York, - - | 367 | Vanilla, - - | 875 |

## ICES.

| | Page. | | | Page. |
|---|---|---|---|---|
| Apricot, - - - | 373 | Lemon, - - - | 372 |
| Cherry, - - - | 371 | Orange, - - | 371 |
| Currant, - - - | 371 | Pineapple, - - | 369 |
| Currant and Rasp- | | Peach, - - - | 373 |
| berry, - - - | 372 | Raspberry, - - | 873 |
| Champagne, - - | 375 | Strawberry, - - | 369 |
| Ice a la Tutti-Frutti, | 373 | | |

## MISCELLANEOUS.

| | Page. | | | Page. |
|---|---|---|---|---|
| Cafe a la Glace, | - 373 | Frozen Peaches, | - 379 |
| Cherry Diplomat, - | 880 | Kirsch Punch, - | - 380 |
| Frozen Fruits or | | Nesselrode Pudding, | 376 |
| Berries, - - | 371 | Pineapple Bisque, | - 877 |
| Frozen Egg-Nog, | - 375 | Roman Punch, - | 371 |
| Fruit Frapees, - | 378 | Royal Punch, - | - 379 |

## MEMORANDUM.

# ICE–CREAMS, ETC.

TO begin with, you must procure the best triple-motion patent freezer, plenty of ice and rock salt (common salt will not do so well). Use pure cream only. You can not expect to make rich ice-cream of milk. Pure cream and pure fruit juices only should be used. When your cream is ready to freeze rinse the can with cold water, also the paddle or flat stick. Be sure the pail rests on the pivot before packing. Cover securely. Have ready a quantity of cracked ice (the pieces should not be larger than a walnut). To do this easily lay the ice in the folds of an old piece of carpet or blanket and pound it with a hammer or mallet. In this way you will not waste any ice or soil the floor. Gather it up with a large kitchen spoon and pack it closely around the cream pail to the height of the freezer. Pack alternately a layer of ice and a layer salt, until the ice reaches the top of the pail. Turn the crank slowly and evenly, the slower you turn the smoother the cream will be, which should be like velvet to the tongue. If frozen too rapidly it will be coarse-grained, and using too much salt is apt to have the same effect. When the water reaches the hole in the freezer and you can not possibly turn any more, your cream is frozen. To make sure of this, however, let John or Bridget take hold of it and turn for five minutes more. Then pour off the water, wipe off the cover of the freezer and uncover very carefully, so as not to have any salt mixed with the cream. Take out the paddle and pack the cream firmly in the pail, cover closely and put thick paper—a cork is still better—into the hole in the cover of the cream pail. Pack well with ice and set it in a cool place, covered with carpet or an old blanket. If your refrigerator is large enough set the whole freezer in it. I wish to state right here that it requires a much longer time to freeze water-ices than cream, and requires more salt in freezing. You will find that ices are much cheaper than creams, though confectioners charge just as much for one as the other. If the freezer does not work easily oil with a little sewing-machine oil, but be very careful not to get a drop into the can of your freezer. I once ate ice-cream flavored with kerosene oil, but I did not take a second mouthful of it, though the hostess playfully assured us all that it was very good for sore throats. None present, however, happened to be afflicted in that way. But I have drifted away from my subject. Well, I would advise you to oil the machinery of the freezer before putting it together. After filling the tub with ice and salt, allow a few minutes for the cream to become thoroughly cooled and then turn the crank until the freezing is complete. Turn slowly at first, and remember that too much salting and too rapid freezing are liable to produce coarseness. A moderate revolution of the can assures smoothness, and will, in freezing, increase the cream to double the original quantity. Do not draw off the water during freezing, but keep the hole in the side of the tub open, to let the water run out.

## NEW YORK ICE–CREAM.

Take one quart of rich, sweet cream and heat it slowly in a farina kettle, in which you have put a vanilla bean (if you haven't the vanilla bean flavor with extract when the cream has cooled off). In the meantime beat the yelks of ten or twelve eggs with one pound of pulverized sugar; add, a little at a time, the heated cream to the beaten yelks. Stir well until all has been added. Return all to the farina kettle and stir until it boils. Stir constantly until thick, remove from the fire and stir until cold. You may do this for some time the day previous. Your cream is now ready to freeze, which do according to above directions.

## CHOCOLATE ICE-CREAM.

(No. 1.) To three pints of cream, rich and sweet, add one pound of pulverized sugar, and dissolve half a pound of sweet vanilla chocolate, which has been previously grated, in part of the cream. Add the latter when the cream is partly frozen.

## CHOCOLATE ICE-CREAM.

(No. 2.) Take one quart of cream, one pint of new milk, two eggs, a teacupful of grated chocolate, double vanilla, two cups of pulverized sugar, a teaspoonful of cornstarch and one of extract of vanilla. Beat the yelks of the eggs, stir them in the milk, add the cornstarch and sugar and let them come to a boil. Then take them quickly from the fire, dissolve the chocolate in a little milk over the fire, stir it all the time. When smooth mix with the milk and eggs, add the cream and vanilla. If not sweet enough add more sugar. Freeze when cold.

## CHOCOLATE ICE-CREAM.

(No. 3.) Grate ten ounces of fine, sweet vanilla chocolate and dissolve it in a pint of sweet cream. Heat it in a farina kettle with an additional quart of cream. Beat the yelks of twelve eggs light with a pound of pulverized sugar; add the boiling cream gradually, very little at a time. When all has been added return to the kettle and let it come to a boil. Remove from the fire and strain through a hair sieve, stirring constantly in one direction until cold. Freeze.

### PEACH ICE-CREAM.

Pare and grate a quart of fine-flavored yellow peaches and mix with a pound of pulverized sugar. Stir gradually into this mixture three pints of rich cream and freeze.

### PINEAPPLE ICE-CREAM.

Pare and grate the pineapple and sprinkle sugar over it. Now freeze three pints of cream with one pound of pulverized sugar. When partly frozen add the pineapple just as it is, or pressed through a hair sieve.

### PINEAPPLE ICE.

Grate one large pineapple and the juice of one lemon to two quarts of water, and one pound of pulverized sugar to each quart of water. Beat the whites of three eggs to a very stiff froth, and add when the ice is almost frozen.

### STRAWBERRY ICE.

(No. 1.) Extract the juice of two quarts of berries by mashing and pressing them through a hair sieve. Use the juice of one lemon and one pound of sugar to each quart of water. Freeze.

### STRAWBERRY ICE.

(No. 2.) Crush two quarts of strawberries with two pounds of sugar; let them stand for two hours, then strain through a jelly bag. Now add as much water as you have juice; also

the juice of a lemon. When half frozen add the
beaten whites of four eggs.

### COFFEE ICE-CREAM.

Put one-quarter of a pound of fresh-roasted
and ground coffee in a quart of boiling cream,
and three-quarters of a pound of sugar, and let
this boil in a closely-covered farina kettle. Set
it away to cool, keeping it closely covered all the
time. Stir the yelks of twelve eggs light, and
add to the coffee cream, again letting it come
to boil. Then remove from the fire and strain
it through a hair sieve and stir until cold.
Freeze.

### TEA ICE-CREAM.

Steep two ounces of the best mixed tea in
three pints of boiling cream. In the meantime
stir three-quarters of a pound of pulverized sugar
and the yelks of twelve eggs or more until thick;
add gradually to the cream, boil up once, strain
through a hair sieve, and stir until cold.
Freeze.

### LEMON ICE-CREAM.

Grate the peel of two lemons into a pound of
pulverized sugar; put the sugar into a quart of
cream and boil; beat the yelks of eight eggs
light and add gradually to the boiling cream
and let it boil up once more. Remove from the
fire and stir until cold, then stir the juice of
three lemons into the cream; do this rapidly

and turn into the freezer at once and freeze, for the acid is apt to turn the cream sour.

### ORANGE ICE.

Take six oranges; grate the peel of three and squeeze out the juice of all the oranges. Add the grated peel to the juice, also the juice of two lemons, one pint of water and one pint of sugar. Strain into the can and freeze.

### ROMAN PUNCH.

Prepare the same as for orange ice, and then add good brandy or Jamaica spirits before freezing.

### FROZEN FRUITS OR BERRIES.

Select the ripest and reduce to a pulp. To each quart add three-quarters of a pound of pulverized sugar and the juice of one or more oranges. Freeze.

### CURRANT ICE.

Take one pint of currant juice, one pound of sugar and one pint of water. Put in freezer, and when partly frozen, add the beaten whites of two eggs. Freeze.

### CHERRY ICE.

Take one quart of cherries, with half the stones pounded in a mortar, and the juice of one lemon. Squeeze out the bruised cherries and stones through a bag over a pint of sugar. I forgot to mention to put the bruised cherries and stones into a pint of water for about two hours before you intend to freeze. A wineglassful of brandy or red wine improves this ice very much; but all ices which have brandy added require a longer time to freeze.

### LEMON ICE.

Take six large, juicy lemons and the grated peel of three; two oranges, the juice of both and the peel of one. Squeeze out every drop of juice, and steep the grated peel of the lemons and oranges in it for an hour. Strain, mix in a pint of sugar and a pint of water. Stir until dissolved, and freeze.

### ORANGE ICE–CREAM.

Is made in the same way as lemon ice-cream, omitting the lemons.

### BANANA ICE–CREAM.

To three pints of cream add one pound of pulverized sugar and six or eight bananas grated into the cream. Freeze. You may boil the cream and add as many eggs as you choose. When cold add the grated bananas and freeze. I like this cream just as well without the eggs.

### CURRANT AND RASPBERRY ICE.

Take one quart of red currants and one quart of red raspberries. Mash to a pulp, squeeze out the juice and mix in a pint of water and a pound of sugar; dissolve the sugar well before freezing. Delicious.

### RASPBERRY ICE.

Take one quart of berries, juice of one lemon and one pint of sugar dissolved in half a pint of water. Mash the berries, extract the juice by squeezing through a cloth.

### APRICOT ICE.

Pare and grate two dozen apricots, and blanch a few of the kernels. Then pound them and add to the grated fruit. Pour a pint of water over them, adding the juice of a lemon also. Let them stand for an hour and strain, adding a pound of sugar just before freezing.

### APRICOT ICE–CREAM.

Make same as peach Ice-cream.

### PEACH ICE.

This is made like Apricot Ice, using two lemons instead of one.

### ICE A LA TUTTI-FRUTTI.

Prepare an Orange Ice, and when partly frozen, add candied fruit, chopped up fine, such as cherries, apricots, peaches, pineapple, etc.

### CAFE A LA GLACE.

Take ten ounces of fresh-roasted and ground coffee. Pour eight cups of boiling water over it; cover quickly and put on the back of the stove, and add three-quarters of a pound of sugar. When cold, press through a sieve, and fill in the can to be frozen. Let it remain in

freezer five minutes longer before you begin to
turn the freezer. Serve in glasses, and put
sweetened whipped cream on the top.

### HAZELNUT ICE-CREAM.

Take ten ounces of hazelnuts or filberts
pounded in a mortar or grated, and boiled in a
quart of cream. Press the boiled cream through
a hair sieve or fine cloth. Beat the yelks of ten
eggs and three-quarters of a pound of pulverized
sugar to a cream; add to the nut cream and
heat again until it boils. Stir until cold, and
freeze.

### TUTTI-FRUTTI ICE-CREAM.

Take three pints of cream, one pound of pulverized sugar and the yelks of twelve eggs.
Prepare just like the other creams. When half
frozen throw in half a pound of crystalized
fruit, peaches, apricots, cherries, citron, etc.,
chopped very fine. Put in also a wineglassful
of pale sherry and the juice of an orange or
lemon. Finish freezing.

### PISTACHE ICE-CREAM.

Blanch half a pound of pistache nuts and
grate with white of an egg. Boil a quart of
sweet cream; beat the yelks of eight eggs with
three-quarters of a pound of pulverized sugar,
and add this to the boiling cream. Stir constantly after removing from the fire until cold.
Boil the nuts with the cream.

### RASPBERRY ICE—CREAM.

Take three pints of rich cream, one quart of berries and one pound of pulverized sugar. Mash the berries to a pulp, strain through a sieve, mix with the sugar and cream, and freeze.

### CHAMPAGNE ICE.

Boil one pound of sugar with one cup of water until it is like syrup. When cold, add the juice of six lemons, one bottle of champagne and the stiff-beaten whites of seven eggs. Mix all thoroughly, fill in the can and freeze, stirring constantly. Add also a very liberal quantity of rock salt to the ice.

### FROZEN EGG—NOGG.

Take one quart of rich cream, and put it to boil in a farina kettle. Beat up the yelks of eight eggs with one pound of pulverized sugar, flavor with grated nutmeg and half a pint of best brandy. Stir the beaten yelks and sugar into the boiling cream; stir constantly for one minute; remove from the fire and stir until cold. Lastly whip in the stiff-beaten whites of four eggs. Freeze.

### VANILLA ICE—CREAM.

To three pints of cream, rich and sweet, add one pound of pulverized sugar and four teaspoonfuls of vanilla extract; mix well and freeze, or boil a vanilla bean in the cream, and let it get perfectly cold before freezing.

### NESSELRODE ICE-CREAM.

Boil one pound of chestnuts and peel and grate them, or mash to a smooth paste with a pint of milk. Beat the yelks of twelve eggs and one pound and a half of powdered sugar, and add three pints of boiling cream, in which you have boiled a vanilla bean and a quarter of a pound of the finest chocolate. Strain and stir until cold. Add some apricot marmalade, candied cherries, preserved figs, and any other kind of candied fruit chopped very fine. Freeze very slowly.

### NESSELRODE PUDDING, WITH MARA- SCHINA SAUCE.

Roast one pound of chestnuts, remove shells, and boil them in wine and sugar until tender. Boil two pounds of sugar with the juice of four lemons. Now press the boiled nuts and sugar through a fine sieve. You may add part of the wine the nuts were boiled in. When cold beat one quart of whipping cream to a froth, like for Charlotte Russe. Lay it upon a hair sieve to let the thin part run off and add a quarter of a pound of the finest chocolate, grated, and freeze. When frozen put a layer of cream in a form, then a layer of apricot marmalade and fig preserves, also the boiled chestnuts. Add as much candied fruit chopped fine as you like, then a layer of cream, and so on until all is used up. Press all very tight in the form. In serving, dump on a platter, and pour a cold sauce over it, which is made of whipped cream flavored with Maraschina brandy and sweetend to taste.

## PINEAPPLE BISQUE.

Take a quart of rich, sweet cream and heat in a farina kettle. In the meantime beat up the yelks of eight eggs with two cups of pulverized sugar. Beat as light as you would for cake. Take the cream and add gradually to this, then return to the farina kettle and boil until thick like custard, stirring constantly. Remove from the fire and pour into a bowl, stirring until cold. When you are ready to freeze the cream, add a can of grated pineapple, or a fresh pineapple, which you have previously grated and sweetened, also a handful of macaroons, pounded finely. When partly frozen add a wineglassful of good brandy.

## STRAWBERRY ICE—CREAM.

Reduce one quart of strawberries to a pulp. Do this with a potato-masher in a large porcelain bowl. Stir into this gradually one pound of pulverized sugar, then stir in three pints of cream, and freeze. Serve in small nests of spun sugar, or fill the cream in eggs made of meringue, and lay one in each nest. The effect is very pretty. Cherry-ice may be served instead of the cream, or both. Of course. this is meant for company only.

### BERGAMOT ICE-CREAM.

Heat a quart of milk almost to boiling point; beat eight eggs light with one pound of pulverized sugar; add the heated milk gradually to the eggs and sugar and return to the fire, boiling in a pail set within one of hot water. Stir the mixture steadily until it thickens. Remove from the fire, stir until cold and flavor with half a teaspoonful of bergamot. Whip a quart of rich cream, add and freeze.

### CHERRY ICE.

Take one quart of canned red cherries, one pound of sugar and the juice of a lemon. It will take longer to freeze than cream. Use more rock salt with the ice in freezing. You may add some red wine if you choose.

### FRUIT FRAPEES.

Line a mold with vanilla ice-cream, fill the center with fresh berries or any other fruit and cover again with ice-cream. Cover closely, and set away to freeze for an hour, packed in a pail with ice and salt.

### CARAMEL ICE-CREAM.

Boil one pound of sugar in a saucepan until it is a brown caramel, and then pour it into a porcelain bowl, and set in a cool place until cold. Then pound to a powder in a mortar, or roll on a board with a rolling-pin until fine. Now boil one quart of cream, beat the yelks of twelve eggs or less until light, add gradually to the cream; also the caramel, remove from the fire, and when cold freeze. You may add an additional flavor of vanilla or orange. Adding whipped cream to any of these creams improves them.

### FROZEN PEACHES.

Set on to boil one quart of water with one pint of sugar. Boil sugar and water fifteen minutes, throw in about one dozen fine peaches which have been sliced and pared, and boil fifteen minutes longer. Rub through a collander or sieve, and when cold freeze. Whip two cups of sweet cream, remove the dasher from the frozen peaches and stir in the whipped cream with a spoon. Let it stand in freezer for an hour before serving.

### ROYAL PUNCH.

Take two quarts of water, three pounds of sugar, juice of six lemons, two oranges, the contents of half a can of pineapples, one wineglassful of brandy, and one-half pint of white wine. Grate the rinds of one lemon and one orange into a bowl and add the juice of all the fruit. Set the water and sugar on to boil with the juice of the pineapple and boil until thick like syrup, then pour the syrup while hot on the grated rind of the lemon, etc., and juice to draw the flavor. Chop up the pineapple, add to the strained juice and freeze. Use red wine if you would have it pink, instead of white.

### KIRSCH PUNCH.

Take two quarts of water, juice of five lemons, one pint of kirschwasser and three pounds of sugar. Mix the ingredients together and strain into your freezer. When nearly frozen, whip the whites of eight eggs very stiff and add to the punch and continue the freezing until done

### CHERRY DIPLOMATE.

Line a mold with white cake, thinly sliced, which you have previously dipped in marachino or some other fine brandy. Then fill in with plain white ice-cream and then put in a layer of cherry-ice and next fill in a layer of candied cherries, and next again a layer of cherry-ice, then a layer of strawberry ice-cream or the plain white vanilla. Finish it up with a layer of cake again and be sure to dip the cake in the marachino. Cover all up tight and pack in ice until wanted.

# CONFECTIONERY.

|  | Page. |
|---|---|
| Burnt Almonds, | 384 |
| Butterscotch, | 386 |
| Butter Taffy, | 387 |
| Butternut and Almond Candy, | 392 |
| Candy of any Flavor, | 383 |
| Cocoanut Caramels, | 383 |
| Cream Candy, | 384 |
| Cream Almonds, | 385 |
| Chocolate Creams, | 385 |
| Cocoanut Cones, | 386 |
| Cocoanut Drops, | 388 |
| Candied Cherries, | 389 |
| Cream Caramels, | 391 |
| Filbert Creams, | 291 |
| General Instructions, | 382 |
| How to Wax Paper, | 387 |
| Hoarhound Candy, | 389 |
| Ice-Cream Candy, | 387 |
| Lemon Cream Candy, | 384 |
| Maple Creams, | 387 |
| Maple Nut Candy, | 388 |
| Marshmallows, | 390 |
| Molasses Candy, | 390 |
| Nut Candy, | 388 |
| Nougat, | 392 |
| Pink Cocoanut Creams, | 392 |
| Prunes, Dates and Figs, | 391 |
| Peanut Candy, | 391 |
| Salted Almonds, | 389 |
| Tutti Frutti Candy, | 392 |
| Uncooked French Creams, | 390 |
| Walnut Chocolate Drops, | 385 |

# CONFECTIONERY.

A BRASS KETTLE, if kept perfectly clean, is best for boiling sugar in for confectionery. Dissolve two pounds of white sugar in one pint of water and place this in the kettle over a slow fire for a quarter of an hour. Pour into it a small quantity of gelatine and gum arabic dissolved together. Skim off at once all the impurities which rise to the surface. The white of an egg may be used as a substitute to make the clarifying process still more perfect, and strain through a flannel bag. If you allow the syrup to boil a few moments longer you will have what is called "Rock Candy." To make other candies bring the syrup very carefully to such a degree of heat that the "threads" which drop from the spoon when raised into cold air will snap like glass. When this desired stage is reached, add a teaspoonful of vinegar or cream tartar to prevent granulation, and pour into pans as directed in the receipts which follow. To make stick candies, pull and roll into shape with buttered hands.

(382)

### CANDY OF ANY FLAVOR.

Take two and a half pounds of refined sugar, one pint of water and one teaspoonful of cream tartar. Mix in a kettle large enough to hold the candy when expanded by heat, and boil over a brisk fire, taking care that it does not burn, applying the heat at the bottom, not to the sides. After boiling fifteen minutes remove a small portion of the melted sugar with a spoon, and cool by placing in a saucer set in ice-water. When cool enough take a portion between thumb and finger, and if it "threads" as it is separated, the process is nearly completed, and great care must be used to regulate the heat so that the boiling may be kept up without burning. Test frequently by dropping a bit into cold water placed near. If it becomes hard and brittle, snapping apart when bent, it is done and must be removed at once, and the flavoring stirred in. Then pour into shallow earthen dishes, thoroughly but lightly greased, and cool until it can be handled; then pull and roll into sticks or any shape desired.

### COCOANUT CARAMELS.

Take one pint of milk, butter about the size of an egg, one cocoanut grated fine, three pounds of white sugar and two teaspoonfuls of lemon extract. Boil slowly until stiff, beat to a cream, pour into shallow buttered pans. and when set cut into squares.

## CREAM CANDY.

Take two heaping cups of white sugar, one wineglassful of vinegar and one tumbler of water. Boil one-half hour, flavor with vanilla and pull like molasses candy.

## LEMON CREAM CANDY.

Take three cups of sugar, one-half cup of vinegar, one-half cup of water and a teaspoonful of butter, put in last, with a teaspoonful of soda dissolved in hot water. Boil fast for about half an hour, until it crisps in cold water; flavor with lemon and pull white.

## BURNT ALMONDS.

Take one pound of almonds and wipe clean. In the meantime put on a pound of sugar with a quarter of a pint of water, let it boil until clear and thick; throw in the almonds and stir with a wooden spoon until you hear them crack. Take off the fire, but keep stirring them; and when dry put in a wire sieve and sift all the sugar from them. Now put that sugar on to boil again, add a little, very little, water and some cinnamon if you like. When this boils throw in the almonds again, and keep stirring until quite dry. Take off the fire and pack in a glass jar. You may add fruit-coloring in sugar the second time it is put over the fire.

### WALNUT CHOCOLATE DROPS.

Take two and a half cups of pulverized sugar, one-half cup cold water and boil five miuntes. Then place in a pan of cold water and beat until cold enough to make into balls and put a walnut in the center of each. By using maple sugar you have maple creams. Take half a cake of chocolate, shave off fine, set it in a bowl on top of a boiling teakettle to melt, and when the drops are cold roll in the melted chocolate with a fork.

### CREAM ALMONDS.

These are made like walnut drops. While making into balls mold an almond meat into the center of each ball; then roll in coarse granulated sugar, and you have delicious cream almonds. Lay on buttered paper until cold.

### CHOCOLATE CREAMS.

Take two cups of sugar, one cup of water and one tablespoonful and a half of arrowroot or cornstarch, one tablespoonful of butter and one teaspoonful of vanilla. Wash the butter, stir the sugar and water together, add the arrowroot and bring to a boil, stirring constantly to induce granulation. Boil for about ten minutes, then add the butter, take from the fire and stir constantly until it begins to look like granulated cream. Add the vanilla. Butter your hands and make the cream into balls the size of a marble, and lay upon a clean board or flat dish (outside).

Take half a pound of sweet vanilla chocolate, grate it, set in a tin pail or saucepan, and put this in another of boiling water, so as to melt the chocolate. When the chocolate is melted to the consistency of syrup, roll the cream balls in it until sufficiently coated and take each one up carefully and lay upon a dish to dry.

### COCOANUT CONES.

Whip the whites of five eggs to a very stiff froth and add gradually the whole of one pound of pulverized sugar and one teaspoonful of arrow-root; last, a fresh-grated cocoanut, or half a pound of desiccated cocoanut. Mold the mixture with your hands into small cones (flour your hands); set these far enough apart not to touch one another, upon buttered or waxed paper, in a long baking-pan. Bake in moderate oven. Be sure to prepare the cocoanut before you begin; lay the pieces in cold water after paring, until all is grated.

### BUTTERSCOTCH.

Boil one pound and a half of coffee sugar (white, but not granulated), half a cup of sweet butter, half a teaspoonful of cream tartar, and just enough water to dissolve the sugar. Boil without stirring until it will break easily when dropped into cold water. When done add one teaspoonful of lemon juice, or ten drops of extract. Pour into well-greased pans, and when almost cold mark into small squares.

## HOW TO WAX PAPER.

Get some one to assist you in holding the paper over the fire, and a third person to rub the wax over it. It may be done in a second. To remove macaroons or any other confection from paper, moisten the paper with a damp sponge on the opposite side and they will come off easily.

## BUTTER TAFFY.

Boil one cup of molasses and one cup of sugar until it candies. Remove from the fire and stir in nearly half a cup of butter and flavor with vanilla.

## MAPLE CREAMS.

Set some genuine maple sugar on to boil with half as much water as you have sugar. Boil until it is brittle when dropped into cold water, and when it is inclined to harden remove from the fire and stir rapidly until it becomes a waxen substance; then form into balls not larger than a marble. Butter your hands well to do this. Put half a walnut kernel on either side. Lay them on a greased platter to cool.

## ICE-CREAM CANDY.

Boil one and a half pounds of moist white coffee sugar, two ounces of butter, one teacupful and a half of water, together with the peel of half a lemon. When done (if done it will become crisp by dropping into cold water) set aside till the boiling has ceased, and stir in the juice of one large lemon (no seeds).  Butter a dish and pour in about an inch thick.  When cool take out the lemon peel, pull until white and form into any shape desire.  If you have no lemon take two tablespoonfuls of vinegar and two teaspoonfuls of extract.

### COCOANUT DROPS.

Take one pound of grated cocoanut, half a pound of confectioner's sugar and the stiff-beaten white of one egg.  Work all together and roll in the hands into little balls.  Bake on buttered tins.

### MAPLE NUT CANDY.

Take one pint of maple sugar, and half a pint of water, or just enough to dissolve the sugar. Boil until it becomes brittle by dropping in cold water.  Just before pouring add a table-spoonful of vinegar, having previously prepared the nut meats; butter the pans, line with nut meats, and pour the candy over them.

### NUT CANDY.

Boil a pound of sugar with a cup of water. After boiling over a brisk fire pour in a dash of vinegar.  Take off the scum as it rises and test by raising with a spoon; if its "threads" snap, pour over chopped cocoanut or any other kind of nuts.  Brazil nuts cut into slices are very nice.  Butter the pans before putting in nuts and candy.

## HOARHOUND CANDY.

Boil two ounces of dried hoarhound in a pint of water for about half an hour; strain and add three pounds of brown sugar. Boil over a hot fire until hard; pour out on well-greased flat pans, and mark as soon as cold enough to retain the marks.

## CANDIED CHERRIES.

Boil a syrup of two pounds of cut loaf sugar and a cup of water; boil until thick enough to pull. Then remove to the side of the stove until it shows signs of granulation. Drop in the cherries, carefully stoned, only a few at a time, and only two or three minutes; remove to a sieve, set over a dish, shake gently and turn the cherries out on white paper.

## SALTED ALMONDS.

Throw the almonds into boiling water and blanch. After they are skimmed lay on a platter for several hours to dry. Put a piece of fresh butter in a spider, and as it melts stir the almonds over and over in it to glaze them. Take them off and set in the oven to roast, stirring often, until they begin to color slightly. Take from the oven, throw on clean paper, spread out and sprinkle with fine table salt, and repeat, so that all will be well sprinkled. Eat cold. Do not get the almonds too brown. Fry well before putting in the oven. They are very appetizing, and serve as a course at progressive dinners.

## MARSHMALLOWS.

Dissolve one pound of gum arabic in one quart of water; strain; add one pound of refined sugar and place over the fire, stirring constantly until the sugar is dissolved and the mixture has become the consistency of honey. Next add gradually the whites of eight eggs, well beaten, stirring the mixture all the time, until it loses its stickiness and does not adhere to the fingers when touched. The mass may now be poured out into a pan slightly dusted with corn-starch. When cool divide into small squares.

## MOLASSES CANDY.

Take one cup of molasses, one cup of sugar, and one tablespoonful of vinegar, and a teaspoonful of fresh butter. Boil until it hardens when dropped in cold water; then stir in a pinch of soda or cream tartar and pour on buttered tins. When cool begin to pull, having previously greased your hands.

## UNCOOKED FRENCH CREAMS.

Break the whites of three eggs into a bowl, and add exactly as much water as you have whites of eggs (measure with the egg-shells). Stir in confectioner's sugar until stiff enough to mold into any shape desired. Flavor to suit your taste.

### FILBERT CREAMS.

Butter or flour your hands, and roll the above French cream around filbert nuts. Have some chocolate melted over a steaming tea-kettle in a bowl, and after the filbert balls are dry, roll them in the melted chocolate by means of a long hat-pin or fine knitting-needle.

### PRUNES, DATES AND FIGS.

Select the finest only. Tear them open and extract the kernels, leaving them whole at the stem end. Insert a piece of cream, and press the fruit together at the bottom.

### PEANUT CANDY.

Boil two cups of sugar with half a cup of water and dissolve half a teaspoonful of cream tartar in a little cold water and add. Boil until it becomes brittle when dropped in cold water. Then add a piece of butter the size of a hickory-nut and boil a few minutes longer. Pour this over the nuts, which have been spread in a buttered tin, and set away to cool.

### CREAM CARAMELS.

Boil together one pint of cream and three pounds of sugar. Add any desired flavoring. Boil until it reaches 260° Fahrenheit. Pour out the mixture on flat dishes to cool, and, as soon as it begins to " set," which is very soon, cut it into little blocks with a sharp blade dipped in cold water. These will be good for some time, and are as wholesome a confection as can be found for children.

### PINK COCOANUT CREAMS.

Use pink confectioner's sugar, or color with fruit coloring; add grated cocoanut; roll into balls; fill each center with a candied cherry.

### TUTTI-FRUTTI CANDY.

Chop seeded raisins, citron, figs and a few candied cherries. Put two cupfuls of granulated sugar and half a cupful of boiling water into a brass or porcelain kettle and boil hard for ten minutes. Take from the stove, pour into a bowl, flavor and stir rapidly with a spoon until it looks like cream. Add the chopped fruit and stir awhile longer. Press thin on buttered tins, cut into squares and wrap in waxed papers.

### NOUGAT.

Blanch one-half pound of almonds in boiling water. When skinned, cut in half through the center and lay on white paper in the oven with door open to dry. Meanwhile, melt half a pound of sugar in a double kettle, without adding a drop of water. Stir constantly until the sugar boils, take off the kettle and stir in the almonds immediately. Pour into a flat greased tin pan, which has been previously warmed. Press the nougat flat to the bottom of the pan. Cut while still warm. Wrap in waxed paper.

### BUTTERNUT AND ALMOND CANDY

Are made same as Cocoanut candy.

# PRESERVES.

|                                        | Page.      |
|----------------------------------------|------------|
| Apple Butter,                          | 405        |
| Blackberry Jam,                        | 402        |
| Blackberry Syrup,                      | 403        |
| Cherries,                              | 400        |
| Cherry Marmalade,                      | 400        |
| Citron,                                | 401        |
| Gooseberry Jam,                        | 404        |
| Grape Preserves,                       | 406        |
| Green Tomatoes,                        | 401        |
| General Instructions,                  | 394        |
| Preserved Peaches,                     | 394        |
| Preserved Pears,                       | 395, 403   |
| Preserved Greengages and Plums,        | 395        |
| Preserved Quinces,                     | 396        |
| Preserved Crab-Apples,                 | 396        |
| Preserved Currants and Raspberries,    | 397        |
| Preserved Raspberries,                 | 397        |
| Preserved Figs,                        | 399        |
| Preserved Blackberries,                | 403        |
| Peach Butter,                          | 404        |
| Quince Cheese,                         | 405        |
| Ripe Tomatoes,                         | 402        |
| Raspberry Jam,                         | 404        |
| Strawberries,                          | 398        |
| Strawberry Jam,                        | 399        |
| Strawberry Marmalade,                  | 400        |
| Watermelon Rind,                       | 401        |

# PRESERVES.

IN making preserves or jellies use none but porcelain-lined or bell-metal kettles, being very careful to have them perfectly clean. Scour with sapolio or sand before using. Take plenty of time to do your work, as you will find that too great hurry is unprofitable. Use glass cans and the best white sugar, and do not have any other cooking going on while preserving, as the steam or grease will be apt to injure your preserves.

## PRESERVED PEACHES.

Select peaches of the finest quality. Weigh them after they are pared and stoned, and allow one pound of sugar to each pound of fruit. Crack part of the stones, extract the kernels, and steep them in a covered vessel in a very little water. Throw the peaches in cold water as soon as they are pared, to keep from discoloring. Make a syrup of the sugar, allowing a pint of water to every three pounds of sugar. Let it boil up gently, and skim until perfectly clear. It is then ready for the peaches. Boil the peaches steadily until they are tender and clear. Then take them out with a perforated skimmer and lay upon large platters to cool. Boil the syrup, add the

water the kernels were steeped in, and boil fast
like jelly.  Skim off all the scum until it looks
clear and thick like honey.  Fill the peaches into
your glass jars two-thirds full, and pour the
boiling syrup over them.  When cold cover with
brandied paper.  This is not necessary if you
use patent glass jars with rubbers.  You may
then seal while hot, screwing tighter as the cans
grow colder.  You may cut up a whole pineapple and add to the preserves.  I like the additional flavor very much, though it does not look
so well as the large halves of the peaches alone.

### PRESERVED PEARS.

Preserve just as you would peaches.  Pare,
divide, take out the cores, but leave the stems
on, and boil a little bag of spices with the syrup,
such as cinnamon and cloves.

### PRESERVED GREENGAGES AND PLUMS.

Wipe the fruit carefully, and discard all that
are imperfect.  Now weigh the fruit and sugar
accurately, and prick each plum or gage with a
needle in several places.  Put the sugar on to
boil, allowing a pint of water to every three
pounds of sugar; lay in your plums; let them
boil about ten minutes; if they begin to break,
take them up sooner; do this carefully with a
perforated skimmer, draining them well, and lay
upon a large platter.  Boil the syrup until thick
and clear, skimming it thoroughly.  Return the

plums to the boiling syrup and boil five minutes
longer; then take them up again and fill in glass
jars.  Pour the boiling syrup over the fruit and
seal.  The remaining syrup makes excellent
jelly.

### PRESERVED CRABAPPLES.

Choose the small, yellow apple for this purpose.  Take only those that are perfect, leaving
the stems on.  Take a pound of sugar for every
pound of fruit and a bag of spices to boil with
them.  Boil the apples as you would quinces,
until tender; then take up with a perforated
skimmer.  Measure the juice, allowing a pint of
juice to a pound of sugar.  Boil the spices again
with the syrup, and add the juice of a large
lemon.  When the syrup is quite thick boil the
apples again in the syrup for fifteen minutes.
Then take them up and fill in jars, pouring the
boiling syrup over all.

### PRESERVED QUINCES.

Choose the fine, yellow, pear-shaped quince.
You may take half a pound of " Sweets " (the
name of a sweet apple used to preserve with
quinces).  Pare, core and quarter them, and
throw into cold water as you do so.  Put the
quinces on to boil in just enough water to cover
them.  Boil until tender, or until you can pierce
them with a straw.  In the meantime, boil the
parings, seeds and cores also, in just enough
water to cover them.  Take up the quinces with

a perforated skimmer and lay upon dishes to
cool.  Strain all the juice, both of the quinces
and parings, through a fine wire sieve or jelly-
bag, and to every pint of juice allow a pound of
sugar.  Boil and skim it carefully, lay in the
quinces and boil twenty minutes longer.  Take
up the fruit and fill in jars; pour the boiling
syrup over them and seal.  Boil the remaining
syrup to a jelly.  If you use half apples be
careful to cut the same size as the quinces.

### PRESERVED CURRANTS AND RASPBERRIES.

Use pound for pound.  Stem the currants by
running a fork along the stems.  Make a syrup
of the sugar, putting in the currants ten minutes before adding the raspberries; boil ten minutes longer.  Take up the fruit with a perforated
skimmer; fill the jars, letting the syrup boil
until thick; pour over the fruit hot and seal.

### STRAWBERRIES PRESERVED WITH CURRANT JUICE.

Allow a pound of sugar to a pound of berries.
Sprinkle half a pound of sugar over every pound
of fruit and let them remain this way in a covered bowl over night.  In the morning make a
syrup of a quart of currant juice and the remaining sugar; add the strawberries, and proceed same as with Strawberry Preserves.

### PRESERVED RASPBERRIES.

These should be preserved same as above.
Do not wash the berries, but pick over carefully.

### PRESERVED STRAWBERRIES.

Allow a pound of sugar to a pound of fruit, and a quart of water to four pounds or more of berries. Put the sugar and water over a slow fire in your preserving kettle, which should be either of brass or copper, and used for no other purpose. See that it is well scoured before using, and use a silver spoon, and do not have any other cooking done while preserving, or your fruit will not keep. While the sugar is boiling pick the berries over carefully. When the sugar has boiled to a syrup take it from the fire and put in the berries, carefully pouring the boiling syrup over them with a silver spoon, Let them remain in the syrup over night. Next day heat to boiling point, fill the cans to overflowing, and seal air-tight. In two or three days line a wash-boiler with hay, set the cans or jars of preserves in it, put sticks of wood between them to prevent jarring or falling over, and fill the boiler with cold water almost up to the neck of the cans, and let them boil about ten minutes. Then lift the boiler carefully from the stove, and leave the cans in the water until perfectly cold. Take them out and screw tighter, repeating this again in a day or so. Then wrap the cans in paper and set in a dark, cool place. The imported berries are all colored with cochineal. You may do likewise if you wish to have them highly colored. I prefer the Mason glass jars for canning and preserving. Always adjust the rubbers carefully, roll the jars in hot water, also the covers, and fill the jars to overflowing, and clap the covers on immediately.

## PRESERVED FIGS.

Lay fresh figs in water over night. Then simmer in water enough to cover them until tender, and spread upon dishes to cool. Make a syrup of a pound of sugar to every pound of fruit. Allow a small teacupful of water to a pound of sugar. Boil until a very clear syrup; remove every particle of scum; put in the figs and boil slowly for ten minutes. Take them out and spread upon dishes, and set them in the hot sun. Now add the juice of as many lemons as you have pounds of sugar, and a few small pieces of ginger. Boil this syrup until thick. Boil the figs in this syrup for fifteen minutes longer. Then fill in glass jars three-quarters full, fill up with boiling syrup and cover. When cold screw air-tight or seal.

## STRAWBERRY JAM.

Take thre quarters of a pound of sugar to every pound of berries, and a cup of currant juice to every two pounds of fruit. Set the sugar and juice on to boil, skim off the scum and put in the berries, boil rapidly, stirring all the time. Put in small jars covered with brandied paper. You may make jelly out of the surplus juice. A better way is to boil the berries for half an hour

with the currant juice, dip out nearly all the
juice and add the sugar, boil rapidly half an hour
longer with the sugar, stirring all the time.

### STRAWBERRY MARMALADE.

To every pound of fruit allow one pound and
a half of sugar.  Boil the sugar until it is thick
syrup, throw in the berries and boil until it is
quite thick.  Put away like jam.

### PRESERVED CHERRIES.

The sour red cherries, or " Morellas," are the
best for preserves.  Never use sweet ones for
this purpose.  Stone them, preserving every drop
of juice, then weigh the cherries, and for every
pound take three-quarters of a pound of sugar.
Set the sugar and juice of the cherries on to boil,
also a handful of the cherry stones pounded and
tied in a thin muslin bag.  Let this boil about
fifteen minutes.  Skim off the scum that rises.
Now put in the cherries, and boil until the syrup
begins to thicken like jelly.  Remove from the
fire, fill in pint jars, and, when cold, cover with
brandied paper and screw on the cover tight.

### CHERRY MARMALADE.

To three pounds of sweet and one pound of
sour cherries allow two pounds of sugar.  Weigh
the cherries when stemmed and pitted.  Make a
syrup of the sugar, add cinnamon bark and
cloves.  Put in the sweet cherries first, adding
the sour ones half an hour after, boil down thick
and cover with brandied paper.

### PRESERVED CITRON OR WATERMELON RIND.

Pare off the green skin and take out all the inner soft part, so as to leave nothing but the hard white rind. Cut it into strips a finger in length, pour about a pint of vinegar over all, and let it remain so so until next day. Then throw them on a clean board to drip and dry each piece. Allow one lemon to two pounds of rind, and add stick cinnamon and cloves, removing the heads of the latter. Add also a very small quantity of blanched ginger root. Allow three-quarters of a pound of sugar to every pound of rind. Boil all together about three hours, remove the citron with a perforated skimmer and boil the syrup until thick, throw over rind, boil over once more next day for about fifteen minutes (be careful to remove all seeds of the lemon) and cut the lemon into thick slices. You may tie the spices in a bag if you so prefer. If you don't mind the trouble, boil the citron first in grape leaves and a little alum, which makes them green and glossy, and throw them into cold water before preserving. A few pieces of blanched ginger is a nice addition to the flavor.

### GREEN TOMATO PRESERVES.

Take seven pounds of nice, even-sized, small, green tomatoes, six pounds of sugar, three lemons, five cents' worth of cloves and cinnamon mixed (use only half of this) and one-half ounce of whole ginger. Pierce each tomato with a fork,

heat all together slowly and boil until the tomatoes look clear.  Don't use the seeds of the lemons.  Take out the tomatoes with a perforated
skimmer and lay on large platters and then fill
in glass jars.  Boil the syrup until very thick,
pour over the tomatoes hot, and seal.  This
tastes like fig preserves.

### RIPE TOMATO PRESERVES.

To twelve pounds of sound, ripe tomatoes take
eight pounds of sugar and three lemons, one-
half ounce of cloves and one ounce of cinnamon
bark.  Scald the tomatoes, pare and cut up
(weigh the tomatoes before scalding them), heat
slowly, add sugar and boil slowly for twenty
minutes, then add spices and lemons (the lemons must be sliced), extract all the seeds and
boil slowly, stirring often with a silver spoon,
and being very careful not to let them burn.
The last hour they will require almost constant
stirring.  Take off the scum that rises and let
it boil until very thick and dark.

### BLACKBERRY JAM.

Weigh the fruit, allowing three-quarters of a
pound of sugar to every pound of fruit.  Put
the fruit on to boil without any sugar, mash it
with a potato beetle and let it boil slowly for
about half an hour.  Dip out most of the boiling
juice before adding the sugar and cook half an
hour longer; then pack in pint jars.  This is
delicious.  Now I will tell you what to do with the

surplus juice, and I know you will be very
thankful, for it is real nice and refreshing as a
summer drink.

### PRESERVED BLACKBERRIES.

Weigh the fruit and allow a pound of sugar to
every pound of fruit. Tie spices in a bag, such
as cloves and cinnamon, and make a thick syrup
of the sugar before you put in the berries. Boil
half an hour and seal when cold.

### BLACKBERRY SYRUP.

To every pint of blackberry juice allow a pint
of sugar and boil rapidly for five minutes by
the clock—five minutes for every pint. Bottle
and cork it. When cold mix with chopped ice
and water, using a cupful to a quart of water.
Very nice.

### PRESERVED PEARS.

Pare the fruit and then weigh. Leave whole,
with the stems on, and allow a pound of sugar to
every pound of fruit. Put a layer of sugar at the
bottom of the kettle, then one of fruit, and so on
until you have used up all of both. Throw a pint
of water over all and heat slowly until the sugar
is melted and the fruit is heated through. Boil
the pears until quite tender, then take them out
with a perforated skimmer and lay upon large
flat dishes until the syrup is thick. Tie up a
small bag of spices, such as cloves and cinnamon bark, and let it boil rapidly with the syrup.
Boil almost to a jelly, which must be clear and

thick. Skim off the scum as it rises, then put in
the pears again. Boil up once, then fill jars and
seal. To prevent the sugar from crystalizing,
which it is very apt to do with fruit like pears,
dissolve a piece of alum, no larger then a pea, in
a little water and add to the boiling sugar.

### GOOSEBERRY JAM.

Pick the berries carefully and boil one hour,
then add a pound of sugar to every pound of
fruit, and boil for an hour and a half longer, stirring most of the time. All jams must be watched
closely and stirred for fear of burning. Gooseberries should be perfectly ripe.

### PEACH BUTTER.

Weigh the peaches after they are pared and
pitted. Allow a pound of sugar to a pound of
fruit. Cook the peaches alone until soft, then add
one-half of the sugar and stir frequently. In
half an hour put in the remaining sugar. Now
watch carefully, stirring almost constantly for
two hours. Boil slowly, and add one-quarter of
the peach kernels. Spice with cinnamon and
cloves, using whole spices.

### RASPBERRY JAM.

To five pounds of red raspberries (not too
ripe) add five pounds of loaf sugar. Mash the
whole well in a preserving kettle (to do this
thoroughly use a potato masher). Add one
quart of currant juice, and boil slowly until it
jellies. Try a little on a plate; set it on ice, if

it jellies remove from the fire, fill in small jars, cover with brandied paper and tie a thick white paper over them. Keep in a dark, dry, cool place. If you object to seeds, press the fruit through a sieve before boiling.

### APPLE BUTTER.

Boil down any desired quantity of sweet cider in your preserving kettle to two-thirds the original quantity. Pare, core and slice as many wine apples as you wish to use. Boil slowly, stirring often with a silver or wooden spoon. Spice with stick cinnamon and cloves, and sweeten to taste. Boil from four to five hours; take from the fire, pour all together into a large crock. Cover and let it stand over night, then return to the preserving kettle and boil down, stirring all the while until it is the consistency of mush, and of a dark brown color.

### QUINCE CHEESE.

Wipe off each quince before paring, core and slice them, weigh your fruit and sugar, allowing three-quarters of a pound of sugar for every pound of fruit and set the sugar aside until wanted. Boil the skins, cores and seeds in a clean vessel by themselves, with just enough water to cover them. Boil until the parings are soft, so as to extract all the flavor, then strain through a jelly-bag. When this water is almost cold, put the quinces in the preserving kettle with the quince water and boil until soft, mash

with a wooden spoon or beetle.   Add the juice of
an orange to every two pounds of fruit, being
careful not to get any of the seeds into the preserves.   Now add the sugar and boil slowly for
fifteen minutes, stirring constantly; if not thick
enough boil longer, being very careful not to let
it burn.   Take off the fire and pack in small jars
with brandied paper over them.   You may mix
sweet apples with the quinces.   Nice for ornamenting.

### GRAPE PRESERVES.

Squeeze the pulp into one bowl and put the
skins into another.   Press the pulp through a
sieve, weigh the grapes before you squeeze them
and allow three-quarters of a pound of sugar to a
pound of fruit.   Put the strained pulp and sugar
on to boil, the skins also, and boil slowly until
thick.   Very nice.   It will be much easier for
you to heat the pulp before straining.

# JELLIES.

|                                      | Page. |
| ------------------------------------ | ----- |
| Apple Jelly, - - - - - -             | 411   |
| Currant Jelly, - - - - - -           | 410   |
| Crab-Apple Jelly, - - - - -          | 134   |
| Cranberry Jelly, - - - -             | 414   |
| Fruit Jelly, - - - - - -             | 413   |
| Grape Jelly, - - - - -               | 410   |
| Neapolitan Jelly, - - - - -          | 412   |
| Peach Jelly, - - - - -               | 409   |
| Raspberry and Currant Jelly, - -     | 410   |
| Red Raspberry Jelly, - - -           | 409   |
| Raspberry Syrup, - - - - -           | 412   |
| Strawberry Jelly, - - - -            | 408   |
| Wine Jelly, - - - - - -              | 411   |
| Wine or Champagne Jelly, - - -       | 414   |

# JELLIES.

## STRAWBERRY JELLY.

PRESS the strawberries through a jelly press,
or boil and mash them to a pulp and strain
through a flannel bag. A good way to do this
is to hang up the bag on a strong nail and let it
drip into a bowl. In the meantime get all your
jelly-glasses ready and roll them in hot water.
Take a pint of juice and a pint of sugar at a
time and no more. You will have better jelly
and it will not take any more time. I always
put a pint of juice into the preserving kettle, set
it on red-hot coals, and as soon as it boils throw
in the sugar and stir with a silver spoon. Then
put fine kindling wood under the kettle and let
it boil hard until it rises clear to the top, allowing it to boil in this way for five minutes by the
clock. It will then be so thick that it will boil
with a "thud," and can not rise any more.
Pour into your glasses, filling them to the brim,
reserving, however, a pint of the juice to repeat
the above. Try this method, and you will never
follow the old-fashioned way again. By adding
lemon juice to the strawberries your jelly will
be firmer (raspberry and strawberry jellies are
never as firm as other jellies). You may boil a

(444)

vanilla bean in the preserving kettle with the berries, which makes a very nice flavor. Try it.

### PEACH JELLY.

Pare the peaches; cut them up in small slices, and crack one-fourth of the kernels, and put all in the jar with the peaches. Heat in a dish-pan of boiling water, but do not add any water to the peaches; stir them from time to time until they are boiled to the consistency of mush. Strain through a bag, and to every pint of juice add the juice of a lemon. Measure again after adding the lemon-juice, and add a pint of sugar to a pint of juice. Boil a pint at a time, adding sugar when the juice begins to boil. Boil fast and hard five minutes. Allow five minutes by the clock for each pint of juice and sugar. Always have the pint measure filled with juice, so as to lose no time in getting the kettle to boil. You may weigh the sugar if more convenient— a pound to a pint. Fill in glasses immediately. When cold dip tissue or fine note-paper in the white of egg, and lay on top of each glass. Cut around with scissors, put on covers, or tie up with stout paper. Each glass should be labeled.

### RED RASPBERRY JELLY.

· Put the berries into a stone jar. Set this in a kettle of warm water, and let it boil, closely covered, until the berries are broken to pieces. Strain through a flannel jelly-bag. If you have none use a stout, coarse kitchen towel, pressing

only a few handfuls at a time. To each pint of
juice allow a pint or pound of sugar. Measure
the juice and set it on a very hot fire in a preserving kettle. As soon as it boils throw in the
sugar; stir with a silver or wooden spoon, and
let it boil five minutes by the clock, and so hard,
too, as to require constant watching, and in a
two-gallon kettle at that, boiling only a pint at
a time. Remember, this is very important, a pint
at a time. Do this, and your jelly will never
fail to harden almost before it is cold. Measure
while your jelly is boiling, so as not to lose a
moment's time. Have jelly-glasses ready,
cleaned and rolled in hot water, so as to prevent
cracking, and have enough kindling-wood at
hand to keep the kettle boiling.

### CURRANT JELLY.

In making this jelly follow the above receipt.

### RASPBERRY-CURRANT JELLY.

Mix equal parts of currants and raspberries,
and proceed as with currant jelly. The flavor
is exquisite and is especially nice for cakes,
creams, charlottes, etc.

### GRAPE JELLY.

Put the grapes on to boil in a stone jar set in
a vessel of water. Do not add any water to the
grapes and let them boil a few hours, then strain
through a jelly-bag or fruit-press. Boil a pint at
a time. When the juice boils hard, add a pound

of sugar. If wild grapes add a pound and a
quarter of sugar. Boil fully five minutes and
proceed as you would with currant jelly. When
cold cover with a paper dipped in white of egg.
Cover and label.

## WINE JELLY.

(No. 1.) Take one pint of wine and two
pounds of sugar. Soak one package of gelatine
in one pint of water, juice of two lemons and
grated peel of one, and a good pinch of cinnamon.
After the gelatine has soaked for one hour, pour
in all the above ingredients and one quart of
boiling water. Stir until all is dissolved, then
strain through a flannel bag. Wet your molds
with cold water, pour in the jelly and set away
in a cold place.

## WINE JELLY.

(No. 2.) Dissolve one box of gelatine in a
pint of boiling water, add one pound of loaf sugar
and a quart of wine. Stir this mixture very
hard and pour through a jelly-bag and then into
a mold that has has been washed in cold water.
When congealed, wrap a cloth dipped in warm
water around the mold and turn out the jelly.

## APPLE JELLY.

Take sour, juicy apples, not too ripe, cut up
in pieces, leave the skins on and boil the seeds
also. Put on enough water to just cover, boil on
the back of the stove, closely covered, all day.
Then put in jelly-bag to drip all night. Next

morning measure the juice. Allow a wineglassful of white wine and juice of one lemon to every
three pints of juice. Then boil a pint at a time,
with a pound of sugar to every pint. Very good.

### NEAPOLITAN JELLY.

Take equal quantities of fully ripe strawberries, raspberries, currants and red cherries. The
cherries must be stoned, taking care to preserve
the juice and add to rest of juice. Mix and press
through a jelly-press or bag. Measure the juice,
boil a pint at a time, and to every pint allow a
pound of sugar and proceed as with other fruit
jellies.

### RASPBERRY SYRUP.

Choose nice, large, fresh red raspberries, weigh
them and allow three-quarters of a pound of
sugar to every pound of fruit. Make a syrup by
boiling a pint of water to every two pounds of
sugar. When the syrup is clear put in the berries and let them boil up once. Then remove
from the fire and let them remain in a covered
bowl over night; then press through a jelly-bag
and boil until clear and thick; when cold, bottle,
cork and seal. The juice of canned raspberries
left over from last season, obtained by pressing
them through a fine wire sieve or jelly-bag, is nice
to mix with lemonade; you will never want a
better drink. Strawberries may be used in the
same way; use quantities of chopped ice and
lemons. Delicious.

### CRAB APPLE JELLY.

Take Siberian crab apples, cut up in pieces, leaving in the seeds, and do not pare. Put into a stone jar, and set on the back of the stove to boil slowly, adding a good-sized dipperful of water. Let them boil closely covered all day, then put in a jelly-bag and let them drip all night. If the apples are very dry, add another dipperful of water. Boil a pint of juice at a time, with a pound of sugar to every pint of juice. Boil five minutes steadily, each pint exactly five minutes, shoving kindling wood under the kettle all the time, while it boils. Now weigh another pound of sugar and measure another pint of juice. Keep on in this way and you will be through before you realize it. There is no finer or firmer jelly than this. It should be a bright amber in color, and of fine flavor. You may press the pulp that remains in the jelly-bag through a coarse strainer, add the juice of two lemons and as much sugar as you have pulp, and cook to a jam.

### FRUIT JELLY.

Take any kind of fruit, fresh, canned or mixed. Peaches, cherries and raspberries are very nice. Add the juice of a lemon, also that of an orange and sweeten to taste. Dissolve a box of gelatine in a little warm water or the juice of the canned fruit. You may add a little wine or other liquor. One box of gelatine is sufficient for two quarts of fruit. This is particularly nice poured into a square mold, to cut into squares and serve with poultry or meats. An ornamental dish for any table.

## WINE OR CHAMPAGNE JELLY.

Pour a pint of cold water over the contents of a package of Cox's gelatine. Let it soak for ten minutes, then add a pint of boiling water and stir till the gelatine is dissolved. Next add a pint of wine, half a pound of sugar, the grated rind of a lemon and its juice, a little grated nutmeg, ground cloves and cinnamon. Stir the beaten whites of two eggs into this mixture and set on a slow fire and stir until it starts to boil, when it should be immediately taken off and strained through a jelly bag. Rinse the bag in boiling water first and suspend it near the fire until strained. Wet a mold with cold water before putting in the jelly and set on ice to cool.

## CRANBERRY JELLY.

Wash and pick ripe cranberries and set on to boil in a porcelain-lined kettle closely covered. When soft strain the pulp through a fine wire sieve. Measure the juice and add an equal quantity of sugar. Set it on to boil again and let it boil very fast for about ten minutes—but it must boil steadily all the time. Wet a mold with cold water, turn the jelly into it and set it away to cool, when firm turn it into a glass salver.

# BRANDIED FRUITS.

|                    |   |   |   |   |   |   | Page. |
|--------------------|---|---|---|---|---|---|-------|
| Cherries,          | - | - | - | - | - | - | 418   |
| French Prunes,     | - | - | - | - |   |   | 419   |
| Melange,           | - | - | - | - | - | - | 416   |
| Peaches,           | - | - | - | - | - | - | 417   |
| Pears,             | - | - | - | - | - | - | 417   |
| Quinces,           | - | - | - | - | - | - | 418   |

(415)

# BRANDIED FRUITS.

## MELANGE.

THIS French fruit preserves is truly delicious,
and should be put up in the month of June.
To every pound of fruit take one pound of
sugar. It requires no cooking at all, and is
therefore easily made. Any child can follow
the directions. Begin with strawberries. Get
the largest and soundest berries in the market.
Pick two quarts and lay them in a new and perfectly clean two-gallon stone jar and cover with
two pounds of the finest granulated sugar.
Stone as many pounds of red, black and white
cherries as you wish to use, and add the same
quantity of sugar. You may also use bananas,
pineapples or oranges. Seed the latter carefully. Be sure to weigh all the fruit, and
allow one pound of sugar to every additional
pound of fruit. Now pour over the fruit a pint
of pure alcohol, in which you have dissolved five
cents' worth of salicylic acid. Tie up the jar
with thick paper, and in season add peaches,
apricots, raspberries, blackberries, large, red
currants; in fact, all kinds of fruit. Greengages and purple and red plums also add both
to looks and taste. Be sure to add the same

(416)

amount of sugar as you do fruit, but no more alcohol. In the fall of the year pack in glass jars; looks very pretty. Keep it in a dry, cool place. There is always a surplus of juice, which makes excellent pudding sauces. Add a little water and thicken.

### BRANDIED PEACHES.

Select only the largest and finest quality of clingstone peaches. Allow a pound of sugar to a pound of fruit, and a pint of the best brandy to every four pounds of peaches. Make a syrup of the sugar with enough water to just dissolve it, and boil about half a dozen blanched peach kernels with it. When the syrup boils put in the fruit and let it boil about five minutes. Remove the fruit carefully upon platters, and let the syrup boil fifteen or twenty minutes longer, skimming it well. Put the peaches in wide-mouthed glass jars. If the syrup has thickened pour in the brandy. Remove from the fire at once, pour over the fruit and seal.

### BRANDIED PEARS.

Pare the fruit, leaving the stems on. Weigh and allow a pound of sugar to a pound of fruit. Heat the fruit and sugar like you would for preserves, adding enough water to prevent burning. Remove the pears to platters as soon as tender—so tender that you can pierce with a straw. Let the syrup boil until thick, having added a small bag of spices in boiling. Let the syrup boil very fast. In the meantime, put the pears in glass jars, fill two-thirds full, add the brandy to the boiling syrup, and take the kettle at once from the fire. Pour boiling hot over the fruit, and seal. Allow a pint of best brandy to every four pounds of fruit. Use none but the best. If you can not afford brandied fruit it is no disgrace, but don't try and put up fruit in whisky or some other cheap stuff.

### BRANDIED CHERRIES.

Select the largest sweet cherries for this purpose, leaving the stems on. Allow half a pound of sugar to every pound of fruit, and a pint of good brandy for every five pounds of fruit. Make a syrup of the sugar, using as little water as possible. Pour it over the cherries and let them remain in the syrup all night. Next day put them in a preserving kettle and heat slowly. Boil about eight minutes. Take up the cherries with a perforated skimmer and boil the syrup fifteen minutes. Add the brandy to the boiling syrup, remove from the fire and pour over the cherries hot, and seal.

### BRANDIED QUINCES.

Select large yellow, pear-shaped quinces, and peel and quarter them. Take out the cores and throw into cold water, until all are pared. Then boil until tender, so they can easily be pierced. Take them out with a perforated skimmer and

weigh. Then take three quarters of a pound of
sugar to a pound of quinces, and boil in a little
over half the quince water. Add stick cinnamon
and cloves (removing the soft heads). Boil until quite a thick syrup. Pack the quinces in
jars, add a pint of good brandy to the syrup and
pour boiling hot over the quinces and seal immediately.

### FRENCH PRUNES IN COGNAC.

Lay the prunes in white wine for two days;
then put on a wire sieve to drip, but do not
squeeze them. When they look dry, which will
be in about half an hour, lay in glass jars with
alternate layers of sugar and stick cinnamon and
a few pieces of mace and a very few cloves.
When the jars are full, fill up with cognac and
seal. Set in the sunniest place you can find for
three days.

**MEMORANDUM.**

# RAW FRUIT DESSERTS.

|  |  | Page. |
|---|---|---|
| Ambrosia, | - - - - | 422 |
| Bananas, | - - - - | 423 |
| Blueberries, | - - - - | 423 |
| Frosted Currants, | - - - | 424 |
| Pineapple, | - - - - | 422 |
| Peaches, | - - - - | 423 |
| Ripe Tomatoes, | - - - - | 422 |
| Raspberries and Currants, | - - | 423 |
| Strawberries, | - - - - | 421 |
| Salade D'Orange, | - - - | 422 |
| Snowflakes, | - - - - | 424 |
| Tutti-Frutti, | - - - | 423 |
| Watermelon, | - - - - | 424 |

**MEMORANDUM.**

# RAW FRUIT DESSERTS.

### STRAWBERRIES.

ALWAYS select the best fruit, as it is the cheapest, and requires less sugar, and where every berry is perfect there is no waste. Never wash strawberries, as it injures their flavor. If they are too "sandy," do not use them raw. Pick the berries and pile them in the fruit dish in the shape of a hill, and when ready to serve, put over them plenty of pulverized sugar. Reserve half a cup of the berries, mash to a pulp, sweeten and strain, and pour sweet cream gradually to the juice, stirring constantly; pour this over the berries when ready to serve, and not before, for fear of curdling. Some object to cream of any kind; in this case it is better to pass the cream around the table.

### STRAWBERRIES.

(No. 2.) Pick nice ripe berries, pile them in a fruit dish and pour over them a gill of rum or wine (rum is better). Then strew plenty of pulverized sugar over them and garnish with round slices or quarters of oranges, also well sugared.

### RIPE TOMATOES.

Select nice, large, well-shaped tomatoes, pare, slice and put on ice. When ready to serve sprinkle each layer thickly with pulverized sugar, and pour over all a pint of whipped cream. Delicious.

### PINEAPPLE.

Peel the pineapple, dig out all the eyes, then cut from the core downward, or chop in a chopping-bowl, and set on ice until ready to serve. Then sugar the fruit well, and form into a mound in a handsome dish. Garnish the base well with leaves or small fruit or any kind. You may squeeze the juice of a fine orange over all.

### SALADE D'ORANGE.

Pare and slice nice, sweet oranges, the seedless "navel orange" being the best. Set on ice. Do not sugar until absolutely necessary, as it extracts the flavor of the fruit and leaves nothing but juice. When ready to serve arrange the slices in a glass bowl and sprinkle powdered sugar over them. You may add a glass of wine if you like the flavor.

### AMBROSIA.

Take eight or nine sweet oranges, peel them, take out the seeds after cutting into slices. Take a large-sized fresh cocoanut, grate it and then put alternate layers of the oranges and cocoanut in a glass dish, and sprinkle pulverized sugar over each layer of cocoanut and orange.

### RASPBERRIES AND CURRANTS.

These berries, mixed, make a very palatable dish. Set on ice until ready to serve. Then pile in a mound, strewing plenty of pulverized sugar among them. As you do this, garnish the base with white or black currants (blackberries look pretty also) in bunches. Eat with cream or wine.

### BANANAS.

May be sliced according to fancy, either round or lengthwise. Set on ice until required. Then add sugar, wine or orange juice. In serving, dish out with a heaping tablespoonful of whipped cream.

### TUTTI-FRUTTI.

Slice oranges, bananas, pineapples and arrange in a glass bowl; sprinkle with pulverized sugar, and serve either with wine or cream. You may use both.

### BLUEBERRIES.

Wash and pick over carefully, drain off all the water, sprinkle powdered sugar over them and serve with cream or milk.

### PEACHES.

Peel fine, ripe freestone peaches. Cover plentifully with pulverized sugar, and serve with whipped cream and plenty of it. The cream should be ice cold. Peaches should not be sliced until just before dining, or they will be very apt to change color.

### FROSTED CURRANTS.

Pick fine, even, large bunches of red currants
(not too ripe) and dip each bunch, one at a time,
into a mixture of frothed white of egg; then into
a thick, boiled sugar syrup. Drain the bunches
by laying on a sieve, and when partly dry dip
again into the boiled syrup. Repeat the process
a third time; then sprinkle powdered sugar over
them and lay on a sheet of paper in a slightly
warm oven to dry. Used on extra occasions
for ornamenting charlottes, cakes, creams, etc.

### WATERMELONS.

Use only those melons that are perfectly ripe.
Do not select those that are very large in circum-
ference; a rough melon with a bumpy surface is
the best. Either cut in half or plug and fill with
the following: Put on to boil some pale sherry
or claret and boil down to quite a thick syrup
with sugar. Pour this into either a plugged
melon or over the half-cut melon, and lay on ice
for a couple of hours before serving. If you
use claret you may spice it while boiling with
whole spices.

### SNOWFLAKES.

Grate a large cocoanut into a raw fruit dish,
and mix it thoroughly and lightly with pulverized sugar. Serve with whipped or plain sweet
cream.

# CANNING.

|                            |            | Page. |
| -------------------------- | ---------- | ----- |
| Blackberries,              | -   -   -  | - 431 |
| Blueberries,               | -   -   -  | 430, 431 |
| Cherries,                  | -   -   -  | - 428 |
| Currants,                  | -   -   -  | 430 |
| Damsons,                   | -   -   -  | - 432 |
| French and German Plums,   | -   -      | 433 |
| General Rules,             | -   -   -  | - 426 |
| Green Corn,                | -   -   -  | 434 |
| Peas,                      | -   -   -  | - 435 |
| Peaches,                   | -   -   -  | - 432, 433 |
| Pears,                     | -   -   -  | - 435 |
| Pineapples,                | -   -      | 436, 437, 438 |
| Quinces,                   | -  -   -   | - 429 |
| Rhubarb,                   | -   -   -  | 428 |
| Strawberries,              | -   -   -  | - 427 |
| Tomatoes,                  | -   -   -  | 434 |

# CANNING.

USE none but glass cans for canning fruits and vegetables. You will find them the cheapest in the end, for you can use them year after year by replacing new elastics for the old ones, which must be done yearly. Keep your canned fruit and vegetables in a cool, dark place, and be sure the place is dry as well. Strawberries and red raspberries lose their color very quickly if exposed to the light. I knew a lady that packed her canned strawberries away in a box for fear of their discoloring. A good plan is to wrap each can in paper. You must pay strict attention to the following rules in canning: Remember it is worth while to put up your own fruit, for it is cheaper and better than the fruit you buy; and then a good housekeeper is proud of her own work, especially in this line:

First. Clean your cans thoroughly and roll them in boiling water; be sure that they are not cracked; fit the elastic firmly around the neck of the can, so when you are ready to screw on the top there will be no time lost, as this has to be done quickly, and there will be no room for the air to get in. Screw tight, this is important.

(464)

Have the tops lying in hot water, so that no time
may be lost in screwing them on. You must
always fill the cans to overflowing, for the fruit
will shrink some as it cools, and that, you know,
is dangerous, for it invites the air to enter.
Screw the top on immediately. Fill one can at
a time, and tighten this one before you go to the
next. Be sure to examine each can as it cools,
then screw tighter. Never put them away until
the following day, and then examine narrowly
again, screwing tighter if needed.

### STRAWBERRIES.

To each pound of fruit use three-fourths of a
pound of sugar. After the berries are picked and
washed, measure or rather weigh the fruit, and
strew the sugar over the fruit. Let them stand
at least three hours, then pour off the juice into
your preserving kettle, and let it boil. Remove
all the scum that rises, and when perfectly clear
put in the berries carefully. Just let them come
to a boil. Put your cans on an old tray right
near the boiling berries. Can immediately and
observe the above rules. To make perfectly sure
of their keeping (for strawberries ferment very
easily), place them in a wash boiler with hay,
and let them come to a boil. Do this after a
few days. I have described how to do this in
some previous receipt. In case one of the cans
is not quite full, and you have more berries to
can, just set the can in hot water until the fruit

is ready. If you have none, why, the best plan
is to use it as soon as possible, for it will not
keep. Follow rules for canning carefully.

## RHUBARB.

Strip the skins from the stalks, and cut into
small pieces as you would for pies. Allow eight
ounces of loaf sugar to every quart of rhubarb.
Set the sugar over the fire with as little water as
possible, throw in the rhubarb and boil ten
minutes. Have the cans ready, and roll each
one in hot water. Have the rubbers at hand,
and the covers also rolled in hot water. Fill
each can to overflowing, clap the covers on immediately, screw tight, see that the rubbers are
on as they should be and screw tighter as they
grow colder. Examine each can the next day
and screw tighter if possible. Set away in a
dark, dry closet.

## CHERRIES.

Prepare in the same manner as you would for
preserving (see Preserved Cherries), allowing
half a pound of sugar to a pound of fruit. After
putting the cherries into the syrup do not let
them boil more than five minutes; then fill your
cans to overflowing, seal immediately and then
screw tighter as they grow cold. Remove the
little bag of stones which you have boiled with
the syrup. The object in boiling the stones
with the syrup is to impart the fine flavor to the
fruit, which cherries are robbed of in pitting.

Cherries canned expressly for pies, which are
scarcely inferior to those filled with fresh fruit,
are put up in the following manner:   Stem the
cherries—do not pit them—pack tight in glass
fruit jars, cover with sweetened water, say about
two tablespoonfuls of sugar to a quart of fruit;
put on the rubbers evenly, clap on the covers
and screw tight.   Line your wash-boiler with
hay, put in the cans, fill in hay between them,
so that they will not knock against each other
in boiling.   Fill the boiler up to the neck of the
cans with cold water, then set on to boil.   Let
them boil fifteen minutes from the time they
begin to boil.   Lift the boiler off the stove and
do not take out the cans until perfectly cold.
Wipe each can and screw the tops as tightly as
possible.   Next day screw tighter if possible.
You may stone the cherries just before using for
pies.   They have a much nicer flavor put up in
this way.   I have never had a single can of fruit
spoil put up in just this simple way.

### QUINCES.

Select the finest yellow quinces in the market;
pare and core, and throw into cold water.   Put
the parings and cores on to boil just as you would
for preserves, and then strain.   Allow a quarter
of a pound of sugar to a pound of fruit.   If you
like them very sweet take half a pound of sugar
to a pound of fruit.   Add sugar to the strained
juice, boil, throw in the quinces and boil until

tender, so they may be easily pierced with a fork.
Have your cans ready, previously rinsed in hot
water. Now pack fruit in jars and fill to overflowing with the boiling syrup, which must be
kept boiling until all the cans are filled and
sealed. Seal each can as soon as filled and do
not forget to fill to overflowing, and as the cans
cool they must be screwed tighter. Look after
them in a day or two and try to screw them
tighter if possible.

### CURRANTS.

Select the large "cherry currants," pick from
the stem; sugar, about half a pound to a pound
of fruit, weighing after being stemmed. Boil
ten minutes and seal hot, as you do other fruit.

### BLUEBERRIES.

(No. 1.) The worst part of the work is the
picking over, which requires a great deal of patience. After picking wash well and fill in glass
jars. I do not mean to just fill, you must jam
them in as tight as possible, using a potato beetle
or some other wooden tool to squeeze in the berries, no matter if they are bruised. Fill to the
brim, clap on the rubbers, then screw on the lid.
When you have all the jars filled, set in a wash
boiler, which has been lined with hay and pack
between the jars also. Fill jars almost to the
neck with cold water, then set on to boil, and
boil about fifteen minutes from the time it begins to boil. Lift the boiler from the fire and

let the jars remain in the boiler until cold. Now examine each jar closely, screw tighter and examine every other day for a week, always screwing tighter. Add sugar when you intend to use them. They are equal to fresh berries, especially for compote.

## BLUEBERRIES.

(No. 2.) Following is another way of canning blueberries or huckleberries: Heat slowly to a boil in a large porcelain kettle. When they begin to boil add sugar in the proportion of two tablespoonfuls to each quart of fruit. Before doing this, if there is too much juice in the kettle, dip out the surplus with a cup. Leave the berries almost dry before putting in the sugar. Boil together fifteen minutes and can. Have the rubbers at hand to clap on immediately, and have the tops rolled in hot water. Fill each can to overflowing, seal and look after them as they grow cold.

## BLACKBERRIES.

Heat slowly, and when they begin to boil add about three tablespoonfuls of sugar to each quart of berries. Boil about ten minutes. Have the cans ready, rolled in hot water. Fill the cans to overflowing. If you have a surplus of juice add more sugar and boil down to a syrup, which is very nice for pudding sauces, or to drink in ice water.

## DAMSONS.

Make a syrup of three-quarters of a pound of sugar to every pound of fruit and allow about a pint of water to every three pounds of fruit. Prick the damsons with a needle to prevent bursting. When the syrup is clear, put in your damsons, a quart at a time. Boil each quart five minutes, not fast, or they will burst badly. Fill up the jars with the fruit, pour in the syrup until it is overflowing and seal immediately as you do other fruit.

## PEACHES.

(No. 1.) In selecting peaches for canning, see that the fruit is ripe and firm of texture, but not too soft. The yellow "Crawford" peaches are nicest for this purpose. Pare the fruit, cut in halves and stone, taking care not to break the fruit, and drop each piece in cold water as soon as it is pared, and leave them in the water until all are pared, halved and stoned. Now prepare enough sugar water to cover your peaches after you have packed them in glass jars. Pack them in tight, and put two blanched peach kernels on top of each can and fill to overflowing with very sweet sugar water. To do this, take about three pounds of granulated sugar, put it in a bowl and fill it with cold water and stir the sugar and water until dissolved. Now place your cans of peaches in a row, and pour a cupful of this sugar water over each can, and repeat it until all are overflowing: now seal tight. Set them in a wash-boiler, filled with cold water, up to the neck. Put sticks of wood and straw or hay, if you have it, between and around the jars and boil steadily for fifteen minutes or more. Lift from the fire carefully and let them grow cold in the boiler. Lift out carefully and screw each one as tightly as possible. Try to screw tighter the next day again. Keep in a dry, cool place.

### PEACHES.

(No. 2.) Prepare same as No. 1. Allow two heaping tablespoonfuls of sugar to each quart of fruit, and scatter between the layers also a few peach kernels, and put a pint of water at the bottom of the kettle before packing in the fruit. After the kettle is filled heat slowly to a boil. Boil five minutes, just long enough to heat every piece through thoroughly. Fill the cans to overflowing, one at a time, and seal each one as soon as filled. When cold, screw tight as possible. You may can peaches whole in this way, using a little more sugar. They are much finer in flavor when whole.

### FRENCH AND GERMAN PLUMS,

Prick with a needle to prevent bursting and prepare a syrup, allowing a pint of water and two pounds of sugar to every three quarts of plums. When the sugar is dissolved put in the plums. Heat slowly to a boil. Let them boil slowly for five minutes, not fast, but they must boil. Lift them out with a perforated skimmer upon platters. When all the plums have boiled, pack in jars three-fourths full, clap on the rubbers evenly around the rim, fill with the scalding syrup until it runs down the sides, and seal without a moment's loss. You may can red plums and greengages in the same way. Boil down the surplus juice for jelly, only adding a little more sugar, say half as much sugar as you have juice.

### TOMATOES.

Scald, remove all the skin, cut out any places that are green or imperfect. Then cut them up and put on to boil, adding a little salt. Boil until perfectly soft, then strain through a collander ; return them to the kettle and boil again. Now can them quickly, sealing air-tight. You may leave them whole if you so prefer.

### GREEN CORN.

Boil on the cob all the corn you can pack into al arge wash-boiler, and boil about half an hour in salted water. Cut all the corn from the cobs, and pack in Mason jars; fill, and pour slightly salted water over all to overflowing. Seal and arrange in a wash-boiler, fill the bottom with hay, and fill the boiler with cold water up to the necks of the cans. Boil about fifteen minutes. Allow the cans to cool in the boiler. Examine narrowly, and screw each lid tighter if possible.

Keep in a dry, cool, dark place. To make doubly sure of its keeping, you may add to the salted water three drams of salicylic acid, and four ounces of salt to one gallon of water.

## PEARS.

Choose "Bartletts" or "Sickles"; pare, and if "Bartletts," cut in halves, leaving the stems on. Throw into cold water as soon as pared, to prevent them from turning dark. Put on sweetened water to boil, and throw in the fruit, not too many at a time. When so tender that you can pierce with a straw, can as you would other fruit. Fill the cans to overflowing. Lose no time in sealing, and so on until all are boiled and canned. It is the easiest fruit to can, and if sealed properly, not a single can will spoil. You may put up the common variety of pears in this way, for puddings, compotes, etc.

## PEAS.

Boil in salt water; drain off all the water, by throwing the peas on a large, clean board and allowing them to get perfectly cold. Then pack in glass jars, air-tight, allowing the salt water to overflow before clapping on the lids. Boil cans and all, like in foregoing receipt. Asparagus and cauliflower are canned in the same way.

## A CHAPTER ON PINEAPPLES.

### HOW AND WHAT TO DO WITH THEM.—DIFFERENT WAYS OF CANNING THE LUSCIOUS FRUIT.

The large, juicy pineapple is the best for this purpose. To begin with have your scales at hand, also a sharp-pointed knife and an apple-corer, a slaw-cutter and a large, deep porcelain dish to receive the sliced pineapple. Now begin to pare, do this carefully, dig out all the eyes as you go along. Lay the pared pineapple on a porcelain platter and stick your apple-corer right through the center of the apple, first at one end and then at the other; if it acts stubbornly put a towel around the handle of the corer and twist it. Behold! the whole core will come out at once. Now screw the slaw-cutter to the desired thickness you wish to have your pineapple sliced. Slice into receiving dish, weigh one pound of fine granulated sugar and sprinkle it all over the apple, and so on until all are pared and sliced, allowing one pound of sugar to each very large pineapple. Cover the dish until next day and then strain all the juice off the apples and boil in a porcelain or bell metal kettle, skimming it well; throw in the sliced pineapples, boil about five minutes and can. Be sure to have the cans rolled in hot water before using; have the rubbers secure (always use new rubbers), and roll

the covers in hot water before screwing them on.
Fill the cans to overflowing and seal immediately, not losing a moment's time. As the cans
grow cold screw tighter and examine daily, for
three or four days, and screw tighter if possible.

ANOTHER WAY.—Prepare the pineapples as
above, allowing half a pound of sugar to two
pounds of fruit. Steam the sliced pines in a
porcelain steamer until tender. In the meantime make a syrup of the sugar, allowing a tumblerful of water to a pound of sugar. Skim the
syrup carefully, put in your steamed pineapples
and can as above.

STILL ANOTHER WAY.—Prepare as in No 1.
Weigh your sliced pineapples and to five pounds
of fruit make a syrup of two and one-half pounds
of sugar. Put the sugar on to boil with one
quart of water, boil and skim carefully. Add
the fruit to the boiling syrup and boil five
minutes. Can quickly, lose no time in screwing on the covers. Screw tight as possible and
tighten again as they grow cool. Examine frequently, always screwing tighter.

AND STILL ANOTHER WAY.—Take off the rind
and trim. Cut into desired slices; a nice way is
to cut round slices then divide into thirds.
Fill into glass cans, and dissolve sugar in water
enough to cover the cans to overflowing, allow-

ing half a pound of sugar to a pound of fruit, and pour this sweetened water over the pineapples. Clap on the rubbers and screw on the covers tightly. Now place them in a large wash boiler, securing the cans from tumbling over, by placing sticks of wood at the bottom of the boiler; a still better way is to put hay or old rags between the cans. Fill the boiler with cold water up to the neck of the cans, and let them boil steadily for at least twenty minutes. Lift the boiler from the stove and allow the cans to get cold in the water they were boiled in, even if it takes until the following day. Then remove each can carefully, screwing each can as tightly as possible. Wipe dry and put away in a cool place. All canned fruits should be examined carefully in one or two weeks' time after being put up. If any show signs of fermenting, just set them in a boiler of cold water and let them come to a boil slowly. Boil about ten minutes, remove boiler from the fire and allow the cans to cool in the boiler. When cold screw tight and put away.

# PICKLES, RELISHES, ETC.

|  | Page. |
|---|---|
| Boiled Beans, - - - - - -´ | 444 |
| Chow-Chow, - - - - - | 449 |
| Cold Slaw, - - - - - | 451 |
| Cabbage, - - - - - | 453 |
| Cauliflower, - - - - - | 454 |
| Cherries, - - - - - | 458 |
| Cucumber Pickles, - - - - - | 459 |
| Dill Pickles, - - - - - | 441 |
| Early Fall Vegetables, - - - - | 443 |
| Green Corn, - - - - - | 446 |
| Husk Tomatoes, - - ᴸ - - | 459 |
| Mother's Dill Pickles, - - - - | 440 |
| Mustard Pickles, - - - - | 447, 448 |
| Nutmegs, or Cantaloupes, - - - | 456 |
| Onions, - - - - - - - | 453 |
| Picalilli, - - - - - - | 450 |
| Prepared Mustard, - - - - - | 455 |
| Pepper Mangoes, - - - - | 454 |
| Plums, - - - - -` - - | 455 |
| Pears, - - - - - - - | 456 |
| Peaches, - - - - - - - | 457 |
| Salzgurken, - - - - - - | 442 |
| Salt Pickles, - - - - - | 442 |
| String Beans, - - - - - | 443 |
| Sauerkraut, - - - - - | 444, 445 |
| Spiced Apples, - - - - - | 458 |
| To Keep Beans Fresh, - - - - | 444 |
| Teufelsgurcken (Hot Pickles), - - | 450 |
| Tomato Catsup, - - - - | 451, 452 |

# PICKLES, RELISHES, ETC.

## MOTHER'S DILL PICKLES.

EXAMINE the cucumbers carefully, discard all that are soft at the ends, and allow them to lay in water over night. In the morning throw them on a clean board to drain, and dry them with a clean towel. Then put them in a wooden pail or jar, along with the dill, putting first a layer of dill at the bottom then a layer of cucumbers, a few whole peppers, then a layer of dill again, and so on until all are used up, and last lay a clean, white cloth on top, then a plate and a stone to give it weight, so that the pickles will be kept under the brine. To a peck of cucumbers use about two large handfuls of salt. Dissolve the salt in enough cold water to cover them. You may add one or two tablespoonfuls of vinegar to the brine. If the cucumbers are small, and if they are kept in a warm place, they will be ready for the table in five or six days. If any of my readers have put up salt pickles that have turned out to be too salty, just pour off the old brine and wash your pickles and then exam-

(440)

ine them closely, and if they are spoiled throw
them away.  Lay those that are sound in a clean
jar and pour over them a weak solution of salt
water, into which you have put a dash of vinegar.
Always examine your pickles weekly.  Take off
the cloth, wash it, and remove all the scum that
adheres to the pail, and lay a clean cloth over
the pickles again.  Do not use more than two
handfuls of salt in the new brine, which must be
thoroughly dissolved.  You will find among Salads a nice recipe wherein salt pickles are used.
(See "Polish Salad," or "Salad Piquant.") It is
a good way to make use of pickles in winter that
have become too salty for ordinary use.

### DILL  PICKLES.

Take two or three dozen medium-sized cucumbers and lay them in salt water over night.  Wipe
each one dry, discarding all that are soft and lay
them in a wooden vessel (which is better than
a stone one) along with grape leaves and green
grapes, if you can get them, whole peppers, or one
or two green peppers, a few bay leaves, a few
pieces of whole ginger, a few cloves and a stick of
horseradish sliced up on top of all.  Use plenty
of dill between each layer.  Boil enough water
to cover the pickles.  Use about one pound of
salt to six quarts of water, and one cup of vinegar.  If you wish to keep them all winter, have
your barrel closed by a cooper.

## SALZGURKEN.

Take half-grown cucumbers; lay them in water over night, then wipe each one dry and reject all that are soft at the ends. Now lay a layer of cucumbers in a new barrel or wine keg (a small vinegar barrel is best), then a layer of the following spices: Fennel, dill, bay leaves, a few whole peppers; then cover with grape and cherry leaves, and begin again with a layer of cucumbers and fill in alternate layers until all are used up. Then boil enough salt and water to just cover them, test the strength of the water by laying an egg in it, if it rises the water has enough salt in it, if not, add more salt. Pour this over the cucumbers when cold. Get a cooper to tighten up the barrel, and roll it in the sun and allow it to stay there for two weeks, turning over the barrel once each day.

## SALT PICKLES.

(For immediate use.) Take nice, large cucumbers, wash and wipe them; lay them in a jar or wooden pail, sprinkle coarse salt over each layer, and add dill, whole peppers and grape leaves, if you have them, also a very few bay leaves. Cover with water up to the brim and lay a piece of bread in the jar; it will help to quicken the process of souring. Cover with a plate and put a clean, heavy stone on top of the plate, in order to keep them well covered with the brine.

Set them in a warm place, say back of the
kitchen stove, for the first three days. They
will be ready to use in a week.

### EARLY FALL VEGETABLES.

Take new firkins or large stone jars, and scald
them well with boiling water before using. Vegetables that are boiled before pickling in a brass
kettle always keep their fresh, green color. In
salt pickling cover your jars or kegs with a clean,
white cloth, then a cover made of wood and last
a heavy stone to weigh it down. The cloth must
be removed every other day, washed and put
back. In doing this, take hold of the cloth at
each corner, so that none of the slimy substance
can get into your pickle, and wash the top and
sides of the jar also. Be particular about this.

### STRING BEANS (RAW).

String the beans very carefully, and cut into
fine short lengths; then sprinkle salt over and
through them, mixing thoroughly, say to twenty-
five pounds of beans, two pounds of salt. Let
them remain in the salt over night. Then pack
the shredded beans as tightly as possible into
jars or kegs, without any of their juice. In two
weeks look them over, remove the cloth and
wash it, etc., as already described. When cooking the beans, take out as many as may be
required for a meal and soak them in cold water
over night. In the morning set on to boil in

cold water. Boil for one hour. Pour off the water they were boiled in, add fresh water, and prepare as you would fresh beans.

### BOILED BEANS.

Select small, young string beans, string them carefully and boil in salt water, in a brass kettle, until tender, and throw them on a large, clean board to drip. Next morning press them into a jar, with alternate layers of salt and beans, and proceed as with string beans.

### TO KEEP BEANS FRESH.

String, shred, and put in a barrel or keg, with the following mixture: Dissolve three drams of salicylic acid in a little hot water, add it and four ounces of salt to a gallon of water and pour over the beans. Cover securely as in foregoing receipts.

### SAUERKRAUT.

Line the bottom and sides of a clean barrel or keg with cabbage leaves. Cut into fine shreds one or two dozen large heads of white, crisp cabbage. Do this on a large slaw-cutter. Now begin to pack: First put in a layer of cabbage, say about four inches deep, and press down firmly and sprinkle with about four tablespoonfuls of salt. You may put one or two tart apples, cut up fine, between each layer, or some Malaga grapes (which will impart a fine flavor to the kraut). When you have put in these four layers pound with a wooden beetle until the cabbage is quite compact and then add more cabbage, and so on until all has been salted, always pounding down each layer. Last, cover with cabbage leaves, then a clean cloth, a well-fitting board, and a heavy stone, to act as weight on top of all. It is now ready to set away in a cool cellar to ferment  In two weeks examine, remove the scum, if any; wash the cloth, board and stone, wash also the sides of the keg or jar, and place all back again. This must be done weekly.

## BOILED SAUERKRAUT.

Take a brisket of beef weighing about five or six pounds. Set it on to boil in a gallon of water, a little salt and the usual soup greens. When the meat is tender take it out, salt it well and put on to boil again in a porcelain-lined kettle, having previously removed all the bones. Add about a cupful of the soup stock and as much sauerkraut as you desire.  Boil about one hour; tie a tablespoonful of carroway seed in a bag and boil in with the kraut.  Thicken with two raw potatoes, grated, and add a tablespoonful of brown sugar just before serving.  If not sour enough add a dash of vinegar.  This gives you meat, vegetables and soup.  Mashed potatoes, kartoffelkloesse or any kind of flour dumpling is a nice accompaniment. Sauerkraut is just as good warmed over as fresh, which may

be done two or three times in succession without
injury to its flavor.

## GREEN CORN.

Place the corn in large Mason jars and pour
a gallon of water over it, in which you have dissolved four ounces of salt and three drams of
salicylic acid (dissolve the acid in hot water).
Another way: Boil the corn, cut it off the cobs,
and pack in jars in alternate layers of salt and
corn. Use plenty of salt in packing. When you
wish to cook it soak in water over night. Pack
the corn in this way: First a layer of salt, half
an inch deep; then about two inches of corn;
then salt again, and so on. The top layer must
be salt. Spread two inches of melted butter
over the top layer and bind with strong perforated paper (perforate the paper with a pin).
Keep in a cool cellar.

Use none but the best vinegar, and whole
spices for pickling. If you boil vinegar with
pickles in bell metal do not let them stand in it
one moment after taken from the fire, and be sure
that your kettle is well scoured before using.
Keep pickles in glass, stoneware, or wooden pails.
Allow a cup of sugar to every gallon of vinegar;
this will not sweeten the pickles, but helps to
preserve them and mellows the sharpness of the
vinegar. Always have your pickles well covered with vinegar or brine.

## MUSTARD PICKLES.

Choose small cucumbers or gherkins for this purpose. Reject all that are specked or mis-shapen. Wash them thoroughly; drain off all the water, and allow them to lay in a tub over night, thickly salted. In the morning wipe your pickles carefully. Lay them in a stone jar or a wooden bucket, in this way: Put in a layer of pickles. Cut up a few green or red peppers; put a few pieces in each layer, also a few cloves (remove the soft heads) and a table-spoonful of mustard seed, and one bay leaf, no more. Then proceed in this way until your pickles are used up. Then take half a pound of the very best ground mustard, tie it in a cloth loosely (use double cheese cloth for the purpose), and lay this mustard bag on top of your pickles. Boil enough white wine vinegar in a bell metal kettle to just cover them; add a cup of sugar for every gallon of vinegar, this does not sweeten them, but tends to preserve them and cut the sharpness of the vinegar. If your vine-gar is very strong, add a cupful of water to it while boiling; it should not " draw " your mouth, but be rather mild. You must see that the pickles are well covered with the vinegar, and pour the vinegar hot over the pickles and mus-tard. If the vinegar does not completely cover your pickles, boil more and add. Lay a plate on top of all to keep the pickles under the vinegar,

and when cold tie up. Look them over in a few
weeks, if you find any soft ones among them,
boil the vinegar over again, and pour it over
them hot.

### DELICIOUS MUSTARD PICKLES
(SENFGURKEN).

Take about two dozen large, yellow pickles,
pare them with a silver knife (to prevent them
from turning dark), and cut lengthwise. Now
take a silver spoon and remove all the seeds and
soft inner pulp  Cut into strips about as long
as your finger; sprinkle salt over them, and so
on, until they are all cut up, then put in a
wooden pail or large china bowl over night. At
the same time take about two quarts of small
pickling onions. scald them with boiling water,
remove the skins, also with a silver knife, and
salt the same as you did the pickles. In the
morning take a clean dish towel and dry each
piece and lay them in a stone jar in the following manner: First a layer of pickles then a
layer of onions, and then some horseradish,
sliced, between the layers; a few whole peppers,
a very few bay leaves, and sprinkle mustard
seed, allspice and whole cloves between each
layer. Remove the soft little heads of the
cloves to prevent the pickles from turning dark;
cover all with the best white wine vinegar; put
a double cheese cloth filled with mustard seed
on top. In two weeks pour off the vinegar care-

fully and boil, and let it get perfectly cold before pouring over the pickles again. You may pack them in small glass jars if you prefer.

## CHOW-CHOW.

Take pickles, cauliflower, beans, little onions and a few green and red peppers. Cut all up fine, except the onions; salt well over night, drain off next morning and put in a large jar. Now mix one gallon or more of best pickling vinegar with a pound of ground mustard (wet the mustard with cold water before using). Put in a bag the following spices: Cloves, whole peppers and mustard seed. Boil the vinegar and spices and then throw over pickles boiling. Add a tablespoonful of curry powder, and when cold tie up, having previously put a cloth with mustard seed over all.

## VINEGAR PICKLES, OR GHERKINS.

Salt the pickles for twenty-four hours and then drain and wipe dry. See that they are all sound, and put in a large jar. Set a gallon of best vinegar on to boil, adding a cup of sugar and a pint of water. Tie a bag of all kinds of pickling spices and let it boil with the vinegar. If you like your pickles very hot lay a few peppers among the pickles. Pour the vinegar over them boiling, and cover with a cloth and plate on top to keep the pickles covered with vinegar. Look them over in two weeks, and if necessary boil the vinegar once more.

### TUEFELSGURKEN (HOT PICKLES).

Pare large, green cucumbers, cut each one lengthwise, take out the seeds with a silver spoon and then cut each piece again so as to have four pieces out of one cucumber. When all are pared salt well and let them remain in the salt for twenty-four hours or more; then dry each piece, put in layers in a stone jar with whole white and black peppercorns, small pickling onions, which have been previously pared and salted over night, pieces of horse radish, a few bay leaves, a little fennel, carroway seeds, a few cloves of garlic (use this sparingly) and also some Spanish pepper (use very little of the latter). Have a layer of the spices at the bottom of the jar. A handful of mustard seed put on the top layer will be an improvement. Boil enough pickling vinegar to cover well. Add a cup of sugar to a gallon of vinegar, boil and pour over hot. Boil again in three days and pour over the pickles after it gets cold, and in two days pour off the vinegar and boil again and pour over the pickles hot. Boil three times altogether.

### PICCALILLI.

Take one-half peck of green tomatoes, two heads of cabbage, nine large onions, about a dozen good-sized cucumbers, half a dozen green peppers and one quarter of a pound of mustard seed. Chop all quite fine. Make a strong brine of salt water, and boil your chopped piccalilli in it for about five minutes. Remove from the fire and press out every drop of the brine; then mix in the mustard seed, and put all in a large stone crock. Boil a gallon of pickling vinegar and pour over hot. It is fit to use as soon as cold, and will keep a year.

### COLD SLAW.

Take a firm, white head of cabbage; cut it in halves; take out the heart and cut as fine as possible on slaw-cutter. Cut up one onion at the same time and a sour apple. Now sprinkle with salt and white pepper and a liberal quantity of white sugar. Mix this lightly with two forks. Heat a spoonful of goose-oil or butter, and mix it thoroughly in with the cabbage. Heat some white wine vinegar in a spider; let it come to a boil and pour over the slaw boiling. Keep covered for a short time. Serve cold.

### TOMATO CATSUP.

(No. 1.) Take one peck of tomatoes, one ounce of salt, one tablespoonful of mace, a teaspoonful of black pepper and one of Cayenne, two of ground mustard and half a teaspoonful of celery seed. Cut up the tomatoes, put them in a porcelain-lined kettle, and boil until all are mashed up. Strain through a collander, add the spices and boil for half a day, stirring constantly the last hour for fear of burning. About half an hour before done add a pint of

best vinegar, and a tablespoonful of brown sugar.
Bottle when cold, and seal. You may omit the
celery seed and mace if you object to their
flavor.

### TOMATO CATSUP.

(No. 2.) Select ripe tomatoes, say about one
peck, and cut them in pieces. Put on to boil,
and boil until soft. Then strain and press
through a coarse sieve. Return to the kettle and
add a bag of the following spices: Two tablespoonfuls of salt, one of black pepper, one teaspoonful of Cayenne pepper, one teaspoonful of
cloves (powdered), one teaspoonful of celery
seed, and two tablespoonfuls of ground mustard. Boil for at least four hours, stirring constantly for the last hour and very often while
boiling. Add a pint of vinegar and a tablespoonful of sugar just before removing from the
fire. Bottle and seal securely.

### TOMATO CATSUP.

(No. 3.) Pour boiling water on a peck of
ripe tomatoes, remove the skins and all bad
spots. Boil slowly in a porcelain-kettle about
three hour, stir often from the bottom especially
when nearly done. Then add four tablespoonfuls of salt, pepper and three of ground mustard, six medium-sized red peppers, chopped up
fine, one-half tablespoonful of cloves, one-half of
allspice; stir all the spices in a pint of best
cider vinegar. Simmer the whole tomatoes and

spiced vinegar mixed thoroughly half an hour.
Bottle and seal while hot.

### PICKLED ONIONS.

Pour hot salt water over the onions, which
should be small and perfectly white.  Peel them
with a silver spoon (a knife would injure their
color, and let them lay in a salt brine for two
days.  Then drain the onions and boil enough
vinegar to cover them.  Throw the onions in the
boiling vinegar and let them boil only a few
minutes.  Take from the fire and lay them in
glass jars, with alternate layers of whole white
peppercorns and a few cloves (removing the
soft heads, which would turn the onions black),
a stick of horseradish sliced, and mustard seed
and dill (used sparingly).  When the jars are
filled heat the vinegar and add a cup of sugar
to a gallon of vinegar.  Cover the jars to overflowing with the vinegar, and seal while hot.

### PICKLED CABBAGE.

Chop fine two large heads of crisp cabbage
and peel and chop fine one quart of onions.
Pack the cabbage and onions in alternate layers,
sprinkling fine salt between each layer.  Let
them remain in this salt until next day.  Then
scald three pints of vinegar, adding one pound of
sugar, one tablespoonful of best ground mustard
(wet the mustard with cold water before adding),
one tablespoonful of pepper, one of cinnamon

and one of celery seed; a teaspoonful of allspice,
one of mace and one of pulverized alum. Pour
this over the cabbage and onions. Do this three
mornings in succession. The last time heat all
together and boil five minutes. When cold
pack in small jars.

### PICKLED CAULIFLOWER.

Clean the cauliflower and boil five minutes in
salted water. Remove and lay in cold water
for one minute, and then cut up and put in jars.
To each gallon of vinegar add one red pepper
pod, two tablespoonfuls of white mustard seed,
one tablespoonful of mace, one-half a tablespoonful of cloves, one of allspice and one of
ginger. Put the spices in a bag. Boil the spices
with the best cider vinegar. Do this once a
week, four weeks in succession.

### PEPPER MANGOES.

Take large green peppers; extract the seeds
and core with a penknife, being careful not to
break the peppers. It takes some ingenuity to
do this. Chop up one head of cabbage after
boiling it in salt water. When cold add one
handful of mustard seed, two tablespoonfuls of
grated horseradish, one nutmeg grated, one clove
of garlic grated, a pinch of ground ginger, one
dozen whole peppercorns, half a tablespoonful
of prepared mustard, one teaspoonful of sugar
and half a teaspoonful of best salad oil. Lay

the peppers in strong salt brine for three days; then drain off the brine and lay them in fresh water for twenty-four hours. Fill the peppers with the above mixture, sew or tie them up with strong thread, pack them in a large stone jar and pour scalding vinegar over them. Repeat this process three times more, at intervals of three days. Then tie up the jar and set it away in a cool, dry place for three months. They will keep forever.

### PREPARED MUSTARD.

Rub together one teaspoonful of sugar, salt-spoonful of fine salt and one tablespoonful of best salad oil. Do this thoroughly. Mix two tablespoonfuls of ground mustard with vinegar enough to thin it. Then add to the mixture of sugar, and, if too thick, add a little boiling water.

### PICKLED PLUMS.

Prick the plums with a large needle then weigh them, and to every seven pounds of fruit use four pounds of white sugar, two ounces of stick cinnamon, one ounce of cloves and a pint of best pickling vinegar. Boil the vinegar, sugar and spices, and pour boiling hot over the fruit, which you have packed in a large jar; repeat this three times. While your vinegar boils the third time, pack the plums in glass jars and pour the syrup over the plums. When cold seal.

### PICKLED NUTMEG, OR CANTALOUPE.

Take fine, ripe melons, pare, take out the seeds and wash, cut into slices about three inches long and two inches wide, lay them in a stone jar and cover with vinegar for twenty-four hours or longer. Then lay the fruit on a clean board to drip; and throw away one quart of the vinegar to each quart remaining. Allow three pounds and a half of white sugar to a dozen small cantaloupes, three ounces of stick cinnamon, one ounce of cloves (remove the soft heads) and two ounces of allspice (whole spices). Boil the spices, vinegar and sugar, adding a pint of fresh vinegar to the old. When well skimmed put in the melons, boil fifteen minutes, twenty is still better; take out the fruit, put it in jars and boil the syrup awhile longer. Skim it again and pour boiling hot over the fruit. Seal when cold.

### PICKLED PEARS.

Pears should always be peeled for pickling. If large cut them in half and leave the stems on. The best pear for this purpose, also for canning, is a variety called the "Sickle Pear." It is a small, pulpy pear of delicious flavor. Throw each pear into cold water as you peel it. When all are peeled weigh them and allow four pounds and a half of white sugar to ten pounds of fruit. Put into the kettle with alternate layers of sugar and half a cup of water and one quart of strong vinegar. Add stick cinnamon and a few cloves (remove the soft heads). Heat slowly and boil until tender, then remove them with a perforated skimmer, and spread upon dishes to cool. skim the boiling syrup and boil fifteen minutes longer. Put the pears in glass jars or a large earthen jar, the former being preferable, and pour the syrup and spices boiling hot over the fruit. When cold seal.

## PICKLED PEACHES.

Select large cling-stone peaches for this purpose. Throw the peaches into cold water as soon as pared, and then weigh. Add four pounds of white sugar to seven pounds of peaches, one pint of best pickling vinegar, half of five cents' worth of stick cinnamon and cloves (remove the soft heads). Heat peaches and sugar slowly. Boil about fifteen minutes, and add the vinegar and spices. Boil about ten minutes longer; take them up with a perforated skimmer and lay them on flat dishes to cool. Then lay them in jars; let the syrup boil until quite thick, pour over your fruit scalding and when cool seal. This quantity fills about four quart jars. In a month look them over, and if they should show signs of fermenting set the jars in a kettle of water, and heat until scalding. But this is not likely to happen if you follow directions closely, and use none but the best pickling vinegar.

### SPICED OR PICKLED CHERRIES.

Take the largest and freshest red cherries you can get, and pack them in glass fruit jars, stems and all. Put little splints of wood across the tops of the fruit to prevent rising to the top. Now to every quart of cherries allow a cup of best pickling vinegar, and to every three quarts of fruit one pound of sugar and a handful of whole cinnamon bark and half of five cents' worth of cloves; this quantity of spices is for all of the fruit. Boil the vinegar and spices and sugar for five minutes steady; turn out into a covered stoneware vessel, cover, and let it get cold. Then pour over the fruit and repeat this process three days in succession. Remove the heads of the cloves, for they will turn the fruit black. You may strain the vinegar after the first boiling, so as to take out the spices, if you choose. Seal as you would other fruit. Be sure that the syrup is cold before you pour it over the cherries.

### SPICED OR PICKLED APPLES.

Pare the apples, "Pound Sweets" are best; crab apples may be pickled the same way, but do not pare. Leave on the stems and put into a kettle with alternate layers of sugar; take four pounds of white sugar to nine pounds of fruit, and spice with an ounce of cinnamon bark and half an ounce of cloves, removing the heads. Heat slowly to a boil with a pint of water; add the vinegar and spices, and boil until tender. Take out the fruit with a perforated skimmer and spread upon dishes to cool. Boil the syrup thick; pack the apples in jars and pour the syrup over them boiling hot. Examine them in a week's time, and should they show signs of fermenting pour off the syrup and boil up for a few minutes, and pour over the fruit scalding, or set the jars (uncovered) in a kettle of cold water and heat until the contents are boiling, and then seal.

### PICKLED HUSK TOMATOES.

This tomato looks like an egg-shaped plum and makes a very nice sweet pickle. Prick each one with a needle, weigh, and to seven pounds of tomatoes take four pounds of sugar and spice with a very little mace, cinnamon and cloves. Put into the kettle with alternate layers of sugar. Heat slowly to a boil, skim and add vinegar, not more than a pint to seven pounds of tomatoes. Add spices and boil for about ten minutes, not longer. Take them out with a perforated skimmer and spread upon dishes to cool. Boil the syrup thick, and pack as you would other fruit.

### CUCUMBER PICKLES.

Let your pickles lie for two or three days in strong brine; take them out and wash in clear water, then put them into a porcelain kettle;

take half water and half vinegar, in which scald
the pickles; when they come to a boil, take out
and put into glass cans, throwing the liquid
away. Then scald in a porcelain kettle, more
vinegar, if two strong add a little water.
Season to taste; and pour over the pickles and
seal while hot. Use none but cider vinegar for
pickling and add a cup of sugar to a gallon of
vinegar.

# BEVERAGES.

|  | Page. |
|---|---|
| Apple Toddy, | 471 |
| Blackberry Brandy, | 462 |
| Barley Water, | 472 |
| Blackberry Cordial, | 473 |
| Chocolate, | 463 |
| Cocoa, | 463 |
| Coffee, | 464 |
| Currant Wine, | 467 |
| Cocoa Shells, | 468 |
| Cold Egg Wine, | 470 |
| Cherry Brandy, | 471 |
| Cherry Syrup, | 471 |
| Dried Flour for Teething Children, | 472 |
| Egg Lemonade, | 462 |
| Egg Nogg, | 469 |
| Elerbier, | 470 |
| Flaxseed Lemonade, | 471 |
| Grog, | 470 |
| Huckleberry, | 462 |
| Hot Beer, | 470 |
| Iced Tea, | 465 |
| Iced Tea, a la Russe, | 465 |
| Lemonade, | 465 |
| Lemonade for Invalids, | 466 |
| Milk Lemonade, | 468 |
| Milk Punch, | 472 |
| Orangeade, | 469 |
| Punch Extract, | 470 |
| Raspberry Vinegar, | 466 |
| Rice Water, | 472 |
| Slippery Elm Water, | 472 |
| Strawberry Sherbet, | 465 |
| Strawberry Syrup, | 467 |
| Sherry Cobbler, | 469 |
| Spiced Red Wine, | 469 |
| Soda Cream, | 468 |
| Tea, | 464 |
| Tea, a la Russe, | 464 |
| Toast Water, | 472 |
| Whip, | 471 |
| Watermelon Sherbet, | 473 |

# BEVERAGES.

I drink to the general joy of the whole table,
And to our dear friend Banquo.—*Shakespeare*

## BLACKBERRY BRANDY.

ALLOW two quarts of blackberries and a pound of cut loaf sugar to one gallon of brandy. Put all in a large jug, cork, and set in the sun for two weeks at least. You may add whole spices, such as cloves and stick cinnamon.

## HUCKLEBERRY BRANDY.

Allow two quarts of huckleberries, one quart of blackberries and one pound of cut loaf sugar to two gallons of brandy. Put all in a large jug, throw in a handful of cinnamon bark, about two dozen cloves and a very little whole mace. Cork, and set in the sun for two weeks.

## EGG LEMONADE.

Grate over the sugar the peel of half the lemons you intend to use, and squeeze the lemons into it with a squeezer. Then beat up as many eggs as you intend glasses of lemonade. If you are making a quantity you may take one or two eggs less. Beat up the lemons and the sugar, next add water in proportion and then shake or beat the whole vigorously for a few seconds. Fill the tumblers half full of broken ice. Before serving shake again.

### CHOCOLATE.

Heat one quart of milk with a pint of water and add a quarter of a pound of grated chocolate. If too thick add more milk, and sweeten to taste. Boil for about five minutes, stirring occasionally. Beat up the yelks of two or more eggs light and add a spoonful of cold water or milk to the eggs before pouring the chocolate into it. This will prevent curdling. Return to the kettle and set on the back of the stove. Should be served immediately. Serve with whipped cream. A good substitute for this is made of the beaten whites of the eggs, thus: Beat up the whites of the eggs with pulverized sugar and cover the surface of each cup with the sweetened meringue before serving. Whipped cream, sweetened, is preferable. The meringue is more economical.

### COCOA.

Take one or two teaspoonfuls of cocoa (according to the size of the cup) and the same quantity of pulverized sugar, add two teaspoonfuls of milk or water, and mix into a paste. While stirring, pour in slowly the rest of the milk or water. Now boil the cocoa for about two minutes in a closely-covered vessel. You may also prepare it according to Chocolate receipt.

## COFFEE.

There are so many ways of making good
coffee that I hardly know which one to give you.
I use a French coffee pot, to begin with, and the
best Java and Mocha mixed. It must be fresh
roasted, and not ground until you wish to use it.
A millful of coffee for a family of eight is a good
rule. Put the coffee in the filterer, pour boiling
water over it, half a cupful at a time, and wait two
or three minutes before you add the other half-
cupful, and so on, until you have the desired
quantity. Then begin to pour one or two cupfuls of the made coffee through the filter again;
but, remember, the water must boil hard. This
is very important if you wish good coffee, but
do not let the coffee boil. Use cream and serve
at once. If it is allowed to stand too long it will
become flat and gray.

### TEA A LA RUSSE.

Lay a slice of lemon in the bottom of each
cup, sprinkle with sugar, and pour hot, strong
tea over it. No cream is used.

### TEA.

Allow one teaspoonful of tea for two cups of
boiling water. Have the water boiling hard and
pour over the tea about half the quantity
required. Cover tightly, and let it stand where
it will keep hot, but not to boil. Let the tea in-
fuse for ten or fifteen minutes, and then pour

more boiling water on it. If you wish to make just one cup of tea use a teaspoonful of tea.

### ICED TEA.

Allow a teaspoonful of tea for each cup, put the tea in a porcelain-lined or china tea-pot, and pour as much cold water on it as you require for your tea. Set this in ice-chest for twelve hours or more. You will find this tea more delicate in flavor than when prepared with the boiling water. It will not have any bitter taste at all, which tea made with boiling water always has, if allowed to stand any length of time.

### ICED TEA A LA RUSSE.

Press the juice of a lemon and a wineglassful of brandy into your tea. Serve in glasses with pounded ice, and sweeten as you would iced tea.

### STRAWBERRY SHERBET.

A delicious summer drink is prepared in the following manner: Crush a quart of ripe strawberries, pour a quart of water over them, and add the juice of two lemons. Let this stand about two hours, then strain over a pound of sugar, stir until the sugar is dissolved, and then set upon ice. You may add one tablespoonful of rosewater. Serve with chopped ice.

### LEMONADE.

Roll the lemons on the table or between your hands until quite soft, say about three lemons to a quart of water; squeeze out every drop of juice; extract the seeds and sweeten to taste.

Do not put the ice in the lemonade, but have it chopped fine and put in the glasses just before serving. When wine is used take two-thirds water and one-third wine.

### LEMONADE FOR INVALIDS.

Pour boiling water over the lemons, being very careful to extract all the seeds. Bottle it and set it on ice. Sweeten only what is to be used and cork up the bottle again and return it to the ice chest. This is both good and economical.

### RASPBERRY VINEGAR.

(No. 1.) Press ripe red raspberries through a sieve, under which you have placed a fine cloth, so as not to have any seeds in the syrup. Pour the juice in a stone jar and let it sour for four or five days (even six days is not too long), then skim of the white sheet of foam that has risen to the surface and boil the clear juice, allowing a pint of sugar to a scant quart of juice. Boil until it is the consistency of syrup, then bottle it, and when cold cork and seal with sealing wax. This is the finest raspberry vinegar made, rather expensive, but two or three tablespoonfuls are sufficient for a glass of chopped ice and water.

### RASPBERRY VINEGAR.

(No. 2.) To six quarts of red raspberries allow one scant quart of white wine vinegar. Pour the vinegar over the fruit into a stone jar, cover and stir the fruit once every day for four or five days in succession, then strain through a jelly bag and boil, allowing a pint of sugar to every pint of juice. Skim off the scum that rises and cook until the consistency of syrup. When cold, bottle, cork and seal. It is not necessary to buy the choicest raspberries for this purpose. Your grocer, probably, may have a quantity of berries on hand that he can not dispose of for table use (which are good enough for this purpose), which you may buy at one-fourth the selling price.

### CURRANT WINE.

Pick, stem and mash the currants, which must be very ripe. To two quarts of juice add two pounds of sugar and one pint of water, stir all together thoroughly, put in a clean cask, leaving out the bung and cover the hole with a piece of lace net. Let it ferment four weeks, then bottle and seal.

### STRAWBERRY SYRUP.

Take three pints of berries and one pound of loaf sugar. After measuring the berries, weigh the amount of sugar required and boil the sugar until it forms a syrup by adding a pint of water to two pounds of sugar. When perfectly clear put in the berries and stir them in the syrup with a silver spoon. Do not mash them or boil. When thoroughly heated remove from the fire and let the syrup run through a jelly bag, but do not press the berries. When the syrup is cold pour into bottles and seal. This syrup is a very refreshing drink, especially for consumptives,

giving a teaspoonful at a dose. It has very soothing qualities. You may make a marmalade of
the berries left in the jelly bag. They will keep
until currants come into the market, then boil
them with the currants, adding as much sugar
as you have fresh fruit.

### MILK LEMONADE.

Dissolve in one quart of boiling water two
cups of granulated sugar, add three-fourths of a
cup of lemon juice, and lastly, one and a half
pints of boiling milk. Drink hot, or cold with
pounded ice.

### SODA CREAM.

Take three pounds of granulated sugar and
one and one-half ounces of tartaric acid, both
dissolved in one quart of hot water. When cold
add the well-beaten whites of three eggs, stirring well. Bottle for use. Put two large spoonfuls of this syrup in a glass of ice water, and
stir in it one-fourth of a teaspoonful of bicar-
bonate of soda. Any flavor can be put in this
syrup. An excellent summer drink.

### COCOA SHELLS.

To one quart of boiling water add two ounces
of cocoa shells which have been previously wet
with a little cold water. Boil together one
hour, strain, add one quart of fresh milk, and
when it reaches boiling point remove from the
fire and sweeten to taste. This is excellent for
invalids.

## EGG-NOGG.

Stir the yelks of six eggs with three-fourths of
a cup of sugar until thick; then add gradually
one quart of rich, sweet milk and one-half pint
of best brandy and a little grated nutmeg.
Beat the whites of the eggs to a stiff froth and
add, mixing well. In winter you may heat the
milk and drink hot.

## ORANGEADE.

Take four large, juicy oranges and six tablespoonfuls of sugar. Squeeze the oranges upon
the sugar, add a very little water and let them
stand for fifteen minutes; strain and add
pounded ice and water.

## SPICED RED WINE (GLUEHWEIN).

Put red wine on to boil, add cinnamon bark,
cloves, and sweeten to taste. Boil covered and
drink as hot as possible. This is an excellent
remedy for diarrhea.

## SHERRY COBBLER.

It is best to mix this in a large bowl and fill
in glasses just before serving, and put a little of
each kind of fruit in each goblet with pounded
ice. To begin with, cut pineapple in slices and
quarters, a few oranges and a lemon, sliced
thin; one cup of powdered sugar and one tumbler of sherry wine. A few berries, such as
black and red raspberries and blackberries, are
a nice addition. Cover the fruit with the sugar,
laid in layers at the bottom of your bowl with

pounded ice; add the wine and twice as much water as wine; stir all up well before serving.

### COLD EGG WINE.

To each glass of wine allow one egg, beat up, and add sugar to taste. Add wine gradually and grated nutmeg. Beat whites separately and mix.

### PUNCH EXTRACT.

Boil two pounds of cut loaf sugar with two cups of water. When clear add the juice of four lemons, and when cold add a bottle of arrack. In serving take one part punch extract and two parts boiling water.

### EIERBIER.

To one bottle of beer beat up the yelks of two or more eggs, with two heaping tablespoonfuls of sugar. Beat until light, and add the beer gradually.

### HOT BEER.

To two bottles of beer allow one pint of milk, and heat each in a separate vessel. Beat the yelks of four eggs light, with half a cup of sugar. Add gradually the hot milk, stirring all the time, and then the boiling beer, stirring constantly. Serve immediately in glasses.

### GROG.

Is made by pouring two-thirds boiling water to one-third arrack or rum, and sweetening.

## WHIP.

Take one bottle of white wine, one-half pound of sugar, in which you have grated the peel of one lemon, adding its juice, a pinch of ground cinnamon and six eggs. Beat all together over the fire until it reaches boiling point, remove from the fire and serve in glasses, hot.

## CHERRY BRANDY.

To one gallon of brandy allow two quarts of cherries. Mash and pound them until all the stones are broken, put in the brandy and add a pound of cut loaf sugar. Set in the sun for two or three weeks, shake daily, strain and bottle.

## CHERRY SYRUP.

Mash and pound the cherries until the stones are all broken, then press through a cloth. Use a pound of sugar to a quart of juice; boil, skim and bottle. When cold seal.

## FLAXSEED LEMONADE.

Steep three hours in a covered porcelain lined vessel five tablespoonfuls of whole flaxseed, one quart of boiling water and juice of three lemons (extract the seeds). Sweeten to taste. If too thick, add more water and then strain. Add ice for drinking, Excellent remedy for coughs.

## APPLE TODDY.

Boil a few apples in a quart of water, and strain when soft. While hot, add a glass of good whisky, some lemon juice and sugar.

## TOAST WATER.

Take slices of toast (be careful not to have them burned), pour boiling water over them, cover closely and steep until cold. Strain and sweeten and add ice if advisable.

## SLIPPERY-ELM BARK WATER.

Pour boiling water over the bark and cover until cold, sweeten and add ice. For diarrhœa.

## MILK PUNCH.

Stir together one tumbler of sweetened milk and two tablespoonfuls of best brandy. Give only a few swallows at a time. You may add an egg beaten light, then you have "Egg Punch."

## BARLEY WATER.

Wash and pick over three tablespoonfuls of coarse barley, set on to boil with two cups of water, add a pinch of salt and strain.

## RICE WATER.

Wash two tablespoonfuls of rice, put on to boil with two cups of water and a pinch of salt; strain and set on ice.

## DRIED FLOUR FOR TEETHING CHILDREN.

Tie up as much flour as your napkin will hold, set it on to boil in plenty of cold salt, and boil at least four hours, slowly but steadily, in an earthen milk bowl. Take out of the napkin; it will now be a solid ball; and scrape off the thick, yellow rind. Grate one tablespoonful, wet it with a little cold water, stir in half a cup

ful of boiling milk, add a pinch of salt and boil
about five minutes. You may give this to baby
in the worst cases of summer complaint. I
know it is a positive cure for loose bowels with
children. Keep it in a dry place and it will
last for some time.

### BLACKBERRY CORDIAL.

To one quart of blackberry juice add one
pound and a half of the best white sugar, half an
ounce of grated nutmeg, half an ounce of powdered cinnamon, a quarter of an ounce of allspice, one quarter ounce of cloves and a pint of
best brandy. Tie the spices in a thin muslin
bag, boil the sugar, juice and spices together for
twenty minutes, skimming well, and add the
brandy. Remove from the fire and set aside in
a closely-covered bowl to cool. When cold,
strain, bottle and seal.

### WATERMELON SHERBET.

Take good, pale sherry and boil down to quite
a thick syrup, with loaf sugar; and then allow
to cool. When cold mix with the chopped meat
of a very fine, sweet melon, use only the heart
of the soft red part, not any near the white rind.
Freeze in a freezer as you would ice, but do not
allow it to get too hard. Serve in glasses. You
may use claret instead of the sherry. If you do,
spice it while boiling with whole spices, such as
cloves and cinnamon. Strain before adding to
the melon.

**MEMORANDUM.**

# EASTER DISHES.

|  | Page. |
|---|---|
| Apple Pudding, - - - - - | 478 |
| Apple Charlotte, - - - - - | 479 |
| Almond Hills, - - - - - | 486 |
| Brod Torte, - - - - - | 485 |
| Chand'eau Sauce, - - - - | 477 |
| Chrimsel, - - - - - | 479 |
| Chocolate Cake, - - - - | 485, 486 |
| Clover-leaf Macaroons, - - - - | 487 |
| Chocolate Macaroons, - - - - | 484 |
| Cinnamon Sticks, - - - - - | 487 |
| Date Tart Cake, - - - - | 485 |
| Easter Table, how to set, - - - - | 475 |
| Filled Crimsel, - - - - - | 480 |
| Filled Matzo Kloesse, - - - - | 483 |
| Grated Apple Pudding, - - - | 479 |
| Hasty Pudding, - - - - | 488 |
| Matzo Kugel, - - - - | 476 |
| Matzo Pudding, or Schalet, - - - | 476 |
| Matzo-Mehl Cake, - - - - | 488 |
| Matzo Kloesse, - - - - | 482 |
| Macaroon Cookies, - - - - | 484 |
| Mandeltorte, - - - - - | 486 |
| Macaroon, - - - - - | 487 |
| Potato Pudding, - - - - | 477 |
| Potato Flour Pudding, - - - - | 478 |
| Prunes, - - - - - | 480 |
| Pies, - - - - - | 481 |
| Raisin Wine, - - - - | 481, 482 |
| Sponge Cake, - - - - | 484 |
| Strawberry Short Cake, - - - | 483 |
| Strawberry Dessert, - - - - | 459 |
| Ueberschlagene, - - - - | 481 |
| Wine Sauce, - - - - - | 482 |

# MEMORANDUM.

# EASTER DISHES.

## CAKES, PUDDINGS, SAUCES, WINES, ETC.

### HOW TO SET THE TABLE FOR THE SERVICE OF THE "SEDAR" ON THE EVE OF PESACH OR PASSOVER.

SET the table as usual, have everything fresh and clean; a wineglass for each person, and an extra one placed near the platter of the gentleman who is to give the sedar. Then get a large napkin; fold it into four parts, set it on a plate, and in each fold put a perfect matzo; that is, one that is not broken or unshapely; in short, one without a blemish. Then place the following articles on a platter: One hard-boiled egg, a bone that has been roasted in ashes, the top of a nice stick of horseradish (it must be fresh and green), a bunch of nice curly parsley and some bitter herb (the Germans call it lattig), and, also, a small vessel filled with salt water. Next to this platter place a small bowl filled with חרוסת, prepared as follows: Pare and chop up a few apples; add sugar, cinnamon, pounded almonds, some white wine and grated lemon peel, and mix thoroughly. Place these dishes in front of the one that gives the sedar, and to

his left place two pillows, nicely covered, and a
small table or chair, on which you have placed
a wash-bowl with a pitcher of water and clean
towel.  In some families hard-boiled eggs are
distributed after the sedar (Easter eggs).

### MATZO-KUGEL.

Soak about six matzos; heat some fat in a
spider, press all the water out of the matzos with
your hands and dry them in a spider of heated
fat.  Now add about half a pound of matzo-meal;
stir the matzo and matzo-meal well with a large
spoon; add by degrees the yelks of ten eggs and
three or four ounces of pounded almonds, and
the grated peel of a lemon.  Add also two large
sour apples, grated, a pinch of salt, and, last,
the stiff-beaten whites of the eggs.  Line a
kugeltopf well with fat, and pour about half a
pound of hot fat over the kugel.  Bake immediately.

### MATZOS PUDDING, OR SCHALET.

Soak about three matzos, press out every drop
of water, and stir the matzos in a bowl with a
tablespoonful of goose fat and a saltspoonful of
salt.  Stir at least ten minutes, or until it looks
like a mass of cream; then add gradually the
yelks of eight or ten eggs, the grated peel of a
lemon and juice; half a pound of sifted sugar,
and, last, the beaten whites of the eggs.  Have
the pudding form well greased, and bake immediately.  Time required, about half an hour.

Must be served as soon as taken from the oven, or it will fall. Serve with chand'eau sauce.

### CHAND'EAU SAUCE.

Take a cup of white wine and about half a cup of water and set it over the fire in a double kettle. That is, set the vessel that contains the wine in another of water to prevent burning. Add the grated peel of a lemon, wet a teaspoonful of potato-flour with cold water, add also the yelks of four eggs, and stir constantly until so thick that it coats the spoon. Serve immediately, or it will get thin again. If the wine is too strong add more water and more eggs.

### POTATO PUDDING.

Stir the yelks of eight eggs with a cup of sugar, add a handful of blanched and pounded almonds and grate in the peel of a lemon. Add also its juice. Have ready half a pound of grated potatoes which have been cooked the day previous. Last add the stiff-beaten whites, not forgetting to add some salt. Grease your pudding form well, pour in the mixture and bake. Set in a pan of boiling water in the oven. The water in the pan must not reach higher than half way up to the pudding form. Time required, half an hour. When done turn out on a platter. Serve with a wine or chocolate sauce. You may bake this pudding in a pudding form without setting it in the boiling water. It must be an iron one. This is a delicious pudding.

## POTATO FLOUR PUDDING.

Take a quarter of a pound of goose oil, stir it to a cream and stir in gradually the yelks of ten eggs and three-quarters of a pound of sifted sugar; the grated peel of a lemon; also its juice, and half a teaspoonful of salt. Add last half a pound of potato flour and the stiff-beaten whites of the eggs. Have the pudding form well greased before putting in the contents. Bake in a moderate oven. Serve with raspberry sauce, made either of jelly or canned raspberries. Take a can of red raspberries, press them through a hair sieve, add a wineglassful of red wine, add sugar to taste, and let it boil hard for about five minutes.

## APPLE PUDDING.

Pare the apples and cut off the tops carefully, so as to be able to use them as covers to the apples. Now scrape out the inside with a knife, being careful not to break the apple. Mix the scrapings with sugar, raisins, cinnamon, pounded almonds and a little white wine. Fill this mixture into the hollow of the apple and clap on a cover for each apple, then grease a pudding dish, lay in the apples and stew them for a few minutes, but not long enough to break them. Make a sponge cake batter of eight eggs and two scant cups of sugar and a pinch of salt and add the grated peel of a lemon and beat until thick, at least half an hour. Add a cup of matzo flour,

sifted very fine, pour over the apples and bake.
Serve with wine sauce.

### GRATED APPLE PUDDING.

Grate six large, juicy apples and add the yelks
of eight eggs and half a pound of pulverized sugar. A better way is to stir the sugar and eggs
alone before adding the apples, the grated peel
of a lemon, and half a cup of finely-sifted matzo-
flour, or a cup of grated sponge-cake crumbs.
Add last the stiff-beaten whites of the eggs. Bake
in a spring form. Strew a handful of blanched
almonds on top of pudding just as you set it in
the oven.

### APPLE CHARLOTTE.

Soak a couple of matzos, press out every drop
of water, add half a pound of finely-shaved suet
and about six apples, cut in very fine slices,
some sugar, raisins, cinnamon, almonds, yelks
of seven eggs and whites beaten to a stiff froth.
Bake about an hour.

### CHRIMSEL.

Soak about three matzos. In the meantime,
seed a handful of raisins and pound as many almonds as you have raisins. Now press every
drop of water out of the matzos, put them in a
bowl and stir them to a cream; add a pinch of
salt, the peel of a lemon, yelks of six eggs and a
cup of sugar, the raisins and almonds, and also
a little cinnamon. Heat some goose oil in a
spider, use enough of it; the more fat the lighter

the chrimsel will be.  Last add the stiff-beaten
whites to the dough.   Then fry a light brown on
both sides; use about a tablespoonful of batter
for each chrimsel; serve with stewed prunes.
Lay the chrimsel on a large platter and pour the
prunes over all.   Eat hot.

### PRUNES.

Wash the prunes well, first in warm water,
then in cold.  Cut up half a lemon, some stick
cinnamon and sugar to taste.  Cook them in the
oven, covered tight, allowing a liberal quantity
of water; stew slowly for two hours; thicken
with a teaspoonful of potato flour, and wet the
potato flour with the juice of an orange before
adding.  If you pour the prunes over the chrimsel leave out the thickening.

### FILLED CHRIMSEL.

Soak about three matzos, press out every drop
of water, and heat a very little goose oil in a
spider, just enough to dry the soaked matzos.
Now add a few handfuls of matzos flour, four
eggs, salt and sugar to taste.  Mix all well and
form eight or ten oblong cakes out of it, to be
filled.  To do this take some dough in your
hand, about the size of a goose egg, and flatten
with the other hand.  Lay them on a clean
board or platter until you have prepared the
filling.  Chop up four large, tart apples, add a
handful of pounded almonds, the grated peel of
a lemon, a handful of raisins, some cinnamon,

about three-quarters of a cup of sugar, a wineglassful of wine; stew this for about five minutes, closely covered; when cool fill half of the
cakes and cover them with the remaining half;
press the edges firmly together (they should be
egg-shaped); dip them in beaten egg, turning
them over and over in it, and fry in hot goose-
fat, pouring the hot fat over them as they fry.
Serve with a wine sauce. Eat hot.

### PIES.

The above dough will answer for any kind of
pies. Finish by putting a meringue on top.

### UEBERSCHLAGENE MATZOS OR MATZOS DIPPED IN EGGS.

Beat up a dozen eggs, very light; add salt
and soak the matzos in the beaten egg. (It is
much better to soak the matzos in milk first
then in the beaten egg.) In the meantime heat
a quantity of goose oil in a spider; dip each
piece of matzos in the eggs before laying in the
spider, and fry a light brown on both sides.
Lay on a large platter and sprinkle with a mixture of sugar, cinnamon and grated peel of a
lemon. The more eggs used the richer they will
be. Delicious.

### RAISIN WINE.

(No. 1.) To every pound of large raisins
allow one quart of water. Chop up the raisins
and put in a stone jar, set in a warm place
(cover, of course), for four or five days, then

press through a coarse cloth, pressing the raisins thoroughly. Strain again through a cloth
or bag as you would jelly. Fill in wine bottles
and put a piece of lemon peel in each bottle;
cork and put in a dry, cool place.

### RAISIN WINE.

(No. 2.) Take two pounds of raisins, seeded
and chopped, one pound of white loaf sugar, and
one lemon. Put all into a stone jar, pour six
quarts of boiling water over all and stir every
day for a week. Then strain and bottle. Ready
for use in ten or twelve days.

### WINE SAUCE.

Take a cupful of white wine and half a cup
of water, a few slices of lemon, a little cinnamon
and sugar to taste. Boil. Wet a teaspoonful of
potato flour and add, stirring constantly. Beat
up the yelks of four eggs and add the wine gradually to the beaten egg. Return to the kettle,
stirring constantly, and add part of the beaten
whites of the eggs, and put the remainder on top
of the sauce, after putting in the sauceboat.
Sweeten the whites also.

### MATZO KLOESSE.

Soak some matzos about half an hour, and
press out all the water. Heat some goose oil in a
spider; cut up part of an onion very fine, heat it
with the goose oil and dry the matzos in it.
Put the matzos in a bowl; break in five or six
eggs, a large handful of matzo flour, some salt

and grated nutmeg and a very little ground
ginger. Mix this thoroughly into the dough.
Grease your hands, and form into little balls
the size of marbles. You can make enough at
once to last a few days. Keep in an ice-chest.
Another way is to use all matzo flour, moistening
the flour with scalding soup stock and proceed
as above. These are very nice for soups.

### FILLED MATZO KLOESSE.

Prepare a matzo dough as for soup kloesse.
Make round flat cakes of it with your hands, and
fill with cooked prunes (having previously removed the kernels). Put one of the flat cakes
over one that is filled, press the edges firmly
together and roll until perfectly round. Boil
them in salt water—the water must boil hard
before you put them in. Heat some goose fat,
cut up an onion in it and brown; pour this over
the kloesse and serve hot. The kloesse are nice
without any filling.

### STRAWBERRY SHORTCAKE.

Beat the yelks and whites of four eggs together with a scant teacupful of sugar, a pinch
of salt and the grated peel of a lemon. Beat
until the consistency of a thick batter, add last
about three-quarters of a cup of matzo flour.
Bake in two layers. Pick strawberries, cut
them in halves, sugar liberally, fill each layer
(this makes two cakes); whip some very rich
cream, sweeten and spread on top of the cakes. If

you haven't the cream whip the whites of five eggs with a quarter of a pound of sugar, and spread over the cakes.

### SPONGE CAKE.

Beat eight eggs very light with two small tea-cupfuls of sugar, a pinch of salt and grated peel of a lemon. Beat until the consistency of a very thick batter, sift a small cup and a half of matzos flour as fine as possible, add the grated peel and juice of a lemon and bake in a moderate oven.

### MACAROON COOKIES.

Blanch half a pound of almonds, cut them into three parts lenghtwise, set a spider over the fire and throw in a liberal handful of sugar. Slightly brown the almonds in this, take off the fire, stir them for a minute and turn on a platter to cool. In the meantime, beat the whites of six eggs to a very stiff froth with one pound of sugar. Stir in the almonds and bake upon greased or waxed paper. A pound of almonds may be used and you have them still richer. Very fine.

### CHOCOLATE MACAROONS.

Grate half a pound of almonds which have been previously blanched. Beat the whites of six eggs with three quarters of a pound of fine sifted sugar. Add one-eighth of a pound of the finest grated chocolate. Bake upon waxed or buttered paper. Drop with a teaspoon, which has previously been dipped in cold water.

### DATE TART CAKE.

Beat one pound of sifted powdered sugar with yelks of fourteen eggs. Beat half an hour at least. Then add half a pound of dates cut extremely fine, one teaspoonful and a half of allspice, the same quantity of cinnamon, two squares of chocolate, grated, and one pound of matzo flour, sifted fine. Add, also, the grated peel of a lemon and the juice of an orange and last the stiff-beaten whites of eggs. Bake slowly in a spring form.

### BROD TORTE.

Beat ten eggs light with two cups of sifted powdered sugar, one-quarter of a pound of almonds, with some bitter mixed, grated or pounded, and one cupful of matzo flour sifted fine. Add the juice of an orange and grated peel of a lemon, one tablespoonful of cinnamon, one teaspoonful of allspice and cloves mixed, and add the stiff-beaten whites last. Bake at once in a slow oven.

### CHOCOLATE CAKE.

(No. 1.) Beat the yelks of eight eggs and half a pound of sugar until quite light, add half a pound of almonds which have been blanched and cut fine, like shavings; one-half pound of the finest sweet grated chocolate, half a pound of finest raisins, seeded and chopped and one cup of matzo flour, sifted very fine. Add the juice of an orange, a wineglassful of wine, and

the stiff-beaten whites added last. A piece of
citron shaved very fine adds to this delicious
cake. Bake also in spring form.

### CHOCOLATE CAKE.

(No. 2.) Beat the yelks of twelve eggs with
half a pound of sifted sugar, half a pound of
grated sweet almonds, half a pound of finely-
grated vanilla chocolate, and one tablespoonful
of ground cinnamon. Add the stiff-beaten whites
last, and bake one hour in a slow oven. Bake in
a spring form lined with greased paper.

### ALMOND HILLS.

Roast half a pound of sweet almonds cut into
strips lengthwise in a spider of heated sugar, not
too brown. Beat one pound of sifted powdered
sugar and the whites of ten eggs to a very stiff
froth. Mix all thoroughly and place little heaps
of this dough on waxed paper, and bake a light
brown.

### MANDELTORTE.

Take one pound of sweet almonds and half an
ounce of bitter ones, mixed. Blanch them the
day previous to using, then grate or pound them
as fine as powder. Beat the yelks of fourteen
eggs with three-quarters of a pound of sifted
powdered sugar until light. Add the grated peel
of a lemon and half a teaspoonful of mace. Beat
long and steadily. Add the grated almonds and
continue the stirring in one direction. Add the
juice of the lemon to the stiff-beaten whites, also

two heaping tablespoonfuls of potato flour sifted in last. Bake immediately in a spring form, in a very slow oven. Bake from one hour to an hour and a quarter.

## MACAROONS.

(No. 1.) Take half a pound of sweet almonds, blanched and pounded (better grated), whites of six large eggs, beaten to a stiff froth with three-quarters of a pound of powdered sugar and bake on wafers or paper.

## MACAROONS.

(No. 2.) Blanch one pound of sweet almonds, grate on almond grater, whip the whites of twelve eggs to a stiff froth with one pound and a quarter of pulverized sugar, and add a tablespoonful of ground cinnamon. Bake on greased paper and sprinkle coarse grained sugar over them.

## CLOVER-LEAF MACAROONS.

Grate half a pound of hazelnuts with the whites of twelve eggs, add one pound and a half of sugar and a little cinnamon, place three little heaps of this dough, not larger than a gold quarter of a dollar, on greased paper and join each little clover heap with a stem made of citron.

## CINNAMON STICKS.

Grate half a pound of almonds, beat the whites of four eggs to a stiff froth, add gradually one pound of pulverized sugar and a tablespoon-

ful of cinnamon. Roll out this dough into half
finger lengths and about as thick as your little
finger. Bake, and when done ice each one with
boiled frosting.

### HASTY PUDDING.

Take any old cake, cut up in slices, dip in
wine or sprinkle some wine over all. Make a
custard with a pint of milk and four eggs. Put
a tablespoonful of potato flour with the yelks,
sweeten to taste, boil the custard flavor and pour
over cake in pudding dish. Beat whites to a
stiff froth, add sugar and spread over all. Put
in oven to brown slightly. Eat cold.

### MATZO-MEHL CAKE.

To the yelks of nine eggs, add two scant cups
of pulverized sugar, stir until the consistency of
batter, add the grated rind of a lemon, two teaspoonfuls of ground cinnamon and two tablets
of chocolate grated, one teaspoonful of allspice,
add the juice of an orange, and half a wineglassful of wine, and three-quarters of a cup of
finely-sifted matzo-mehl and a handful of almonds finely pounded, last add the stiffly-beaten
whites of the eggs in which you have added a
teaspoonful of baking powder (or a lump of
ammonia finely powdered). Bake in a moderate oven for three-quarters of an hour; try with
a straw.

## STRAWBERRY DESSERT.

Line a dish with macaroons, wet them with wine, put over this a box or quart of strawberries, and sugar them well. Now beat the yelks of eight eggs with two small cups of sugar, grated peel of a lemon and half its juice. Beat the whites to a stiff froth, add half the yelks, pour over all in your pudding dish. When baked spread the other half of the whites on top, having previously sweetened the remaining whites with sugar. Bake a light brown. Eat cold, with whipped or plain cream.

**MEMORANDUM.**

# BILLS OF FARE.

|                          |   | Page. |
|--------------------------|---|-------|
| Monday,                  | - - - - - - | 491 |
| Tuesday,                 | - - - - - - | 491 |
| Wednesday,               | - - - -. - - | 492 |
| Thursday,                | - - - - - - | 492 |
| Friday,                  | - - - - - - | 493 |
| Saturday,                | - - - - - - | 493 |
| Sunday,                  | - · - - - - - | 494 |
| Plain Sunday Dinner,     | - - - | 494 |
| Thanksgiving Dinner,     | - - - - | 495 |
| Kaffee Klatch,           | - - - - - | 496 |
| Portable Lunches,        | - - - - - | 496 |
| Pink Tea,                | - - - - - - | 497 |

(490)

**MEMORANDUM.**

## MENU FOR MONDAY.

### BREAKFAST.

Fruit.    Oat Meal.    Boiled Eggs.
Bread.    Butter.    Coffee.

### LUNCH.

Cold Roast or Poultry.
Baked or Fried Potatoes.    Pickles.
Preserves.    Tea.    Cake.

### DINNER.

Roast Veal.    Baked Sweet Potatoes.
Horseradish.    Beets.
Prunes.    Cake    Tea.    Coffee.

## MENU FOR TUESDAY.

### BREAKFAST.

Fruit.    French Toast.    Coffee.

### DINNER.

Farina Soup.
Roast Mutton, with Jelly.    Potatoes.
Stewed Tomatoes.    Pickles.
Peach Pie.

### SUPPER.

Paprica.    Graham Muffins.
Chocolate Souffle.    Canned Plums.
Tea.    Coffee.

## MENU FOR WEDNESDAY.

### BREAKFAST.

Fruit.     Omelets.     Bread.
Butter.     Coffee.

### DINNER.

Green Kern Soup.
Breast of Mutton, with Carrots.
Lemon Pie
Cheese.     Fruit.

### SUPPER.

Veal Cutlets.     Green Peas.     Mashed Potatoes.
Tea.     Coffee.     Floating Island.
Cup Cake.

## MENU FOR THURSDAY.

### BREAKFAST.

Fruit.     Potato Pancakes.     Steak.
Coffee.     Chocolate.

### DINNER.

Soup Schwamchen.     Brisket of Beef.
Sauer Kraut.     Kartoffel Kloesse.
Apple Sauce or Baked Apples.

### SUPPER.

Mutton Chops.     Baked Sweet Potatoes.
Neapolitan Blanc Mange.
Cake.     Tea.     Coffee.

## MENU FOR FRIDAY.

### BREAKFAST.

Fruit.    Poached Eggs on Toast.
Oat Meal.    Coffee.

### DINNER.

Barley Soup.    Fried Calf's Liver.
Velvet Potato Puffs.    Canned Corn.
Beets.    Cheese Pie.
Pickles.

### SUPPER.

Speckled Trout.    Potatoes.
Various kinds of Coffee Cake.
Apple Mohn.    Cheese.    Prunes.
Pistachio Cream.    Coffee.    Chocolate.

## MENU FOR SATURDAY.

### BREAKFAST.

Fruits.    Fried Perch.    Kuchen.
Coffee.

### DINNER.

Noodle Soup, with Chicken.
Young Duck, with Cauliflower.    Potatoes.
Pickled Pears.    Cocoanut Pie.

### SUPPER.

Marinirter Herring or Herring Salad.
Potatoes Cooked in their Jackets.
Cake.    Apple Snowballs.
Coffee.

## MENU FOR SUNDAY.

### BREAKFAST.

Sweetbreads.        Olives.        Milk Toast.
Coffee.

### DINNER.

Soup a la Julienne.        Roast Turkey.
Cranberries.
Beef, with Horseradish Sauce.
Sweet Potatoes.        Asparagus.        Cold Slaw.
Stewed Tomatoes.        Plum Pudding.
Roman Sauce.

### SUPPER.

Cold Turkey.        Neapolitan Salad.
Neapolitan Fruit Cake.
Coffee.

### PLAIN SUNDAY DINNER.

Noodle Soup.        Fish, Sweet and Sour.
Ducks, dressed with bread.
Red Cabbage.        Sweet Potatoes.
Pickled Peaches.        Mustard Pickles.
Suet Pudding cooked with Pears.
Coffee.

## THANKSGIVING MENU.

Blue Points on Shell.

Consomme Julienne.      Bisque of Lobster.

Boiled Black Bass a la Maitre d'Hotel

Boiled California Salmon, Sauce Piquante.

Hollandaise Potatoes.

Celery.      Olives.      Dressed Lettuce.

Chicken Patties.

Boiled Fowl.      Smoked Tongue.

Roast Beef.      Spinach.

Turkey,  Chestnut Dressing.

Broiled Quail on Toast.

Sweetbreads,  Filet.

French  Cream  Fritters  d'Orange

Champagne Punch.

Roast Prairie Chicken.      Haunch of Venison.

Mallard Duck.

Boned  Turkey en  Aspic.

Pate de Foie Gras en Aspic.

Green Peas.      Browned Sweet Potatoes.

Asparagus. Tomatoes.

English  Plum  Pudding, Brandy  Sauce.

Mince Pie.                                    Apple Pie.

Pumpkin Pie.

Fruit Cake.                              Macaroons.

Cream Puffs.

Confectionery.

Neapolitan  Ice-Cream.      Wine Jelly,

Mixed Nuts.

Raisins.      Dates.      Figs.

Fruit.      Café  Noir.      Cheese.

### KAFFEE KLATCH MENU (NO. 1.)

Oysters on Half Shell.
Smoked Tongue.    Pressed Chicken.
Heringsalat.
Fromage de Brie.        Neufchatel.
Kaffee Kuchen.
Bread Torte.    Almond Cake.    Chocolate Tart.
Tutti-Frutti.    Nuts.    Raisins.
Assorted Fruits.

### KAFFEE KLATCH MENU (NO. 2.)

Oysters on Half Shell.
Hot Rolls, Butter.        Soft Shell Crabs.
Roast Turkey.
Mushroom and Sweetbread Salad.
Aspic (Sulz).    Veal Patties.    Kuchen.
Neapolitan Ice-cream.    Fruits.    Nuts.
Coffee.

PORTABLE LUNCHES.—Cold corned beef, nicely
sliced, bread, butter, pickles, fruit. Carry sugar
in an envelope. Cold veal, radishes, sliced and
salted, hard-boiled eggs, sandwiches of cold
boiled ham or corned beef, smoked beef, boiled,
pickled or smoked tongue, chicken salad, pressed
meats, cold roast beef, sardines, salmon, smoked
or canned, herring, sardellen, olives, summer
sausage (cold steak is also nice if cooked rare),
cold poultry, cake in variety, pies and cheese.

## PINK TEA.

"Pink Teas," just now so fashionable, are rather novel if carried out to the letter, and an expensive way of entertaining, too, yet, as the old saying is, one might as well be dead as out of fashion. So all those who wish to be fashionable come and listen, and I will give you a few hints in regard to getting up a " Pink Tea." As a matter of course the table linen should be in harmony. If you possess a tablecloth with a drawn-work border, line the border with pink cambric. If not, cut the cambric the width desired and sew it on to any tablecloth and cover it with some cheap lace inserting; it will look very pretty. You may draw pink ribbons through the napkins. Suspend sash ribbons from the chandeliers in dining-room to reach half way down the center of the table, or, better still, to reach the four corners. Your lamps all over the house should have pink shades. They may be of pink paper; the dishes also of a delicate pink shade, which you may borrow for the occasion. Arrange the white cakes on high cake-stands, lined with fancy pink paper, or pink napkins, and put the pink frosted cakes on low cake-stands lined with fancy white paper or napkins. The flowers for decoration must also be of pink. Serve the creams and ices in novel designs made of pink paper, such as baskets, boxes, buckets, freezers,

cups and saucers, shells, wheelbarrows, vases, etc.
I am not able to tell you all the different designs
they have for this purpose. You may procure
these and many more beautiful designs at almost
any fashionable caterer's. Each guest should
have a pink boutonniere, or a white hyacinth,
tied with a pink satin ribbon. Have miniature
fans placed for each guest, with a card attached
containing his or her name. These are to be
taken home as souvenirs. Serve the butter in
pink individuals, each piece of butter moulded
differently and garnished with a wreath of parsley. A handsome center-piece for the table is
indispensable, so get a large fruit-stand and trim
it prettily with ferns, smilax and flowers, or have
an ornament of spun sugar for a center piece.
If you live where there are no caterers you may
try this: Make a large nest of macaroons, oval
in shape. Join the macaroons with sugar boiled
until it candies and have this filled with charlotte russe and resting on a rock of spun sugar.
You may color the charlotte russe pink and the
effect will be beautiful, for the spun sugar will
look like crystal. A nice way to serve charlottes at a "Pink Tea" is to hollow out large
"Acme" tomatoes, skin them carefully, cut off
the tops and scoop out the inside, set on ice
until wanted, then fill with whipped cream and
ornament with candied cherries. (At a "Yellow
Tea" you may substitute oranges for this pur-

pose.)   Your waitress should wear a pink cap
and a pink apron.   Illuminate the table with
pink "fairy lamps" or a chandelier of candles.
Menu the same as for "Kaffee Klatch."

**MEMORANDUM.**

# WEDDING MENU.

## FOR EVERY MONTH IN THE YEAR.

|                                      | Page |
| ------------------------------------ | ---- |
| November, December, January,   -   - | 501  |
| February, March, -   -   -   -   -   | 502  |
| April, May,   -   -   -   -   -   .   | 503  |
| June, July, August,   -   -   -   -  | 504  |
| September, October,   -   -   -   -  | 505  |

**MEMORANDUM.**

NOVEMBER, DECEMBER AND JANUARY.

Oysters on Shell.
Hock.

---

Tomato, with Noodles.
Celery.

---

Baked Black Bass.      Boiled White Fish.
Deidesheimer.

---

Roast Beef.      Boiled Capon.      Roast Duck.
Roast Turkey.
Champagne.

---

Sweetbreads.      Green Peas.
Apple Fritters, Rum Sauce.
Oysters Baked on Shell.   Macaroni with Cheese.
Champagne.

---

English Snipe.      Saddle of Elk.
Champagne.

---

Boiled and Mashed Potatoes.      Spinach.
Sweet Potatoes.      Sweet Corn.
Stewed Tomatoes.

---

Dressed Lettuce.      Mayonnaise of Chicken.

---

Bridal Cake.      Fruit Cake.
Fancy Cakes.      Wine Jellies.
Tutti-Frutti.      Bon Bons.      Fruit.
Coffee.

FOR FEBRUARY AND MARCH.

Celery, with Drop Dumplings.

---

Shad, filled with Oysters.      Salmon.
Trout Mayonnaise.
Old Sherry.

---

Saddle of Lamb, with Green Peas.

---

Cauliflower.      String Beans.
Veuve Cliquot.

---

Cutlets of Sweetbreads a la Bechamel.
Spring Chicken with Asparagus.
Young Pigeons on Toast, with Apple Compote.

---

Mayonnaise of Celery.      Turkey.      Shrimp.

---

Tomatoes.      Olives.      Radishes.
Strawberries.

---

Wedding Cakes.      Charlotte Russe.
Macaroon Cream Pudding on Ice.
Fruits.
Almond Tarts.      Small Cakes.
Fancy Ices and Creams.      Macaroons.
Stuffed Kisses.
Coffee.

### FOR APRIL AND MAY.

Chicken, with Croquettes.

---

Boiled Pickerel, Sauce Hollandaise.
California Salmon, Sauce Mayonnaise.

---

Turkey, stuffed with Italian Chestnuts.
Tame Duck, with French Peas.

---

Tenderloin Smothered with Mushrooms.
Chicken Fricassee, with Asparagus.
Smoked Beef Tongue with Spinach.
Stuffed Pigeons a la Jardiniere.
Spring Chicken with Jelly.

---

French Fried Potatoes.     Saratoga Potatoes.

---

Chicken.     Potatoes.     Lettuce.

---

Cucumbers.     Radishes.     Olives.
Celery.     Mixed Pickles.
Cranberry Sauce.

---

Pineapple.     Peaches.     Green Gages.
French Prunes.     Florida Oranges.     Grapes.
Bananas.     Raisins.     Almonds.
Pecans.     Walnuts.     Filberts.
Brazil Nuts.     Candy Pyramid.     Ornaments.
Stuffed Kisses.     Wedding Cake.
Fancy Cakes.     Wine Jelly.     Orange Pudding.
Ice-cream and Ices in Figures.

### FOR JUNE, JULY AND AUGUST.

Little Neck Clams.
Haute Sauterne.

---

Chicken Soup, with Noodles and Dumplings.

---

Filet de Bass a la Normande.
Pommes a la Parisienne.
Salmon.      Trout, Sauce Mayonnaise.

---

Sweetbread Patties, with Green Peas.
Filet de Boef, with Champignons.
French Fried Potatoes.
Fricassee of Spring Chicken with Asparagus.

---

Young Pigeons stuffed with Lettuce.
Tame Duck, with Apple Compote.
Turkey, with Cranberry Sauce.
Punch a la Romaine.
English Plum Pudding, with Brandy Sauce.

---

Lobster.   Mayonnaise of Chicken.   Cucumbers.
Celery.

---

Olives.      Young Onions.      Radishes.
Salt Pickles.

---

Ornaments.      Macaroon Pyramids.
Bride's Cake.      Assorted Cakes.
Dessert of Fruits.      Strawberries.
Neapolitan Ice-cream.
French Coffee.

## FOR SEPTEMBER AND OCTOBER.

Blue Points.
Old Sherry.

———

Chicken Soup, with Noodles.

———

Celery.    Olives.

———

Filet of Pike a la Hollandaise.
Wine.

———

Turkey, with Cranberry Jelly.

———

Sweetbreads Braze.
Fricassee of Young Chicken, with Imported
Asparagus.
Squabs on Toast.    Rice Coquettes.

———

Potatoes Parisienne.    French Peas.

———

Lobster.    Chicken.
Champagne.

———

Fruit Ices.    Pistache Ice-cream.    Meringues.
Fruits.
Coffee.

**MEMORANDUM.**

# VALUABLE HINTS.

| | Page. |
|---|---|
| Family Medical Case | 507 |
| Black Cashmere, How to Renovate, | 514 |
| Black Silk, How to Clean, | 514 |
| Croup, | 508 |
| Cold, | 510 |
| Cure for Hoarseness, | 513 |
| Cement for Glass and China, | 514 |
| Facts Worth Remembering, | 516–520 |
| Gargle for Sore Throat, | 508, 511 |
| How to Preserve the Hair, | 513 |
| Hoarseness, | 512 |
| How to Make a Bacon Bandage for Sore Throat, | 513 |
| Nervousness, | 511 |
| Nose-Bleeding, | 512 |
| Sore Throat, | 510 |
| To Mothers, | 508 |
| Tar Smoke for Diphtheria, | 512 |
| To Relieve Vomiting or Cramps, | 512 |
| To Relieve Neuralgia, | 513 |
| To Remove Dandruff, | 514 |
| To Restore Injured Furniture, | 514 |
| To Clean Diamonds, | 514 |
| To Remove Inkstains, | 515 |
| To Remove Tar, | 515 |
| To Bleach Cotton or Linen Clothes, | 515 |
| To Prevent Fading and Shrinking, | 515 |
| To Clean Carpets, | 515 |
| Whooping Cough Tea, | 512 |

**MEMORANDUM.**

# THE FAMILY MEDICINE CASE.

## HOW TO CONSTRUCT IT.

In the first place keep your medicine case out of the children's reach, and in a dry, cool place. Have drawers at the bottom large enough to hold pieces of flannel and nice, soft, old linen rags (such as old linen handkerchiefs) and cotton batting, lint, two salt bags, a rubber water bag, bandages, large pins, syringe, etc. Have also one or two smaller compartments in one of the drawers for medicine dropper, camel's-hair brushes, sponges, arnica, court plaster, scissors, etc.

The two lower shelves should be wider apart than the upper ones, for large bottles, and the space between the higher shelves need not be more than five or six inches. Place all poisons such as tincture aconite root, zinc sodine, arnica and carbolic acid, on the top shelf.

## WHAT TO PUT IN IT.

Sweet oil, camphorated oil, spirits of camphor, castor oil, sweet spirits of nitre, tinc. of iron, syrup ipecac, ipecac powder, tinc. arnica, turpentine, spiced syrup rhubarb, alcohol, carbolized and plain cosmoline, tinc. aconite root, tinc iodine, paregoric, ammonia, cream tartar, brandy, glycerine, powdered borax, mustard for plasters and foot baths, lime water. Children's laxatives, such as castoria, cream tartar and Rochelle salts.

Have a pocket made on the inside of the door of the case to hold a teaspoon and tablespoon, and keep a tumbler on the lower shelf of your case, also a wide-mouthed bottle containing sugar. This precaution may save you from running up and downstairs during the night. Another precaution: Have a pair of warm slippers at hand, to slip on if necessity compels you to leave your bed at night. You will then be able to fall asleep as soon as you return to bed, which you could not do with cold feet.

*Gargle for a Sore Throat.*—Take equal parts of glycerine and tincture of iron, mix well in a bottle. Use half a teaspoonful in a little water as a gargle; no harm done if you happen do swallow a part of it. Dose for children, five drops in a teaspoonful of water. If you notice molecules or little white specks on the tonsils this gargle is especially good and often prevents diphtheria. Gargle every two or three hours, an hour before meals or an hour after. You may swab the throat with this occasionally. If the patient coughs at the same time, rub the chest well with equal parts of camphorated oil and turpentine; when using at bed time heat the mixture. The way to do this is to mix it in a bottle and set the bottle in hot water, heat a flannel also and saturate it with the oil, lay across the chest, pretty high up, so as to cover the lower part of the throat at the same time, pin carefully to the night dress, so as to keep it in place. If the tonsils are much swollen rub the mixture along the glands and back of the ear; put a piece of heated flannel over the ears, fastened on top of the head. Do this two or three nights in succession if necessary.

## TO MOTHERS.

*Croup.*—As your children are liable to take severe colds, coughs, croup, etc., always remember that "an ounce of preventive is better than a pound of cure." This is a true saying, and that is principally what I wish to talk about.

Croup, how the words frighten young mothers! And well it may; still, when attended to in time, and with proper treatment and care, there need not be any worry and fright. Infants rarely have croup, at least not until about twelve months old, but from that time until the age of two years they are more liable to take it than at any other period. The liability lessens after two years, but there are exceptional cases that have croup up to ten years. Croup is more likely to prevail when we have strong easterly winds.

To prevent our little ones from taking serve colds at night, which they often do, have long Canton flannel night drawers made for them which button up to the throat and cover the feet, yes, completely cover the feet. In order to do this the bottom of the drawers must fit like a sock. Insist on having them made in this way, for I speak from experience. I happened to read somewhere that is was injurious to have the feet covered at night; I cut them off for one of the children under my care, and behold, that very night he took a severe cold, for children will kick off the bed-clothes at night, no matter what you do, so try my way. Have the feet left on the night drawers, and do not cover your children too heavily at night. Leave a window open somewhere to ventilate the room. In the mornings throw open your windows, top and bottom, about the time that you go to breakfast. In this way the rooms will be ventilated thoroughly. Do this every day.

Keep a four-ounce bottle of turpentine in your medicine case, also one of ipecac, which will have to be renewed every two months, as it spoils easily. The turpentine will be of use very frequently. As soon as your children, young or old, take a cold, saturate a flannel with turpentine and pin to the night dress, across the chest, so that when they sleep they will inhale it. Remember to pin on the outside of the dress, for if you bring it in contact with the bare skin it will be apt to burn the little ones. You may rub the chest with it by diluting it with camphorated oil, using say half of each; rub well over the chest, under the arms and across the back. You will also find this an excellent remedy when children complain of pains in their bowels; then heat the turpentine by setting the bottle in hot water, mix sweet oil with it, about equal parts, rub the stomach well with it and put hot flannels across the bowels, have them hot and dry; relief is sure to follow.

Croup almost always comes on during the night, especially at midnight. When you have once heard a croupy child cough you will find no difficulty in detecting croup the second time. When a very young child is hoarse there is every reason to believe that it is going to have the croup. If a child

breathes heavily and has a "crowing" cough you
should send for the family physician at once, especially if you are inexperienced. In the meantime
give small doses of Ipecac, till the child must be
made to vomit.

Keep up the temperature of the room, do not
let the fire get low at night; have hot water steaming in the room the child sleeps in, which is
easily done if you have a gas stove. Lime water
is still better. The temperature of the room must
be kept above seventy-five degrees. Remember
to keep Ipecac in the house, and saturate flannels
with turpentine and camphorated oil mixed; they
may be heated separately and then mixed in a
saucer. Apply to the chest. For an ordinary
cough, small doses of Ipecac, say from five to ten
drops, every hour or two, will often rid your child
of a cough. And if you possibly can get your child
dren to take cod liver oil every winter, say from
the first of October to the first of April, the first
thirteen years of their lives; it will regulate their
whole system and strengthen them; it will be like
giving them so much food too. Children from five
to ten years old should take a teaspoonful three
times a day, after meals, and older ones a tablespoonful night and morning, after meals. In order
to get children to take the oil you must bribe them
to take it by giving them nice fruit or other delica-
cies. When they are old enough they will crave it
and through it you will save many a doctor's bill.

## VALUABLE HINTS.

*Cold.* – To break up a bad cold, take a strong mustard
   foot-bath on going to bed, wipe the feet quickly
   and dry, then take a strong, hot lemonade. In the
   morning dose yourself with quinine, and keep it up;
   take a dozen pills, two grains each, in two days.

*Diphtheritic Sore Throat.* – Put the patient to bed immediately and let him gargle with a mixture of glycerine and tincture of iron, equal parts, say a teaspoonful of this mixture and two teaspoonfuls of
   water. You may also swab the throat with it every
   two hours, using it pure. If the patient have

much fever give aconite every two hours. Mix six drops of aconite with twelve teaspoonfuls of water in a goblet, and give a teaspoonful of this mixture every two hours until the fever is allayed. A strong mustard foot-bath is advisable. If the patient's bowels move too often give mild doses of paregoric after each movement. When the fever has gone down give quinine every two hours for three or four days. Under fifteen years of age, one grain capsules. Keep on a strictly milk diet, and when the fever has disappeared give brandy and milk as a stimulant, say one teaspoonful of brandy to six of milk or cream. One teaspoonful of this every two hours. It is necessary to keep up the strength of your little patient, and if it shows signs of being chilly give the brandy and milk hot. You may also mix the brandy in with the paregoric half a teaspoonful of each in hot water sweetened with sugar. Keep the patient in bed until well, and guard against taking cold. Keep the little ones in the house and out of the room, for it is very contagious, and a child having the disease in a very mild form is very apt to give it to another member of the family, which may turn out serious. Place saucers of crude carbolic acid in each room, particularly in the water closet, and keep some in the vessel used in the patient's bed-chamber. Ventilate the room by opening windows in the adjoining room. Do not let any person use the same spoons, goblet or any dish used by the patient. It in always best to send for a physician at once.

*Nervousness and Noise.*—If you are nervous and suffer from noise, or if you desire to think without being disturbed, just take a bit of spermacetti ointment of about the size of a pea, tie it up in a small piece of linen, and place it deep in the ear, leaving the end hang out; not a murmur of sound can be heard. This quiets the nerves and does no harm, and the plug can be removed at will.

*Gargle.*—One tablespoonful of alcohol and four table-spoonfuls of water. This is said to be a sure cure for the worst form of sore throat. Gargle every hour.

*Nose-bleeding, How to Stop.*—Dr. Gleason says the following remedy for nose-bleeding has never been known to fail in a single instance: In the case of a child a wad of paper should be inserted in its mouth and chewed hard. It is the motion of the jaws that stops the flow of blood.

*To Relieve Cramps in Stomach and Vomiting.*—Apply a spice poultice to the pit of the stomach. Make the poultice with ground cloves, allspice, ginger, pepper and Indian meal, wet with essence of peppermint and a very little water. Apply after putting the patient to bed.

*Whooping Cough Tea.*—This tea is invaluable in whooping cough, asthma and also for common coughs. There are seven different "teas" which you may procure at any first-class druggists. Buy five cents' worth of each, have them well mixed and when you wish to use the tea take all you can hold between your fingers and pour one pint of boiling water over it. Cover and allow it to steep for ten or fifteen minutes—not boil. Add a lump of rock candy each time you steep new tea. Names of the teas as follows: Marshmallow Root, cut, Garraw Herb, Couchgrass, Iceland Moss, Licorice Root, cut, Mallow Flowers, Centauri Minons Herb.

*Tar Smoke for Diphtheria.*—Pour equal parts of liquid tar and turpentine into a tincup and set fire to it. A dense resinous smoke arises which obscures the air of the room, the patient immediately experiences relief. The above from Dr. Delthil, in the Paris Figaro; it is also a specific for croup. Pour about two tablespoonfuls of liquid tar and an equal quantity of turpentine in an iron pan or cup, light it, set on the register in room, near the bed if possible. I have tried it, it certainly brings relief in croup.

*For Hoarseness or a Cold.*—Beat the white of an egg to a stiff froth, add a scant teaspoonful of glycerine, the juice of a lemon and two tablespoonfuls of honey, stir it up well and let the patient take a teaspoonful of this mixture every two hours, oftener if necessary.

*How to Make a Bacon Bandage for Sore Throat.*—Cut the bacon in strips one quarter of an inch in thickness and two or three inches in width and long enough to pass entirely around the throat. Remove the bacon rind and any lean meat there may be in it to prevent blistering the throat or neck. Sew the bacon to a strip of flannel so as to hold it in position and prevent its slipping and then apply the bacon to the throat and neck. Pin it around the neck, so that it will not be uncomfortably tight. The throat and neck should be completely swathed with the bacon. If after an application of eight hours the patient is not better apply a new bandage in the same manner.

*Cure for Hoarseness.*—Roast a lemon in the oven, turning it now and then, so as to cook all sides. It should not break, but be soft all through. While the lemon is warm, cut a piece from one end, fill with as much sugar as it will hold, and eat on going to bed, or heat some honey and mix juice and honey and eat while warm.

*To Relieve Neuralgia.* — Towels wrung out of hot water give prompt relief for neuralgia in the face or head when applied to the parts affected.

*How to Keep and Promote the Growth of the Hair.*—A lady with a fine growth of hair nowadays is the exception. Why? Because of the neglect of giving it a good brushing at least once a day, twice is better, night and morning. The most injury done to the hair is the habitual use of the curling iron. It is better to singe off the hair when uneven than cut it. Equal parts of castor oil and whisky mixed is a good tonic for the hair, rubbing a very little into the roots at a time with your finger tips. Twice a week is sufficient, as it will make the hair strong and glossy. Wash the head at least once a month in warm soapsuds to which you have added a little ammonia. Take fresh water for a second wash (it must be hot this time) and add a little borax, then rinse in clear hot water. Lastly, let cold water be doused all over the head. This will prevent taking cold. Rub dry with coarse towels and then fan.

*To Remove Dandruff.*—Two ounces of cantharides, two ounces of glycerine, two ounces of bay rum, and one ounce of water. Shake before using. Part the hair about an inch apart and rub the mixture well into the scalp with the tips of your fingers.

*Cement for Glass and China.*—A very strong cement may be made for glass and china by diluting the white of an egg with the same quantity of water. Beat it up thoroughly, add enough powdered quicklime to make a thin paste. It must be applied immediately or it will lose its virtue.

*To Restore Injured Furniture.*—Moisten the dent with warm water, then lay over it a folded brown paper and apply a warm iron until the moisture has evaporated.

*To Clean Diamonds.*—Wash them in warm suds, then rinse them in clear water in which you have added some ammonia, then dry them with a soft linen handkerchief, the older the better, or chamois skin; last run tissue paper through and all around the setting of the diamond.

*Black Cashmere.*—How to renovate. Steep two ounces of soap bark in a quart of warm water for a couple of hours, then strain and add it to the water the Cashmere is to be washed in, do not use any soap to the goods. When washed rinse in warm water which has been well blued and iron on the wrong side when half dry.

*Black Silk, How to Clean.*—Purchase a few ounces of soap bark at any drug store. Steep two ounces of the bark in a quart of warm water for a few hours. Rip and brush the silk, remove all the threads left by former stitches. Spread the pieces on a lap board or clean table and sponge the silk with the infusion, which you have previously strained; sponge the silk on both sides and rub off the lather with a clean piece of silk. Do not wring the silk, but simply spread the different pieces upon a clean sheet laid over the carpet and pin the pieces down at the corners. When dry the silk will look like new.

*To Remove Ink Stains.*—Saturate the spots with spirits of turpentine and let it remain several hours. You can rub it out easily after that.

*To Remove Tar.*— Rub with lard or butter, then rinse with warm soap and water.

*To Bleach Cotton or Linen Clothes.*—Take one pound of chloride of lime, dissolve and strain it into about three pails of water. Leave your clothes in it over night. Then rinse well and dry. This will also remove mildew.

*To Prevent Ginghams or Calicos from Fading and Shrinking.*—Dip them and allow them to remain in a pailful of cold water in which you have put two or three tablespoonfuls of sugar of lead. Allow them to remain in the water for two or three hours or longer. Do this before making up the material, wring and hang up the goods and iron on the wrong side before quite dry. It will pay you for the trouble, for the ginghams will always look like new, and never shrink if properly taken care of.

*To Wash Carpets.*—To every pail of water add one large tablespoonful of ammonia, and one large tablespoonful of beef gall. Scrub with a clean brush, and rinse with clean tepid water.

#### MISCELLANEOUS.

When going from a warm room out into the cold, always keep the mouth closed and breathe through the nostrils, in order that the air may be warmed before reaching the lungs.

Never go to bed with cold or damp feet.

Never bathe immediately after a meal, nor when the body is fatigued.

If the feet are tender or painful after long walking, great relief may be had by bathing them in tepid salt water.

Fine loaf sugar sprinkled over proud flesh will remove it with less trouble than any other remedy.

Never use anything but light blankets as a covering for the sick.

Almond meal used instead of soap keeps the skin smooth in winter and will ward off sunburn in summer.

Arris Root will yield a more delicate and lasting odor than any other sachet powder.

Sliced onions in a sick-room absorb all the germs and prevent contagion. It is a good plan to hang an onion in the nursery.

Hot water taken freely before bedtime cures indigestion, it has a soothing effect upon the stomach and bowels.

Do not rub the face with camphor applications or vaseline, as it it apt to make the hair grow where it is unbecoming.

Put salt on clinkers in your stove or range while they are hot, after raking down the fire, and they will be easily removed.

## FACTS WORTH REMEMBERING.

*Care of the Hands.*—When your hands become badly stained from kitchen work, wash them first in cold water, then rub them well with dry powdered borax; now wash them with very warm water and soap, and if the stains still remain rub them well with lemon juice, cleaning the nails at the same time by rubbing them in the lemon. Before drying pour a few drops of glycerine into the palm of the hand and rub well into the skin and wipe perfectly dry. Do this before retiring at night and you will find that your hands will soon become soft and white.

*The Teeth.*—Brush your teeth twice daily, particularly before retiring at night. Brush the teeth occasionally, say once a month, with finely powdered pumice stone, and run a thread of white silk floss between each tooth daily. Use warm water instead of cold. Powdered borax and camphor whiten the teeth beautifully, but use this but seldom.

*Dried Currants, How to Clean.*—Rub them between your hands, in warm water first, then in cold, and repeat this many times, always renewing the water; then lay them on a clean flannel cloth and rub dry; the stems will adhere to the flannel

*Raisins, How to Clean.*—Raisins should be cleaned dry by rubbing them between two cloths.

*How to Preserve " Dill " for Winter Pickles.*—Put fresh green dill in wide-mouthed jars and pour vinegar over it. You may use both the dill and vinegar on your pickles.

*To Clean Glass Decanters.*—Crush egg shells into bits, put into the decanter three parts filled with cold water. Shake thoroughly up and down.

Having accepted an invitation to dinner, it is proper to be at the house half an hour previous to the time set for dining. And do not leave, under any circumstance, until half an hour after dining; however, a dinner party rarely breaks up until late, as music, games, etc., usually follow.

You may use the liquor left from pickled peaches, pears, or cherries, for seasoning red cabbage, beans, etc.

The liquor left from brandied peaches may be utilized in mincemeat. In baking mince pies add an apple chopped up fine, the juice of an orange and a very little sugar just before baking. You will find this quite an improvement.

When broiling steak heat the gridiron before putting on the meat, and the steak will not stick.

It is a good plan to make parsley butter in the summer for winter use. Melt the butter, boil until clarified, then throw in as much chopped parsley as you desire. It is very convenient to use in winter, when greens are scarce, for gravies, etc. You may do the same with goose or any other kind of fat.

In breaking eggs for baking or frying, break each one separately over a cup, it is the safest way; if the egg is bad no harm is done. If you were to run the risk of breaking your eggs all in one bowl you might spoil a whole dozen or more, for it takes but.a few drops of a bad egg to do this.

If a little flour is sprinkled over meat that is to be minced it will not adhere too closely to the chopping-knife

Clear boiling water will remove tea stains. Hold the fabric firmly and pour boiling water through the stain, thus preventing its spreading.

Milk that has just turned can be sweetened and made fit for use by stirring in a little soda.

To remove cakes from deep pans easily, butter the tins, sides and bottom, and line with buttered paper as well, cutting it to fit the tin exactly. When your cake is baked allow it to get perfectly cold, then return to the oven, keep it there only long enough to warm the tin through, then turn the cake upside down and it will slip out easily.

Kerosene Oil will soften leather boots that have become hard from exposure. Also good for harness when hard from dampness.

An uncomfortably tight shoe may be made perfectly easy by laying a cloth wet in hot water across where it pinches, changing several times. The leather will shape itself to the foot.

Sulphuric Acid will remove spots from brass that will not yield to oxalic acid. It may be applied with a brush. Great care must be taken that none drops on clothes or skin, as it is ruinous to garments and cuticle. Polish with rottenstone.

Lamp chimneys wiped and polished with old newspapers have a better polish than when wiped with a cloth.

When putting away the silver tea or coffe-pot which is not in use every day, lay a stick across the top under the cover. This will permit fresh air to get in and prevent the mustiness that is so often found in them.

A ripe tomato will clean the hands after paring fruit. If very much stained use a lemon; digging your fingers into it will also clean your finger-nails.

Always keep a basin of water in your sink in which to dip your kitchen spoons after using; also one to wash your hands in, and put a hand towel on a roller. One has to use it constantly while cooking or baking.

One ounce of salicylic acid put in a barrel of cider will prevent its turning sour.

When putting away stoves for the summer wet a rag with kerosene oil and rub them all over with it. This will prevent rusting.

Keep your bread in a large, square, tin box or an earthen jar. For cake use a tin cake box with shelves in it; a novel picnic basket may be made in the same way.

Never lay fresh meat directly on ice. To keep meat fresh without ice, sprinkle a very little powdered salicylic acid over it.

A teaspoonful of borax put in the last water in which clothes are rinsed will whiten them.

Flannels should be ironed on the wrong side with an iron barely hot. Iron until dry.

Egg stains may be removed by rubbing with common table salt.

If your table celery happens to be frozen lay it in clear cold water to thaw out.

By putting concentrated lye in your wash-basins, with boiling water, once a month, you will keep them sweet and save many a plumber's bill.

To remove iron taste from new iron kettles, boil a handful of hay in them.

Old wall paper may be cleaned by rubbing with a loaf of stale bread. Cut the loaf in half and rub gently on the wall.

To rid the kitchen and closets of cockroaches, put powdered borax in all corners and allow it to remain there all year. Renew every three months at least. This will positively rid a house of roaches.

In cutting hot bread use a hot knife, and it will not be clammy.

In putting away knives wrap them in paper to prevent rusting. Never in woolen cloth.

In winter clean windows with a sponge dipped in alcohol.

Yellow soap and whiting, mixed together in a little water into a thick paste, will effectually stop a leak in your boiler.

Salt will curdle milk. In preparing mush, gravies and sauces, salt should not be added until the dish is prepared.

Keep salt and pepper on a shelf near your cook-stove; it will save you many a step.

Have your fire ready to light before going to bed and have your breakfast materials at hand, and it will be so much less work in the morning.

In dusting a silk dress never use a brush; wipe carefully with a piece of soft flannel, shaking the flannel occasionally.

In sewing, change your position frequently, it will help to rest the body.

Rusty flat-irons should be rubbed over with salt, and then with beeswax.

To beat the whites of eggs quickly and well, be extremely careful not to get any of the yelks in with the whites, then add a pinch of salt and set on ice for a little while. If for an icing add the sugar as soon as you begin to beat, a little at a time, until stiff; add a few drops of lemon to whiten the icing.

In baking macaroons and kisses, use washed butter for greasing the tins. Bake in a moderate oven or dry in a cool oven for two hours. Another and still better way to prepare the pan is to sprinkle it lightly with flour, over the butter, and then shake or blow it off.

Almonds for confectionery should be dried in the oven after blanching, and they will pulverize more easily. In making candy drops or macaroons, or pulling candy, grease the hands.

Eat salt with nuts, to aid digestion.

Sugar for fried cakes should be dissolved in milk to prevent the cakes from absorbing the fat while frying.

When loaves of bread do not retain the dent of the finger they are ready for the oven.

### PROPORTIONATE WEIGHTS AND MEASURES.

1 lb. of Butter equals 1 quart.

1 lb. of Loaf Sugar equals 1 quart.

1 lb. of Flour equals 1 quart.

1 lb. 2 oz. of Indian Meal equals 1 quart.

1 lb. 2 oz. of Brown Sugar equals 1 quart.

1 lb. 1 oz. Powdered sugar equals 1 quart.

1 tablespoonful of salt equals 1 ounce.

10 unbroken hen eggs equal 1 lb.

A teaspoon contains about twenty drops of a liquid.

A wineglass contains about four tablespoonfuls.

A so-called quart bottle contains about a pint and a half.

One gallon equals half a peck.

16 tablespoonfuls half a pint.

Four large tablespoonfuls equals half a gill.

Eight large tablespoonfuls equals one gill.

A common sized tumbler equals half a pint.

# Home Confectionery...

**I**S dedicated to "*our young ones*" especially those living in "*country towns*," where fresh and pure candies are not to be had at any price.

CANDY MAKING as a past-time, is not to be surpassed. By carefully following these receipts you will have good quantity and fine quality at very little cost.

It has been my aim to make all receipts as simple and explicit as possible, so that any child may make its own sweets. The receipts given are all wholesome and will be found economical.

Remember that practice makes perfect.

AUNT BABETTE.

# INDEX.

—

## CANDIES REQUIRING NO COOKING.

Almond Creams, No. 1 ............................... 8
    "    "  No. 2 ........................... 8
Chocolate Cream Drops ............................ 12
    "  Cherries ............. ............... 8
    "  Kisses ............... ............. 11
Cherries in Cream .................................. 13
Chocolate Nut Creams ......................... ..... 16
Coffee Creams ..................................... 15
Cream Dates, Prunes and Figs ...................... 13
English Walnut Creams ............... ............. 13
Fruit Slices ....................................... 14
Foundation French Cream ........................... 7
French Creams and Spiced Chocolate ..... .......... 10
    "  Cocoanut Creams ........................... 11
Filbert Creams ..................................... 15
Kisses or Cream Meringues ......................... 11
Lemon Creams ...................................... 9
Nut Creams .. .............................. ...... 14
Neapolitan Creams ................................. 12
Orange Creams ..................................... 9
Peppermint Creams ................................ 9
    "  Drops ..................................... 14
Pink Creams ....................................... 14
    "  Cocoanut Creams ......... .......... 15
Uncooked Spiced Chocolate Creams ................ 10
Unboiled Creams ................................... 7
Rose Creams ....................................... 11
Spiced Chocolate .................................. 8
    "    "  Creams ............................. 9
Wintergreen Creams ................................ 10
Walnut Maple Sugar Creams ........................ 13

1

# INDEX.

## CANDIES THAT REQUIRE COOKING.

Almonds Grilled....... 30
Almond Nut Candy.... 26
"       Candy........ 34
"       Caramels...... 31
Almonds Roasted in Oil. 31
Blanched Almonds.... 31
Boiled French Cream... 33
Burnt Almonds........ 19
Butternut Candy....... 34
Butter Scotch ......... 22
Butter Taffy........... 23
Candy of Any Flavor... 18
Cocoanut Caramels.... 19
Cream Caramels....... 37
"     Candy.. ..... 19
Coffee Cream......... 32
Cream Almonds....... 20
Chocolate Cherries..... 27
Chocolate Caramels.... 28
"     Caramels, No. 2. 29
Chocolate Creams....21, 38
Cocoanut Cones....... 22
"          Drops....... 24
Candied Cherries...... 25
Cough Candy ......... 29
Everton Taffy......... 27
Filbert Creams......... 38

General Instructions.... 17
How to wax Paper..... 22
Hoarhound Candy..... 25
Ice Cream Candy...... 24
Lemon Cream Candy... 1
Maple Creams......... 23
Maple Nut Candy...... 24
Marshmallows......... 35
Molasses Candy ....... 35
Molasses Taffy......... 27
Nut Candy............ 25
Nut Creams........... 32
Nougat............... 36
Old Fashioned Molasses
    Candy.............. 33
Pine Apple Chips...... 27
Peanut Candy......... 36
Pink Creams.......... 33
"    Cocoanut Creams. 38
Prunes, Dates and Figs.. 36
Salted Almonds........ 34
Tutti-Frutti Candy..... 37
Uncooked French Cr'ms 35
Vanilla Caramels...... 30
Walnut or But'rnut Glace 26
Walnut Chocolate Drops 20

# HOME CONFECTIONERY

CANDIES REQUIRING NO COOKING.

### UNBOILED CREAMS.

For the novice it is advisable to try unboiled candies at first, as their preparation is
much easier than those requiring the fire.
Candy boiling requires some practice before
you acquire the desired state of boiled sugar.
For these unboiled French creams, none but
the best confectioner's sugar will answer: it
may be obtained at all first-class groceries.

### FOUNDATION FRENCH CREAM.

Take the white of one or more eggs. add an
equal quantity of cold water. The surest way
to measure the water is to fill a half egg-shell
full to the white of each egg. Then stir into
the eggs and water as much confectioner's
sugar as it will require to make it stiff enough
to roll into any shape desired. Flavor to
taste.

### ALMOND CREAMS, No. 1.

Blanch and chop or grate the almonds and mix them thoroughly through the French cream. Mold into any shape desired.

### ALMOND CREAMS, No. 2.

Shape or mold the French cream oblong and press an almond into its side. Then roll it in granulated sugar or melted chocolate.

### CHOCOLATE CHERRIES.

Roll each candied cherry into melted chocolate. If desired cover each cherry with French cream, and then roll into the chocolate. Use a long hat pin for this purpose.

### SPICED CHOCOLATE.

Take two cupfuls of brown sugar, one-half cupful of hot water and three-fourths ($\frac{3}{4}$) of a cupful of grated chocolate and a piece of best butter, the size of an egg. Boil the ingredients until thick and test by dropping the drops from a spoon into cold water—if the drops harden, remove from the fire. Add allspice, ground cloves and cinnamon, mace, if desired, a very little of each, about a half teaspoonful. Pour into buttered tins and when cool cut into desired sizes.

### SPICED CHOCOLATE CREAMS.

Make as in above receipt. Roll into balls
and turn them over into melted chocolate.

### ORANGE CREAMS.

Grate the rind of an orange into a bowl,
then squeeze the juice over it and strain
through a piece of cheese-cloth. Add a pinch
of tartaric acid and stir in as much of the finest confectioner's sugar as it will take to mold
into shapes.

### LEMON CREAMS.

Made according to above receipt. You may
roll them into balls and cover them with chocolate. Very nice.

### PEPPERMINT CREAMS.

Break the white of one egg into a bowl, add
to it an equal quantity of cold water; then
stir in as much of the best confectioner's
sugar as will take to make it very stiff, stiff
enough to mold into shape. Flavor with
three drops of oil of peppermint. Grease very
lightly a large baking tin, drop the creams on
it with the aid of a teaspoon and lay them

far apart. When all are in, wet the back of a teaspoon with cold water or alcohol and press each peppermint flat with the back of the spoon. Wet the spoon each time in cold water. You may color these a pretty pink with fruit coloring or cochineal.

### FRENCH CREAM AND SPICED CHOCOLATE.

Press layers of French cream between layers of spiced chocolate.

### UNCOOKED SPICED CHOCOLATE CREAMS.

Take the white of one egg and add half an egg-shell full of water, so as to have as much egg as water. Stir into this as much confectioner's sugar as will make it stiff enough to mold. Grate as much chocolate as you wish to add and add ground spices, such as cinnamon, cloves, allspice and mace. Roll these balls—which you must make with the hands slightly buttered or dipped in cold water. Have some chocolate ready to roll them in, as you would chocolate creams.

### WINTERGREEN CREAMS.

Made the same as peppermint creams. Flavor with wintergreen instead of peppermint and color pink.

### ROSE CREAMS.

Made the same as other uncooked French creams—color pink and flavor with a few drops of rose water.

### FRENCH COCOANUT CREAMS.

Make either boiled or uncooked French cream, and add as much grated cocoanut as desired. Do this while the cream is still soft. Add sufficient confectioner's sugar to mold into balls or flat cakes. You can make a variety by coloring part pink with fruit coloring, or brown by adding chocolate to the cream before adding the cocoanut.

### CHOCOLATE KISSES.

Beat up the whites of two eggs with two cups of confectioner's sugar and about three ounces of chocolate. Drop on buttered paper, which you have put in a large baking tin. Drop from a spoon, dipped in cold water. Bake fifteen minutes.

### KISSES OR CREAM MERINGUES.

Beat very stiff the whites of two eggs with one pound of confectioner's sugar. Add half a teaspoonful of vanilla and one heaping tea-

spoonful of arrowroot. Bake on buttered
paper, with the oven door slightly open, and
watch closely.

### NEAPOLITAN CREAMS.

Make the French cream receipt, either
boiled or unboiled, and divide into as many
parts as you have coloring—leave one uncolored (white); color one pink, one brown, one
yellow, etc., just as you fancy. To color
pink use fruit coloring or cochineal syrup
and color the brown either with chocolate or coffee, which is done quickly while
the cream is still soft. Press the different
colored creams, first separately, then together;
cut into squares or any other shape desired.
Color yellow, with the yolk of an egg.
You may have quite a variety in this way,
making some white, brown and yellow; others
pink, white and brown. It is necessary to
work the cream while soft very quickly, so as
not to allow it to harden before molding.

### CHOCOLATE CREAM DROPS.

Roll some French cream into cone-shaped
forms and lay them on waxed paper or a
greased platter, until they are hard, which
will take from three to four hours. Then

melt some grated confectioner's chocolate in a farina kettle (set in boiling water). When the chocolate is melted, roll the creams in it, one at a time, by the means of a long hat-pin. Slip them on waxed paper to dry.

### CHERRIES IN CREAM.

Take a candied cherry and cut it almost in two and fill it with French cream.

### CREAM DATES, PRUNES AND FIGS.

Remove the pit with a knife and fill the cavity with French cream.

### ENGLISH WALNUT CREAMS.

Have your walnuts ready to use but use only the perfect ones (the broken ones can be used for some other purpose). Make some French cream, and shape into balls the size of a hickory nut and place a half meat upon either side of the cream ball, pressing it into the cream. Place upon waxed paper to dry.

### WALNUT MAPLE SUGAR CREAMS.

Mix a quantity of grated maple sugar with the French cream, and roll the same as walnut creams.

### NUT CREAMS.

Use any kind of nuts or mixed nuts and chop them up as fine as desired. Mix with French cream.

### PEPPERMINT DROPS.

To one tablespoonful of glucose add one-third of a cupful of boiling water. Stir in enough of the best confectioner's sugar to make it stiff enough to mold. Knead it thoroughly, like dough, and flavor with about five drops of oil of peppermint. Shape into balls as quickly as possible and lay them on flat tins. Press them flat.

### FRUIT SLICES.

Chop up seedless raisins, currants and citron, a few candied cherries or any other candied fruit, if desired. Mix all into some French cream. Do not add as much sugar as usual to the French cream. Cut into squares half an inch thick, and wrap in waxed papers.

### PINK CREAMS.

Break into a bowl the white of one egg and add to it an equal quantity of cold water;

then stir in as much confectioner's sugar as
it will take to make it stiff enough to mold.
Flavor with vanilla or rose, and color with a
few drops of fruit coloring. Form into balls,
and flatten out. Lay upon paper to dry.

### COFFEE CREAMS.

Make according to above receipt and instead
of using plain water, use extract of coffee.
Make as follows: Take one tablespoonful of
finely pulverized coffee and pour two tablespoonfuls of boiling water over it. Let it
steep awhile, then strain and use it, instead
of plain water.

### FILBERT CREAMS.

Pound some filberts to a powder in a mortar and mix in with some French cream.
Shape into balls and when hard roll them in
melted chocolate like chocolate creams.

### PINK COCOANUT CREAMS.

Take some French cream and add a
quantity of freshly grated cocoanut. Color
with a few drops of fruit coloring and roll it
into balls. You may dip these in melted
grated chocolate or flatten out as desiuns as

## CHOCOLATE NUT CREAMS.

Have a quantity of finest vanilla chocolate grated. Make a French cream, not as thick as usual. Stir in the grated chocolate and grated or pounded nuts. Shape into balls, then flatten out on waxed paper. A good plan is to stir in the chocolate and nuts as soon as you begin the French cream. You will then know exactly how much confectioner's sugar to take.

L
add .

## PART II.

### CANDIES THAT REQUIRE BOILING.

A brass kettle, if kept perfectly clean, is best for boiling sugar in for confectionery use. Dissolve two pounds of white sugar in one pint of water and place this, in the kettle, over a slow fire for a quarter of an hour. Pour into it a small quantity of gelatine and gum arabic, dissolved together. Skim off at once all the impurities which rise to the surface. The white of an egg may be used as a substitute to make the clarifying process still more perfect. Strain through a flannel bag. If you allow the syrup to boil a few minutes longer you will have what is called "Rock Candy." To make other candies bring the syrup very carefully to such a degree of heat that the "threads" when dropped from the spoon into cold air, will snap like glass. When this desired stage is reached, add a teaspoonful of vinegar or cream of tartar, to prevent granulation, and pour into pans as directed in the receipts which follow. To make stick candies, pull and roll into shape with buttered hands

## CANDY OF ANY FLAVOR.

Take two and a half pounds of refined sugar, one pint of water and one teaspoonful of cream of tartar, and mix it in a kettle large enough to hold the candy when expanded by the heat, and boil over a brisk fire, taking care that it does not burn, applying the heat to the bottom, not to the sides. After boiling fifteen minutes remove a small portion of the melted sugar with a spoon, and cool by placing it in a saucer set in ice-water. When cool enough take a portion between thumb and finger, and if it "threads" as it is separated, the process is nearly completed. Great care must be used to regulate the heat so that the boiling may be kept without burning. Test frequently by dropping a bit into cold water; if it becomes hard and brittle, snapping apart when bent, it is done and must be removed at once, and the flavoring stirred in. Then pour into shallow earthen dishes, thoroughly but lightly greased, and cool until it can be handled; then pull and roll into sticks or any shape desired.

### COCOANUT CARAMELS.

Take one pint of milk, butter about the size of an egg, one cocoanut grated fine, three pounds of white sugar and two teaspoonfuls of lemon extract. Boil slowly until stiff, beat to a cream, pour into shallow buttered pans, and when set cut into squares.

### CREAM CANDY.

Take two heaping cups of white sugar, one wineglassful of vinegar and one tumbler of water. Boil one-half hour, flavor with vanilla and pull like molasses candy.

### LEMON CREAM CANDY.

Take three cups of sugar, one-half cup of vinegar, one-half cup of water and a teaspoonful of butter put in last with a teaspoonful of soda dissolved in hot water. Boil fast for about half an hour, until it crisps in cold water. Flavor with lemon and pull white.

### BURNT ALMONDS.

Take one pound of almonds and wipe clean. In the meantime put on a pound of sugar with a quarter of a pint of water; let it boil

until clear and thick; throw in the almonds
and stir with a wooden spoon until you hear
them crack.  Take off the fire, but keep stirring them; and when dry put in a wire sieve
and sift all the sugar from them.  Now put that
sugar on to boil again with a little, very little,
water and some cinnamon, if you like.  When
this boils throw in the almonds again, and
keep stirring until quite dry.  Take off the
fire and pack in a glass jar.  You may add
fruit coloring to the sugar the second time it
is put over the fire.

### WALNUT CHOCOLATE DROPS.

Take two and a half cups of pulverized
sugar, one half cup of cold water and boil
five minutes.  Then place in a pan of cold
water and beat until cold enough to make
into balls and put a walnut in the center of
each.  By using maple sugar you have maple
cream.  Take half a cake of chocolate, shave
off fine, set it in a bowl on top of a boiling
tea-kettle to melt, and when the drops are
cold roll in the melted chocolate with a fork.

### CREAM ALMONDS.

These are made like walnut drops.  While
making into balls mold an almond meat into

the center of each ball; then roll in coarse granulated sugar, and you have delicious cream almonds. Lay on buttered paper until cold.

Take two cups of sugar, one cup of water and one tablespoonful and a half of arrowroot or cornstarch, one tablespoonful of butter and one teaspoonful of vanilla. Wash the butter, stir the sugar and water together, add the arrow-root and bring to a boil, stirring constantly to induce granulation. Boil for about ten minutes, then add the butter, take from the fire and stir constantly until it begins to look like granulated cream. Add the vanilla. Butter your hands and make the cream into balls the size of a marble, and lay upon a clean board or flat dish (outside). Take half a pound of sweet vanilla chocolate, grate it, set it in a tin pail or saucepan, and put this in another of boiling water, so as to melt the chocolate. When the chocolate is melted to the consistency of syrup, roll the cream balls in it until sufficiently coated and take each one up carefully and lay upon a dish to dry.

### COCOANUT CONES.

Whip the whites of five eggs to a very stiff froth, and gradually the whole of one pound of confectioner's sugar and one teaspoonful of arrowroot; last, a fresh-grated cocoanut, or half a pound of desiccated cocoanut. Mold the mixture with your hands into small cones (flour your hands); set these far enough apart not to touch one another, upon buttered or waxed paper, in a long baking-pan. Bake in a moderate oven. Be sure to prepare the cocoanut before you begin; lay the pieces in cold water after paring, until all is grated.

### HOW TO WAX PAPER.

Get some one to assist you in holding the paper over the fire, and a third person to rub the wax over it. It may be done in a second. To remove macaroons or any other confection from paper, moisten the paper with a damp sponge on the reverse side and they will come off easily.

### BUTTERSCOTCH.

Boil one pound and a half of coffee sugar (white but not granulated), half a cup of sweet butter, half a teaspoonful of cream of tartar, and just enough water to dissolve the sugar. Boil without stirring until it will break easily when dropped into cold water. When done add one teaspoonful of lemon juice, or ten drops of extract. Pour into well-greased pans, and when almost cold mark into squares.

## BUTTER TAFFY.

Boil one cup of molasses and one cup of sugar until it candies. Remove from the fire and stir in nearly half a cup of butter and flavor with vanilla.

## MAPLE CREAMS.

Set some genuine maple sugar on to boil with half as much water as you have sugar. Boil until it is brittle when dropped into cold water, and when it is inclined to harden remove from the fire and stir rapidly until it becomes a waxen substance, then form into balls not larger than a marble. Butter your hands well to do this. Put half a walnut kernel on either side. Lay them on a greased platter to cool.

### ICE-CREAM CANDY.

Boil one and a half pounds of moist white coffee sugar, two ounces of butter, one teaspoonful and a half of water, together with the peel of half a lemon. When done (it will become crisp by dropping into cold water), set aside till the boiling has ceased, and stir in the juice of one large lemon (no seeds). Butter a dish and pour in about an inch thick. When cool take out the lemon peel, pull until white and form into any shape desired. If you have no lemon take two tablespoonfuls of vinegar and two teaspoonfuls of extract.

### COCOANUT DROPS.

Take one pound of grated cocoanut, half a pound of confectioner's sugar and the stiff-beaten white of one egg. Work all together and roll in the hands into little balls. Bake on buttered tins.

### MAPLE NUT CANDY.

Take one pint of maple sugar and half a pint of water, or just enough to dissolve the sugar. Boil until it becomes brittle by dropping in cold water. Just before pouring add a tablespoonful of vinegar. Having previously prepared the nut meats, butter the pans, line with nut meats and pour the candy over them.

### NUT CANDY.

Boil a pound of sugar with a cup of water. After boiling over a brisk fire put in a dash of vinegar. Take off the scum as it rises and test by raising with a spoon; if its "threads" snap, pour over chopped cocoanut or any other kind of nuts. Brazil nuts cut into slices are very nice. Butter the pans before putting in nuts and candy.

### HOARHOUND CANDY.

Boil two ounces of dried hoarhound in a pint of water for about half an hour, strain and add three pounds of brown sugar. Boil over a hot fire until hard, then pour out on well-greased flat pans, and mark as soon as cold enough to retain the marks.

### CANDIED CHERRIES.

Boil a syrup of two pounds of cut loaf sugar and a cup of water; boil until thick enough to pull. Then remove to the side of

the stove until it shows signs of granulation.
Drop in the cherries, carefully stoned, only a
few at a time, and for only two or three minutes; remove to a sieve, set over a dish, shake
gently, and turn the cherries out on white
paper.

### WALNUT OR BUTTERNUT GLACE.

Take one pint of granulated sugar and
three-fourths of a cupful of boiling water,
boil until it will crack if plunged into ice-
cold water.   Do not stir the sugar while boiling.   Dip the nuts carefully into the boiling
candy by means of a long hat-pin.   Lay each
one on slightly buttered tins or marble, to
cool and harden.   Sliced oranges or other
fruits may be dipped into this glace and you
have fruit glace.

### ALMOND NUT CANDY.

Take any quantity of blanched almonds
desired, and the same amount of sugar, the
best confectioner's.   Set the sugar over the
fire to dissolve and as soon as dissolved throw
in the almonds, stirring rapidly.   Pour all
into tins which you have previously buttered.
Press flat with a buttered knife.   Don't allow
the sugar to boil.

### CHOCOLATE CHERRIES.

Roll each candied cherry into melted chocolate. If desired cover each cherry with French cream and then roll in the chocolate. Use a long hat-pin for this purpose.

### EVERTON TAFFY.

Boil two cups of brown sugar in half a cupful of water, until it will harden when dropped into cold water. Add butter the size of an egg; set back on the stove and boil once more. Flavor to suit the taste.

### MOLASSES TAFFY.

Take one cupful of brown sugar, one cupful of molasses and butter the size of a walnut. Boil and test by dripping a few drops into cold water. If it hardens pour out into buttered tins or plates. When cool cut into desired squares.

### PINE-APPLE CHIPS.

Pare, core and slice the pine-apple quite thick. Take half a pound of confectioner's sugar to a pound of fruit; sprinkle it over the fruit so as to have each slice sugared and let it remain in a covered dish until all the sugar is dissolved. Set on to boil slowly until each chip is clear. Set away until the following day. Remove all the syrup and place the chips singly on glasses or porcelain dishes to dry in a very moderately heated oven.

### CHOCOLATE CARAMELS, No. 1.

Set on to boil one cupful of fine granulated sugar, one cupful of New Orleans molasses, and one-fourth cup of sweet milk. Add a piece of butter the size of an egg. Let this boil steadily in a porcelain lined kettle. In the meantime grate a heaping cupful of best chocolate, add it to the boiling candy but not before it has attained the right consistency (try it by dropping some from the spoon into cold water, if done it will harden immediately, if not let it boil until it is). Let it boil briskly; it will have the consistency of cake batter and thread from the spoon when sufficiently boiled. Try again in cold water; if it hardens put in the grated chocolate and let it boil again for two minutes. Take from the fire, and flavor with a teaspoonful of vanilla. Pour into a large tin pie-plate, which has been previously buttered; when almost cold, cut into squares with the back of a knife, which you must dip into cold water occasionally.

It should be boiled steadily fifteen minutes by the clock. The success of making good candy depends on the boiling, if you fail, try again; candy making is a profession and it takes practice to learn the art.

### CHOCOLATE CARAMELS No. 2.

Take one cup of molasses, one cupful of white sugar and one-half cup of sweet milk in which you have rubbed smooth two teaspoonfuls of sifted flour. Stir all together and when you think it has boiled enough, add a lump of butter the size of an egg and test the candy as in above receipts. When done add the grated chocolate of which you should have a heaping cupful and let the candy boil up for a few minutes. Flavor with vanilla and remove from the fire and pour into a well greased tin plate or on a marble slab; when cool cut into squares and wrap in wax paper.

### COUGH CANDY.

Soak a gill of whole flax-seed in half a pint of boiling water. In another dish soak a cupful of broken bits of slippery elm, also in half a pint of boiling water. Let both soak for two hours or more, then strain both through a fine cloth into a porcelain lined dish and set on to boil with two pounds of granulated sugar. After boiling hard for ten minutes add the juice of two lemons and boil until it turns to candy. Test by dropping a few drops into cold water.

### VANILLA CARAMELS.

Mix one half of a pound of white sugar with eight large tablespoonfuls of sweet cream (one gill), one large tablespoonful of honey, butter the size of a hazel nut, and four tablespoonfuls of hot water. Boil these ingredients until the right consistency is reached; to ascertain this, drop some into ice-cold water, if it crackles when coming into the water, it is right; add a teaspoonful of extract of vanilla and pour upon a marble slab or buttered tin. Cut into squares when cool.

### ALMONDS GRILLED.

Used as you would "salted almonds" at teas, luncheons, etc. Very often both are served together using half grilled and half salted in the same dish. I do not recommend this; it is better taste to serve each separately. Blanch the almonds, then dry them in an open oven, or by laying them between two cloths and patting them until dry. Set on a cupful of sugar (confectioner's) wet with one-fourth of a cupful of water and let it boil until it threads from the spoon. Then throw in the almonds and let them boil. Stir them occasionally, until they change color. Remove from the fire and stir the syrup until it is all sugar. Lay them upon a platter to cool.

### ALMONDS BLANCHED.

Put the almond meats into a dish and pour boiling water over them. When cool the skins will come off readily.

### ALMONDS ROASTED IN OIL.

Blanch one heaping cupful of almonds, and pour over them one tablespoonful of best olive oil. Let them lay at least two hours, then sprinkle a teaspoonful of fine salt over them and brown them in the oven. Not too brown. Rub off the salt before serving.

### ALMOND CARAMELS.

Set a cupful of sugar on to boil, without water. As soon as the sugar is melted throw in a cupful of almonds, not blanched.

Remove from the fire at once. Take up each almond separately and lay on waxed or buttered paper.

## NUT CREAMS.

Mix in chopped nuts of any kind with the French cream (see receipt for French creams) and form into balls or other fancy shapes. You may color them with any kind of fruit coloring and give any desired flavoring. Then roll them in melted chocolate or coffee cream. Roll with a hat pin, using the latter as a means to take up the candies without touching them with the fingers.

## COFFEE CREAMS.

Take one heaping tablespoonful of pulverized coffee and pour a wine glassful of boiling water over the coffee. Cover the cup and let it steep for about five minutes. Then strain through some cheese cloth and make your French coffee cream, according to French cream receipt, using the coffee instead of water, and sugar according to quantity of coffee, about one cupful of sugar to a.wine glassful of coffee.

### BOILED FRENCH CREAM.

To one-half cupful of hot water, add two cupfuls of white sugar and boil briskly for five minutes, without stirring. If the boiled sugar threads when dropped from the spoon, remove from the fire. Try a teaspoonful on a saucer, if it creams and you can make a ball of it with your fingers, it is of right consistency. Pour all into a bowl and stir rapidly with a silver spoon. If it does not cream readily, set it back on the fire and boil it a minute or two longer. Flavor when it begins to cool with a teaspoonful of vanilla, or any other flavoring desired. This is the way all French cream candies are made.

### PINK CREAMS.

Made like French creams and color with fruit coloring, adding a few drops at a time, so as not to get it too dark, or use pink confectioner's sugar.

### OLD FASHIONED MOLASSES CANDY.

Take one pint of molasses, one half pint of sugar and a piece of butter about the size of a walnut, and one tablespoonful of pure glycerine. Boil hard over a brisk fire about

twenty minutes. When boiled thick, try by
dropping a few drops in ice-cold water and if
hard enough to retain their shape, it is ready
to take from the fire. Have a well buttered
platter ready to pour the candy on. Just
before removing the candy from the fire stir
in half a teaspoonful of cream of tartar and
flavor with vanilla.

### SALTED ALMONDS.

Throw the almonds into boiling water and
blanch. After they are skinned, lay on a
platter for several hours to dry. Dissolve a
little gum arabic in a spider with as little water
as possible; when dissolved throw in the
almonds and turn them over and over again
until all are glazed. Then take them off and
set in the oven to roast, stirring often, until
they begin to color slightly. Take from the
oven, throw them on clean paper, spread out
and sprinkle with fine salt. See that all be
well sprinkled.

### BUTTERNUT AND ALMOND CANDY.

Are made the same as coconut candy.

## MARSHMALLOWS.

Dissolve a pound of gum arabic in one quart of water, strain, add one pound of refined sugar and place over the fire, stirring constantly until the sugar is dissolved and the mixture has become the consistency of honey. Next add gradually the whites of eight eggs, well beaten, stirring the mixture all the time, until it loses its stickiness and does not adhere to the fingers when touched. The mass may now be poured out into a pan slightly dusted with corn-starch. When cool divide into small squares.

## MOLASSES CANDY.

Take one cup of molasses, one cup of sugar, one tablespoonful of vinegar and one teaspoonful of fresh butter. Boil until it hardens when dropped in cold water, then stir in a pinch of soda or cream of tartar and pour on buttered tins. When cool, begin to pull, having previously greased your hands.

## UNCOOKED FRENCH CREAMS.

Break the whites of three eggs into a bowl and add exactly as much water as you have whites of eggs (measure with the egg-shells).

Stir in confectioner's sugar until stiff enough to mold into any shape desired. Flavor to suit your taste.

### NOUGAT.

Blanch one-half pound of almonds in boiling water. When skinned, cut in half through the center and lay on white paper in the oven, with door open, to dry. Meanwhile, melt half a pound of sugar in a double kettle, without adding a drop of water. Stir constantly until the sugar boils, take off the kettle and stir in the almonds immediately. Pour into a flat greased tin pan, which has been previously warmed. Press the nougat flat to the bottom of the pan. Cut while still warm; wrap in waxed paper.

### PRUNES, DATES AND FIGS.

Select the finest only. Tear them open and extract the kernels, leaving them whole at the stem end. Insert a piece of French cream, and press the fruit together at the bottom.

### PEANUT CANDY.

Boil two cups of sugar with half a cup of water and dissolve half a teaspoonful of cream

of tartar in a little cold water and add.   Boil
until it becomes brittle when dropped into
cold water.   Then add a piece of butter the
size of a hickory nut and boil a few minutes
longer.   Pour this over the nuts, which have
been spread in a buttered tin, and set away
to cool.

### CREAM CARAMELS.

Boil together one pint of cream and three
pounds of sugar.   Add any desired flavoring.
Boil until it reaches 260 degrees Fahrenheit.
Pour out the mixture on flat dishes to cool,
and as soon as it begins to "set" which is
very soon. cut it into little blocks.

### TUTTI-FRUTTI CANDY.

Chop seeded raisins, citron, figs and a few
candied cherries.   Put two cupfuls of granulated sugar and half a cupful of boiling water
into a brass or porcelain kettle and boil hard
for ten minutes.   Take from the stove, pour
into a bowl, flavor and stir rapidly with a
spoon until it looks like cream.   Add the
chopped fruit and stir a while longer.   Press
thin on buttered tins, cut into squares and
wrap in waxed papers.

### FILBERT CREAMS.

Butter or flour your hands, and roll the above French cream around filbert nuts. Have some chocolate melted over a steaming tea-kettle in a bowl, and after the filbert balls are dry, roll them in the melted chocolate by means of a long hat-pin or fine knitting-needle.

### PINK COCOANUT CREAMS.

Use pink confectioner's sugar, or color with fruit coloring; add grated cocoanut; roll into balls; fill each center with a candied cherry.

### CHOCOLATE CREAMS.

Take one heaping tablespoonful of gelatine and dissolve it in six tablespoonfuls of warm milk, one heaping cupful of sugar and half tablespoonful of best butter and one tablespoonful of glucose and a pinch of cream of tartar. Stir over the fire until it boils then remove and stir until it is of the desired consistency ready to roll into balls. Butter the hands to do this. If not thick enough return to the fire and boil again. When all are rolled, melt some confectioner's chocolate and roll the balls in it. Take a long hat-pin to handle the balls with. Lay them on waxed paper to dry.

MEMORANDUM.

MEMORANDUM.

CPSIA information can be obtained
at www.ICGtesting.com
Printed in the USA
BVHW042023170420
577867BV00009B/62

9 780341 940685